The Stewarts
They staked a place in history by capturing
THE SPIRIT OF AMERICA

Stephen—The new leader of this bold family. He built his father's business into a booming shipping dynasty then sought to conquer America's overland routes.

Thaddeus—The nephew Stephen raised like a son. At an early age he displayed the unyielding ambition that drove the Stewarts to greatness and his friendship with Abraham Lincoln revolutionized Westward expansion.

Marguerite—Thaddeus' beautiful cousin. Family pride demanded that she suppress her love for Thaddeus. But her endless devotion to him led her husband down a fateful path.

Ruth—Thaddeus' wife. Torn by desires she could not control, she stood to lose the man she fought so desperately to win.

John—Stephen's son. His scandalous actions were an embarrassment to the family and his insane jealousy plunged Thaddeus into grave danger.

Francesca—Marguerite's sister. She despised all Stewarts—including Marguerite—and used her wealth to become Thaddeus' most powerful enemy.

Bantam Books by Charles Whited
Ask your bookseller for the books you have missed.

CHALLENGE: The Spirit of America, I
DESTINY: The Spirit of America, II

The Spirit of America ★ Book II

DESTINY

CHARLES WHITED

An Arthur Pine Associates Book

BANTAM BOOKS
TORONTO · NEW YORK · LONDON · SYDNEY

DESTINY

A Bantam Book / August 1982

ISBN 0-553-22615-0

Published simultaneously in the United States and Canada

Bantam Books are published by Bantam Books, Inc. Its trademark, consisting of the words ''Bantam Books'' and the por-
trayal of a rooster, is Registered in U.S. Patent and Trademark
Office and in other countries. Marca Registrada. Bantam
Books, Inc., 666 Fifth Avenue, New York, New York 10103

PRINTED IN THE UNITED STATES OF AMERICA

H   0987654321

Prologue

From a thousand pulpits the warnings came. "I tell you, my brethren, the railroad is an abomination in the sight of God. Man was not made to go at such terrific speeds. The heart will stop, the blood be caused to boil. I shudder at the moral consequences for young females. Danger to life and limb will be devastating, maiming and killing, showering sparks across this land. You farmers, your hens will refuse to lay, your cows will go dry. Woe betide us. And what's more, it is against our democratic principles to place such economic power in the hands of the few greedy men who shall own railroads..."

Thaddeus fidgeted. He was nine years old. His skin prickled. His starched white collar was hot. He stared at the angel in the stained glass window. He waited until the service was finished. And then he dutifully followed his Uncle Stephen as the crowd flowed up the aisle. Women murmured down to him, smelling of eau de cologne. A line formed at the double doors, where the sunlight streamed through. He ached to be outside. Slowly, slowly, they approached the sunlight. The parson was shaking everybody's hand. "Mighty fine sermon, Parson," Uncle Stephen said. Thaddeus gravely shook the parson's hand. The parson was a cadaverous man with a nose like a rooster's beak. He patted Thaddeus on the head and said, "Good lad."

The buggy was waiting. Uncle Stephen clamped the metal claw which served for his left hand onto the side of the buggy and swung his brass-studded peg leg aboard. He undid the reins of the pony. "Now then, Thaddeus."

Thaddeus followed him up and sat in silence until the buggy was moving. Then he said, "Uncle Stephen, can we go and see another train?"

Thaddeus glanced up at the man's partially-masked face and saw the smile lifting there. "My boy, you've been reading my mind. We'll do it right away!" He flicked the pony into a trot.

Two weeks went by. They joined a crowd of laughing yokels on the outskirts of Baltimore, watching the steam engine *Tom Thumb* race a big gray mare belonging to a rival stagecoach company. The tiny locomotive belched and chuffed. "Hah, hah, teakettle on a track!" jeered the crowd. Engine and horse went the full thirteen miles of track. The horse won. Red-faced officials of the B&O departed in a huff. Later, it was said that they gave *Tom Thumb* back to its inventor, a man named Peter Cooper.

"Uncle Stephen, I hear there's a new railroad out of Charleston, in South Carolina. Can we go? Can we go?"

The Charleston and Hamburg line was experimenting with faster methods of moving small, open, carriage cars along the track; faster methods, that is, than mule power. It was a breezy spring day. The conductor was resplendent in a dark coat with brass buttons. "Ladies and gentlemen, please take your seats. We are about to raise the sail." They climbed aboard, Stephen and Thaddeus in a front seat, their friend Crippled Wolf in the back. The Omaha Indian wore his favorite costume, a gray stovepipe hat, green split-tail morning coat, beads, braids, and buckskin trousers. ("Upon my word, Maude, do you see that Indian?")

The seats filled at last, the sail billowed, the cars began to move. Faster and faster they went. "My heavens, Thaddeus, we must be doing seventeen miles an hour!" They came to a curve, got halfway around, and the train blew off the track.

Two years passed. Again the scene was Charleston. A stubby engine huffed clouds of live steam. The engine was named, happily, *The Best Friend of Charleston*. An engineer stood on the platform behind the boiler, stoking wood into the firebox. A steam safety valve hissed at his elbow. The locomotive snorted, chuffed, jerked into motion. Gathering speed, the steam valve hissed louder. And louder. And louder. The engineer, irritated, shut it down. "Uncle Steph..." *The Best Friend of Charleston* blew up. The engineer was dead in the wreckage.

Thaddeus grew taller and lankier, his body advancing into the awkward stage of adolescence. His fascination for trains matured apace. "Uncle, the Mohawk and Hudson has built seventeen miles of track between Albany and Schenectady.

They're in direct competition with Uncle Nathan and the Erie Canal. Can we go?"

Such impudence! Directors of the new railroad had the gall to name their first steam locomotive *De Witt Clinton* after the New York governor who had been father of the competing Erie Canal. As the railroad plotted to snatch away the canal's booming freight business, the name was salt rubbed in the wound. The maiden run was made on a broiling summer day. "She'll haul three open passenger cars, Mr. Stewart, and a half a dozen flatcars of freight. Glad to have ye aboard, sir. And the lad. And the, uh, Indian." They perched on hard wooden seats, clutching their hats. The *De Witt Clinton* lurched forward on a head of steam. The speed was breathtaking, the smokestack disgorging a fiery trail of sparks. Thaddeus, Uncle Stephen and Crippled Wolf beat at smoking embers showering their clothing. As the train whooshed past a crowd of spectators, a lady's parasol caught on fire. Her shriek was lost in the rumble and wind.

Thaddeus became the thoughtful teenager, ever doodling, ever scribbling in his diary. "Uncle, what a shame that trains can run only in daytime. With proper lights, they could operate at night, too." Reflectorized candles didn't work, for the wind blew them out. Thaddeus doodled and pondered. "I've got it, Uncle! We'll let the engine push a flatcar carrying a bonfire built on sand."

Trainmen were skeptical. "Well, I don't know, Mr. Stewart." A gold piece dropped into the hand of the reluctant engineer. The good man became more flexible. "What the hell, we'll let the boy try."

A pinewood bonfire was lit on a flatcar. The train chuffed off into the night. A feeble light was cast for a short distance down the track, but only when the fire was at its height. Thaddeus wearied of throwing on wood. He ran out of logs and pine knots. The disgruntled train crew, unable to light their way back home, spent the night in the forest. Uncle Stephen shrugged. "Nothing ventured, Thaddeus, nothing gained."

In the year 1842, Thaddeus was thirteen years old. The state of Illinois had great plans for building more than a thousand miles of railroad. Fifty-nine miles were completed. A mighty steam locomotive *Northern Cross* chugged the entire distance at eighteen miles an hour. But the line was doomed. Prairie grass, silent and swift, grew over the tracks faster than it could be cut away. Portions of the trip were unbearably slow as passengers were constantly getting off the train to form bucket brigades for water. Within seven years the Illinois Railroad gave up and shut down. The once-mighty *Northern Cross* gathered rust in a barnyard, a dead leviathan. Thaddeus and Uncle Stephen made the trip between Meredosia and Springfield behind a plodding mule. Illinois was left millions of dollars in debt.

There were those who saw the demise of the *Northern Cross* as the handiwork of God Almighty and the iron horse itself as an instrument of Satan. The Illinois Railroad, they declared, was dead for all time, and good riddance.

"Do you believe that, Uncle?"

"Of course not, Thaddeus."

"Neither do I."

I

Death was a presence. It had neither form nor substance, but it was there. Death was a magnitude. The old man bent his mind to it as he would to any adversary. "You will not take me easily, Death," he thought. "I'll make you exact each measure of my destruction." Ninety years of living, after all, taught a man things. It taught him not to surrender easily his belongings to a robber. And what was more precious than life, and more common a robber than Death? This he knew instinctively, without having to give it thought. Anyway, clear hard thought was no longer possible. Everything was sensation, light and shadow, and recurrences of the reality that he called pain. This was deep in his being, the pain. It stabbed through his vitals, making his big body shudder and gasp, and then it went away. At intervals between jolts, it flickered and teased at him. The rest was light, shadow, whispers, and gentle hands.

The old man's eyes opened briefly. The pain had diminished. A fly stood on the white bedspread. He focused on the fly, watching the creature rubbing its forelegs. "O tiny blob of life," he thought, "how superior you are to me now. Once I could squash you as a nuisance; now you walk over me with impunity." His thoughts drifted back into their semiconscious state. The hours passed. He napped. Life measured itself in the comings and goings of women in long dresses. He had learned to identify the whispers of their dresses as they walked. This one was Moon Flower, the Indian woman. She had hard, strong hands. That one was Betsy, the black. Her hands were light and unsure. And this one...ah, this one was Catherine. Hers were strong but gentle hands, and soothed him most.

And so they came and went, the women, in light and darkness. The hands puffed up his pillow, shaved him, bathed

5

him. It became a bother. He would have preferred to be left alone more.

The pain struck him again. He gritted his teeth. He groaned. His mind fought back. No, Death. You will not take me easily.

"Father, here is some broth. Open your eyes."

He opened his eyes. He saw the blur of her in soft daylight, the fine sheen of golden hair backlighted by the windows. Catherine. It was Catherine. The spoon came. He opened his mouth. The spoon deposited its warm, thick broth upon his tongue. He tasted, but no longer identified the taste. He swallowed, worked his mouth, grunted acknowledgment. Catherine went away. Time passed. He slumbered. He dreamed. He awakened. It was night.

"Martha," he said.

A voice whispered, "What did he say? What was it he said?"

"I don't know. He mumbles."

The fools. Isaiah concentrated his will and spoke again, through a mouth and tongue thick as cotton. "Martha."

"He wants Martha. Shall we bring her? She is so depressed, poor thing."

"Yes. Bring her." This was Catherine's voice.

He dreamed of Martha. So young and full of fire, always laughing. They were in the shack together, and he grabbed her around the waist and locked his arms, lifting her aloft. Her laughter filled his mind. He knew again the firm fullness of her thighs and breasts. Martha's eyes danced with that curious sparkle. The young, full mouth laughed and said, Oh, Isaiah...

"Isaiah? Isaiah? He won't wake up. Isaiah?" It was a raspy, dry voice. He opened his eyes again, and looked into the wrinkled face and rheumy eyes of a woman in a wheelchair beside his bed. Her hair was thin and gray, her neck long and wrinkled like a turkey's. He blinked. This was Martha? But it couldn't be Martha. Not his beloved Martha. This crone...

Time is the greatest thief of all.

"Isaiah." Her hands touched his face. They were old and veined, but strong. Clarity returned to him. Martha. He said, "Martha, will you fix dinner?"

He slept again.

When he awoke, a man was bending over him making noises in his throat. The man's hands felt of him, here, there.

The man put his ear to Isaiah's chest and listened. "Amazing," the man said. "Absolutely amazing." The man saw that his eyes were open. He smiled. "Isaiah, you're absolutely amazing." The man fussed in a black leather bag, mumbled instructions and went away. He heard Catherine's voice, saying, "Thank you, Doctor."

The doctor shook his head and muttered. "A wondrous thing."

The doctor went down the stairs. He reclaimed his stovepipe hat in the parlor. He nodded officiously to the black-garbed women seated about the room, whose gossip had been stilled by his arrival. He said, "Another day. Maybe two." Someone sobbed. The doctor put on his hat. He followed the servant girl out the front door, admiring the roundness of her buttocks.

"What did he say?" piped an old woman from the shadows.

"He said, 'Another day. Maybe two.'"

And so the word trickled out of the great white-pillared hilltop house, as news from a deathwatch always does. "Another day. Maybe two." It floated on the gray October afternoon down the hill and into the homes and workplaces of Pittsburgh. The wait hung over the city like smoke. In the taverns where men from the blast furnaces, river barges, and boatyards gathered to slake their thirst, the talk was of little else. The dying of Isaiah Stewart was an event of significance.

"Another day, I hear. Maybe two."

They were leathery men with deeply seamed faces and dark cloth caps. The grime of Pittsburgh burrowed into their pores. They bore the smell of old sweat and coal fires and crucible steel. Many spoke a smattering of Middle-European tongues. Few could read or write or figure. They had toiled since boyhood in mines, in steelmills, in foundries, and aboard the riverboats of the Ohio and Mississippi rivers. From such hard usage, men aged early and died before their time. And so there was a familiarity with death. Death closed the gap between rich and poor, employer and laboring hand, manor-born and shack dweller. This was more than a deathwatch, then; it was a celebration of shared experience. Isaiah Stewart, the man who'd built a dynasty in boats and freight business, the shrewd bargainer and taskmaster, the builder of a family empire, at last one of their own.

In narrow, bustling streets, overshadowed by tall houses

built by ironmongers of wood and native stone, people watched
the arrival of strangers with fresh interest. Not that outsiders
were anything new. Pittsburgh was a city of strangers. From
its earliest days the human tide had flowed through, on
wagons and horseback and afoot, heading west. It was the
tide of strangers that had enriched boatbuilders such as Isaiah
Stewart. Generations of immigrants had paid their hard-earned
cash for his flatboats, keelboats and scows, or booked passage
on the great Stewart steamers that now thrashed up and
down the Ohio River, splitting the hills with mighty whistle
blasts. But now certain strangers were different, and could be
identified by the fine cut of their expensive woolen garments.
They wore black for mourning, and by their manner, their
fine horses and carriages, obviously they were arriving for the
dying and the funeral that would follow. They made a regular
procession up the winding, tree-lined brick road that led to
Stewart House, followed by the murmurs of Pittsburgh.

"Well, he's a tough one, and that's a fact. I been knowing
Isaiah for fifty years. Worked for him at the boatyard when I
first come down the Allegheny. In the morning you'd go to
work before daylight and there he'd be, standing on his porch
dressed in a suit, hat, greatcoat and linen stock, checking his
pocket watch. If you was a minute late, your foreman heard
about it. Old Isaiah could not abide lateness in a man.
Drunkenness, fighting, cussing, yes; but not lateness."

"I never knowed him ask a man to do a job of work he
wouldn't do himself."

"That's true."

"I ain't surprised to hear that he dies hard. Isaiah Stewart
is a stubborn man."

"Caw, you'd be stubborn, too."

"How do you mean, mate?"

"I mean, to die and leave all them millions behind, you'd
be stubborn too."

John Colby Stewart opened one eye and surveyed the
room, taking in the unfamiliar items and giving them identifi-
cation: sagging dresser with a cracked mirror, man's picture in
yellowing tintype, dusty chair piled with his own rumpled
clothes, wall clock with a broken face, wallpaper decorated
with small roses. The window admitted gray morning light

through soiled panes. There was an odor of musk, dead cigar smoke, cheap perfume.

He rolled over. Beside him, the girl still slept. She was sixteen, no more. Her mouth was swollen and slightly ajar in sleep. Red hair lay in a tangle on the pillow. The features were cherubic, the lashes long and dark. Penny Louise, she called herself. It sounded phony, but no matter. There were a thousand like her in the river towns, homeless and adrift. One name was as good as another. Penny Louise, he thought, I'm glad to meet you. We ain't been formally introduced. I'm John Colby Stewart. That's right, Stewart. One of *the* Stewarts. That's my granddaddy's house on the hilltop yonder. You can see it on a clear day. My granddaddy's the richest man in Pittsburgh. He's in his big bedroom behind them white pillars up there, a-dying. And I'm lying in bed with a river whore named Penny Louise and gettin' another hard-on.

She stirred, rolled over and bared a small, creamy breast with a pink nipple. He moved his face down close to the nipple and studied it. There were pink nipples and there were brown nipples. This he had already learned at the age of eighteen. He wondered if his cousin Thaddeus knew there was a difference in nipples. Probably not. Thaddeus had never lain with a woman, he'd stake his life on that. Old pisspot straight-arrow Thaddeus probably never even pulled his pork. He hated Thaddeus. And then he took the nipple between his teeth and bit down on it.

She came out of her sleep with a shriek. He guffawed loudly. Frantic hands struck out, pushing him away. The red mouth contorted in rage. "You! You! You . . . !" She looked down in horror. Blood welled from a tooth mark on the nipple. She clutched at the wound in pain. "You bastard!"

The blood and rage excited him more. He felt himself swelling and stiffening. As she rolled away, fighting at the covers, he grabbed her hair and yanked her back, screaming. Then they were fighting and clawing in the covers. She spat into his face. His member was poker stiff. He tried to force her thighs apart. Blood spotted the sheets. He laughed again at the sight of it and grabbed her around the throat in a hammerlock.

"I'll break it," he said. "I'll break your pretty little neck. Lie still. Lie still, I say!" His grip tightened.

"All right," she whispered. Her body stopped thrashing.

He was breathless and exhilarated. She lay in the vice of his arm grip. He sensed his absolute mastery of her in the lock of his arm. When she spoke again, her voice was a rasp. "You're insane," she said.

"Roll over."

"What? No."

"Roll over, face down."

"Please. I . . . I hurt."

"Do as I say."

"Not again, please. Not that way again, please."

"Roll over now, or"—his grip tightened—"or I swear I'll break your fucking neck."

"Please . . ."

But she rolled over, face down. He ordered her onto her knees. He rose up behind her, positioning his member. He thought of Thaddeus. He drove himself into her.

Her body convulsed with shock and pain. "Oh, God!" she cried. "Oh, my God!"

The sky was the color of slate. It pressed down upon the panorama of surrounding hills, washing them of their autumn hues. A breeze dislodged dying leaves that fell in brown swirls. Down across the valley, smoke billowed from a score of open stacks, spreading an acrid veil over the city. Even at Stewart House, its hilltop crowned in white-pillared majesty, one caught whiffs of smoke day and night from the crucibles and foundries of Pittsburgh.

Thaddeus paced the verandah, his mood as somber as the weather. He looked down at the smoky city caught in the V of its converging rivers, their dark surfaces as still as old grass. A fitting time, he thought, for a man to die. The enormity of that consumed his mind. A misty drizzle began. Tiny beads of water stood on the broadcloth of his black suit. He paced, forward and back. A dozen times he paused to peer up at the great double windows of his grandfather's room as if to find some sign of life there. In his mind's eye he remembered the face of Isaiah Stewart—that broad, rough-hewn face he loved so well—looking down from those windows. He imagined the deep voice calling, "Grandson, come up. There's something I want to show ye." But there was nothing now. The windows remained shut. The panes stared back at him like sightless eyes. The drizzle beaded the glass with silver.

"Thaddeus. I wondered where you were."

The voice interrupted his dark reverie. Catherine stood in the shelter of the portico. He strode over and took her hands. They were cold. Fatigue etched the fine, aging face of his aunt, but seemed to give it a luster. Her blond hair, touched with gray, was drawn back in a tight bun.

"Is there any change?" he asked.

She shook her head, took his arm and matched his stride as they walked the portico. "Your grandfather is a proud man. He will not yield easily. He suffers..." She bit at her lip and stood at the balustrade, looking down at the city. As always Thaddeus was conscious of her tallness. At age nineteen he was a full six feet two, and his aunt came to his shoulder. Height, proud posture gave her a regal look. "I rather wish it were over," she said.

From here they could see the Monongahela River and the cluster of buildings and works that made up the thriving Stewart compound. Sounds of work drifted up through the drizzle. Boats of every type crowded the ways and racks. They made a thicket of stacks, masts and scaffolding. Out from the boat works, along the riverfront, spread the other major Stewart enterprise, the freight yard compound. Conestoga wagons stood hub to hub and were constantly coming and going. Teamsters whiplashed their animals. The corral teemed with horses, mules, oxen.

"It amazes me," Catherine said.

"Yes."

"There was nothing on that riverbank when your grandfather and Miss Martha came. Nothing. They lived in a shack down there and almost starved the first winter."

Thaddeus spied the raw superstructure of Catherine Stewart's own new vessel, the steamboat *Monongahela Pride*. The craft was to have twin stacks, huge boilers, ornate deckwork, a vast central salon. On the rivers, nothing afloat would match her for size and speed. Thaddeus thought of the strength of this woman and of how much she had brought to the family, by her marriage to Uncle Stephen. A legendary beauty, her steadfastness to a maimed and disfigured husband was part of the lore of river folk. More, she was a shrewd businesswoman who'd worked with her husband to expand the empire, so that now—in this year of 1848—Stewart steamboats dominated the Ohio, the Mississippi, the wild Missouri, the Kanawha. And where the steamboats couldn't go, the freight wagons did.

"Have you seen John Colby this morning?" Catherine asked. "I can't find him anywhere."

"Not since last evening, when he left for town."

"I see." She frowned. But the proud face masked its feelings. Thaddeus did not pursue the subject.

They made small talk. She was reluctant to go back into the house, indulging for the moment a quiet respite. She looked wistfully down the hill, across the sloping grounds cut by a winding drive. In summer the great yard was a place of breathtaking beauty, shaded by tall elms. But this was late October. The grass was browning, the leaves would soon be gone, the fall rains were setting in.

"Francesca and Marguerite will be arriving soon. Do you remember when we visited them in New York, Thaddeus? It was years ago. I hear that Marguerite's quite a beauty now. And then the whole family will be represented, except for—"

"Except for Maybelle," he said.

Her smile was a quick abstraction. "Yes. Except for Maybelle."

They were quiet again. It was a gift they shared, this ability to be comfortably silent in each other's company. Thaddeus also shared it with Uncle Stephen. He sensed his good fortune to have such people in his life, to be the ward of this handsome woman and the husband for whom she had fought so valiantly and won. They were also the only parents he had ever known, his closest friends. He often wondered why John Colby, their natural eldest son, did not feel the same.

"Your grandfather wants to see you," Catherine said. "It might be a good idea to go up now."

"All right."

"Shall I go with you?"

"No." He had known the summons would come, had to come. He withdrew his arm gently from hers. "I'll go alone."

The house was filled with shadows. He passed through the parlor, aware of dark-clad men and women sitting on settees, following him with their eyes. So many had come, old friends and distant relatives and people whose names he did not know at all, drawn by the long and labored dying of a patriarch. And still more came, filling the guest rooms and all the beds and extra cots; moving about the cavernous reaches of Stewart House at all hours, gliding like strange shadows; filling the dining room and kitchen with their murmuring talk and gossip. It was a reunion in black, an event of magnitude unlike any other. Thaddeus saw the burden so many guests

put on his Aunt Catherine, his Uncle Stephen and the rest of
the family and servants. He wished they would honor the
dead simply by going away. Sometimes he felt like shouting,
Get out; leave us to our trial. But he kept his tongue.

Francesca. In fantasy, she sensed their appreciative whispers. And always there were the covetous looks. Francesca.
Tall and willowy, haunting them with her dark eyes. This was
her daydream. In reality, it was not so. In reality, Marguerite
was the one they fancied. Francesca frowned, thinking of
Marguerite. Prissy, mincing Marguerite, tossing her blond
hair just so, looking back at the men with those soft blue eyes
so full of innocence. God, she despised Marguerite. Marguerite was the pilferer of Francesca's dream. Well, she would
keep the prissy little sister in her place, keep her from
straying, insist on the rectitude of her behavior. That was it.
Father would approve. Father had loved his Francesca, favored her, told her she was smart. In the years after Mother
died, when Nathan Stewart had lived alone in the mansion by
the Hudson, still building his canal and shipping empire and
resisting the onslaught of the hated railroads, it was Francesca
on whom he depended. While Marguerite went away to
boarding school, being a busybody and frittering away her
time at study, it was Francesca who was the dutiful one,
taking the place of Mother in the house.
    And then, of course, Father had died. Died in that terrible
accident, run over by the train. Of all things! Drunk, they said
he was. Standing in the tracks while the train rushed down
upon him at Syracuse, and striking out at its cyclopean
headlight with his umbrella. Well, it was a lie. Father was not
drunk. Father hardly ever drank. She loved Father. And then
Father was gone. And Francesca took charge of the mansion
by the Hudson and, ultimately, Father's business affairs.
    Now, ironically, the death of the patriarch Isaiah Stewart,
their father's father, had brought Francesca and Marguerite
together again. At Francesca's insistence they had taken the
slow route through the Erie and Ohio canals, then by steamboat to Pittsburgh. They could have made the journey more
quickly by going through Philadelphia. But this would have
meant riding the train part way. Francesca would have walked
first. "I've never ridden one of those infernal things," she
announced, "and I never shall!" And so they came by water

all the way, finally boarding at Cincinnati the mighty *Princess of the Ohio*, flagship of her cousin Stephen's steamboat fleet, for the final leg of the journey.

She dreaded going to Pittsburgh. Death held no attraction for her. It was family duty, nothing more. Of what earthly interest was Isaiah Stewart beyond being her grandfather? Francesca stood imperiously on the foredeck of the *Princess of the Ohio*, drawing up her furs against the morning chill. Not far away, Marguerite strolled the upper deck. Francesca felt again the old twinge of envy, imagining that the eyes of the crewmen were on Marguerite. Had the girl no shame? She pursed her lips and stood more stiffly, eyes fixed on the browning hills sliding past. From aft there came another blast of the steam whistle. The sound ricocheted across the river valley. A male voice cried, "By the mark, three!" Francesca dabbed at her face with a hanky. Finally, she turned and glared at her sister. Marguerite came over, her bright, oval face flushed and youthful.

"What is it, Francesca?"

"Must you flaunt yourself before every male on this river?" The words came out an angry hiss.

"Really, Francesca. Let's not start that again. I'm not flaunting myself. I'm taking a walk around the deck. Heavens, how you do carry on."

"It's not decent."

"You're such a prig."

"I'm thinking of your welfare. A girl can't be too careful when traveling. There's so much riffraff on board. All those men in the salon, gambling and telling ribald stories. What must they think of us?"

"They probably don't think anything at all. And what if they did? It's natural for a man to want to look at a pretty woman."

"And I suppose you think you're pretty."

Marguerite made a face. She held her breath briefly and then exhaled. "Francesca," she said, "you are the limit."

Francesca relaxed, smiled and abruptly changed the subject. Instinctively, she knew the subtle art of making her point and then leaving it alone. Now it was time to soothe and beguile. She gave her sister a motherly pat on the cheek. "I do worry about you, Marguerite. You might catch a chill out here. Shall we go inside?"

"No. I like it out here." Marguerite leaned on the railing,

anxious to put the bad feelings aside. "This is beautiful country. Absolutely breathtaking."

Francesca grimaced. "Beauty is in the eye of the beholder." Her eyes took in the rolling, muddy Ohio and the rocky hills flanking it on both sides. Rugged and cheerless, these hills were, their faces frequently cut by forbidding limestone cliffs. She longed for the familiar strong countryside abounding along the Hudson, where the distant Catskills rose as wispy blue-green eminences. The people they had met weren't to Francesca's liking, either. She saw them as loutish and rough-hewn, the men profane, the women cowed or too defiant, everyone in need of a bath. All were either moving west in pursuit of some folly of a dream or thinking about it. My word, she thought, was there no sophistication on this frontier? She missed the polite society of New Yorkers, even though she seldom mixed socially with them. Unexpectedly, however, her thoughts were brought up short.

"This was Father's country," Marguerite mused, gazing at the passing hills. A cold river breeze spanked into their faces. The surge of the steamboat raised bursts of spray. "To think that he traveled on this same river, and looked at these same hills. Isn't that something, Francesca?"

"Humph," Francesca said.

Shortly after noon, her worst impressions were realized. The *Princess of the Ohio* rounded a final bend and churned into the smoky environs of Pittsburgh itself. It reminded her of a woodcut scene of Hell. Fires from ironworks and coke ovens lit the darkening afternoon. Everywhere sooty stacks belched smoke and soot. What light there was from a lowering October sky seeped down through a veil of pollution. The *Princess of the Ohio* nudged to berth in an unbelievable jumble of steamers, barges and soot-blackened coal scows. Francesca pressed a hanky to her nose.

"Phew!" she said.

Fifteen minutes later the two women were settled into a hired carriage that went lurching through the crowded streets. Ancient wooden and brick buildings loomed darkly all around them. The driver bellowed, "Make way there! Make way there! Make way!" and forced his horses through the noisy crush. Odors of coal smoke and raw sewage assailed them. Along crowded sidewalks, top-hatted dandies and fancy women rubbed shoulders with tattered workmen, hawkers of sweets and lotteries, tradesmen and patent medicine vendors.

Marguerite watched from the carriage window, wide-eyed. "What a fantastic place, Francesca! It's absolutely the most incredible town I could imagine."

Francesca sniffed. "Pooh. Pittsburgh is a cesspool. I shudder to think of what lies ahead of us these next few days. If it weren't for family obligation, I'd turn right around and go home."

But Marguerite was not listening. As the carriage began ascending a wooded, winding road, she glimpsed a stone mansion crowning the hilltop, its gray-white pillars gleaming.

"Oh my," she said.

Late afternoon sunlight broke through a bank of clouds, casting the autumn landscape in a golden glow. A buggy came smartly up the driveway, tassels dancing, drawn by a pair of matched grays. The horses picked up their feet daintily and tossed their heads in splendid show. A lone man sat tall on the buggy seat. A smile lit his dusky features. He wore a gray suit of excellent cut, the collar trimmed in black velvet, a striped cravat with diamond stickpin, a black beaver hat, and handmade Italian boots of soft black leather. On the seat beside him, a greatcoat lay across a black traveling valise. The grays swung in beneath the portico of Stewart House, hooves crashing on the paving stones.

"Whoa!"

Merman, the Negro house servant, rushed out to seize the bridles but stopped, confused. The newcomer shouted, reining the skittish horses. "Grab them, man! Take the bridle!" Seeing Merman's discomfiture, he laughed, teeth flashing. But the tone of command was enough. Merman sprang to the horses, grabbing leather beneath their foaming mouths.

The driver leaped nimbly down and peeled off a black leather glove as Catherine came out, followed by Thaddeus. The latter hesitated, eyes widening, but Catherine moved swiftly forward extending her hands.

"Captain Stewart," she said. "Welcome to Stewart House!"

He bowed, brushing his lips to her hand. She turned her smile to Thaddeus. "Thaddeus, this is Captain Francis Drake Stewart, owner and master of the clipper ship *Typhoon*."

"Delighted." Thaddeus took the captain's handshake and found it pleasantly strong.

Merman, still holding the horses, was stammering something. His eyes were white saucers. Catherine heard the last of his question, ". . . take this fella around to the back, Miz Stewart?" She tossed her blond hair and laughed. "Thank you, no, Merman. I don't think that would be appropriate. I will have you see to his horses, though."

Thaddeus grabbed the greatcoat and valise from the buggy as Catherine took Drake Stewart's arm and escorted him into the house. "You're just in time for dinner. You must be starving after your journey."

"But Mister Thaddeus," Merman protested, plucking at Thaddeus' sleeve. "That man's a Negro!"

"Only on his mother's side," Thaddeus replied, pushing through the double doors with his burden. "On his father's side, he is my second cousin."

The arrival of Francis Drake Stewart created a sensation. As a large group of would-be mourners gathered for dinner, reaction ranged from stupefaction to outright hostility. Murmurs rippled through the crowd awaiting summons to table.

"Who'd you say that darkie be?"

"Francis Drake Stewart. He's the grandson of Isaiah Stewart's late brother Bartholemew."

"Ye mean old Bart Stewart, of Cape Cod?"

"The same."

"This was Captain Ward Stewart's boy, then. I knowed Ward was a hell-raiser, but this . . ."

"Handsome devil, nonetheless. Wouldn't you say so, Cora?"

"Hush, Evangeline."

"You know what they say about Nigra studs."

"Evangeline!"

"Some cheek, coming here at a time like this."

"It's Catherine's doing. I understand this black is the only surviving member of old Bart's side of the family."

"Of all things."

"But his father. I thought . . ."

"Ward Stewart's dead. Blew his brains out with a horse pistol not three months ago, I heard."

"Upon my word."

"Before doing so, he took out a newspaper advertisement in Boston, acknowledging that he was the father of Francis Drake Stewart and giving him full legal rights as his heir."

"Heir to what? Ward had been in prison for murder. Didn't have a farthing."

"Heir to the Stewart name. Isn't that enough?"

"And this man's mother?"

"Slave woman from the West Indies. Ward Stewart was once captain of a slaver ship, you know. Brought her over from—"

The talk abruptly stilled as Catherine Stewart appeared in a glow of lamplight at the head of the wide mahogany stairway. Quietly awed, the guests moved to the foot of the stairs. She came down on the arm of her husband, Stephen. They made a strangely compelling couple: the woman, slender and proud in her bearing, still strikingly attractive in her fifty-eighth year; the man, a bizarre figure both handsome and grotesque. Though he was tall and superbly Stewart, Stephen's left leg was a brass-studded peg, his left hand was a metal claw, and the left side of his face was covered with a flesh-toned silken mask. The right side of the face still bore the finely chiseled features that once had stirred the blood of every female in Pittsburgh. They were followed down by their nine-year-old twin children, Bradley and Colette.

Thaddeus stood with Francis Drake Stewart and his cousin Marguerite in a dark vestibule, watching. His heart swelled with pride for his guardian aunt and uncle. He sensed the impact they had on others. It was always so, and always would be so. Marguerite's hand touched his arm. "Beautiful," she whispered. Marguerite's sweet-scented nearness seemed to make his head swim. His glance wavered as the crowd parted to let the Stewarts through. Impulsively he reached for Marguerite's hand and squeezed it. Her body pressed lightly against him. His chest constricted with pleasure. The crowd began to drift toward the great dining hall.

There was no gaiety at dinner. Thaddeus sat at one end of the great mahogany table surveying a scene of faces above expansive white cloth, gleaming silver settings, formal plates, steaming bowls and tureens of food. The servants worked with quiet efficiency tending to plates, water goblets, wine. Thaddeus sipped at a fine claret, measuring its luster in the light. He was conscious of the strangeness of it all. They were gathered as if one had given a party, he mused, but forbade laughter. Pressing down on everyone was the reality of why they were here, the unspoken awareness of the struggle going on upstairs.

Even Stephen had lost his customary vivacity. Catherine

picked at her food, preoccupied. His cousin Francesca, tall and prim—a pretty woman, Thaddeus thought, if only she could relax—was an island unto herself. The twins, normally talkative, were silent. Francis Drake Stewart, for whom Thaddeus had taken an instant liking, caught his eye and smiled. Old Martha sat in her wheelchair and sniffed. The other guests—an ironmonger, two merchants from the city and their wives, plus half a dozen others whose relationship to the family was obscure—took the cue and were quiet.

Only Marguerite seemed herself. Consciously Thaddeus avoided looking directly at her for fear of betraying his feelings. This blond cousin stirred within him more excitement than he could be comfortable with. If he gazed at her directly, then surely the others would know. Worse, she would know, see it in his face and reject him for a fool. And yet he knew that he could not remain aloof; she sat directly opposite him, and he had the overwhelming sensation that her eyes were waiting, blue and clear and terribly magnetic. He had only to look at her to find them. Finally he looked. And they were there.

He smiled, dabbed at his mouth with a handkerchief. "Well, everyone is here, practically the entire family." His voice seemed unnaturally loud, the words empty. He was aware of the others looking at him, studying him, weighing the worth of his statement. Marguerite's eyes widened, locked onto his. They seemed to be for an instant on two levels of communication, one level excruciatingly intimate. His stomach tightened.

"Except for Maybelle," someone said. "Maybelle and her children."

Startled, Thaddeus looked down the table, seeking the speaker. There was a collective intake of breath.

Who had dared say it? Heads turned. All eyes now sought one face. Old Martha's. She had been chewing a morsel of food, the face deeply creased and the mouth and eyes buried in folds of flesh. She wore a black taffeta gown and black choker at the throat caught by a single diamond brooch. The brooch struck fire from the lamplight. The old mouth stopped chewing. A white crumb stuck to the thin bottom lip. Martha's voice rasped: "How dare you!"

Catherine said softly, "Mother."

"How dare you speak that name in this house with Isaiah on his dying bed." Martha's eyes flashed, seeking the miscreant. The tongue darted out, knocking free the crumb. "That name is forbidden in this house."

"Mother, that was a long time ago." This was Stephen speaking now. He put down a water goblet and looked at his mother with one eye. The unmasked side of his face was intense. "This is Maybelle's home and family, too. We cannot hold to such a ban forever."

"Shame on you," Martha said. "All of you, shame. Have you no regard? No one fought Isaiah Stewart on this more vigorously than I. Maybelle . . . She was my daughter as well. But you know him, know how he is. Mule-headed. Maybelle disobeyed her father—oh, so headstrong and willful she was, just like him—and defied his authority. Left her parents, she did, to go downriver with that . . . that Arab drummer man." The words came out in a rush, like a fury too long pent up. Then they lapsed. Martha became aware of where she was. "That is, well . . ."

Maybelle. There it was, out in the open like a naked wound. Maybelle. Thaddeus wished that he could speak, but held his tongue. It was not his place to speak. The taboo had held for so long, throughout his conscious memory. Maybelle's name was whispered, even in Pittsburgh, and always within the context of Isaiah Stewart's unforgiving wrath toward this wayward daughter. It was said that she had come to no good, gone downriver to New Orleans, became a scarlet woman, opened a house of ill fame. But that was talk, and talk was cheap. Of one thing, however, Thaddeus was certain, and that was the taboo. The name Maybelle Stewart had never been mentioned in Stewart House, never. Until now.

A maid entered the dining hall with a whisper of starched cloth. She went to Catherine's side and murmured, "He's asking for you."

Catherine left her place and hurried away, clutching at her gown.

Thaddeus would later regret what happened next. It was his own fault. Casting about for a quick change of subject, he had come up with the topic that fascinated him most. And, of course, his Uncle Stephen had picked it up with enthusiasm.

"They are planning to extend the railroad clear to Pittsburgh," Thaddeus said. "Probably in three years, we'll get on the train here and ride it all the way to Philadelphia."

"That's going to make a tremendous difference in shipping

time, too. Not to mention costs," the visiting ironmonger said. "Railroads are really cutting costs on freight."

"But isn't that going to hurt your business, Stephen?" asked one of the merchants. "Why ship by wagon if you can send it cheaper and faster by rail?"

Stephen cut into a wedge of roast beef, forked a morsel into his mouth and chewed thoughtfully. "It would hurt if we were unwilling to change, Hiram. The point is, we can be flexible. There's plenty of freight business for all. The way I see it, railroads have their limits, just as riverboats and canal barges have theirs. Trains can carry the goods from city to city and from state to state, but somebody's got to haul the goods from the train depot to the inland town and from the town to the farm. And then there are vast areas of this country that aren't served by railroads, and may never be served by them. This means there will always be a profitable business in overland freight wagons. The Stewart freight line isn't going out of business. Riverboats aren't in any danger either, as far as I can see. It will be a long time before there's a direct rail link from, say, Pittsburgh to New Orleans, touching the major cities in between. Besides, slow-moving bulk cargo, like coal and crushed stone, cotton, farm commodities, even a lot of industrial goods, will always be shipped cheaper by water."

"What Uncle Stephen's saying," interjected Thaddeus, "is that we're going to need every means of transportation to meet the demand. This country is growing at a fantastic pace. Why, the National Road is open now all the way to Illinois, and crowded every mile of the way during the warm weather months. But for fast, cheap transportation, the railroad is the most dramatic development in history. Why, a transcontinental railroad would—"

Someone guffawed. "A transcontinental railroad to where?"

"Why, to the far west, of course," Thaddeus said. "To the Pacific coast. To California!"

"What on earth for? Who could possibly want to go to California?"

Laughter rippled around the table. Unaccountably, the talk was growing boisterous. Thaddeus, like all true believers in a cause, was unabashed by the ridicule of others.

Finally, a female voice sliced coldly through the tumult. "Young Thaddeus suffers from the empty-headedness of inex-

perience. What he is suggesting, of course, is absolute bal-
derdash. The railroad will not survive in this country, because
good Americans simply will not tolerate it!"

Heads swiveled. Thaddeus looked down the table into the
eyes of Francesca Stewart. They were twin steel chips in a
face of fury. His mouth worked at protest, but a warning
frown from Uncle Stephen caused the words to die on his
lips. The table talk hushed.

"I'm appalled," Francesca said, "to hear Stewarts speak
openly in favor of this monstrous creation. Have you no
loyalty, no indignation? Must I remind you, all of you, that
my own father, Nathan Stewart—he was your brother, Uncle
Stephen, and Isaiah Stewart's eldest son—was killed by a
locomotive? Run down like a dog!"

"Francesca!" Marguerite protested.

Thaddeus felt his temper rising. Francesca lectured about
the ruination railroads would wreak upon America, their
direct competition to Stewart financial interests, their noise,
their pollution, and the corruption which their enormous
economic power threatened to foist upon the nation's body
politic. Finally Thaddeus could take no more. He stood up
abruptly, knocking over his chair.

"That's enough!"

Francesca, startled, fell silent.

Thaddeus fought to bring his anger under control. White-
faced, he glared at Francesca and whispered, "This is insane."

He picked up his chair and sat down again.

Dinner advanced morosely to its finish. A scraping of chairs
signaled the end. The diners drifted into the parlor. Men
headed for the library and cigars. Thaddeus was talking with
Francis Drake when Marguerite came to him. She wore a
light wrap. Her mouth was pensive.

"Would you gentlemen do me a favor?" she said.

"Of course."

"I need a breath of air. A walk. Would you escort me?"

Francis Drake's smile flashed. "Delighted." The dark eyes
glanced at Thaddeus. "What say, Thad?"

He mumbled something. Marguerite stepped between them,
taking each by the arm, and together they walked out.
Despite his own dark mood, Thaddeus again felt the delightful nearness of her. Marguerite's voice flowed musically,
speaking pleasantries. His old discomfort returned in the face
of small talk. What a dolt he was, so clumsy at the simplest

social graces. He could not chitchat. Frances Drake, he observed, had no such inhibitions. Bantering, laughing, this mulatto cousin kept up a running exchange with Marguerite as they stepped into the evening chill. The coal smoke of Pittsburgh wafted up from the valley.

Marguerite wrinkled her nose.

"What's wrong?"

"That smell. Is it always so strong?"

Thaddeus laughed. "Worse. This is a clear night. But that's Pittsburgh. We don't mind actually. Coal smoke means prosperity. It comes from the works. We make nearly everything in Pittsburgh, y'know. Even glass."

He was comfortable. Here was a subject he could discuss without shyness. Aware of the light pressure of her hand on his arm, Thaddeus talked on about Pittsburgh. Not until they had strolled almost the full depth of the yard to the edge of the woods did he become aware that he monopolized the conversation. He caught himself, stammered, blushed. "Forgive me. I didn't mean to carry on a monologue."

Francis Drake laughed. "Don't apologize, cousin. You do a monologue quite well. I've learned more about Pittsburgh in ten minutes than I could from a guidebook."

"Absolutely," Marguerite said. "I didn't realize anyone really had strong feelings about this town."

"I was born here, grew up here," Thaddeus said. "I'm not exactly unbiased."

Francis Drake broke stride and began patting at his pockets and muttering. He said, "I hope you two will forgive me. I left my pipe behind."

"We'll go back," Thaddeus said.

"No, no, don't you dare. I'll run and get it. You two continue your stroll." With a wave and a flashing smile, Drake was gone.

They watched his lean frame move swiftly up the hill, long legs eating up the yards. He mounted the lighted verandah and vanished into the house.

"Fascinating cousin," Marguerite said.

"Do you like him? I'm glad. I'm rather pleased with Drake. Adds spice to the family, don't you think?"

"Between Francis Drake, Maybelle, and you, I'd say there's quite a bit of spice." Marguerite held his arm more tightly and they swung onto the driveway, walking down the hill. "The Stewart blood runs hot, I'm told."

"Really? Who says?"

"Francesca." Marguerite chuckled lightly. The sound was like music. "And not with approval, I might add. My sister can be quite prudish. Fire and ice, you know."

The confrontation at dinner nagged at Thaddeus's mind. He felt a powerful need to make amends. This seemed as good a time as any. "I'm sorry for the way I acted with your sister. I should have been more tactful. She does have reason to feel strongly. After all, your father was..."

"Killed by a train?" Marguerite sighed. "Well, that's certainly true enough. But it wasn't the train's fault. Trains can't think, after all. Even you've got to admit that."

He caught the teasing inflection in her voice and smiled in spite of himself. "True enough."

"Besides, Francesca can be terribly assertive. I honestly think sometimes she wishes she were born a man instead of a woman."

"Are you not happy with your sister?"

Marguerite shrugged.

"Francesca's all right in her way. After father died, she felt responsible for me. We're only two years apart in age, but two years between sisters can make a tremendous difference. Francesca has a need to be dominant. It's her nature. But I suspect that she's awfully lonely deep inside."

"I understand she's done amazingly well in business."

"True. When it comes to business, Francesca is a match for any man."

"How did you two come to..."

Marguerite anticipated his question. "How did we come to this state of affairs?" She chuckled, with an edge of bitterness. "I guess you'd call it fate."

Marguerite seemed to welcome a chance to talk, to unburden herself to someone who would listen, who cared. The sisters had inherited the fruits of their father's steamship and freight empire, on the Hudson River and the Erie Canal. Their wealth was reckoned in millions. When Francesca reached age twenty-one, she filed a lawsuit to take personal charge of the businesses—the river steamers, the canal packet boats, the freight warehouses. Her father's former associates cringed. The all-male management threatened revolt. "A woman," they declared, "has no head for commerce. She'll ruin us."

Francesca won her suit. Her first act was to fire all the men who had opposed her takeover and replace them with people of unquestioned loyalty. She raided rival companies for management talent, then viciously undercut competitors for freight business to build volume business. Within a year, the voices of derision were stilled along New York's docks and wharfs. Francesca Stewart, just turned twenty-three, was a competitor to be reckoned with.

But among the sisters, things did not run smoothly. Marguerite had an independent nature, refused to be bossed like a hireling. Clashes were frequent and bitter, and all the more so because Marguerite attracted males as strongly as Francesca repelled them. The sisters drifted apart. "And now," Marguerite admitted, "I'm afraid there's no love lost between us."

Thaddeus thought of his own strained relations with his cousin, John Colby. The two had been brought up as brothers, and yet John Colby's animosity at times became open, naked hatred. Thaddeus started to speak of it, and then changed his mind. A more compelling mood possessed him. "But you're so different," he said, "so beautiful and"—he caught himself, flustered, but stumbled on—"and desirable."

Her face turned to him. In the dim light, he could not tell if she was smiling or teasing. Thaddeus suffered another flash of embarrassment. Damn his clumsiness!

"Desirable?" she asked. The face of Marguerite Stewart was a light oval in the shadows, almost translucent. Her beauty, at this closeness, seemed ethereal. They had stopped walking and she half turned, her breast lightly brushing his arm.

"What?" he said.

"You used the word 'desirable.' Do you find me so, Thaddeus?" Her voice dropped almost to a whisper. He had the distinct impression that Marguerite was trembling. His mind must be playing tricks! He drew back from her slightly.

"I . . . mean to say that you're a young woman of charm and, uh, personality. Not at all like your sister."

"I see."

They walked on, not touching now. But his mind was in turmoil, his heart hammering. Did his senses deceive him?

It was she who broke the silence. "What is Maybelle really like?"

"Maybelle?"

"I've heard dreadful things. Father never spoke of her. But Francesca says that Maybelle had the morals of an alley cat.

She calls Maybelle an evil Stewart, one who inherited the bad seed. Do you believe that?"

"Do you mean, do I believe what they say about the Stewart blood?"

"Well, yes. That too. Is there something in our nature that... that's not what it should be?"

Thaddeus let the question seep into his mind. Should he tell her of his own father? The weakling of Isaiah Stewart's offspring, Burl Stewart had been a drunkard and erstwhile religious fanatic who fled downriver, came back a changed man, and eventually was murdered along with his wife and small daughter. Only Thaddeus, who was visiting his grandfather at the time, survived. They said that Burl took to his grave dark and mortal secrets of his past. And what of Maybelle Stewart? She had become, it was said, a bordello queen in New Orleans, fled to St. Louis when her lover was slain and finally went overland to California with two bastard children by different fathers. Should he speak of Maybelle? And then there was the other branch of the family which had produced Francis Drake Stewart. Drake was the son of Ward Stewart, the slaver captain, and a black woman in Jamaica. Ward Stewart had committed a murder, gone to prison, had his freedom bought by this illegitimate mulatto son, and died a suicide. How much did Marguerite really wish to know? And what purpose was there in telling her?

"Every family has its skeletons in the closet," he said. "Ours is no different."

It was not enough. He sensed her vexation at being rebuffed. And so, quietly, he told her the truth, at least as much of it as he knew. There were also things about her own father, Nathan, that she did not know. Nathan Stewart had carried on a stormy love affair, it was said, with Lucy Durange, the wife of a New York business tycoon, and then died an alcoholic.

When Thaddeus finished speaking, they walked in silence, deep in thought. Finally he realized that they had walked off the hill and were now on the river road. A cold breeze came off the Monongahela. A half-moon stood high over the Pennsylvania hills, outlining the woodlands in ghostly silhouette. Marguerite shivered and took his arm again. It was such a natural act, taking his arm, and the pleasurable sensation poured through him with a molten warmth. The rest happened as an automatic response for both. At one instant they were apart, two separate lives in the night; at the next, he had folded her into his arms and their mouths met. Her lips were soft and afire. As he drew her to him, she moaned and tightened her arms around his neck. The fire of it inflamed his mind, his chest, his loins. As his manhood swelled in response, he tried to draw away, but she pressed against him. Their breathing came in gasps, punctuating the night.

"Marguerite," he said. "Marguerite."

Abruptly, they separated. The flush of joy and embarrassment was in his face. Her eyes glowed from dark orbs. A trick, he thought. A trick of the light.

"What are we doing?" she whispered. "I don't know what's come over me."

They locked hands, turned and walked back up the road. Moonlight sifted through the trees. The empty road fell away before their feet, and they seemed to float. His mind was a mad swirl, his chest seemed on fire, his testicles ached.

"This is unbelievable," she said.

"Yes. How do you feel? What do you feel?"

"I feel... I feel lighter than air, like a thistle. I have wonderful pains, like needles, running all through me. I want..."

His arms encircled her again. Again, they came together. Their mouths met hungrily. They strained against each other and felt a joyful, moonstruck, spectacular madness. Around them all nature held its breath. The damp hollows of the night waited expectantly. The moon rode high, sliding in and out of fleecy clouds. Then...

"Please. Thaddeus, no." She pushed away, gasping for breath.

He backed away from her again. They linked hands, staring at each other. They turned and walked. The road steepened, winding through the night. At last the white pillars of Stewart House rose into view, and behind them the windows glowed with lamplight.

They were separate once more, climbing the porch side by side, hands apart, communing in their shared silence. At the door he whispered, "I shall never forget this evening."

"Nor I," she said.

They entered the house.

Francesca was waiting for her in their shared room upstairs. Marguerite walked in and the flush of happiness was upon her, too powerful to be subdued.

Francesca glared. "For shame. Your behavior is positively sinful."

"What are you saying?"

"You are trifling with the forbidden fruit."

"Francesca . . ."

"You little fool. Thaddeus Stewart is your first cousin!"

Just before dawn, Isaiah Stewart died.

"How lovely is thy dwelling place, O Lord of hosts! My soul longs, yea, faints for the courts of the Lord. Even the sparrow finds a home and the swallow a nest for herself . . ."

Parson Millsap Canaday was pleased. Yes, pleased. He fixed his eye upon the great mahogany coffin with its sheen of polished wood and gleaming brass fittings. Massed behind the bier were the floral tributes, tier upon tier of them, rising to the ceiling of the altar alcove. A splendid scene. "Blessed are those who dwell in thy house," he contined, "ever singing thy praise." His voice had never been in better form. Positively mellifluous, it was, with a rich timbre that rolled out over this host of mourners. Even the weather cooperated. Sunlight poured down through the massive stained-glass windows of the sanctuary, breaking into varicolored beams to illuminate, almost with a heavenly light, the bier of the dear departed. Ah! He completed the psalm and went into his text. "We are but putty in the hands of the Lord, molded out of dust and ashes. Ashes to ashes, then, and dust to dust. Only the soul lives on and is immortal. We are gathered here to pray for the immortal soul of Isaiah Stewart, a good and righteous man, a builder and a prince of commerce, that he may find eternal rest in the presence of our Lord Jesus Christ, the Savior who is in heaven." Parson Canaday put his hands together in a favorite gesture of piety and looked to heaven. He bowed his head in silent supplication and the organist, taking his cue, came up with the haunting strains of "Prelude to the Glorious Host." Yes.

It was a feather in his cap, indeed, to have so notable a funeral. Nothing of this magnitude had occurred before in the thirty-odd years of his ministry. Parson Canady felt it a blessing from Almighty God, for one could speculate pleasurably upon how the church's budget stood to be enriched. Every pew was filled and the crowd overflowed into the churchyard. The great and near-great of Pittsburgh were all here. The governor of Pennsylvania sat in the second row, behind the Stewart family. From the White House there had come a special emissary, bearing a message of presidential condolence.

The parson would love to have lengthened the service considerably with a full choir, a grand musical program and a two hour sermon in keeping with the enormous importance of the deceased. But Stephen would not hear of it. "My father was not a churchgoing man, Parson," Stephen Stewart had said. "He would not hold for great display now. The fact that we are having a funeral at all is in deference to the living, not the dead."

Well, nobody in Pittsburgh had ever said the Stewarts weren't a strange lot. Headstrong, they were; headstrong and handsome and fiercely independent. Isaiah Stewart and his family had fueled the town's gossip for so long, Parson Canaday reflected, that one more log on the fire wouldn't matter much. The parson, shepherd to an ever whispering flock, glanced down at the family pew. His face was composed in piety but his mind worked at conflicting thoughts. The hell-raising grandson, John Colby, sat in his black mourning suit, sullen and defiant; that one, Parson Canaday sensed, would come to no good. The tall, handsome Thaddeus held the hand of his Aunt Catherine, who grieved behind her black veil; Thaddeus was the brilliant offspring, the one most likely to make something of himself. Other faces flicked across the parson's consciousness: the widow Martha, her grief masked in the countenance of old age and blunted by the knowledge that she would join Isaiah soon; the two female cousins from New York, daughters of the dead Nathan Stewart, seemed to have no love lost between them; the disfigured Stephen—egad, the suffering that man had gone through—his twin children, Bradley and Colette, and his Indian friend, Crippled Wolf; the handsome colored cousin, Francis Drake, about whom all Pittsburgh prattled. Indeed, the parson thought, the Stewarts are a strange and oddly predestined lot.

"May the Lord cause His face to shine upon you, and give you peace."

The organ music swelled. The parson stepped back from his pulpit. The black-clad pallbearers rose and came forward. Ushers pushed open the double doors, flooding the sanctuary with afternoon sunlight. Things were moving along quickly. Here, too, the parson was disappointed. He had hoped—

suggested delicately, in fact—that the coffin would be opened one last time, permitting the bereaved to see their loved one before his final journey. The ritual of viewing always made for a fitting conclusion, the parson thought. Again, Stephen Stewart would have none of it. In the face of this strong veto, even the mortician had been somewhat offended. The good man was, after all, quite proud of the work they'd done at cosmetics for the deceased. The parson hoped that even now Stephen would change his mind. But no. The pallbearers advanced in somber procession, surrounded the casket, hoisted it by its brass fittings and bore it majestically out to the waiting hearse. The black-caparisoned horses tossed their plumed heads as if anxious to be off.

Parson Canaday and the mortician exchanged commiserating glances, the meaning of which each clearly understood. How much better it would be if families left these things to the professionals.

The grief came upon her in a rush. As they had prepared to leave Stewart House for the funeral, Catherine was clear-eyed and composed at one moment, racked with sobs the next. Quickly she had dropped the black veil over her face and kept it there. The funeral service was mercifully brief, thanks to Stephen's insistence. Parson Canaday meant well, she supposed, but as Stephen had said, the man was also inspired by his own self-interest. And so the church portion of the ritual was done, and now the somber caravan of mourners' carriages and buggies rattled along slowly through clear autumn sunlight up Cemetery Hill toward the family graveyard. Catherine was amazed at the size of the crowds. They overflowed the church, and lined the cemetery road. She looked through the mesh of veil at passing faces, somber and work-worn for the most part, ordinary laboring men, their wives, their children. The men stood with their caps off in respect, and the stoic faces seemed to share, or at least to understand, what Catherine was feeling. This was an oddity of sorts, for she did not fully comprehend it herself. All she knew was that the death of Isaiah Stewart was for her an enormous loss.

"Are you all right?" It was Stephen speaking. He sat closely beside her, holding her hand. The strength of his presence gave her a powerful sense of support. "You're not ill or anything?"

"I'm all right," she said. "It just came over me, that's all. He was such a strong old man, durable as gnarled oak. And now he's gone."

Old Martha sat in silence across from Catherine, seemingly lost in her thoughts. The children and their cousin Marguerite were crowded in beside her. Martha's ancient face expressed no emotion. Her eyes were quite dry. Abruptly, she raised her voice over the noise of the carriage. "Where is Isaiah?"

Catherine was befuddled for a moment, unable to reply. She reached across and took Martha's hand. The hand was heavily veined and dry to the touch. "Grandmother..."

"Is Isaiah in the hearse up there?" Martha looked up the curving dirt road to where the shining black hearse labored on the final ascent, its crystal windows flashing sunlight and the plumed heads of the horses bobbing with rhythmic grace. "He's in the hearse, isn't he?"

"Yes, Grandmother."

"I see." The old lips pursed, the eyes turned back and seemed to lose their focus. "Isaiah died, didn't he? Forgive me. I forgot." She was silent again.

The procession rounded the brow of Cemetery Hill. The great line of carriages and buggies broke apart in quest of parking places. It had rained the night before, so the many wheels and horses' hooves quickly churned up mud. Mourners climbed down from their vehicles and picked their way up the slope to the grave, muddying shoes, trouser cuffs and dress hems.

The grave was an open wet wound in the grass, flanked by piles of earth. A fresh tombstone stood at the head, its face newly chiseled with the legend "Isaiah Stewart, 1758-1848. Rest in Peace."

Catherine stood with Stephen and Martha, forcing herself to look down into the grave as the pallbearers brought the casket and placed it for lowering. She thought, "And here is where it all ends, Grandfather. Here, in this hole in the ground. The miracle of life, of all things you tried to do and did do, and of your thoughts and dreams, come down to this. You were a strange man in so many ways and I cannot say that I truly understood you. And yet you loved me, and showed me that you loved me. You took me in when I was but an orphan child working in your stables; you made me a part of this family and gave me a heritage that I would not otherwise have had. And you made it possible for me to have the most precious gift of all, the love of your son Stephen. I cannot imagine life without Stephen, Grandfather..."

The parson strode to the graveside, opened his leather-bound Bible, cleared his throat and began to read. His somber phrases flowed out upon the clustered black-garbed masses and quickly evaporated in the immense silences of the hilltop. Scraps of phrases intruded upon Catherine's consciousness but did not remain. She looked across the grave into the face of her eldest son, John Colby, and was startled. For it bore an expression of... of almost malicious pleasure. It was true that Grandfather had disliked the boy and their relationship was never close, but surely John Colby could not be so empty of feeling now. Catherine resolved to speak with him about it, and also about his frequent absences from Stewart House lately. But the resolution quickly dissolved as the pallbearers undid the restraining straps and prepared to lower the casket into the grave.

"The Lord is my shepherd," Parson Canaday intoned. "I shall not want..."

II

"Heeee yiyiyiyiyiyi!"

The herd was a living storm. It thundered around him in a mighty gray swirl that shook the earth. The Indian felt a surge of fear. He kicked at the pony's flanks with bare heels, driving the terrified animal sidelong against the pack. Ahead, leading bisons of the mass began to pour over the edge of the bluff. Plunging and bellowing, the horde tumbled down fifty feet into the bottom of a boulder-strewn ravine. Unless he broke free, Standing Bear would be borne with them, a chip in the torrent.

"Yiyiyiyiyiyi!"

Again he gave the keening cry and struck out with his feathered spear. A crack widened in the mass, making a narrow passage, and then another. Bison stench filled his nostrils. Dust choked him. Everywhere, charging beasts grunted, sweated, bulled forward head to flank, eyes rolling dumbly white.

At the brink, his pony broke into the clear.

He brought the animal around and reined in, breathing hard. The herd roared and tumbled down. Necks snapped and leg bones shattered. Abruptly the remaining mass veered sharply and swept westward down a gentle slope. The ravine was left its struggling, bleating carnage.

He spoke to the pony and caressed its trembling neck. "Kani wallihey," he murmured. "Be still." And now he let his anger rise, flowing powerfully and making the taste of gall upon his tongue. It had been a stupid maneuver on someone's part, driving the pack against him like that. Who?

Standing Bear glanced across the mud-churned track. A lone Indian sat rigidly on his pony, watching him. It was the warrior, Black Feather. Eyes glittered back at him from a face ravaged by pockmarks. Wordlessly Black Feather turned his pony away and snicked it to a trot.

The man's hatred was as vast as a stormy sky.

"Ayee, Standing Bear, I thought you were killed. An amazing escape. We saw you and could do nothing. It was as if the great river had swept you up." His friend Hawksblood rode in close. The brave sat on his speckled pony loosely, his sinewy body caked with sweaty dust. His eyes searched Standing Bear's face. "You are all right, my brother?"

"Yes." Standing Bear slipped a tomahawk from his waistbelt and nodded down at the ravine. "Let us hurry and finish."

They rode side by side into the ravine. Other braves were already at work killing off the injured bison. They used tomahawks, spears and knives. Some of the men carried smoothbore rifles but did not use them. Powder and ball were too precious to be wasted. There was a stench of blood.

A young brave came to him wiping blood from a hunting knife. This was one of the loyals, not of Black Feather's faction. "It was Black Feather," the brave said. "He brought down a big bull with his spear, causing the herd to turn into you."

Standing Bear drove his tomahawk into the brain of a struggling female bison. The great body stilled. "I know," he said.

By the time they finished, the sun was a blaze of molten copper. Heat waves shimmered above the western horizon. Now the squaws came to cut up the meat and salvage the hides. Standing Bear rested on his haunches, cleaning the tomahawk. There would be many robes for the lodges from this hunt and much meat to dry for the winter. Shemkuk would be pleased.

The thought of his father warmed him. He squinted toward the far western mountains, their peaks touched with fire. He had never climbed the peaks but had often seen their ghostly whitecapped mirages rising from the hot land. Someday they would carry Shemkuk to the mountains for his final rest. The prospect, however remote, bore heavily upon Standing Bear. His father's strength and wise counsel was so essential to these people. How could Standing Bear, or anyone, ever pick up the burden of being chief of his Cheyenne tribe? A chief must think for his people and practice restraint. "The wise leader," Shemkuk was fond of saying, "leads with his thoughts, not his passions. Let others be hotheads. Survival of the people is not their responsibility."

Survival of the people. Standing Bear wondered if the burden would be too great. This was his eighteenth summer of life. He put the thoughts from his mind.

Black Feather returned after sunset accompanied by the dozen young braves who always followed him. Standing Bear avoided confrontation, waiting for the other to make the first move. Brush fires lit the ravine as the women labored through the night, singing and chattering. Finally Black Feather approached him. "We found another group of white man's wagons," he said, motioning toward the east. "They're camped beyond the big valley."

Standing Bear masked his sudden concern. Silently he cursed himself for not putting out scouts. He had almost allowed them to be taken by surprise. The smirk on Black Feather's face indicated that he was not alone in recognizing the blunder. Standing Bear rose up and slipped the tomahawk back into his waistbelt. "We will keep an eye on them," he said.

He spread a buffalo robe on the ground, lay down and went to sleep.

They were up and mounted before first light, moving silently single file toward the gray smudge of dawn. As the sun came up, Standing Bear shaded his eyes and peered ahead. Dust plumes advanced from the east, moving wisps that caught the sunrise like tiny blobs of smoke. Beneath them he could make out the jerky white shapes of canvas-topped wagons on the move.

They tethered their ponies in cottonwood and hurried up the slope toward a rocky outcropping. The place was at the base of a great butte and commanded a panorama of low hills and the broad valley. Standing Bear put his back to Black Feather and climbed the last hundred yards alone. The other braves were watchful as he ascended the outcropping and squatted.

The wagon train was even larger than one that had come through a month earlier. He counted twenty wagons. As the dust swirls grew, he tried to put Black Feather from his mind. Hatred was the burden of the bearer. But his rival's hatreds were limitless, and extended even to those whites down there. On the trek from the bison kill, Black Feather had talked of raiding the wagons for whiskey and women in defiance of Shemkuk's strict orders against unprovoked attacks on whites.

Two hours passed. The sun blasted down as if to wither every bush and scrub tree. Heat baked his back and skull. Standing Bear did not stir. Only his eyes shifted, taking in the dust-blown train, the tall armed riders watching the hills, the plodding mules and oxen, the women in their shapeless long dresses and faded sunbonnets. Up from the valley came the clatter of white people on the move. He never ceased to wonder at the enormous quantities of goods they needed for survival: the pots and pans and kettles, the kegs and crates, the heavy furniture of dark wood for their lodgings. Much of it they threw away as the miles got harder and water became scarcer, so that the wagon trail was littered with droppings of travelers who had gone before.

Truly, the white man was an enigma. In hottest weather he wore heavy clothing, boots, belts and broad-brimmed hats. His women did not look like women at all, but formless hulks. They covered their bodies, Standing Bear's father said, out of shame. Unsuited for harsh terrain and weather, bringing their young and old, cattle and pigs, dogs and cats, the white men pushed westward. Suffering and sickened, they buried their dead in the ground or beneath mounds of stones.

But there were good and kind whites just as there were good and kind Indians. This he knew from his childhood, when the white plainsman call Van Harrison had come to the village of Shemkuk. Harrison, a lean, hawk-faced man with pale blue eyes, had remained with them for more than a year. He had taught the boy Standing Bear to shoot a rifle and to read the lines on parchment called a map. He had taken a wife from Shemkuk's tribe, named Eyes-of-the-Night. And then they had left, never to return. He lay on the high rocks now, watching the wagon train and thinking of Harrison.

The wagons snaked beneath the butte. Standing Bear backed away from the outcropping and went to his pony. The others followed. As he mounted, Black Feather stayed him.

"What will you do, son of Chief Shemkuk? Will you join us to attack the whites?"

Standing Bear looked down the row of the flinty black eyes. Of the fifteen braves accompanying them, he could be certain of the loyalty of only three. He kept his face as empty as the plain, betraying neither decision nor weakness. "Black Feather need not ask such a question," he said. Gathering the rope bridle, he turned his pony away.

The choice was slim. He could take his three braves and return to the village, leaving Black Feather to do as he pleased, or follow the wagons in hope that his presence would discourage his restless rival. He decided to follow the wagons.

Shemkuk's Cheyenne had spent this summer in the low hills. Game was plentiful and the old ones were spared the usual northward trek for the summer. To the west, the land gave way to desert before reaching the mountains. Game and water were scarce and no Cheyenne saw reason to go there. Only white men went into the desert, to cross it in utter misery and maddening thirst, leaving behind the bleaching bones of their animals. Standing Bear and his Cheyenne rode westward, keeping out of sight of the wagon train. At last they descended into the stifling reaches of shimmering heat and scorching sand.

In late afternoon of the third day, the whites made camp in a sandy waste dotted with clumps of mesquite. As Standing Bear took up his vigil on a rocky hillock, he heard a woman cry out and saw people running toward a travel-worn wagon.

From the activity he soon deduced that someone had died. At nightfall the travelers gathered around a small fire. A man garbed in black made a long, sad speech and then the group sang a mournful song, its sound floating out across the desolate land.

Black Feather moved to Standing Bear's side. "Now is the time, while they are busy making songs for the dead."

Standing Bear did not reply.

"My men will move from that side over there, and yours from this," Black Feather persisted. "Are you ready?"

"If you do this, Black Feather, you do it alone—"

"You speak like an old woman."

"—and in defiance of my father's wishes."

Black Feather grumbled. "Shemkuk thinks with more caution than good sense. He does not think as a Cheyenne warrior chief. And we let the whites roll over our hunting grounds without striking back."

Standing Bear half-smiled. At last he understood why Black Feather discussed the attack with him at all. He was afraid to move on the wagons with only twelve warriors. If Standing Bear agreed to participate, Black Feather would have a greater number of braves and also the approval of the chief's son. This would solidify the attack and enhance the warrior's authority. Now Standing Bear was more sure of his ground.

"Your words," he told Black Feather, "pour as water upon the sand."

At daybreak three men from the wagons went into the desert collecting stones. They heaped the stones in a mound and dug a deep hole in the sand. Another group carried out a body wrapped in white winding cloth and lay it beside the hole. The people gathered around for more solemn speech-making and singing. A woman wept. They lowered the body into the hole, covered it with sand, and piled the stones over the grave. One of the men lashed two sticks together in the form of a cross and stuck the symbol into the sand at the head of the grave. Then the wagonmaster shouted, people climbed onto the wagons, whips cracked, and the train jerked into westward motion again.

Sunlight poured down from a cloudless sky. Heat blasted the earth, radiating shimmering waves of stifling air. A rattlesnake slithered across the wagon tracks, leaving S-curves in the sand.

The Cheyenne watched them go, and this time did not follow.

Standing Bear led the braves back to the village of Shemkuk. No one spoke, for each rider was acutely conscious of the strain between the rivals. Black Feather rode stiff-backed with wounded pride. This was, of course, the problem between them. Pride. Black Feather was a resourceful and brave warrior of great physical strength, but he was afflicted with a deep and bitter envy. He lacked the physical attractiveness to match his strength, for he was badly scarred from a childhood attack of smallpox. The face of Black Feather was a mass of pits and pockmarks. Women shunned him.

Standing Bear, by contrast, was a young man of great physical beauty. It was said that he could have any maiden of his choosing, even if he were not the son of a chief. Women's eyes followed wistfully his every move among the lodges of the village. And so when the scouting party rode in, the usual crowd of adoring young females jostled for the privilege of taking the reins of his pony.

Standing Bear leaped to the ground and pushed through to the lodge of Shemkuk. An ancient squaw squatted at the entrance, stirring a pot of broth over a low fire. In response to Standing Bear's questioning glance, she jerked her head toward the lodge. "He awaits you." Standing Bear ducked into the entrance, adjusting his eyes to the gloom. It was hot and there was the odor of stale tobacco smoke and his father's sweat.

He heard a cough and the familiar deep voice. "You have returned, my son. That is good."

Shemkuk lay on a buffalo robe, his pipe and tobacco within reach. The chief's naked torso was strong and muscular, well defined. The eyes gazed calmly from deep sockets. Shemkuk's long hair was plaited and dressed with bear grease.

"And what did you find out there?" Shemkuk asked.

Standing Bear told him of the bison which they had run over the high bluff and killed. He praised the work of the huntsmen, and of the squaws who had butchered the meat and brought it home. He spoke glowingly of the provisions this would make for the winter. At last he fell silent under his father's scrutiny.

"What else?"

"Another wagon train of the whites," Standing Bear said. "We followed them for three days to the edge of the desert."

"And was it large, this wagon train?"

"Twenty wagons."

"I see." Shemkuk sighed. "There will be many, many more."

"They have not harmed us, Father."

"Not yet. But by their very numbers we must come to conflict. The white man intends to take this country. He will claim all of these lands, the lands of our fathers and our fathers' fathers. There will be no more open hunting grounds for the Cheyenne, the Sioux, the Arapaho. These people that you see passing in their wagons are but the beginning. They are as numerous as the sands and as unconquerable."

"But what of the treaties. I hear—"

"Treaties, my son, are meaningful only to adversaries of equal strength. The white man makes treaties now, and will continue to do so only for as long as they suit his purposes. Beyond that . . ."

Shemkuk paused, gathering his thoughts. The talk was painful to him, Standing Bear could see, but necessary. The pain was that of a man in dread for the future. Standing Bear waited in silence and watched his father's face.

". . . Beyond that, I fear there will be no concern for the Indian. No concern at all."

"Perhaps, then, Black Feather is right. Perhaps we ought to attack their wagon trains, make known our strength. Father, there are no warriors like the Cheyenne."

"Black Feather!" Shemkuk spat the name. "A fool and a scoundrel. He broods darkly, filled with malice, but suggests nothing positive. Such men would counsel conflict and death but offer nothing by which the Cheyenne can live. Remember, my son, without life there is nothing. It is all very well to die prematurely, and perhaps that is our people's fate. But if we must die, let it be for a purpose. First, we must seek after wisdom, keep our wits about us, consolidate our strengths. And that"—he looked sharply into the face of his son—"and that will be your task someday when you are chief."

"What should I do about Black Feather?"

Shemkuk groped for his long carved pipe. He shredded tobacco into the blackened bowl. He waited while Standing Bear went to fetch a burning stick from the old squaw's fire. He lit the pipe and puffed deeply, suffusing his face and head in smoke. He settled back.

"A wolf is worth keeping if you can break him to the leash. Otherwise . . ." Shemkuk shrugged.

It was late afternoon when Standing Bear emerged from the lodge of his father. Smoke from the cookfires lay over the tepees clustered along the valley by a small creek. Still water reflected leaning trees, bathed in backlight from the waning sun. He went to the creek, stripped naked and plunged in head first, feeling the velvet softness of cool water about his body. Surfacing in a shower of bubbles he looked back to the bank and saw several young women gathering to watch him swim. They giggled with a silvery, shivery sound. He smiled and waved, then struck out upstream, swimming with powerful strokes. He swam for a mile, beyond the great bend in the creek, and then stopped again, treading water, to watch ponies grazing in a green meadow cut by slanting sunbeams.

He swam to shore and came out of the creek, water streaming off his body, and dropped down in the soft grass. After a while he heard light footfalls. It was one of the young women, Willowwand. Her face glowed with excitement and she wore a blossom in her hair.

She removed her chemise and lay down beside him. Her nearness stirred his manhood erect. Gradually the sunbeams lengthened and purple twilight came down. Crickets began to sing in the tall grass. He moved over Willowwand and slowly entered her. She gave a small animal cry. A fish jumped in the creek.

Life poured, rich and full.

III

Such fuss it was, such excitement! In the terrible, terrible urgency to be ready on time, Ruth fidgeted in the chair while her mother coiffed the curls of her auburn hair. "Now just a touch here, and a little there. Ruth, stop fidgeting." Marilyn Barrett plucked the last hairpin from her mouth, set it firmly and stepped back, exhaling triumph. "There!"

"Mother, we're going to be late!" The warm brown eyes

scolded from the mirror, the pretty bow of a mouth turned
down in exasperation. "We've still got my dress to do." Oh,
the torment of being dressed by one's mother. Oh, the fuss
and bother. Her mind was a swirl; the sheer rushing pleasure
of expectation filled Ruth's bosom until she thought she
would explode. She was in her bedroom with its starched
white curtains and crocheted spreads, female possessions and
female wearing apparel and, of course, her favorite dolls,
watching her with their big blue eyes from the pink shelf.
(Hello, Mary Beth. Hello, Susan Penelope. Hello, hello,
hello.) Around her, the urgency of it was just too much. Too
much! Oh, dear.

Mother had preferred the blue gown with its bell-like
sweep backed with crinoline. But Ruth didn't like the blue
gown. Too frilly and lacy. She preferred the wine-colored
one. It looked older, more mature and the bodice was a bit
more daring. That was it. She smiled at her mirrored reflection, thinking of the bodice of the wine-colored gown and the
discomfiture of the young men as they would hover about
her, trying to keep their eyes from straying. Oh, such fun!

"You're sure you won't wear the blue?" Marilyn Barrett said.

"No, Mother. How many times must I tell you no. It's too,
too little-girlish. Now, please..."

"Very well."

And so it went, with the fixing of hair, the struggling into
petticoats and frilly pantaloons and, finally, the gown itself.
The fabric was silken and flowed over her like a warm,
smooth presence. It poured down in wine-colored splendor
upon her body, while her mother straightened and pinned,
puffed and combed and dabbed. Ruth swirled before the
full-length mirror and giggled.

"Ruth, please."

"Am I pretty, Mother? Do you think I'm pretty?"

"You're lovely, my dear. Positively lovely. Now, let me get
this one curl, right here .."

"Am I beautiful? Tell me I'm beautiful, Mother."

Marilyn sighed. "Yes, dear, you're beautiful."

"Oh, I love this. I love going to the ball. It's such a
splendid thing to do, so terribly exciting. Will I get a lot of
dances, Mother? Do you think they'll want to dance with
me?"

"My dear, they'll dance your pretty legs off, if you let
them. I daresay you'll be exhausted."

"Oh, wonderful. Isn't that wonderful? I think it's wonderful."

And finally, finally, the last pin was in place, the last stay secured, the last puff puffed. Ruth Barrett swept from her bedroom into the great upper hallway with its polished woods and brass urns. She did a little skipping step for the upstairs maid Caroline. She descended the broad, curving mahogany stairway on tiny feet. That's what Miss Fernwood had taught them at finishing school. It was terribly, terribly important for a young lady to descend stairs properly. ("Now remember, Miss Barrett, tiny feet. Tiny, tiny feet.") And below, she saw the adoring, upturned face of her father, looking uncomfortable as usual in his formal wear, and the noncommittal smile of the butler Herndon, and the other faces of middle-aged guests, all pale and round and polite, there among the gleaming furnishings and the ferns.

"Ruth, you look divine!"

And because she had chosen not to accept the invitations of any of the male escorts who'd vied to take her to the ball—there had been at least a dozen such requests—she accepted a corsage of small budded tea roses from her father, who promptly stuck himself with a pin. "Ouch!"

"Father!"

It was lovely, so lovely, all of it. One did not have to think. There was no time. Ruth's appearance galvanized them all into a flurry of gathering up and putting on, of shrugging into wraps and furs and black evening capes with their scarlet silk flashings. The men, portly and grave, produced tall top hats and silver-headed walking sticks. She recognized the banker Helms; the ironmonger Marchant, a funny little Frenchman with a wispy mustache; the broker Petersen; and the tall man named Huldane, who did something with her father's locomotives. In bright clusters trailing scent and making conversation, the party swept out of the graystone Barrett mansion into the biting cold. Carriages waited in line, their horses blowing fog. Hooves clip-clopped on the shining cobblestone drive as each enclosed carriage advanced, oil lights gleaming, and took on its passengers.

Ruth slipped into the lush darkness that smelled of leather and fine wood, accompanied by her parents and the funny little ironmonger. Her excitement increased as the carriage doors slammed and the coachman whistled the horses forward into the night. Philadelphia glowed under a light coverlet of fresh snow. She watched wide-eyed from the carriage window as they went swiftly down fairylike streets caught in the magic spell of a winter's eve. Here and there, housetops were fringed with icicles from recent thaws and freezes; lighted windows glistened through candlelit frost crystals. The others were speaking pleasantly, but she paid no attention. She let herself retreat into that delicious little never-never land that since childhood had given her such delight. Ruth emptied her mind of all thoughts except lovely thoughts and watched the passing scene from the carriage window. She let the spell remain even when they had swept up the curved gravel driveway of the Bernhart mansion, with its ornate granite facade resembling a Bourbon palace and its liveried footmen hurrying to snatch open carriage doors.

"Ah, here we are. Thank you, my man. Ruth, your hand?"

Ruth alighted on her father's arm. They seemed to flow into the great house. Her impressions were of splendidly dressed people, crystal chandeliers, murmured greetings, music. Ah, the music. It poured out from the ballroom itself, a magnificent room of tall, draped windows, high mirrors, and a grand carved ceiling with gold leaf and painted cherubs. She let her reverie hold, taking this hand and that, curtsying to the brush of mustachioed kisses on her fingers, speaking pleasantries. And then there came the customary rush of the young men. They seemed to materialize on all sides, the handsome blades of Philadelphia society, home from the colleges at Boston, New Haven, New York, Amherst. There was good-natured jostling and teasing. Her dance card quickly filled. She heard the whispers.

"Who is she?"

"George Barrett's daughter. He's in locomotives."

"Lovely creature."

"Yes, stunning."

The flattery soothed and pleased her like a warm balm. Accepting the uplifted hand of husky, blond Cawther Fotheringay, she moved onto the floor for her first dance of the evening. Ruth danced with the grace and lightness of a feather. On tiny feet. Tiny, tiny feet.

Years later, she would often think back upon this event, trying to remember when she first noticed Thaddeus Stewart. It was during the fourth dance. Or was it the fifth? Her partner had turned her around, so that she could see her reflection in one of the great mirrors, and she glimpsed Father talking with a tall young man. Fifteen minutes later, the two were still engaged in what must have been an intense and mutually engaging conversation. She asked her dancing partner, Marvin Kaskott, "Who is that tall young man with Father? Do you know him?"

Kaskott glanced over, bored. "Oh, that fellow. He's not from Philadelphia. I think he's from Pittsburgh, or some such place. He's certainly not worth your attention, my dear."

Ruth canceled her next dance, saying she was fatigued. The disappointed escort delivered her to her father.

"Ah, here she is now!" George Barrett beamed with paternal pride. "Ruth, I want you to meet a young friend of mine, Thaddeus Stewart. Thaddeus, my daughter Ruth. She's home from finishing school."

Ruth smiled up at Thaddeus. He was tall, much taller than he had seemed from across the ballroom. His features had a quality of chiseled refinement that she found quite attractive. The eyes were gray with dark lashes and somehow oddly preoccupied. There was about him, in fact, a certain air of distractedness, as if his mind were too busy to be bothered with trifles. Thaddeus Stewart's evening wear, for example, was of impeccable style and cut, but worn somewhat carelessly, a waistcoat button not fully buttoned, the lapel showing a spot of something, the white tie a trifle off-center.

"Mr. Stewart." She curtsied, offering her hand, but he did not take it immediately. He seemed flustered. Then as she began to lower her hand, he reached for it. His lips brushed the back of her glove in a perfunctory way.

"It's very nice to meet you," he said.

She noticed that his hands were broad and powerful. A little thrill passed through her.

"And what are you and Father talking about so earnestly, while the rest of the world dances around you?" Ruth smiled her most fetching smile, letting the light play in her eyes. He did not seem to notice.

"Trains," George Barrett said.

"Trains?"

"Mr. Stewart is completing his courses in the engineering school. We met two weeks ago when he came to the shops to see our new locomotive the *Barrett Limited*. It will have four driving wheels and a new lubricating system—"

Ruth giggled at Thaddeus, wrinkling her pretty nose ever so slightly. "Father," she said, "you know I don't know the first thing about trains."

"Your father is developing a very powerful engine in the *Barrett Limited*," Thaddeus said gravely. "I think it's just the sort of machine the railroads will need for mountain work. A more powerful engine means the builders can compromise a bit more on the grade tolerances, especially in very rugged country." He turned to George Barrett again, as if dismissing Ruth from his mind. For the first time in her life, she felt that there was something more important in the consciousness of a young, virile male than the charms of Ruth Barrett. "This can make a tremendous difference," Thaddeus was saying, "when the transcontinental railroad is built."

"Did I hear you say something about a transcontinental railroad?" The speaker was a bewhiskered, heavyset man wearing spectacles. He had been standing with another group near Ruth, and now peered at Thaddeus with a bemused smile. "Young man, did I understand you correctly?"

"You did, sir."

"Asa!" George Barrett exclaimed. "Asa Whitney, as I live and breathe!" Excitedly, the locomotive-maker made introductions. "Thaddeus, Ruth, this is Asa Whitney of New York. Fantastic man and a very successful merchant. Do you still run your China clippers, Asa?"

"Indeed I do, George. Trade with China is flourishing. That's why I've tried to sell those blockheads in Congress my railroad idea, but they won't hear of it."

"But, Asa, it's a very sound proposal."

"Certainly it is. That's why I barged into your conversation." Whitney turned to Thaddeus. "Forgive me, Mr. Stewart, but the fact is that I've been trying to sell the federal government on a transcontinental railroad for several years now. My China clipper ships bring tea and other goods from the Far East. These are fast ships which can cross the Pacific in wonderful time. Unfortunately, there is no direct route to our markets in the eastern United States. We've got to portage our goods across the Isthmus of Panama—unloading and loading again and using two seagoing vessels in the process—or spend six weeks beating our way around Cape Horn. If we had a transcontinental railroad with a railhead on the Pacific coast, those goods could be transported across the country in a fraction of the time and at a fraction of the cost. My idea—"

"Listen to this, Thaddeus," George Barrett interrupted. "Here comes the intriguing part."

"My idea is to finance the railroad by means of a special federal land grant," Asa Whitney said. "They've got millions and millions of unused acres in the west, absolutely worthless to anybody except rattlesnakes and wild Indians. And they'll remain worthless until somebody provides a means of access to the Pacific. Western development in this country is stymied without fast, efficient transportation. And the most logical means, the most practical and feasible, is the railroad. If Congress would grant me a swath of land from Michigan Territory to the Pacific, by damn, I'd build a railroad, sell off the land as it's opened up for settlement, and use the profits to pay for everything. I've been preaching this in Washington till I'm blue in the face, from the White House to Congress and anyplace else I can draw a crowd."

"And they won't accept it?" The face of Thaddeus Stewart had taken on a glow. "They won't accept your idea?"

"Accept it!" Asa Whitney snorted. His face turned so red that Ruth feared he would have a seizure. The spectacles slipped down his nose and he pushed them back into place with a pudgy finger. "They laugh me right out the door. Those damned politicians—begging your pardon, Miss Barrett— those fools won't even give me the courtesy of a fair hearing. Daniel Webster himself, who's supposed to be such an all-fired brilliant fellow, stood up in Congress and said, 'What on earth do we need with that wasteland anyhow? Build a railroad out there? I submit to you gentlemen of this august house that Mr. Whitney has quite lost his senses.'"

Asa Whitney stopped speaking. In his zeal, the voice of the merchant had risen to such volume that others were disturbed and even nearby dancers were distracted. He looked about apologetically, and then abruptly extended his hand to Thaddeus. "I'm sorry, Mr. Stewart. I get incensed over this. Let me give you a piece of advice. If you're of a mind to build railroads as a career, do yourself a favor and forget about it. There's nothing more frustrating than trying to sell common sense to fools." Bowing to George Barrett and Ruth, Whitney turned on his heel and walked away.

"Well..." George Barrett said.

Ruth made a face. "Now, Father, that's quite enough talk about railroads for one evening. After all, this is supposed to be a ball. Surely Mr. Stewart is interested in something other than noisy old trains." She turned a coy glance at Thaddeus and smiled. "Aren't you, Mr. Stewart?"

Thaddeus was grinning vacuously.

"Of course you are." Ruth slid her hand around his arm and nudged him gently toward the dance floor. "And Mr. Stewart is also going to ask me to dance. Isn't that right? You do dance, Mr. Stewart?"

Thaddeus felt his face reddening. "Well, now that you mention it . . ."

George Barrett smiled brightly, recognizing his daughter's intentions for the first time. "How silly of me, monopolizing Thaddeus this way. Of course. You two young people go dance and enjoy yourselves. My word, what bad manners I have."

"Miss Barrett, I believe this is my dance." The speaker was a muscular youth wearing the dress uniform of a military school. Glancing at Thaddeus with undisguised bravado, he offered his arm. "Shall we?"

Ruth curtsied, smiled. Her eyes filled with mischief. "I'm dreadfully sorry, Mr. Brannon, but I've promised this dance to Mr. Stewart." She took Thaddeus's arm. "Mr. Stewart, Mr. Brannon."

"Well, really, I don't—" Thaddeus began.

"Tah-tah," Ruth said, gaily dismissing Brannon and swinging onto the crowded floor.

Oh, the delight of it all. She was absolutely ecstatic. The men were so attentive, so handsome in their evening clothes. And now she had drawn to herself this dashing new one, Thaddeus Stewart. He was tall, taller than the others. He held her firmly but not with the sudden familiarity that seemed to possess other young males. From the instant she put her hand on his shoulder for the dance, Ruth knew that he was different. For reasons she could not understand, even the physical presence of Thaddeus Stewart seemed to thrill her. Very quickly she discovered that he did not dance well. His timing was a trifle off and he seemed uncomfortable and unduly quiet. But even this enhanced his attractiveness for her. And when they did a turning step and he accidentally pressed close to her, Ruth Barrett almost shivered.

"You and Father were so engrossed in your conversation, I felt absolutely left out," she said, bowing her lips in a pretty pout. "Aren't you sorry, Mr. Stewart?"

"Your father is a very interesting man. He has a mechanical mind. I'm fascinated by his new locomotive design."

"Oh, those silly old locomotives. He is forever going into

the shop and coming back all greasy and smelling of oil and soot. Do you do that, Mr. Stewart? Of course, you don't. I can't imagine you ever smelling of oil and soot." She made a pretence of sniffing. "You smell divine. So... so manly and delicious."

Ruth looked up at him with that big-eyed, little-girl look that never, never failed to intrigue them. By a kind of animal instinct, she could sense the immediate softening and warming of the most stuffy male when she gave him The Look. It implied, after all, so many things. It was a mixture of helpless innocence and yet almost lascivious admiration, a sweet dependence, and a promise of pleasures untold. And this, this strangely implied dual personality, this blending of the natural femininity and the womanly guile, was the essence of the mystique of Ruth Barrett. The response among males was usually instant, always predictable, practically automatic. She gloried in their fascination, fed upon their desires, and having dominated, was satisfied. It always happened this way. Always.

Thaddeus Stewart talked of trains. He talked of somebody named Uncle Stephen, who was somewhere out west—St. Louis, she thought he said—and of someone else named Marguerite who was his cousin. Ruth felt a stab of jealousy.

"How close is this cousin, Marguerite?"

"Oh, she's my first cousin."

"I see." The jealousy subsided.

Jealousy! It couldn't be. She had never, never been jealous of a male in her life. And this one... this one she hardly knew at all. Who was Thaddeus Stewart? Somebody out of Pittsburgh. They said his family was terribly rich, but then, who wasn't terribly rich? One did not move in Philadelphia social circles unless he was terribly rich.

"My Uncle Stephen and Aunt Catherine are opening a new base of operations just south of St. Louis. He has in mind to start a stagecoach line into the west. Now that they've found gold in California, he knows a stage line will flourish."

What utter nonsense, Ruth thought. Gold in California. Stagecoaches. Steamboats. Trains. She pressed closer to him, looking up into his face like a startled little girl. But he seemed not to notice. His hands—broad, powerful hands they were—moved across her back as they turned with the music. His face was lean and handsome, and a stray lock of his hair tumbled onto his forehead. She had a terrible urge to lift her hand and smooth it back. She had never known a young man who was so self-assured. And his physical strength seemed to give off magnetism. This time, she did shiver.

Three hours later, her mind alive with fantasy, Ruth Barrett stepped into her bedroom, tossed her coat onto a chair and stood enraptured. Her dolls were waiting as always: waiting, watching, listening. She was bursting with the news. And which of them would hear it first? Raggedy, of course. Raggedy was her oldest and best friend, and also the most discreet. She went to the shelf and drew Raggedy down. She poked at Raggedy's button eyes and tweaked Raggedy's button nose. And then she whispered, oh so quietly, into Raggedy's ear, "Raggedy, guess what. I'm in love! Oh, dear, I'm so much in love that I don't know what to do. And if he doesn't love me back . . . oh, Raggedy, if he doesn't love me back I shall surely die!"

At his lodgings across the town, Thaddeus Stewart sat in his evening clothes at a handsome writing desk, took out inkwell and paper and sharpened a fresh writing quill with a pocket knife. His thoughts were afire from the brief talk with the merchant Asa Whitney. Imagine, federal land grants clear across the country! Certainly it would make possible the dream of the transcontinental railroad, of this there could be no doubt.

Thus, his mind was on trains, and he savored again scraps of talk with Whitney and George Barrett. The locomotive-maker's sharing of Thaddeus's excitement warmed him, for the production of sturdy, long-distance engines was as vital to the railroad as the dreams of the promoter, the politician, the trailblazer and the engineer. And now Thaddeus Stewart had the dawning resolve that in order to succeed in what he set out to do, he would have to be all four things at once. Promoter. Politician. Trailblazer. Engineer.

Ruth Barrett flicked lightly across his mind. George Barrett's daughter was certainly attractive—a beauty, one had to admit. But she seemed to have no interest in things beyond herself. Indeed, the prattle of that entire social set seemed shallow and lacking in substance. His attention turned eagerly now to the letter he was about to write. To Marguerite.

Dear, sweet Marguerite. They corresponded at least twice a week, and usually more often than that. Her latest letter, subtly scented and written in a fine, flowing hand, lay at his elbow. He read it again by the lamplight. It was chatty and newsy as always. But he sensed between the lines of com-

ment about the weather, the social whirl of New York and her
vexations with Francesca, a more subtle message. It was
there, indeed, in the little code words and expressions they
had both come to use, signals that managed to convey amid
the commonplace their uncommon depth of feeling, one for
another. How he longed to see her again! There was so much
to talk about, so much to tell her. But even in the rush of his
fervor, Thaddeus knew that to harbor such feelings was
wrong. Marguerite remained his first cousin, and he was
hers, and there could be nothing beyond that. Nothing.

Oh, the cruel ironies of life.

For an instant, he wished that he could think of Ruth
Barrett in the way that he thought of Marguerite.

He dipped the new quill and quickly began to write: "My
dear, dear cousin..."

IV

All Pittsburgh celebrated. Half the city had converged at the
Stewart boatyard to see this launching. So huge was the new
steamboat that some swore she would never float. Others
speculated that she would topple over from the sheer weight
of that massive superstructure the moment she slid down the
ways into the Monongahela.

Stephen stood on the platform overlooking the crowd.
Everything was decorated in red, white and blue bunting:
the platform, the great vessel, the high overhang of planking
from which Catherine was to dash a bottle of French champagne against the bow. Bright June sunshine poured down. A
light breeze stirred the flags. From the shade of a huge
striped awning, set up on a verandah overlooking the boatyard,
the Pittsburgh Brass Band and Marching Ensemble struck up
a medley of martial tunes.

Stephen missed the company of Thaddeus. The lad had
gone to Philadelphia after his grandfather's death to complete

his engineering studies. The twins, Bradley and Colette, were away at boarding schools. The eldest son, John Colby, remained in Pittsburgh but was seldom at home. Stephen frowned, thinking of this wayward boy. He had heard disquieting rumors. John Colby displayed no interest in anything of substance and no desire to complete his education. There had been angry scenes between father and son. Stephen's despair was tinged with guilt. He worried about John Colby, but did not love him.

How different was his nephew Thaddeus. Thaddeus wrote every week. The letters from Philadelphia, done in a strong, firm hand, were a source of real pleasure. Stephen read them again and again. Thaddeus wrote with enthusiasm about his mechanical interests, especially as they pertained to railroad engineering.

"I have met a fine gentleman here in Philadelphia. His name is George Barrett and he manufactures a small but sturdy locomotive. I attended a formal dress ball and met his daughter Ruth. She is nineteen and one of the beauties of young Philadelphia society, I'm told. Frankly, Uncle, I was quite nervous about it. I don't socialize well and am not an accomplished dancer. My ear for music is scant. Marguerite says the deficiency also troubled her father and seems to be a family trait. This is somewhat surprising, because I could never imagine your late brother Nathan being deficient in anything..."

And there it was again, Stephen mused, the constant mentions of Marguerite. Really, he should have had a man-to-man talk with Thaddeus about women before the lad left home, and especially about the hazards of falling in love with one's own first cousin. The lad was so naive about some things.

"Where's that beautiful wife of yours?" Captain Ezekiel Potter shouted, to be heard above the music.

Stephen scanned the slope with its broad walkway of flagstone leading to the old Stewart house. The tall clapboard structure was now converted into offices and additional workshops. But still it was the house in which Stephen was born and reared, and thus, was filled with memories. Now, of course, they lived in the graystone mansion on the hilltop, but he missed the old place down here.

At last he saw Catherine emerge from the front door, tall, blonde, walking with that self-assured carriage that he knew and loved. Damn, that woman could still set his blood to racing. "Here she comes, Captain. Right on time."

There was a stirring. The crowd surged toward the platform. Dignitaries appeared; the mayor in his top hat, morning coat and sash of office; the police chief, resplendent in dark blue uniform and polished brass buttons, and sporting a magnificent black mustache; a member of Congress; assorted state legislators and local aldermen, their wives and children; leading merchants, ironmongers, industrialists and river entrepreneurs. Catherine mounted the platform and took her seat.

Stephen glimpsed another familiar face below the platform. It gave him a feeling of revulsion. Tall, black-garbed Winifred Custer, owner of the rival Black Diamond Line, returned his glance with something between a smile and a smirk. Stephen despised Custer without really knowing why. They were fierce competitors on the rivers. Crewmen of Stewart and Black Diamond vessels had engaged in savage brawls on the docks of New Orleans and Louisville. Black Diamond men were a cutthroat lot, drawn from gin mills and jails of the river towns. But his hostility toward Custer went deeper than business rivalry.

"Ladieeees and gentlemen . . ." The mayor spoke through a megaphone. The band straggled into silence. The crowd quieted. His Honor, a florid man of enormous girth, bowed and raised his arms. "My friends, this is a proud day, I say a prooouuud day, for Pittsburgh! We are gathered here for a truuuuly momentous event, the launching of the twentieth major steamboat to be produced by the Stewart boat works."

Twenty of them! Stephen himself could hardly believe that this very yard had produced so many in only seven years, but it was true. Five of those vessels were now drawn up along the near shore, freshly painted and flying their flags, to provide free excursions, complete with food and refreshments for the multitude that afternoon. And even as the *Monongahela Pride* sat poised to slide into the water (they had used a hundred pounds of grease to slicken the skids), other steamboats were being built at new Stewart boatyards in Cincinnati, Louisville, New Orleans. Soon they would open yet another new compound near St. Louis.

"And I am pleased to announce," His Honor droned on, "that your mayor and a joyous company of leading citizens will ride the *Monongahela Pride* on her maiden voyage to

Cincinnati. And there, I am told, this magnificent vessel—the newest and most powerful afloat—will take on all challengers in a massive one-hundred-and-ten-mile downriver race to Louisville. It will be the most stupendous competition of its kind ever run!" As the crowd raised a cheer, the mayor turned to Catherine. "And now, Mrs. Stewart, if you please..."

Acknowledging the applause, Catherine mounted a bunting-draped catwalk leading to the towering bow. From where Stephen sat, the enormous superstructure dwarfed her and everything else in sight. Beside him, Captain Potter took a swig from his pocket flask and belched softly. "Beautiful. Absolutely beautiful."

"The steamboat?"

"No sir. Your wife."

"I hope she breaks the bottle first crack," Stephen mused. "Y'know, it's bad luck if she don't."

"She'll break it, right enough. A woman like that can do anything she sets her mind to."

Catherine drew back the ribbon-bedecked champagne bottle. Stephen could just hear her voice, speaking in the sudden immensity of space and time as the crowd hushed. "...christen you, *Monongahela Pride!*" She swung.

The bottle did not break. Not until the second strike did it burst, spewing glass and foam. The band struck up a martial air. The crowd buried the music in its roar. Workmen knocked loose the last wooden chocks restraining the behemoth on her perch. With creakings and groanings, *Monongahela Pride* slid stern-first down twin steel tracks into the murky water of the river for which she was named. The river surface divided beneath her, sending wavelets streaking for both shores. The great steamer gave a sigh, a gush of steam, and a whistle blast that rolled down the river valleys and ricocheted into the hills beyond.

"Damn!" Stephen Stewart shouted. "What a sight!"

Forty minutes later, the last guests and dignitaries stepped onto the gleaming lower deck from the gangplank. Captain Potter stuck his head out of the many-windowed pilot house high above. "Cast off yer lines! Take in yer gangway! Smartly now!" With another whistle blast and a belch of steam, the massive paddlewheels came to life, raising twin boils of white-water surge. *Monongahela Pride* moved gracefully into midstream, leaving dual wakes and a flock of wheeling water birds.

The vast central salon filled with celebrants. While a string ensemble played sprightly tunes and sunlight beamed down through masses of crystal windows, the glittering assembly drank from fountains of champagne and feasted from sideboards heaped with delicacies. Catherine Stewart, costumed in a gown of aqua satin set off by a single diamond brooch bearing the Stewart symbol, moved among her guests. Admiring male eyes followed her.

"Hell of a woman, that."

"You're right, my friend. And it takes a hell of a man to keep her."

"A man like Stephen Stewart?"

"Absolutely."

Stephen left the salon, with its noise and cigar smoke, and climbed to the wheelhouse. To the west, beyond the bow flags, the afternoon sun stood high in a blaze of glory. The air was fine and the breeze spanked his face.

Captain Potter reigned supreme up here. Stephen noticed with admiration that the captain was clear-eyed and showed no trace of his earlier nips from the bottle.

"How does she handle, Captain?"

"A smoother vessel never drew water on this river, Mr. Stewart." The heavy gnarled hands moved lovingly over the spokes of the great wheel. "Yes, sir, this a boat that you can be proud of."

"And the new engines?"

"Plenty of power. More than enough power. My compliments to your designer."

"Thank you."

"Uh, just who is your designer, Mr. Stewart?"

The exposed side of Stephen Stewart's half-masked face lifted in a smile. "I am."

They massed on the Cincinnati waterfront in a joyous horde. A thousand throats cheered welcome as the *Monongahela Pride* moved with stately power toward her berth and deckhands flung their lines ashore. As the guests filed down the gangway, there were more speeches of welcome and paeans of praise. Bands played. Flags fluttered. Whistles blasted from a mass of steamboats arrayed along the Ohio. After the welcoming ceremony, Stephen, Catherine and their municipal hosts moved to the city's finest restaurant for feasting and wine. Then, giggling and tipsy, they went off to the pent-house suite of the city's finest riverfront hotel.

"Darling, will she be ready for tomorrow?"

"We have Captain Potter's word on it. He vowed to work through the night on final adjustments, if need be."

"Good. I'd hate for the *Monongahela Pride* to lose on her maiden run. We want her to be not only the most sumptuous, but also the fastest. Do you agree?"

Silence.

"Stephen?"

"Mmmmmm?"

"Stephen Stewart, I think you've got something else on your mind..."

"Hush, woman."

Catherine sighed. "Oh, Stephen. That's nice. That's very nice. Do it again."

The morning of the Great Cincinnati-to-Louisville Steamboat Race dawned clear and balmy. By sunup, crowds poured down to the waterfront and at ten o'clock there was barely standing room left. Bands pumped out lusty tunes. Gamblers did a brisk business laying sideline bets. On the Ohio the finest steamboats afloat built up boiler fires. They spread along the waterfront paddlewheel to paddlewheel, a vast gleaming fleet breathing smoke from a forest of stacks.

Stephen had awakened in a buoyant mood. They rose early, breakfasted on the balcony of their riverfront room, watched the Ohio River come to life in sparkling sunlight and wakening boat traffic, and then decided to walk the half-mile to the landing. They were accompanied by the Indian, Crippled Wolf. Bystanders plucked at their sleeves, held up babies for Catherine to hug, and thrust out leaflets advertising the Great Steamboat Race for them to sign. As they neared the landing, it was necessary to push through the boisterous mass.

"Stephen! Stephen Stewart!"

The shout came from the depths of the crowd. A gray-haired giant emerged, sporting a full growth of beard beneath a black flat-brimmed hat. "Stephen! Hold up a minute, lad!" The giant was followed by several other men, all wearing black broadcloth suits and flat-brimmed hats. The giant enveloped Stephen's hand in a meaty grip. "Stephen Stewart, blessed be! A sight for sore eyes you are." His bear hug brought Stephen off his feet, while Catherine looked on bemused. "I ain't seen you since the *Washington* blew up, and that's nigh twenty years ago. You look fine, my lad. Just fine."

Stephen's one eye widened in sudden recognition. "John Boniface!" He turned to Catherine. "It's John Boniface!" And then there was a mutual back-pounding to the delight of the surrounding crowd, and a chorus of I'll-be-damneds! and Hallelujahs!

"Catherine, this man is the roughest, meanest, finest Indian scout and mountain man in the West. We were on the Lewis and Clark expedition together—ain't that right, John?—and John Boniface just happened to be on a passing keelboat the day the *Washington* exploded. He helped haul me from the water, or what there was left of me. By God, what a coincidence." Stephen pumped the scout's big hand. "There's not a more insatiable appetite for liquor and women on this river, eh, John?"

Boniface's big face lifted in a gentle smile. "It ain't that way no more, Stephen. I've mended my life, rid myself of the bad habits."

"And what are you doing in Cincinnati?" Stephen asked.

Boniface turned to the three men accompanying him. "This here's Elder Patton, Elder Morse, Elder Thatcher." The black hats bobbed in acknowledgment. "We're agoing west, Stephen, a small band of us. Going to find the New Jerusalem."

"I don't believe I know that town."

"Ain't no town yet, my friend. But we're goin' to find the place God intends for it to be, and build it. We'll be moving down the Ohio later today on flatboats, behind your race. Then we'll head west of the Mississippi out into God's country."

"Wild country, you mean. You've been there often enough. Ain't nothing out there but rattlesnakes and prairie dogs."

"That's the wave of the future, Stephen. Mark my words."

"I believe you, John Boniface. In fact, I believe you so much that Catherine and I intend to set up a new boatworks and western depot on the Mississippi, just south of St. Louis. That's where we're going now."

"Now? I thought this was a steamboat race."

"It is. It's also the maiden voyage of our newest boat, the *Monongahela Pride*. And when the race is done, down at

Louisville, she'll carry us on to St. Louis to start building a
compound and offices for the Stewart Lines." Stephen smiled.
"You and your people are welcome to go with us."

Boniface shook his head. "Thank you, Stephen, but no.
We've got to pick up some brothers and sisters along the way,
and our belongings are all stashed on the flatboats. The Lord
intends for us to travel in the old-fashioned way for now. So
that's what we intend to do."

"If you pass through St. Louis, at least stop and see us."

Boniface tipped his hat to Catherine. "Might just do that,
Stephen."

Stephen, Catherine and Crippled Wolf left Boniface in the
crowd and made their way down to the water's edge. The
Monongahela Pride floated in flag-fluttering splendor, surrounded
by a huge crowd. The waterfront was filled with vessels of
every description. The Stewarts boarded the *Monongahela
Pride*. As Catherine and Crippled Wolf went below, Stephen
climbed to the top deck, shook hands with Captain Ezekiel
Potter and looked out across the mass of vessels awaiting the
start of the race. Steamers bore the names *Dixie Belle, Delta
Princess, Pittsburgh, King Creole, Pride of Natchez*. He
recognized *Cotton Queen*, flagship of his arch-rival Black
Diamond Line, the *Rimfire II*, and *Star of the Delta*.

"Captain Potter, I'd say we're in for a bit of competition."

"Mr. Stewart, they all want to beat the *Monongahela
Pride*. That's about as fine a compliment as you could ask
for."

A launch set out from *Cotton Queen*. Even from the
distance, Stephen recognized its towering passenger. Moments later, Winifred Custer stepped onto the deck of the
Monongahela Pride. The owner of the Black Diamond Line
came quickly to the point.

"Mr. Stewart, I would like to offer you a wager, just to
make the race interesting."

Stephen studied his visitor. Winifred Custer, a hulking,
beetle-browed apparition who wore black broadcloth and
stovepipe hat in the warmest weather, was no man to be
trusted.

"What's on your mind, Mr. Custer?"

Custer rubbed his hands together. The long face creased in
a smile. The dark eyes glittered. "We've fought a lot over
freight business on this river, Mr. Stewart. You and your wife

have cost me fortunes in revenue, by your way of doing business."

"All perfectly honest, Mr. Custer."

"I'm not saying it ain't honest. Fair's fair in love and trade, I say. Your boats' speed and your cut-rate prices are a way of forcing the competition, no more, no less."

"Well, then . . ."

"Well, then, I say that my *Cotton Queen* can take the measure of any steamboat afloat, and that includes this gargantuan firetrap of yours."

"Now hold on there!" Captain Potter sputtered.

"It's all right, Ezekiel," said Stephen. "Mr. Custer never pretended to have good manners. Go on, Mr. Custer."

Custer beamed. The black eyes shifted. "Mr. Stewart, I own twelve fine steamboats including the *Cotton Queen* over there. I'm prepared to wager my entire fleet on the *Cotton Queen* against your *Monongahela Pride*."

"And?"

"In return, if you lose, you'll get out of the bulk cargo business on the Ohio River."

"You're out of your mind."

"On the contrary, Mr. Stewart, this is a sane and sensible proposition. If you lose, you lose this vessel, the *Monongahela Pride*, whatever it's worth to you. And you'll still have the entire Mississippi River and any other navigable stream in America on which to ship freight. You'll surrender to me the Ohio. If you win, you gain my vessels, worth a fortune."

A signal gun went off on the riverfront. The smoke drifted over the crowd. There was a rising murmur of expectation.

"That's the ready shot, Mr. Stewart," Captain Potter muttered. "It's almost time."

"Take it or leave it, Mr. Stewart," Winifred Custer said. "Do you believe in your boat or don't you? Maybe all the hot air isn't just in the steam boilers."

"By God, one more remark like that . . !" Ezekiel Potter said.

"Damn!" said Stephen.

"Take it or leave it," said Custer.

"I'll take it!" Stephen said.

"Good! Good! Hee-hee-hee! Oh, that's good!" Winifred Custer did a little dance, hopping gleefully to the rail. Quicker than Stephen expected him to move, the gangling black-clad figure was over the side. "Ho-ho-ho, Mr. Stewart!

Hah-hah-hah! Now we'll see who's king of this river!" Custer shouted, as his launch was rowed away.

"Mr. Stewart, I think you've made a bad bargain this time."

"Well, Captain, it's my bargain."

Lines were cast off. Commands barked across the river front. On shore, officials huddled over a small signal cannon. Stephen eyed the *Cotton Queen* and cursed himself for a fool.

"Booooom!"

Steam whistles blasted. Stacks belched black smoke. Paddlewheels came laboriously to life, their blades kicking up sunlit explosions of water. The mighty white fleet churned into motion on a ponderous sweep downstream.

A thunderous cheer broke out on shore.

The river was a moving spirit of its own, a thing of hidden traps and endless caprice. Men became experts in its navigation, but none could call himself a master. The river knew no master. Today's shoal was tomorrow's deep; today's channel was tomorrow's sandbar. Spring floods could wreak havoc on the channels, their mighty seasonal flushings causing a great dislodgment of flotsam, dead trees, brush and jagged upthrust logs, to bedevil navigation and alter the riverbed. Woe betide the unwary, for a snag could disembowel the sturdiest boat.

Stephen was mindful of all this as the *Monongahela Pride* surged resolutely downstream, smashing wavelets into spray and jockeying for advantage in the mass. No one, not even the most seasoned of steamboat skippers, had seen anything like this race, for never had so many vessels gone wheel-to-wheel at once. Across the wide river they ranged, with many more trailing behind the ragged first line. The racket of engines and blatting steam whistles was deafening. Frantically, captains spun their wheels to avoid collisions, bellowing curses and commands.

"Make way, there!"

"Ye damn fool, you're bound to wreck us both!"

"Hard right! Hard right, I say!"

Ezekiel Potter did not join the jousting. The bearded skipper of *Monongahela Pride* sucked wordlessly at an ancient pipe as he watched the melee. Stephen noticed that his great steamboat had fallen back, avoiding both the lead and the pack. They chugged along in the second rank of vessels, the engine loafing at three-quarter speed. Occasionally Captain Potter exchanged a word with his pilot, a grizzed, crippled veteran of the river named Penchant Povey. They seemed a strangely compatible pair, Potter and Povey. Ashore, such men rarely drew sober breath; on the deck of a steamer, they worked with a single mind, communicating by glances, grimaces and shrugs.

Stephen resolved to keep his own counsel. One who built steamboats did not necessarily excel at running them. Besides, Catherine had insisted that once underway, Potter's word would be law. Now, however, she emerged from below decks and scanned the fleet ahead with concern.

"Captain Potter?"

"Yes, ma'am."

"Why are we lagging behind?"

Ezekiel Potter smoked his pipe, reflecting upon the question. Anyone else would have gotten a silent rebuke. But one did not rebuke Catherine Stewart. The captain knocked his pipe meditatively against a stanchion. "Well, Mrs. Stewart, you'll have to ask Povey."

"I'm not asking Povey, Captain. I'm asking you."

"Povey is wary of the riverbed along here. He don't trust it. His knee is acting up."

"His knee? What's Povey's knee got to do with it?"

"Mrs. Stewart, when Povey's knee acts up, it means that things ain't right. Don't ask me why, because I don't know. But I never seen it to fail. So right now, we're hangin' back. Besides, there's plenty of time."

Catherine looked at Stephen, her blue eyes flashing. "I've heard a lot of pilots' superstitions, but I never heard of a trick knee deciding how to run a boat. Stephen, what do you think?"

Stephen shrugged, masking his deep misgivings. The foolish wager with Winifred Custer nagged at his mind. He'd let the man badger him into it, for God knows what devious purpose. And now he was stuck with a bargain he never should have made. "I don't rightly know, Catherine," he said. "Ezekiel is your captain."

"That's true. But this is a Stewart vessel, and the owner has final say. Especially when it comes to a race with the reputation of the firm at stake." She turned back to Captain

Potter. "Captain, the *Monongahela*'s engine is second to none. Is that correct?"

"Correct, ma'am."

"Then I say, full steam ahead."

Beneath their feet, the engine throbbed a powerful rhythm. Behind them, the driving arms pumped and great paddlewheels churned up white water. A steady breeze swept into their faces. All around, the fleet belched black smoke and ran pell-mell with the current, turning a broad bend in the river flanked by broadening slopes of green hills. Potter looked at Povey. Povey studied the low hills and the river ahead, saying nothing. "But, ma'am . . ."

"Full steam ahead, Captain."

Ezekiel Potter sighed. "Full steam it is, then."

Captain Potter reached for the lever to signal. His hand stopped. From ahead there came a splintering, crunching sound as two vessels, the *Rimfire II* and *King Creole* came together broadside. Stephen looked forward in time to see *Rimfire II*'s port side wheel shatter against the sturdy hull of the other boat. Steam whistles erupted in frantic shrieks. The two vessels swung violently apart at the bows but were locked by wreckage astern.

"Hard right!" pilot Povey shouted.

"Man, you'll run us aground!"

"Hard right, damn you, Potter!"

"Right it is."

Stephen only half heard the exchange. His eyes were riveted to the spectacle in front. A moment's difference and it would have been them. As if in slow motion, a third boat, his own *Pittsburgh*, advanced upon the crippled *King Creole*. The wheelman seemed frozen to his spokes, unable to turn the craft. So thick was the sudden melee of boats that there was no place to turn. *Pittsburgh* rammed *King Creole* at an angle astern, driving her back into *Rimfire II*. Then all three vessels lost way, wallowing and taking on water. He caught sight of the captain of *Rimfire II* jumping up and down in a seizure of frustration. It reminded him of some bizarre ritual dance.

Monongahela Pride skirted the curved afterdeck of *Pittsburgh*, missing by inches, and rushed for the rocky flank of the near shore. A line of jagged granite boulders rose from the water's edge like giant's teeth.

Penchant Povey pointed a gnarled finger toward the rocks. "Make for that strip of smooth water, just this side of 'em!"

"Where?"

"There, under the lee of the bank."

"I see it. There don't seem room."

"There's room."

"Shouldn't we stop and help the wrecked boats?" Stephen shouted.

Captain Potter glanced at the mess astern, his teeth clenched on the pipe stem. "Don't know why we should. Ain't nothing hurt but the boats and their pride. Besides"—he took the pipe from his mouth and jabbed it toward downstream—"your competition ain't missing a piston stroke."

Stephen followed the pipe thrust. Through a veil of steam and billowing smoke he could make out, five hundred yards ahead, the handsome lines of *Cotton Queen*. As sunlight poured down and the air cleared, he caught his breath at the beauty of the sight. *Cotton Queen*'s mighty paddlewheels churned foam at maximum speed. Smoke chuffed from her stacks in a black plume mixed with sparkfire. At her bow, spray exploded like silver in the sunlight. Proud flags, Old Glory and the pennants of the Black Diamond Line, whipped in the wind generated by her dashing progress. By God, he thought, nothing man-made was more beautiful than a riverboat running at speed.

Like *Monongahela Pride*, the *Cotton Queen* had hung back at the start, biding her time. Her shrewd skipper, a Scottish rogue named Ian McCheever, had figured in the same way as Ezekiel Potter on the chance of multiple collisions in that frantic pack. The accident had torn a wide gap in front of *Cotton Queen*. McCheever dashed through, to the lusty hurrahs of his crew.

"Stephen," Catherine said, "we'll never catch him now!"

"What about that, Captain Potter?" Stephen said.

Ezekiel Potter's eyes crinkled. "We'll give him a run for his money anyhow, and that's for sure."

A run for the money. In times to come, river folk would remember this, the most splendid race ever to be run on the Ohio. And while the great steamboats thrashed and chuffed away the miles in a grand excitement, with fortunes in side wagers riding on their wakes, the real contest was between *Cotton Queen* and *Monongahela Pride*. Within two and a half hours of the start, at half the hundred-and-ten-mile distance to Louisville, *Monongahela Pride* made her successful dash through the narrow deep into which Povey had directed her. Leaving the shattered *Rimfire II*, *King Creole* and *Pittsburgh* behind, the behemoth at last reached open water ahead of the crowd. Even Stephen was astonished at the powerful thrust of engine as Captain Potter signaled, "Full speed!" She surged ahead, paddlewheels beating up a half-ton of riverwater at each revolution, stacks belching and steam whistles blasting as if to clear the way by sheer force of sound.

They swept grandly past the last of the pack. Stephen saw that the other vessels' railings were lined with cheering crew members. Caught up himself in the excitement, he clumped down from the top deck on his peg leg, working his way to the lower deck and the engine room. Black stokers, streaming sweat, rhythmically shoveled coal from the huge after-bin into the maw of the firebox.

"Pour it to her, lads!" Stephen shouted gleefully. "Give her the coal now!" Grinning and shouting, the stokers picked up the pace until the firebox glowed red, then slammed the iron doors and stood panting for breath.

Cotton Queen was a fast boat, fitted with sturdy new engines built in Philadelphia. It was said that few rivals could stay on the same river with her, much less match that dazzling speed. But now, inch by inch, *Monongahela Pride* closed the gap. By the time Stephen climbed back to the top deck, Ezekiel Potter was jumping up and down and Catherine had ripped off her picture hat and was waving it, shouting, "We're going to catch her, Captain. We are closing!"

A scant one hundred yards separated the vessels now. *Monongahela Pride*'s performance was exhilarating. Stephen sensed that she had reserves to spare. He reflected now upon Catherine's insistence that they install over-size boilers built of extra heavy plate. The new engine was driven by the largest piston ever forged. He relished the exhileration of its performance.

"Oh, oh. Watch it, Potter!"

It was Povey speaking. The pilot had remained silent until this moment. Now he squinted toward the *Cotton Queen* as they halved the distance again and Potter began to swing out to find passing room. As *Monongahela Pride* heeled to her left, *Cotton Queen* did the same. Potter widened his swing until they were moving at a quarter-slant to the river. *Cotton Queen* veered in at an even sharper angle. Stephen nervously checked his pocket watch. They were averaging nearly twenty miles an hour, counting the current flow, and four hours and thirty minutes had elapsed since the starting gun. By now the pack was far behind, a distant cluster under their broad smoke plume. Ten miles to go, Stphen told himself.

"Ten miles, I fancy," Captain Potter said, echoing his thoughts. "Mebbe less."

"Less," muttered Povey. "And he"—the pilot gestured forward with a quick nod—"ain't playing it fair. Blocking us, that's what."

"Can't we swing around him?"

"This here boat's fast, Mr. Stewart, but she don't fly. Unless we sprout wings, we're in a tight spot. Look over yonder."

Stephen followed Povey's gaze. They were approaching the left bank of the Ohio, on the Kentucky side. The water was muddier and its surface showed tiny swirls and curling configurations.

Ezekiel Potter grunted. "Snags. Ian McCheever knows what he's doing. Them's sunken snags, and he figures to force us into 'em. The devil..."

"Bring her around, then," Povey ordered.

"You'll take us into the middle. He can play this game for nine miles easy." But even as he protested, Captain Potter spun the wheel back to his right. The bow of *Monongahela Pride* came around smartly. So quick was the maneuver that the *Cotton Queen*'s wheelman was caught unprepared. The lead vessel made a shallow cut to maintain blocking advantage, but lost precious distance. Aslant of the downflowing current, the two racers plowed back the width of the river, consuming another five miles in the maneuver.

"One more crossing, the other way, and I think we'll do it!" Ezekiel Potter said.

"We don't have room," Povey replied.

"What do you mean, no room?"

"There's shoals midstream. I can see 'em from here."

"Shoals? Bosh, man, that river's thirty feet deep out there."

"Mud flat, then. Submerged." Povey pointed. "See?"

"Well, I'll be damned."

Shoals they were, giving telltale signs of disturbed water surface. Looking farther, even Stephen could see the cause. Spring floods from a stream flowing into the Ohio here had disgorged a bar of silt that reached out like a finger into the river. The distance was an illusion. It was not midstream at all; actually, they were very close in to the Ohio shore now, and the gentle land terrain indicated a shallow riverbed.

"We're running out of space," Captain Potter said.

Stephen tensed, watching *Cotton Queen* and the approaching bar. Captain Potter timed his last cut superbly. Stephen's heart lifted. *Cotton Queen* hesitated on her responding backswing. She was taking too long! Ezekiel Potter spun his wheel and bellowed, "Eureka! By heaven, McCheever, you've screwed yerself! Begging your pardon, ma'am . . ." Now, *Monongahela Pride* had a decisive advantage on the angle. Indeed, it was so steep that the steamer was running almost laterally across the current in order to clear the obstruction. *Cotton Queen* still had not made her cut and was caught in the hook of the bar.

It was Catherine who spoke. "He's going to run the bar."

Potter paled. "That's suicide. She'll break in half."

The setting sun laid a glare upon the river. Penchant Povey screwed his face into a mask, his gaze trying to penetrate the blinding light. Finally, the pilot grumbled, "No she won't. McCheever knows what he's doing."

"I say you can't run a bar like that. There's logs buried under there big as a house."

"He's got a wedge."

"A wedge?"

Povey licked his lips. "He's got a wedge." The pilot jabbed a gnarled finger at a spot in the glare. "There, I can see it. Smooth water, maybe twenty, thirty feet wide!"

It was too late for *Monongahela Pride*. With a sickening feeling, Stephen checked their course and speed. They were fully committed to the turn, taking them around the bar. *Cotton Queen* gave a whistle blast of triumph. A fresh torrent of black smoke and sparks gushed from her stacks. She rushed forward through the break, paddlewheels thrashing. On the top deck, silhouetted against the blazing sky, the towering figure of Winifred Custer jumped up and down so strenuously that his stovepipe hat fell off.

"I'll turn . . ." Captain Potter shouted, his voice choking furiously. The old man's eyes bulged and his mouth worked in an apoplexy of indecision.

"Hold your course!" Povey snapped. "Ye want to run us aground?"

And so they held to the turn, their long, plodding sweep

consuming an infinity of time. In his agony, Stephen felt that
they had stopped; *Monongahela Pride* was caught suspended
in time and space while his life and hopes rushed away
downriver on a blast of steam whistles and flaunting paddlewheels.

"My God," he groaned.

Catherine took his arm and squeezed it. "It's all right,
darling. Custer's a scoundrel and he tricked us, that's all. It's
nothing to be upset about."

"Nothing to be..."

Beyond the mud bar, *Cotton Queen* dug her paddlewheels
into open water again and surged toward midstream, with
nothing between her and the finish line but water and
wheeling birds and a sky awash in violent orange sunset.

"Damn!" said Ezekiel Potter. His teeth clamped down on
the ancient pipestem, biting it through. The pipe clattered to
the deck, showering sparks. "Double damn!"

They swept the final miles in utter misery. Ahead, *Cotton
Queen* lay her proud wash astern. As they rounded the last
big bend, steaming into Louisville, Stephen became conscious of a new sound, a dull roaring that steadily rose in
volume. At last he recognized with a shock that it was the
cheering of massed spectators along the bank of the Ohio, so
many that they resembled a great human anthill.

"Look at them, Stephen!" Catherine's face glowed with
excitement. "You'll never see another spectacle like this in a
lifetime!"

"Jesus Christ Almighty," snapped Ezekiel Potter.

One hundred yards ahead, *Cotton Queen*'s whistle blasts
split the quiet of the darkening hills. A cannon boomed on
shore. The evening sky erupted in the pop, clatter and boom
of fireworks, showering down in tendrils of fire.

Stephen Stewart watched in utter misery.

An hour later, he faced Catherine alone in the deserted
dockside office of Stewart Lines in Louisville.

"Lost the *Monongahela Pride*?" she said in disbelief. The
blue eyes burned into his. A guttering lamp cast lurid shadows over empty desks and filing cabinets. Captain Potter and
Penchant Povey had beaten a strategic retreat. Stephen's
humiliation was absolute, and compounded now by the agony

of confession. "What are you saying, 'We lost the *Monongahela Pride*?'"

"Correct that, then. I lost the *Monongahela*. And the Ohio River freight business, too."

Catherine's mouth opened, but she was unable to speak. Her expression said, Surely this is a joke. But the dawning awareness was evident. It was not a joke. She sat down slowly in a swivel chair. Stephen, had never seen her more beautiful than now—beautiful, proud, indignant. With an expanding dread, he sensed that he could lose more than a steamboat and a business. On one level of his mind, he phrased the words that he would speak; on another, he reflected that no two human beings ever totally understand themselves, much less each other. A marriage, like a business, was built on respect, on giving and taking, on faith. How much stress could any relationship withstand before it began to crumble?

"I did it," he said. "And for the life of me, I can't defend what I did."

He tried to explain what had happened. He told her of his dislike for Winifred Custer. He described the man's sudden visit in the waning moments before the starting cannon, his challenge and Stephen's own stung pride. Foolish pride, how ruinous it could be! Angered, he had lashed back, accepted the challenge and that abominable wager. Now, of course, it all made sense. Custer had suckered him. Already, Captain Potter had the reports. Ian McCheever and Custer had brought the *Cotton Queen* downriver ten days before, carefully inspecting the sandbar and the river above it. Folks had thought it strange to see the steamboat going back and forth across the river. They thought McCheever was drunk.

When Stephen finished speaking, Catherine sat in silence for a long time. Then, wordlessly, she got up from the swivel chair, walked out of the office and into the night. Stephen waited for an hour, two hours. A grandfather clock ticked in its darkened corner. He lit a cigar and smoked, watching the ash lengthen and finally drop to the floor. He rummaged in a cupboard and found a bottle of Beam's Kentucky bourbon, pulled the cork with his teeth, tilted the bottle and drank. The liquor burned its way down his throat, but made him feel no better. He had never been more intensely isolated. Finally he sat down in the swivel chair where she had sat and nodded off to sleep.

It was dawn when she returned. Outside, the waterfront was littered with the debris of last night's revelry. She pushed open the door and came into the office. Her boots were covered with mud. She came over to him, smiled, caressed his hair, bent down and kissed him on the mouth. Her scent was a pungent mix of perfume and sweat from the exertion of walking all night.

"I love you," she said.

"Where did you go?"

"I walked. I must have walked ten miles, collecting my thoughts."

"And?"

"Maybe this is a blessing in disguise. Anyhow, I'm going to look at it that way. It will force us to expand in other directions. We'll build another passenger steamboat, even more luxurious than the *Monongahela Pride*. We'll make it a floating palace, with excursion rates, gambling tables, music and entertainment on board. We can develop a whole fleet of them, refitting our best boats. As for cargo, we'll concentrate on the Mississippi and its other tributaries. There's a tremendous undeveloped opportunity there. I figure we can get around Mr. Custer's Ohio freight coup somewhat by striking a bargain with another line."

This was the Catherine who always amazed him, the woman rising to meet a challenge, using her mind and will. He remembered, as she talked, the bizarre circumstances in which they'd met. She was the twelve-year-old daughter of a dead teamster, dressed in boy's clothes chewing tobacco, an expert with whip and rifle. In fact, he had brought her to Pittsburgh after her father's death on a lonely Allegheny mountaintop thinking that she was a boy. And she had worked for months as a stableboy named Jamie before the truth came out. The Stewart family had taken her in and their ward suddenly blossomed into a beauty in dresses and curls.

Stephen had loved her then as ardently as he did now. Their only separation had been for the three years before their marriage when he was off on the Lewis and Clark expedition. And when he lay virtually dead of burns following the explosion of the *Washington*, this woman had gone from Pittsburgh, down the Ohio, up the Mississippi and onto the wild Missouri River to find and bring back Crippled Wolf, the Omaha medicine man with his powerful herbs and potions, to save his life. Stephen could not imagine life without Catherine; and he knew now that her feelings were the same.

"So we'll go to St. Louis, as we'd planned, and build the western compound. You can start expanding your stagecoach lines. There's a gold rush starting now. Mark my words, it's going to change the West. I feel it in my bones."

"Yes." he said. "Yes, I agree with you."

She looked at him again, a long, searching look. And then she smiled. "Promise me one thing, though."

"Name it."

"From now on, leave the steamboat business to me."

He laughed and drew her to him. "Delighted."

The warmth and fullness of her electrified him. The kisses were lingering and ardent. Her mouth softened and her breathing quickened. Her scent burned his senses. The grandfather clock measured off five minutes, ten . . .

"Oh, Stephen, not here in the office. Darling, somebody might come in. Besides, there's only the floor . . ."

He laughed again, released her briefly, went to the door and locked it.

V

It was a land of smoky blue distances and mist rising from the river in the heat. In the wet years, white water birds wheeled up at some disturbance, circled in the distance like startled white moving specks against the mounded hills, then bunched up in white clouds and scattered. In summer, thus, they coasted over the land, subsisting on the rich grain morsels from the earth, alighting upon the deep green fold of the bank beyond the rice field where Shingling Chou and his father, Wang-to, toiled knee-deep in black muck with the water buffalo, plowing the ricebed. In summer the water birds were there and in winter they were gone, Shingling knew not where. Some said they flew all the way to the land beyond the great mountains he had never seen, the land they called Tibet.

And so life was a timeless rhythm of hot, steamy summers under a merciless sun that burned Shingling's shaven head and turned his skin the color of wood, summers for plowing with the buffalo, that great shaggy mud-dripping beast moving ponderously through black water. "Hyee!" Shingling's father would shout, cursing the beast and guiding the plow with its wooden blade forward to turn the submerged muck. They worked in mud-soaked shorts, barechested, barefooted, day after day. They plowed and they planted the rice, bending and stooping to set each shoot into the rice lake.

Shingling and his father would go to the river sometimes to bathe in the yellow water among the rocks. Sometimes Shingling's father brought a teapot and cups of porcelain. He would boil water over a low stick fire and pour it upon the tea leaves and they would drink as the sun went down and the night drew its purple folds over the river, with its drifting sampans. At such times, Shingling would take out his small flute of yellow bamboo, the one his father had carved for him, and put it to his lips and play. At other times, in the evenings, he accompanied his father to the temple where they sat among the guttering butter lamps to burn incense, watching the ash go long and gray and thinking their private thoughts. Afterward they would walk home in the moonlight along the twisting road to where Shingling's mother and younger brothers and sisters waited with supper.

Shingling's father was a quiet and reflective man. Wang-to did not enjoy idle talk. So they shared many silences together, man and boy. But when he did talk, Shingling's father often expressed a wisdom beyond the boy's understanding. One evening by the river they watched a group of naked village boys diving and splashing off a moored sampan in the light of the rising full moon. Beyond the river, the rounded twin mountains which they called Sheh and Shah loomed up from their valleys of mists, and Wang-to said, "Someday, you may wish to leave this valley, Shingling, and go beyond those mountains to the sea, and onto the sea by boat to other lands. There is a land called Gum San, the Golden Mountain. There the roads are paved with gold and a man can grow rich from his own labors. In Gum San, you are not shackled to the land, the rice lake and the buffalo." Wang-to sighed a wistful sigh, as if expressing to this eldest son his own dreams. "And I have heard it said that in Gum San they worship different gods, gods with white faces and round eyes and wearing a light above their heads. There is a man in our province who speaks of them, and we should go to hear him. His name is Hung Hsiu-ch'uan, and he is a wise man who has read books and had dreams of this white god. He has many followers, this Hung Hsiu-ch'uan."

One day they went to a house in the village where a meeting had been called. The weather was cold and the abundant rice had long been harvested. The province had stored great quantities of wheat as well, and the green vegetables had flourished. In the temple, there was much joyful burning of incense. But Shingling's father seemed to have much on his mind, and the other farmers and villagers were clearly troubled and fearful. The wealthiest man in the village, who could count many blessings in his storehouse and grainery, who possessed many taels and had even acquired two female slaves, addressed the meeting. As symbols of status, he wore a floor-length robe of blue silk and his long hair was contained in a sack hanging at the nape of his neck. "As most of you already know," he said gravely, "I have been informed that the banditti of Feng Tsieng How expect our valley to pay a share of our bounty. We have until tomorrow to reply. Each family is expected to pay one-third of its grain and other foodstuffs for tribute."

The announcement caused an outpouring of denunciation. Several of the farmers questioned what the government intended to do to protect them against extortion and banditry. The wealthy landowner spread his hands in a gesture of helplessness. "One lives as best he can." And the soldiers? Were they here merely to play finger games in the village and consume the food of their unwilling hosts? It was so. Everyone knew the answers, of course, and the questions themselves were but exercises in hollow rhetoric. It was Shingling's father, Wang-to Chou, who finally rose to speak a new thought. "Perhaps, then, we should seek help elsewhere. These banditti of Feng Tsieng How are but one of many groups. If we pay tribute to one, the others shall expect to be paid as well. And where shall it end?" Shingling's father looked around the room into the blank faces and knew he would find no support here. The fear was palpable and deep-rooted. These men might complain loudly, but clearly, they would rather pay tribute than resist. And so the meeting broke up with nothing resolved. Wang-to walked the two miles to their farmhouse without speaking. Shingling knew that his father had made up his mind not to pay tribute to bandits.

It was at about this time that Shingling Chou became conscious of Tzu Hsi. She was the daughter of the neighboring farmer, Chou Li, who was his father's closest friend. Shingling was fourteen years old now, and Tzu Hsi was a year younger. When she walked to the village with her father, Shingling noticed the grace of her movements and the lovely warmth of her eyes. They seemed to linger upon his face, those eyes, as their parents spoke of the troubles of the day and Shingling's father expressed his intention not to give into the banditti.

Shingling at first had looked away in embarrassment, but then he forced himself to return her gaze and to let a smile play upon his lips. Chou Li was saying to Wang-to, "But how can you resist? You have no arms, and even your eldest son is but a boy yet. The soldiers will not help." Shingling's heart fluttered in his chest and his face felt hot, as if from a fever, as the eyes of Tzu Hsi glowed into his. They caused his stomach to tie into knots.

Shingling heard his father reply, "I don't know what to tell you, Chou Li, except to say that what the banditti get from me they shall have to take." And then the men parted to go their separate ways, and the memory of Tzu Hsi's eyes warmed Shingling's mind all the way home. Her eyes also disturbed his dreams at night, and he awoke strangely light of heart and short of breath and could not even eat his rice and fish at breakfast.

The banditti came the following day. Shingling saw the farmers running from their fields and heard the shouts of alarm. And then he looked into the distance to where the long line of armed men, some of them on horseback, snaked down from the hills toward the valley. Even his grandfather, a crippled ancient who shared their hearth, sensed the sudden anxiety among them and asked, "Who are those men coming down from the hills?" Shingling's father ordered all shutters drawn and the doors bolted. They waited in the dark house through that afternoon and all that night and the next day. Occasionally, they heard shouts from the direction of the village, and on the second morning smoke columns from burning houses appeared on the horizon. Heavy smoke came from the direction of the wealthy landowner's farm, which was five miles away.

The second night there was a frantic pounding on the door and voices crying for admission. It was Tzu Hsi, her mother, and two sisters. The banditti had come to their farmhouse, taken their father as a hostage, pillaged their food supplies and slaughtered their water buffalo. The banditti feasted on the meat and then two of the soldiers had raped Tzu Hsi's mother. Then they set fire to the house and left, taking Chou Li, bound and trussed up on a carrying pole. The females fled to the house of Shingling's father for refuge.

"Are they coming here next, the banditti?" Shingling's mother cried.

"They went back toward the village. Someone said the troops finally had been ordered to resist them, but I don't know that for truth. Oh, my poor, dear husband! The suffering he must be going through!" The good woman seemed to think nothing of her own ordeal and shame.

The plunderers of the bandit leader Feng Tsieng How did not return. At nightfall of the third day the long column ascended into the hills, prodding along numerous hostages, male and female, who labored under great sacks of booty. Far behind them moved a band of soldiers, waving their swords and exploding firecrackers in a show of mock courage, but no one was fooled. The soldiers, as usual, had struck their corrupt bargains with the banditti, and now playacted pursuit in a gesture to save face. Shingling's father watched their departure. "There will be others," Wang-to muttered dourly.

In the valley, survivors were in shock. Rapings and beatings had been commonplace during two nights of terror and at least ten young men and women had been carried away, to be enlisted as banditti or sold into slavery. No one had been killed, but this was not the result of either mercy or generosity of spirit; the banditti did not care. The people of the village thus emerged fearfully, knowing now that having been assaulted once it was probable that other outlaws would come also.

Shingling's father cursed the prosperity which had turned into such bad fortune for them all. He pondered deeply the matter, wondering how a man could protect his home and loved ones. "We are helpless, and the government is power-less to stop this banditry," he said. "And so there seems little alternative but to become a bandit myself."

It was said matter-of-factly, and no one took him seriously at the time. Shingling's father was known as a decent, hardworking man, scrupulously honest in his dealings. It was laughable to think of Wang-to Chou as a member of a bandit horde. But Shingling knew him better, and realized that his father was not a man to idly speculate. When Tzu Hsi whispered to him about it, asking, "Does your father really mean to become a bandit?" Shingling could only shrug.

"We'll have to wait and see." The wait was not long. There came a night when Shingling awoke with his father's hand upon his shoulder in the darkness. His father spoke in a whisper.

"I leave you now, my son. You are the man of the house. You must take the lead and see to the crops and animals. I go now to join Hung Hsui-ch'uan, who has gathered many people to him under the banner of the Christian religion. They are called the T'ai P'ings, and they band together in strength and brotherhood. Some of them are men who were of the banditti. In this way, I hope to gain us a measure of protection, for it is said that marauders do not dare assault the family of a T'ai P'ing. Watch after your mother, your brothers and sisters." And then he was gone, slipping into the night with the stealth of a cat.

The winter passed and the spring came. Now it was Shingling who guided the plow from dawn to dark behind the oxen, sloshing and turning the black soil. And it was his younger brother, Won, who came along behind. The boys were lithe and wiry, their skin bronze from the sun. Shingling drove the buffalo, the great beast sinking up to its yellow eyes in black muck and water, and his mind was busy with thoughts of Tzu Hsi. She and her mother lived with Shingling's family, more or less permanently, and shared their fields and daily work. It was Tzu Hsi who brought to Shingling and Won their lunches of rice, boiled tea and bean sprouts. She treated him, the male head of the family, with great defer-ence now, keeping her head bowed while he ate and speaking only when spoken to. When they were walking, she followed several paces behind, as was the custom. Shingling had not expected his status to change so dramatically and was not comfortable with it. He treated the women with respect, as his father had always done. ("You cannot do enough kindness for a woman, my son," his father had once told him, "for without her, a man is nothing. A man truly has no power over a woman that she does not grant him willingly, just as he has none over the wind and the stars, for each belong to different worlds from him.") But he longed to touch the hand of Tzu Hsi, and was not content unless he was near her. He wished ardently to reach the age of maturity, in order to take her for his wife. Even though he was the head of the household, he was only sixteen.

That was the summer of the drought.

It came upon them quietly, creeping over the land like a shadow. One hardly noticed that the rains of the spring were late. One day flows into the next and the next, and people expect a thing to happen because it has always happened before. It is difficult to conceive of change. One simply did not think of the monsoon not coming; one might as well consider that he would stop breathing, as for the rains not to fall. And this year, too, the clouds gathered as they always had, or at least started to gather on the horizon. But they simply hung there, day after day, not billowing in the usual towering masses, flecked with lightning and rolling with thunder. They lay as distant and tantalizing puffballs, dry and light, and coasted there. A week passed beyond the normal start of the rains, and then two, and then three.

In the third week, the talk began. Two farmers meeting on the road or in the fields cast thoughtful eyes at the far horizon and said to one another, "Do you think it will come today?"

"Well, I don't know. Maybe today, but surely tomorrow."

"Yes, it will rain tomorrow."

"Yes, tomorrow." Tomorrow came, and the tomorrow after that, but still no rain.

The days and weeks flowed imperceptibly into the hot, dry summer. Shingling plowed behind the buffalo, occasionally turning his face to the sky. The water lowered in the rice lakes. The soil grew hot and dank, permeating the air with its odors. He found the going harder as the water in the fields declined. His feet began to stumble in the thickening muck. The air was hot and heavy and harder to breath. The buffalo suffered, beating at the swarming flies with its tail, breathing in deep, shuddering breaths that seemed unnaturally loud in the still afternoons.

In the midst of all this, word came to Shingling that his

father was now one of the right-hand men of the religious leader Hung Hsiu-ch'uan but that there had been fighting between these people and government troops. "It is a rebellion, they say, and your father is much involved," whispered one of the headmen of the village. "I have heard that there is a price on his head." Shingling was joyful to learn that Wang-to was well, for it was the first news they had had of him since his departure. He took this word home to his mother, whose tired face came alive. But he chose not to inform her that his father was also a hunted outlaw. It was better to see his mother smile, if only for a moment.

The rains did not come. Heat eddied up from the rice beds and stood shimmering over the land. The outlines of Sheh and Shah blurred in the heat. The white water birds disappeared. Shingling's brother planted the rice in shallow pools and exposed mud. But the mud began to dry to a thick, cakelike texture, and the tender shoots exposed to the heat shriveled and died. Only the rice in the surviving pools endured, and it was thin and sickly. There was no bountiful harvest that year. By autumn, the smallest, poorest farmers and their families faced the certainty of hunger. Men went with downcast eyes to the moneylenders, and placed their lands up for loans.

"What will you do, my son? How do you intend to handle this?" It was his mother speaking. Already she was growing thin, as were the other children and Tzu Hsi and her mother and the old man. Shingling replied that they should bide their time, eat frugally of what stores they had left and hope for the best. The autumn slipped past them without rain. The winter came, and was cruel.

More travelers appeared on the road, strangers, ragged and bone thin, heading south toward the city of Canton. In the house of Shingling's family, they ate the last of their beans and grains and rice, doling it out grain by grain. As they ate, strangers hovered by the doorway in hope that something, anything, might be thrown away. Nothing ever was.

All the dogs and cats strangely disappeared. There was not a pig or a chicken left in the valley. Even the crows had abandoned the fields. The winter deepened, the suffering intensified. It was said that some children had disappeared in the village. There was an outcry against the strangers who came trickling through from famine-stricken areas to the north. But then meat appeared on the black market of the village, was quickly bought up and consumed; and the people of the valley stopped speaking against strangers, instead looking fearfully and guiltily to one another, keeping their children close underfoot.

"Could they really do that?" Tzu Hsi asked. She had grown so thin that the bones of her face and body protruded. The soft eyes were unnaturally large and she had developed a persistent, dry cough. "Could they really eat the children, Shingling?"

He shook his head. "Of course not," he said. But he said it only as a means of allaying her fears. In his mind there was the dreadful awareness that it was true.

One day Shingling's mother said, "Shall we kill the buffalo?" The thought had been in the minds of all the adults but had not been spoken aloud before. The buffalo still survived in the fenced enclosure behind the house; on several occasions Shingling had driven off prowlers in the night who'd ventured back there. The beast was all skin and bones and seemed barely able to stand. Shingling thought of his mother's question.

"If we kill the buffalo, we will have nothing with which to plow in the spring," he said.

He went to bed thinking that on the morrow, he would have to make a firm decision about the buffalo. In the darkness, he heard the coughing of Tzu Hsi. He thought of the emaciated condition of his mother and younger brothers and sisters. The weight of responsibility pressed down upon him, and he felt acutely his own youth and inexperience. He wished that he could have gone to school, so as to be able to read and write and learn more of the world and his place in it. Shingling felt ignorant and alone.

The men came after midnight. He was vaguely aware that someone was moving about in the road outside, for his dreams were disturbed. He awoke abruptly, eyes staring into the night and ears straining to hear. There, the sound came again. A tapping at the door? No. It was only the wind. But it came again, more persistent this time, a tap. He slipped off of his pallet into the cold darkness and moved barefooted to the window, gently pushed aside the heavy curtain and peered out. There were four of them that he could see, four men gathered in the roadway in the dim light of a quarter moon. He thought he could make out the gleam of a sword blade, unsheathed. The men were warmly dressed in quilted coats and fur headpieces. Shingling felt a tremor of fear. Were these banditti again? He had no weapon with which to defend the family except an ancient heavy cutting knife which had been his father's. It was more tool than weapon and designed for hacking at underbrush, not human throats. Hurriedly he moved to a cupboard and found the knife, but felt small reassurance from its heft. Then, while others stirred and the voice of his mother whispered, "Shingling, what is it?" he returned to the door.

"Yes? Who is there?"

"It is I, my son. We've brought food."

The voice of his father filled him with a rush of delight. Fumbling with the latches, Shingling snatched open the door and stepped into his father's strong embrace. Wang-to was heavily armed with a sword and a rifle of English make. He wore sturdy boots of animal skins and was bundled in a coat of fur. Whispering hoarsely, he ordered the men in the road to keep careful watch, then picked up several bundles and came into the house.

As Shingling lighted their last oil wick, his mother came from her bedroom and fell at her husband's feet with a cry of joy. He gathered her up and enveloped her in his arms. Quickly he opened one of the packages. The odor of cold cooked rice drenched Shingling's senses. His father placed the rice on the table and bade them eat. Everyone dug into the cold mass with fingers and stuffed it voraciously into their mouths. There was a glorious lip-smacking and chewing and swallowing. Shingling could not believe that food could taste so good; he detected in this cold rice the flavor of the meat juice in which it had been cooked. How succulent! How wonderful! How filling!

The children and the old man crowded into the room to have their shares, as Shingling's father opened another parcel and yet another. Like a wizard, he produced lamp oil and dried beans, dried rice, a sack of grain and, wonder of wonders, tea! Shingling's mother, moving with an alacrity he had not seen in months, rummaged for her best teapot, set it on the brazier and brought water to a brisk boil. She made tea for the family and for the men outside as well. One by one, they came in to warm themselves and drink, smacking their lips appreciatively. But the men did not tarry long, and each quickly returned to his vigil on the road. This reminded Shingling that his father had not returned without peril and could not long remain. And so it was that in less than an hour's time, Shingling's father uttered his reluctant farewells, kissed each of them in turn and slipped out to join his companions on the road. By the time first light began to pearl over the twin domes of Sheh and Shah, the men had climbed to the ridgeline and were gone.

Shingling patted his full belly with a grateful sigh. They would not have to kill the water buffalo after all.

Things improved after that. Men came frequently to the valley at night, bringing food to the village and farms. Shingling was not surprised to discover that numerous male heads of families and strong sons had gone to join the T'ai P'ing followers of Hung Hsiu-ch'uan. The legions of the religious-military leader swelled steadily, it was said, until it reached the proportions of an army. Hung kept himself aloof, an austere ascetic preaching equality of men and the renunciation of idols.

Gradually the spring came, and one morning Shingling awoke at dawn to the sound of rain. The family dashed outside shouting and laughing, and even the old man scooped rainwater into his hands and danced out onto the road. The event was cause for celebration throughout the valley, and families went to the village that day to share what meager foods they possessed. The village elders even managed to produce fireworks. Within weeks the spring rainy season was upon them, and the drought was clearly broken.

But the joy in Shingling's family was subdued. Tzu Hsi's persistent cough, contracted during the long suffering of the winter, did not improve. Her appetite was poor and her body refused to gain weight. While the rest of the family gradually restored flesh and health, the girl languished. Shingling had said nothing at first, thinking it discourteous of him to make comment. But finally he could no longer keep silent. He spoke with Tzu Hsi, for the first time taking her hands in his. Even the glowing eyes, he saw, had lost their luster and her hands were hot and dry to his touch.

"Tzu Hsi, I am sorry that you are not feeling well."

"It is nothing. A touch of the night air, no more." Her face forced a wan smile. "I shall be better in another week, Shingling. I'm sorry to be a bother to you."

"You are no bother. I have never spoken of this, and perhaps it is not the time. If I offend you, I shall pluck out my tongue. But I think you've known that my heart is warm

in your presence. I look upon you as one who's blessed with
beauty and grace, and sometimes your eyes are in my dreams.
Does that trouble you?"

"Trouble me?" A flicker returned to the eyes. The mouth,
thin as it was, lifted expressively. "I have dreamed of nothing
else, Shingling. Since I was a child, you have always been
part of my heart, and it would do no good to pretend
otherwise. I have felt too unworthy even to dream that you
would notice me. You are the man of the house now, far above
my humble station. And"—the eyes dulled again as a fresh
thought intruded on her mind—"and I have no dowry."

"You are your dowry. Nothing else is needed, for there is
no gold that can buy what's in my heart."

After this talk with Tzu Hsi, Shingling's spirits briefly
soared. He returned to the fields with Won and the buffalo,
and at times felt as tall as the sky and as light as a zephyr. The
climate and the land smiled upon their efforts, and by early
summer the plantings were done with the promise of an
abundant crop.

While nothing was spoken again of his feelings for Tzu Hsi,
there were small hints from his mother that the two families
in these unusual circumstances could omit the usual process
of parental arranging. Tzu Hsi's health showed slight improvement as the weather warmed, and she could sit outside
in the sunshine and walk about the garden. But her strength
was not lasting. Even the sunlight did little to restore her
color from the pallor of sickness. She lost weight again and
the coughing returned. There was about her a ravaged look,
normally associated with the dying. Shingling insisted that a
physician be brought to attend her, and this was done. The
good man, who had come from another village, merely shook
his head and said there was little he could do. He left
potions, several kinds of herbs and instructions for her treatment, and went away. A short time later, Tzu Hsi asked for
Shingling and he went into the room which they had made
for her and sat by the bed.

"I am going to die, Shingling," she said. "I saw it in the
physician's eyes. But I suspected it even before he came."

"You cannot die. You are too young. Besides, I cannot let
you die. You must be well for both of us."

She turned her face away, the face that now seemed to be
losing life every day and was so terribly thin. Her voice was a

whisper, like the sound of dry leaves. "I have loved you always and love you now. You are my lord and master."

"We shall be married, then. I shall ask our mothers to approve it, and my father's uncle in the village—"

She shook her head. Her eyes nested dully in dark hollows. A cough seized her, deep and rasping, and wracked her frail body with its violence. When it passed, she lay back and took his hand in hers. "You are a strong and virile man and cannot have a sickling for a wife," she said. "And anyway, it is too late."

He left her with an ache in his heart.

Six days later, Tzu Hsi lapsed into unconsciousness and died. They buried her on a slope commanding a view of the entire valley.

The summer yielded a fine rice crop.

The Hsien Magistrate was distraught. He read the message again carefully, so as not to miss a single nuance. There was no need. The thing was clear and the orders of the Mandarin precise. The magistrate sighed, pushed the paper aside, and dismissed the courier. He rose from his polished desk and went to his window to look out over the village.

He was an old man, old and tall and frail. His skin was like parchment and his eyes were buried in folds of aging flesh. A wispy, drooping mustache bracketed his mouth. He wore a robe of red silk and a small round hat; affixed to the robe's breast was his green badge of power. He had worn it for twenty years as the Hsien Magistrate for this village, the village of his birth. Behind him, the office had that patina and odor of quality and age. It was a place of tapestries and tiles, lacquered furnishings and fine floor vases. In summer the servants kept fresh flowers on his desk, always; but this was still the early spring, and it would be weeks before the first blossoms. And so there were dried plants giving off a spicy odor in the desk vases.

The day was sunny but chilly. From here he could see the familiar twin rounded hills, Sheh and Shah. They were a constant part of his life, these hills, and rarely out of his sight. In eighty-three years of life, the Hsien Magistrate had left this valley only six times. The last time was to be received by the Mandarin in Canton. He had not been comfortable in the city,

for it was crowded and noisy and filled with ruffians of every sort.
There were also too many foreign devils for his liking, giving
off strange odors and strutting about in their tight clothing
and coats that would not even button. How ridiculous. And
so the Hsien Magistrate had returned happily to the village,
back among the things that were known. It was said that the
Mandarin's invitation to Canton had been extended for the
purpose of offering the magistrate a higher position, beyond
the valley. Delicately, however, he had let his preference be
known, and it was honored. The offer was never made. Now,
in the worrisome presence of this message from the Mandarin, he almost wished he had done otherwise. It was not
always pleasant to govern those whom you have known since
they first drew breath.

The Hsien Magistrate suddenly felt quite old and ineffec-
tive. He sensed that events larger than life were coming
together and passing him by. He felt himself a pawn in the
system and unworthy of his office. Of what value was responsibility if it could not be used to help one's friends? He
picked up a small bell and rang for his secretary. The man
arrived with a low bow.

"You have heard, I suppose?" the Hsien Magistrate said.

"I have heard, sire. One can no more keep bad news secret
than to stop the wind in the trees."

"So." The Hsien Magistrate stared out upon the village.
Passersby moved briskly, huddled in their cotton coats. They
wore the conical hats of peasants. He sighed. "I have lived
eighty-three years in this village, and nothing like this has
ever happened before. I wonder what the Manchu are about.
Are the T'ai P'ing so troublesome that such extremes are
necessary?"

"I cannot say, sire. The followers of Hung Hsi-ch'uan have
committed grave assaults upon the government and are in
rebellion in the north. Perhaps it is the ardor of religion that
inspires them, and allegiances with the English. It is said that
Hung is much admired by the foreign Christians for his
worship of the god known as Jesus."

"But our men did not join the T'ai P'ing for that," the
Hsien Magistrate said. "Those who did so were impatient
with the failure of the government to protect us against the
banditti. Surely our lords know that. Our men would have
returned to their fields had the militia taken stronger measures to keep order."

"That is true, sire. Do you wish to write that in your reply?"

"Yes. Yes, that is the thought I wish to express. Please convey to my lord the hope that such extremes will be unnecessary; that these condemned men from our village are not outlaws in the strictest sense of the word and their transgressions were not committed out of disloyalty to the empire." The Hsien Magistrate paused to collect a further thought, then continued. "And perhaps I should suggest that such extreme measures might not serve the purpose of chastening the families of this valley, but could raise their rancor unnecessarily. We have suffered much from the famine without relief, and were it not for help brought by the T'ai P'ing many more would have starved."

The secretary's eyebrows lifted in surprise. "You wish for me to write that, sire?"

"Yes. Write it and bring it to me for signature."

The secretary withdrew. The Hsien Magistrate turned back to the window and pondered. If his words were taken as impertinent, then so be it. He was an old man with not much longer to live, and the burdens of office grew heavier each year. Let them take away his badge, if they wished. He gazed at the looming presences of Sheh and Shah; he was sick at heart and acutely conscious of his remoteness from the pinnacles of power in Peking and Canton. In the great amorphous complexity which was China, the Hsien Magistrate counted for as little as a grain of sand.

When the secretary returned and the message was dispatched, the Hsien Magistrate went to the temple and remained there for the rest of the day, sitting cross-legged on the floor among the guttering lamps. The townsfolk, sensing his ordeal of spirit, kept their distance. He went to the temple every day for a week, until one day the courier returned. The message was explicit: "The executions will be performed on the day of the next full moon. The wife, eldest brother, and the eldest son of each condemned person are ordered to be in attendance, but without explanation."

With a heavy heart, the Hsien Magistrate ordered that the message be sent out to the specified homes in the valley.

The day was cloudy and threatening rain. Shingling drew up his quilted jacket against the late autumn chill. For weeks rumors had rippled through the valley about the summonses, until it came to be regarded as an ill omen to receive a messenger from the Hsien Magistrate. In time, the messenger had come to their house, too, causing Shingling's mother to cry out in fear. He had attempted to calm her but had little success, for her intuition was dark and brooding. "Oh, my dear husband," she cried, "how I worry for him!" Because the summons from the magistrate had been insistent, threatening arrest if the named individuals did not appear on the appointed day and time, Shingling managed to convince his mother that they had no other choice but to go.

They arrived at a field on the slope beyond the village and found several hundred people already there, standing in the raw wind under a leaden sky. Practically everyone was from the valley, and it did not take Shingling long to recognize them as families of T'ai P'ing men. This gave him a powerful sense of foreboding, but he attempted to drive it out of his mind. The Hsien Magistrate, after all, was a kindly old man, considering his rank and power, and had never been harsh or cruel in his official actions. Everyone in the valley knew him, for he had lived here forever and was as much a part of their lives as the twin mountains, Sheh and Shah. Most people had never in their lives encountered any governmental official having greater authority than the magistrate. Only a few had ever seen a mandarin, and then only a glimpse when such a fearsome official and his retinue passed on a street while the witness was visiting Canton.

Shingling and his mother found a place in the crowd and stood quietly, awaiting events. Everyone had taken up a position facing where two carved chairs had been placed. The chairs, one slightly larger than the other, looked as if they had come from the Hsien Magistrate's office. Deliberately he thought of this, as he studied the worn faces of the valley peasants and pondered the bleakness of the terraced land. Finally there was no more to occupy his mind and his thoughts drifted to his father—did any of this have to do with his father?—and, ultimately, to Tzu Hsi. This was the first day he had not visited the grave. There simply had not been time, and his mother had needed him more. We must attend to the living first, he thought. He clasped his hands behind him and rocked on his heels.

An hour passed. Two. At last, from the direction of the village, a gong was sounded. This was followed by the rhythmic

banging of cymbals. Shingling watched what appeared to be
an official procession coming up the long dirt road from the
temple. He recognized in the lead the tall, thin figure of the
Hsien Magistrate being borne on a palanquin by eight carri-
ers. Behind him, on an even larger platform, rode a dignitary
in robes of silk. The second man was preceded by menacing
armed sentries and escorted by retainers, musicians and
standard-bearers. Behind this group strode two gigantic men
wearing orange tunics and gold crowns decorated over the
ears with pheasant feathers. Attending these two were several assistants who bore massive curved swords with wooden
handles. To the beating and clashing, the processionists made
their way to the field. As the Mandarin arrived, the crowd
quickly prostrated itself to the ground, Shingling and his
mother following the example of the others. For the first time
in his life he tasted fear, for the Mandarin wielded the power
of life and death. His bodyguards, at his whim, could pluck a
luckless spectator from the crowd and pack him off to jail, or
worse, cut him down with a sword stroke.

The Mandarin dismounted from his palanquin, ascended
the canopied platform and settled into the larger of the
chairs. His eyes seemed to take in everything—the crowd,
the retainers, the humble rock village—and nothing. To
Shingling, the eyes penetrated, analyzed, moved on. They
were the color of slate. As the crowd rose to its feet again, the
Hsien Magistrate took the smaller chair. Nothing was said.

The people of the valley stood hushed, hardly daring to
draw breath. Soldiers trooped up the hill now and took
positions all around the field. Another, larger procession
began making its way from the village, led by officials on
horseback. As they ascended the road, Shingling saw that
eighteen pairs of pole-bearers followed the horses. Between
them, the pole-bearers carried large wicker baskets of the
type used for carrying live hogs to the field, a chill of
recognition swept over him. The baskets did not contain
hogs, but men; eighteen men, each dressed in the rough
cotton garb of a prisoner, were shackled hand and foot in the
wicker cages.

A murmuring rose from the spectators as this parade of
misery neared the field. The sound was a rippling of involuntary vocal response, inspired first by a kind of dumb curiosity
and then by rising alarm. As the procession made its final
turn and moved into the middle of the field, the awareness of

what was to take place suddenly smote the crowd. The murmur became a gasping and then several women moaned, among them Shingling's mother. It was an agony of sound, causing several of the soldiers to look nervously about and grasp the sword hilts at their belts. The Mandarin gave no sign of response. The Hsien Magistrate stared straight ahead from his chair, as one in a trance.

Events moved swiftly now, almost too swiftly for Shingling's startled mind to grasp. The pole-bearers placed their burdens on the ground and a squad of soldiers opened the baskets one by one and dumped their contents as they would dump live goats in a butcher's corral. Fresh gasps came from the watchers as they now saw the dreadful condition of the prisoners. Each man was skin and bone, and bore the marks of beatings and torture. Several were bleeding from the mouth and nose. None had the strength, it seemed, to rise immediately from where he had been flung on the ground.

One of the last to come out of his basket was Shingling's father. A wave of nausea passed through Shingling as he saw the pitiable shape of the once vibrant man, Wang-to. The powerful arms and hands were reduced to sticks, the massive neck to a slender post, the eyes which had once stared boldly from a broad peasant's face now glittered feverishly from a skin-covered skeleton. Shingling's mother cried, "Oh, no! no! No!" and started to rush onto the field but he grasped her arm and held it, whispering for her to quiet herself and give her husband courage. The soldiers now walked down the line of prostrate men trying to rouse them to their knees with kicks and cuffs, but only a few were able to respond. Shingling's father came to his knees briefly, as if to demonstrate a last surge of dignity, but then toppled again onto his side.

One of the Mandarin's assistants shouted an order. The two giants in orange tunics and gold crowns now stepped forward. Behind them, the sword-bearers unsheathed two huge blades. Shingling had never seen such weapons. Each blade flashed in the light, broad as a man's thigh and thick at the back like the blade of an axe, but sweeping down in a tapered curve to the heavy wooden haft.

"Our Lord!" the giants called to the Mandarin, each performing a low bow. "We are prepared."

"Proceed, then." The voice of the Mandarin sounded thin and high-pitched.

Each executioner was handed his blade. The first giant

moved into position commanding a line of nine condemned. He placed his booted feet wide apart, grasped the sword hilt in both hands and deliberately set his body flat-footed. Beneath the massive bulk of the swordsman's height and girth, the prisoners awaiting their fate seemed as puny as ground ferrets. An assistant stepped behind the first condemned man. The swordsman's eyes flickered acknowledgment. He lifted the blade over his head and nodded.

With a quick movement the assistant bent down, locked his hands beneath the arms of the prostrate man, grasping him by the shoulders, and abruptly jerked him to his knees. The motion caused the head to swing upward and outward and the neck to stretch. In the blink of an eye, the neck was fully extended; at this precise instant, the executioner swung. The blade came down with a whoosh of air and chopped the head from the body. A woman screamed as the body fell, its neck gushing blood and fingers and feet twitching violently. As the head rolled free, the eyelids fluttered.

Swiftly, rhythmically, the work advanced: swing and chop, swing and chop. When the first executioner had chopped nine heads, he stepped aside with his bloody sword so that the second could take charge. Not one blow missed its mark or had to be repeated; each sword stroke severed neck and spinal column in a single slice. And behind the advancing swordsmen and their assistants, the torsos poured a torrent of blood into the dark ground of the killing field.

Shingling's father was midway in the second group. As the executioner stepped to him, lifting the blade, Shingling's father stirred on the ground and looked back at the crowd as if in search of the face of his son. Shingling waved his arms vigorously. The eyes flicked to him and locked in an instant that Shingling would remember to his dying day. A ghost of a smile worked at his father's lips. Then the assistant seized him, the smile was flung aside, the body jerked upward, the sword swept down.

Chop!

The sound ricocheted through Shingling's brain and shook him to the marrow. As his mother screamed, he drew her fiercely to him and kept his eyes riveted to the scene. "Good-bye, my father," he said aloud. "I shall remember what you taught me, and live in your behalf."

When the last head had rolled, the executioners stepped aside. The tunics and lower garments of both giants were now

splotched with blood and their boots drenched in it. They
bowed to the Mandarin. The assistants moved swiftly from
head to head, grabbing up each by its hair and flinging it into
a basket. When all the heads had been thus gathered, the
Mandarin and the Hsien Magistrate rose from their chairs,
remounted the palanquins and were borne away, followed by
their retainers, the soldiers, executioners and bearers with
their empty wicker baskets. As the cymbals clashed and the
standards fluttered back down to the village, the crowd began
to move in bewilderment, as people do in the aftermath of a
storm. Like sleepwalkers, they converged to the center of the
field to reclaim the bodies of husbands and sons. For many, it
proved painfully difficult now to identify the headless corpse
as their own. Several families argued over the claiming of a
body and women fell to the ground to wail in fresh paroxysms
of grief and frustration.

They buried the body of Shingling's father on the slope
beside the grave of Tsu Hsi.

Shingling made his decision as he and his brother Won
shoveled the earth into their father's grave. However, he did
not hasten to announce it. Things had to be stabilized first,
the next spring's planting done and the younger boys properly prepared to assume responsibilities. When the rice was in
to his satisfaction, and the daily rains assured another good harvest, Shingling told his mother what he intended to do. It
was his father's dream, he said, and in time he would be able
to send money back to the family, perhaps even send for
them. He could see no future in remaining longer in the
valley. His mother wept and helped him to gather his few
belongings. He said good-bye to her and the others and then,
on his way out of the valley, stopped at the graves of Tsu Hsi
and his father.

"I am leaving now," he told them, "and I probably shall
never return here. I go to Gum San, to a place called
California. It will be difficult, but I hear that others have
managed to go there from Canton. I will make a new life in
California. It is said that the streets are paved with gold."

He left the graves and walked toward the south on the
road. The setting sun laid a smear of color across the evening
sky. In the distance, a cloud of white water birds erupted
from the edge of a rice field and made a sweeping flight
directly over his head, their wings beating against the im-

mense silences of China. He watched the birds until they vanished over the brooding mounds of Sheh and Shah.

It was a good omen, he thought. It was a very good omen.

VI

They came off the river ragged and half-starved, six men, nine women, and five children. They had survived an attack by brigands along the Ohio three weeks earlier and somehow made it all the way to St. Louis by raft. Two men bore festering wounds that refused to heal. Everyone's clothing was in tatters, their faces drawn and hollow-eyed from lack of food. Men and women alike had toiled to haul the raft upriver on the Mississippi. This merciless labor had left their flesh flayed raw by thorny underbrush and frequent falls on the rocky shore. To compound their misery, the November weather was consistently unpleasant, with raw, blustery days and early snow flurries.

"Stephen! Stephen, come quickly!"

It was Catherine who spied them first as they labored upriver along the near shore. She ran down to the water, gathering her skirts. Stephen stumped after her as fast as his peg leg would carry him, trailed by the two children, Bradley and Colette, and Crippled Wolf. The Indian cradled an old smoothbore rifle.

"Bring it in here. That's right. Tie off here, at the dock. You poor, poor souls." Catherine beckoned and shouted. By the time Stephen reached her she was already mooring the rickety craft to a stanchion beside one of the berthed steamers. "Come on, now, all of you."

"Thank the Lord. Bless you, Catherine. Bless you!"

Stephen gasped. "John Boniface!"

The giant was an apparition, gaunt and disheveled, his clothing in rags and his face buried in a wild tangle of gray whiskers. He wore the remnants of a black greatcoat and a round, flat-brimmed hat. His outdoorsman's eyes were even paler than they had been in Cincinnati. At his command the others disembarked and gathered in a miserable cluster. Catherine, Stephen and Crippled Wolf herded them up the broad wooden steps to an unpainted new building. Its raw facade bore a large sign facing the river, "Stewart Line, St. Louis Depot." Several hired workmen dropped their tools and came running to help carry the travelers' meager belongings up from the raft.

As doors slammed against the cold, Stephen brought out several bottles of brandy to warm the refugees, but these were politely declined. "Thank you, but we don't hold to drinkin' alcohol," John Boniface said. As Catherine hurried away to see to the preparation of food, the leader stared at Stephen. "The Lord be praised," he said. "We are saved."

"What in God's name happened to you?"

Painfully, Boniface recounted their misadventures. It was not an uncommon recital, for travelers on the rivers always ran the risk of being waylaid by cutthroats and thieves. They had fought as best they could, but were limited in what they could do. The outlaw band had robbed them, raped two of the women in a drunken orgy and then vanished into the woods. "We were lucky," said the big scout, "to escape with our lives."

As tables were set up and cooking odors wafted from the kitchen, the mood quickly turned to celebration. Stephen and Boniface talked volubly of shared adventures and bygone friends. The scout's memory returned to the day of Stephen's miraculous rescue from the riverboat explosion nearly thirty years before. "Some of your carcass fed the fishes that day."

Stephen laughed. "That's a fact."

"So I guess we could count ourselves lucky," Boniface said.

The big scout sipped tea laced with extra sugar. He glanced at the corner of the room, where Crippled Wolf strung beads on a rawhide thong for the entertainment of the children. The Indian spoke softly to them, his words bringing small ripples of laughter. The children also drank tea and snacked on beef jerky and hard candy. "That'd be the Omaha medicine man," Boniface said gravely.

Stephen nodded. "We are brothers."

"There is no closer kinship between men." Boniface smiled. "It is a status Indians have, the blood brotherhood, that's generally denied to white men. I think we're the poorer for lacking such bonds of friendship." His glance took in his traveling companions. "But there are other bonds between people. Ours is a bond of devotion of God, and not to man. I think that's what got us through this ordeal so well. It was the will of God."

Stephen saw the opportunity to question Boniface further, but instinctively refrained. A man's religion was his own business, and he'd disclose as much as he cared to in due time, or not at all.

"You've labored hard on this place," Boniface said, looking around at the unfinished building in which they sat. "I'm glad to see it. I heard about the race, and your loss of the *Monongahela Pride* and the Ohio River freight business. I'm afraid you were cheated, my friend."

Stephen sighed. "Perhaps. But it forced us to expand our operations in new directions, and that's worth a lot. Catherine and I have worked like hell on this compound, but it's damned rewarding. By next summer, you won't recognize the place."

"By then we shall have found our New Jerusalem, I hope," Boniface said wistfully. There it was again, Stephen thought; the religious reference, the talk of finding an El Dorado. Was the man addled in the head? Boniface continued, "Somewhere out there, somewhere in the mountains, we'll find the place. And we'll put down roots, plant our crops, make the desert bloom and build our tabernacle."

Catherine's voice called to them from a makeshift dining room. "Come and join us, gentlemen, before supper gets cold."

The food was hearty and abundant. Catherine, the house servants, and several women of Boniface's group had prepared a feast of meats, soups, and steaming platters of vegetables. The latter were provided from the basement pantry, where Crippled Wolf's wife Moon Flower had seen to the stocking of a fine winter's supply of foods preserved in airtight jars. As the dinner company gathered at extra tables, fashioned from planks thrown over sawhorses and covered with muslin cloth, Boniface led them in a fervent prayer thanking God for their salvation. He concluded: "And may Thy grace and abundance continue to bless the lives of our dear friends, Stephen and Catherine, who brought us from the river and shared with our starving, miserable company their bounty of spirit and joy and life-giving food. They shall always be welcome as friends in the New Jerusalem."

Stephen watched with pleasure as his starving guests attacked the mounds of food. The warmth of the room had created an embarrassing secondary problem—a heady mix of odors arising from bodies long unwashed permeated the room to the visible dismay of several of the women in Boniface's company. To this was added the stench of infection from the wounded men; one had been knifed in the side and the other suffered from a long festering gash on the thigh. "I'm terribly sorry," Boniface said. "I know how offensive this must be to you, Mrs. Stewart."

Catherine smiled and shook her head. "Mr. Boniface, a few odors are nothing. We are all together, and that's what matters. We'll attend to first things first, and first comes food for the body. Besides," she said, glancing at Stephen, her blue eyes alight, "you should have been around when Stephen was enduring his infected burns. Now that was an odor."

The scout accepted this in the matter-of-fact manner of one who has lived long and experienced much. Abruptly changing the subject, he asked Stephen, "And what will you do next, my friend?"

"We're expanding all over the map," Stephen replied. "Cincinnati, Louisville, St. Louis, New Orleans. We're starting to build steamboats here on the Mississippi. I also need a western base of operations. We're sending out freight wagons to the settlements beyond, and I'm hoping to open a stagecoach line."

"A stagecoach line?"

"That's right. They've discovered gold in California."

Boniface sighed. "Yes, I heard about that back on the Ohio. The whole country's got gold fever. It's spreading like wildfire. Everybody's talking about going west."

"You're going to see big changes in this country," Stephen said.

Boniface grew thoughtful. "Woe betide us," he murmured darkly.

"What's that you said?" Stephen asked.

The scout shook his head. "Nothing."

Boniface forked a slice of smoked ham and looked thoughtfully into Stephen's face. As always, the flesh-covered silk mask covered the scarred left side of the face. "God was merciful to you, Stephen," he said.

"Yes, I quite agree," Stephen said.

"Merciful?" said one of the women. The handsome, unmutilated side of Stephen's face had intrigued her since their arrival. Surely this poor man had been positively beautiful once. "How can you say that God was merciful, Elder Boniface?"

The scout turned his attention back to his plate. "Why, Sister Linda Anne, God left Stephen with one perfectly good eye." He patted his lips with a napkin and burped softly. "After all, he could have taken them both."

They arrived in the early afternoon three days later. The vanguard was a mean lot, idlers and drifters from the city, hard-used waterfront scum. Stephen found them hanging around the main gate of the compound as he and John Boniface came from town with another wagon load of supplies. He recognized the hostile eyes, the ugly set of tobacco-stained mouths.

"Who ye got there with you, Mr. Stewart? Who's the big fella?" The speaker was a scarecrow of a man, squinty-eyed and filthy. He moved as if to block the gate, saw that Stephen did not intend to slow the wagon, then stepped aside. The wagon rattled into the compound and the gates were slammed behind it by Crippled Wolf and one of Boniface's men who had been waiting. Stephen climbed down stiffly and squared his broad-brimmed hat.

"Who are those men, Crippled Wolf?"

"Don't know. They come from town one hour, two hours ago. Hang around the fence."

The other man, whose name was Cate, spoke to John Boniface. "They know we're here, Elder. The word's out in town."

"Any trouble?" Boniface said.

"Not yet. But there'll be more of 'em by nightfall, I expect. You know how it is."

"Yes. I know how it is."

There was loud banging on the compound gate. Stephen frowned, tripped the latch open and stepped through. Crippled Wolf moved behind him. The Indian carried his smoothbore rifle.

"Mr. Stewart, I guess you know what kind of folks you're harboring." This time the spokesman was a fat man, whom

Stephen recognized as a dockhand from town. Several other men were arriving by buggy and horseback. These newcomers looked more prosperous. Two of them were merchants. "I guess you know that, Mr. Stewart."

"I have no idea what you're talking about. What's the meaning of this?"

One of the merchants climbed down from his buggy and pushed through the group. "I'll tell you what we mean, Mr. Stewart. We mean there's no room in St. Louis for that kind of trash. Your friends in there are polygamists and anti-Christians. They've got neither moral scruples nor common decency. And this community, Mr. Stewart, won't stand for it."

Several of the men muttered agreement. "That's right."

"You tell 'em, Squire Fox."

"Yo're darned tootin'."

"They've been run out of towns all over the east."

"Corrupting decent people, corrupting women and children."

Stephen held his ground, not speaking. He sensed a movement. Crippled Wolf had shifted the smoothbore rifle, and Stephen heard the click of the hammer drawing back. He backed off half a step, so that his back pressed against the gun. The men seemed not to notice. They closed around him, all trying to speak at once. He smelled their whiskey breaths. Automatically his mind swiftly summarized their position.

The new Stewart compound, ringed by tall board fencing, was several miles south of the St. Louis city limits. He had selected a bluff well above average flood level for his main structures, with a long, sloping riverfront for racks and ways. This provided ample room to assemble the great shallow hulls of a new generation of steamboats, big, ornate craft that would provide luxury salons, private staterooms and plenty of cargo space on the lower deck. Older boats also could dry-dock here for repairs. There was no thought of withstanding any kind of seige, but subconsciously Stephen had not ignored the idea completely in these troubled times. If necessary, the compound would serve, and his workmen could be called upon to do battle.

John Boniface and his group had spent the first night in the main building, where they bathed and tended the wounds of the injured men. They had been up again the following dawn, preparing to push on. Stephen had given indignant protest. "John Boniface, you're insane! Winter's coming on. It's no time to be traveling with women and children. Besides, you don't have nearly enough supplies to strike out inland. Stay with us until spring, and we'll see to it you're properly provisioned."

The scout seemed strangely reluctant. "There are some things you aren't aware of, Mr. Stewart, and we don't wish for you and your wife to get involved in our troubles. I'm much obliged, but you've done enough already."

Stephen was adamant. "My friend, there's no trouble too big for us to help handle. I insist. You must stay here at least until after Christmas. We'll lay in supplies. Your people can get properly rested. Then we'll talk about it again."

Boniface, seeing the sad shape of his companions and acknowledging ruefully that he had no other choice, finally gave in. Then, groping for words, he confessed that their straits were even worse than it seemed. "We're penniless. Back in Ohio, those outlaws made off with nearly everything we had in this world."

That settled it. "Don't speak another word," Stephen said. "We intend to help. You can consider it a loan."

And so for two days they had made wagon trips into town, buying up everything the Boniface party might need: lanterns and candlewax, guns and ammunition, tents, harnesses, medicinal goods, blankets, boots, clothing, anything and everything. If the activity drew curious comment and sidelong glances, Stephen paid no attention. Arnold Bradford, who was Boniface's righthand man, and several of the others also made trips. All seemed to heed Boniface's warning to keep to themselves and not to mingle with townspeople more than was absolutely necessary. Stephen thought this odd, but made no mention of it. Only once had Boniface indicated that their westward journey was also a flight of sorts. They were returning to the compound on the final trip, rocking together on the wagon seat as it lurched along over muddy ruts and potholes in the river road. Boniface had looked up at a gloomy sky threatening snow. "The Lord is strange in his ways, Mr. Stewart, but we've got to accept them. He's testing us, that's all. We've been tested many times before, for we are the lost tribe of Israel. We intend to push on with your help. It's Providence. We'll go out there"—he turned his big, bearded face to the west—"and find the New Jerusalem far from the wrath of the gentiles. We'll cause the desert to bloom."

Well, Stephen reasoned, everybody has his own form of worship. One man's was as good as another's. At least he was instinctively certain of one point: John Boniface and his people weren't outlaws, and intended nobody harm.

"Hangin's too good for 'em!" the scarecrow shrieked, his spittle spraying in Stephen's face. "And for all we know, Stewart, you're one of 'em yourself, converted to the faith. That's what they do, ye know; convert ignorant Christians to their heathen faith."

"Yeah! How many wives you got, Stewart? Two or three, I'll wager."

"Hold on there, Lowderback. There ain't no call for that."

"I say if he's harboring them, then he's one of them. Or leastways, he ain't no better. Birds of a feather—"

"Let's get the Mormons!" someone shouted from the rear of the crowd.

"Right! Get the Mormons! Tar and feather 'em! Drag 'em out and—"

Someone pushed forward against Stephen. It was the merchant, Squire Fox. "I figured you for a heathen all along anyhow," he said. "That mask. I always wanted to see what was under that mask. How do you know it ain't some satanic religious symbol?" His hand lashed out at Stephen's face. Before Stephen could react, Squire Fox's fingers had grasped the silken mask and had ripped it away.

"My Gawd!"

The crowd gasped and shrank back. Squire Fox's mouth worked as he stared at the mutilation that had once been a human face. Purple welts of melted and dried flesh ran in all directions. Stephen Stewart's eye socket was an empty, ravaged hole. The ear was a jagged rim. Skin had drawn away from the mouth, exposing the teeth as if in a living skull. Forehead and head bore no resemblance to human form. The effect was that of half a mottled death mask, grinning and sightless, a living horror.

Boooom!

The smoothbore rifle went off like a cannon, its report smashing against Stephen's eardrum. As his hearing numbed on that side and a dull ringing set in, someone seized his arm with an iron grip and hauled him backward into the compound. He was trying to shake the ringing from his head as the heavy gate slammed shut and the lockbolts slipped into place.

"Damn it, Crippled Wolf!" he shouted. "Couldn't you point that blunderbuss in some other direction?"

"Sorry, my brother."

"Bad enough to have my hidden beauty exposed, I've got to be deafened and manhandled to boot. And why the hell are they calling me a Mormon?"

"You men get up on that stockade with your weapons and stay there till I order you down," John Boniface bellowed. The big scout had herded his own men and several Stewart workmen into position along the top of the heavy fence. Already their rifles bristled along the top, aiming down at the startled crowd of townspeople on the other side. Boniface confronted Stephen, and began to speak, looking directly into his host's unmasked face. "Mr. Stewart, I . . . Jesus Christ . . ." Boniface swallowed, the words frozen in his throat.

Stephen chuckled. "Arresting sight, ain't I?"

"I never thought . . . I never knew . . ."

"Well, now you know. And if you tell me you're sorry you helped drag me out of that river, John Boniface, I'll have Crippled Wolf break your neck."

Boniface recovered, forcing his eyes not to waver. "I've seen prettier sights." He laughed nervously.

"Good."

Crippled Wolf moved to Stephen's side and held up a bit of fabric. It was the silken mask. Stephen nodded wordlessly. The Indian carefully tied the mask back into place.

"I meant to tell you, Stephen, about us being Mormons and all," John Boniface said. "I . . . I made a mistake, I guess. But I figured with all the trouble we've had—trouble everyplace we've been—there was no need to include you in it. I figured that if we just moved along quickly, there would be no problem."

"There's no problem, John Boniface. If some folks don't like Mormons, that's their business, not mine. I don't hold much with religion one way or the other. But I don't like for other people to try to tell us or our friends how to live. So you folks just make yourselves at home. And as far as I'm concerned, you can defend that stockade till hell freezes over." Stephen turned to the Indian. "Crippled Wolf, better get some men and unload this wagon." Then he stumped on his peg leg across the compound yard and into the main house.

Darkness came early this time of year. The onset of night brought uneasiness to the compound. Stephen considered sending a man upriver to bring back the St. Louis constabulary, but then thought better of it. No need to blow things out of proportion by hasty action. Besides, by midnight he and Boniface had agreed upon a better plan. While armed sentinels kept watch from the wooden palisade facing the road, everyone hurried with the preparations.

The crowd outside the fence had grown considerably, but consisted mostly of riverfront louts and human refuse from the saloons and public houses, drawn for sport. Several bonfires were lit and drunken laughter erupted from time to time, interspersed with storytelling and bawdy songs. As evening wore on, the cold deepened and there were flurries of light snow. Men clustered closer around the fires. In time, those who had conveyances began drifting away back to town, leaving their companions a dispirited lot, out of whiskey and too cold and hungry even to argue among themselves. The respite would be short-lived, however; of this Stephen was certain. Trouble would return on the morrow, and probably bring reinforcements.

Several older steamboats were moored at the wharf, among them Catherine's small, fast steamer, *Jamie*. The craft was a durable little stern-wheeler with an oversized boiler and piston driver. Her extremely shallow draft would negotiate creeks, backwaters and sloughs. This made *Jamie* a valuable all-around workboat. Stephen had built her as a wedding present for Catherine nearly thirty years ago and gave her a complete overhaul at least once a year. *Jamie* was as riverworthy now as the day she was launched.

Stephen had discussed his plan with Catherine following the late afternoon confrontation at the gate. Then he presented it to Boniface. The big scout was astonished. "You'd do that for us? But what if we run her aground or sink her? I don't know those waters too good. I could make it by canoe, maybe, but not by steamboat. Besides, I don't know the first thing about engines."

"Crippled Wolf does," Stephen said. "He's an expert. He'll go with you."

In the cold darkness, a human chain was formed from the main building down to the wharf, handing down all the accumulated supplies for the Boniface party. When they had loaded everything aboard the *Jamie*, there was still room for three horses and all the people. It was two o'clock in the morning when the engine was fired and she pushed off without running lanterns into the black Mississippi. A thin new moon stood high and cold, casting the wooded river-banks into ghostly silhouette. Stephen and Catherine stood bundled in their woolen cloaks, listening to the retreating sounds of *Jamie*'s stout engine and watching the diminishing plume of her chimney stack. *Jamie* breasted the current, chuffed northward and vanished around a bend.

"They'll be heading west on the Missouri River after daylight," Stephen said, "and then it's all the way to the Platte, and beyond. If any vessel can make it, the *Jamie* can. At least, till the freeze sets in."

"Where will they stop, Stephen?"

He sighed and shook his head. "Some place called New Jerusalem, ultimately. Boniface will know it when he gets there. Then Crippled Wolf will return home to us."

The townspeople came back in force soon after daybreak. This time the entourage of wagons and buggies was led by several substantial citizens, Squire Fox among them. The Squire's face was round like a melon and flushed from the cold. Most of the men carried rifles or sidearms.

The compound gate stood open. There was no one in the main yard. Stephen's hunting dogs signaled the arrivals with spirited barking. Squire Fox and the leaders entered the compound warily, guns ready. They seemed confused. Not until they moved to the front of the main building was there a sign of human life. The front door creaked open slowly and Stephen Stewart stepped out, yawning and adjusting his suspenders.

"Well, well, well," he said pleasantly. "'Morning, Squire Fox. Gentlemen." He sniffed the cold air coming up from the river and inspected the sky. "Looks like it's going to be a nice clear day."

"Where are they, Stewart?"

"Where's who?"

"You know who. Them Mormon friends of yours. Where are they?"

Stephen smiled. "Oh. They're gone, Squire Fox."

"Gone? Gone where?"

"Gone west, same as everybody else nowadays. They never intended to stay in St. Louis anyhow."

The guns lowered. The men glanced sheepishly at each other. Some of them glared at Squire Fox. There was a clearing of throats, an indecisive shuffling.

Stephen's smile broadened. He clapped the nearest citizen on the shoulder. "Well, you fellows must be cold and hungry after that trip from town so early. So come on in the house. There's coffee on the stove and breakfast is cooking." He turned and led the way as, wordlessly, they followed.

"Catherine," he called cheerily, "we've got guests for breakfast!"

VII

Men still looked at her, and that was fine. Life moved on. Aging was a natural course of it, but a woman could age gracefully, keep her figure, work her wiles. And so even now, as she walked in Portsmouth Square daintily lifting her hems out of the dust, Maybelle felt their eyes, heard their whispers.

"My, my."

"Handsome woman."

"That's a fact. And you should've seen her when she was younger." Here a tall stranger lifted his top hat, there a grizzled prospector turned with an open-mouthed stare. She smiled, nodded, took her compliments.

"Harlot." This was open, a female voice without pretence of whisper. "Bawdy house madam. Thy sins will find thee out!" Maybelle's smile faded; her eyes flashed at the shadowed crone. The harpie scuttled away in a flurry of black taffeta, spitting a final epithet. "Whore!"

Around her, San Francisco surged. The town today was a constant uproar of hammering, banging, carousing, brawling, singing, shooting. New buildings, constructed with prefabricated wooden sections brought in by the schooners, sprang up overnight. The harbor was a mass of vessels, great numbers of them empty and rotting in their berths, their captains and crews having joined the rush to the hills. The dirt streets and plank sidewalks teemed with every describable human variety, from Yankee adventurers to seraped Mexicans, Negroes, Peruvians, Chileans, renegade Frenchmen, Chinese Celestials in their blue quilted jackets, insolent southerners, millionaires and paupers, beggars and thieves.

"'Morning, Miss Maybelle."

"Good morning, Mr. Finch."

Away from town, the countryside was soft and languorous and the summer a presence felt as well as seen. Wildflowers danced in riotous array on rippling grasslands reaching back toward the blue mountains. Streams leaped and tumbled in frothy delight. The land was benign, for the grazing of cattle and wild horses and deer. Hawks winged over the cliffs. The sea fringed the coast in white froth. But all that was away from town, where nature remained pristine.

In town, the hand of man wrought its dreadful changes in the insane rush for riches. Man cut dirt streets around the hills and flanked them with shanties and shacks and tents. Man dug his privies, filled the air with his noise and odors of sawdust, sweat, manure. Man brought his horses, his wagons, his greed, his guns, his profanity, his brawlings and drunken songs and fartings, his tobacco spit, his dust...

"Ma'am, look out!"

The shout came from behind her, along with a wild and rumbling clatter. Confused, Maybelle turned. From out of the late afternoon shadows, bolted a runaway horse team, wild-eyed, harness streaming. Hooves thundered into Portsmouth Square, sending pedestrians flying. Maybelle felt herself frozen to the spot, unable to move. Someone seized her around the middle with a grip of iron, and yanked her bodily aside. The panicked horses pounded past her, flinging sweat. Gasping for breath, she felt suddenly ill and undone. Her flowered hat had fallen off. She stooped to recover it from the dust and her red hair tumbled into her eyes, so that for an instant she could not see. As the arm released its grip from around her waist, she turned to thank her savior and looked into the smiling face of a young Chinese. He wore a conical hat of matted straw, a cloth coat and sandals. His hair was braided in one long pigtail. He bowed and jabbered something in his native tongue.

"Thank you," Maybelle stammered. "Mister... Mister..."

The man bowed again and turned away, walking hurriedly.

"Wait," she shouted. "Wait!"

Maybelle began to move after him, but as she did someone came running up behind her. "Are you all right, ma'am?"

"Yes. Yes, I..." She looked at the man, a tall easterner in city clothes. He was clean-shaven, middle-aged, with friendly brown eyes. "I'm all right. I just..." She turned again, looking for the Chinese youth. He was gone, vanished into the crowd. "That man saved my life."

"Who?"

"The Celestial. He saved my life. He pulled me out of the path of those horses. I... I couldn't move."

"Well, you're all right now." The tall man smelled of tobacco and shaving soap. He wore a vest with a gold watch chain and high boots of soft brown leather.

"Are you the man who shouted the warning?"

"Yes."

"Thank you."

"I couldn't reach you in time. The Chinaman was nearer."

A crowd had gathered, murmuring excitedly. The tall man took Maybelle's arm. "Shall we move along? No need to attract attention." As she fell into step, trying to match his long stride, he made practiced small talk. "I'm new to San Francisco."

"You're here to find gold," she said. It was not a question but a statement. All of them were here to find gold. Riches lay just beneath the surface, just over the next hill, just beyond the draw. "You're here to get rich. Pick up gold nuggets right off the ground. Isn't that so?"

He smiled. She liked the smile. It was open and honest, which was something rather special these days. "In a way, yes," he said. "But not precisely as you describe. I'm a businessman."

"A businessman?"

"I deal in cards."

"You're a gambler!"

"Yes."

Maybelle's laughter was involuntary and bubbled from deep inside. It burst over her in gales. As his handsome face mirrored consternation, her laughter renewed itself, doubling in force. Finally she was compelled to sit down on a stone and recover herself. "A gambler!" she gasped. "You look like—"

"Like a parson," he said mildly. "Or a merchant. A dealer in stoves, perhaps?"

"Yes," she laughed again. It was too much, too, too much. "A dealer in stoves."

"Well, I am a gambler. That is to say, I deal in games of chance. Three-card monte is my game." He bowed. "David Hatfield, ma'am."

Maybelle was exhilarated. "Well, Mr. Hatfield, I'm going to invite you to a party. Just for the hell of it. A party at my place."

"Your place?"

Maybelle reached into her purse and fished out a card. The card read: *The Golden Door, Maybelle Stewart, Prop*. "Tonight, ten o'clock sharp," she said.

"What's the occasion?"

"Why, the gold strike, Mr. Hatfield. There's gold in California, and we're going to celebrate it!"

"And what, may I ask, is the Golden House?"

"It's a whorehouse, Mr. Hatfield. I run the finest whorehouse in San Francisco."

Now it was his turn to laugh.

There were twelve of them working for her now, twelve of the most accomplished prostitutes in San Francisco. Pleasure was her business, and that's what the men of this all-male town paid for. Pleasure, and the company—if only for a few moments—of a woman.

"Let's get those lamps lit up, girls. Give us your bright smiles. That's it. That's the ticket. Tonight, we open the Golden House, the grandest house of entertainment in all of California. We'll make it a night to remember!"

It warmed her to stroll through the parlors. How they had worked to finish these rooms on time! Glowing lamplight bathed the red plush chairs and gleaming woods shipped by schooner around the Horn from the east. Lace curtains adorned the windows. A scent of incense delicately wafted to the nostrils, helping to subdue the cigar smoke. The lamps guttered with fresh whale oil. The cellar was stocked with fine wines and whiskeys. One flight down, the newly refurbished restaurant awaited its first patrons, and a pianist—one could find everything in the gold fields, even a drunken classical pianist—fingered the notes of an etude. Maybelle took it all in with a proprietary eye, picking flaws here, dressing a hostess there, changing a table setting, rearranging a bouquet of fresh wildflowers.

At last the doors opened and the patrons flooded in, men young and old, short and tall, some bearing the pallor of office and bank, others bronzed by the hot sun of the diggings. Men lacking jackets and neckties were turned away, some of them noisily unhappy. For this purpose, she posted burly bouncers at the front door.

The piano struck up its melodies, a soft patina of sound against the backdrop of conversation that Maybelle so dearly loved. The sounds haunted her and took her back to earlier days. Lamps glowed in their glass chimneys, candles guttered on their posts, shadows danced in all the right places. And light, blessed, warm, deceptive light, played on white feminine bosoms, working its own special magic.

"Ah, the changes I've seen in just eight years in this town." She swirled a glass of wine, holding it more than sipping. Her listener was an eager middle-aged man who had more on his mind than talk. No matter. "Sometimes I ask myself, has it really been that long? Eight years ago we came down from those mountains in a few battered wagons drawn by half-starved oxen. We were a handful of settlers and a few whores who'd managed somehow to survive that dreadful trek." As she spoke, deep in nostalgic reverie, several guests drifted to her side with their hostesses. Maybelle was conscious of her listeners and responded to the presence of an audience. A very special audience, she thought; they all understood.

"We left our dead scattered along a thousand miles of trail." It was true, of course. What she neglected to tell them was that when Maybelle Stewart, queen of the whorehouse madams of New Orleans and St. Louis, arrived on that wagon train in this dusty, squalid town of San Francisco, she was pregnant, bearing the daughter of the dead trail boss Van Harrison.

Her heart still ached at times over that man. She woke from troubled dreams in which the tall, lean, sunblasted plainsman held her, soothed her and spoke deeply into her soul: "Easy, Maybelle. Easy, honey. It ain't so bad."

Well, it wasn't so bad.

"It wasn't so bad," she said aloud. "I opened a cafe on the waterfront, and my girls went to work serving food. Hell, this town didn't have enough men to keep one girl busy, much less ten." Laughter rippled through the room. "But I had a hunch, a real strong hunch, that this town, this state, was going to amount to something. And then, up there at Colonel Sutter's place on the American River, damned if they didn't strike it rich!" Applause and cheers filled the parlor. She hoisted her glass. "So let's drink to that, ladies and gentlemen. Here's to striking it rich. Here's to bright yellow gold!"

It was a rousing party. A fine opening, she thought, a good omen for a new business. Some of the customers even brought flowers. As morning light finally sifted over San Francisco, the last reveler made his tipsy way out of the Golden House. The litter in the parlors gave evidence to the merriment of the night, with empty cups and glasses, cigar butts, the stale smell of old smoke and the flowers already starting to droop in their vases.

The girls speculated about Maybelle over morning coffee.

"She's a strange one, that. I never seen an older woman that had so many men agog for her, and she don't tumble for any of 'em. Wish to Gawd I had that fatal charm."

"That's Maybelle for you. She always had 'em lined up, some proper gentlemen, too. I've heard it said that back in St. Louis, senators, congressmen, even governors came calling. And in New Orleans she had a place called the Nocturne that the swells talked about all over the world."

"That might be so, but she's a soft touch if you ask me. Give a loafer the shirt off her back."

"Now, Flo."

"She's got every dime sunk into this place, every dime she owned and could scrape together. And do y'know what she did last fall? She went and grubstaked drunken old Charlie Prime to a gold claim. Give him three, four hundred dollars right out of her pocket, so's he could buy a mule, a blanket, tools and grub."

"Anybody'd be a fool to stake that man. Charlie Prime ain't drawed a sober breath in years."

"Maybelle done it."

"That's Maybelle, all right."

"You can count on it."

"Shhh, girls. Here she comes."

She swept into their presence humming brightly and wear-

ing a yellow gown decorated with small red roses, her favorite
flower. "Ladies," she said, "time to get some shut-eye. Another big night tonight."

They shuffled groggily off to bed.

In the next ten days, the Golden House thrived as no
new business had ever thrived in San Francisco. It was a
reflection of the gold boom itself. From the earliest part
of that summer it was clear to Maybelle that the surge of the
previous summer would be doubled, even tripled during these
spectacular months. Into the Golden House came the daily
news of what was happening. The hills and trails now teemed
with seekers after gold. They came by ship, some around the
storm-tossed Cape Horn, some by steamer and the short land
journey across the Isthmus of Panama. And they came by the
overland trail, braving hunger and thirst, desert and mountain, grizzlies and Indians and outbreaks of cholera. They
were drawn by the spectacular tales of gold strikes on the
Tuolumne River, the Stanislaus, the American, Carson Creek,
Angel Creek. New camps flourished on the sites of dry
washes, rich gullies and bends in a stream. Sullivan's Creek.
Jamestown. Big Bar. Rough and Ready. Hangtown.

"Hangtown? Didn't that used to be called Dry Diggings?
How come they call it Hangtown, Duke?"

"Why, fer the hanging, Miss Maybelle. Hanged three of
'em, they did, two Frenchmen and a Chilean. First these
fellas had tried to rob a Mexican cardplayer. We put together
a jury, found 'em guilty and gave 'em thirty-nine lashes
apiece. Then while they was still laying up in the shack after
the floggings, a fella comes along and says they was the three
that did a robbery and tried to kill a man at the Stanislaus
diggings. We had a jury of nearly two hundred miners fer
that one. Found all three guilty as sin. The miner we'd
picked as judge says, 'What's to be the punishment, then?'
And the crowd hollers, 'Hang 'em!' The crowd was all pretty
well liquored up by now, naturally, so it probably wasn't the
fairest trail ever conducted. Still and all, crime's crime. They
gave them fellas thirty minutes to pray to their Maker, shoved
them onto a wagon, set the ropes from a tree limb, bound
their arms and lashed the horses. They went kicking into
eternity."

"Did any of them speak in his own defense?"

The miner named Duke stroked his grizzled jaw and squinted

into a whiskey glass. "Miss Maybelle, I can't rightly say that they did. Couldn't none of 'em speak a word of English."

If the Golden House was Maybelle's ticket to fortune, Vanessa was her reason for living. The child was turning nine now, a joy and a beauty. Her mind was quick, her manner saucy and spoiled. "Maybelle," friends chided, "you're too indulgent with that child." Maybelle knew, sensed that Vanessa needed a firmer hand. But she had come unexpectedly, a gift late in life; and she was Van Harrison's child. And so Maybelle indulged Vanessa, dressed her in little girl frocks, fixed her pretty red curls, and saw that she had a nanny in attendance.

Maybelle often thought of Brack, the son whom she had never fully understood. He had always seemed so cold and distant. And this was strange, for Brack's father Maurice, the dapper Frenchman who had been murdered in New Orleans, had been a kindly man, a lover of fine music and fine wines. It was Maurice who had given Maybelle her appreciation of life's more elegant pleasures. How odd, she thought, that Brack would turn out as he did. Oh, she had cause to be proud of him, right enough. When they'd left St. Louis, Maybelle and her girls in the wagon train heading west, she placed Brack with Senator Thomas Hart Benton's friends. And they had seen to his enrollment at Harvard College in the east. From the few letters she received, one from Senator Benton, another from the Harvard dean, two from Brack himself, he had performed handsomely at Harvard, graduating summa cum laude. The boy had a shrewd mind for finance, it was said. There was talk of finding him a position with a New York banking firm.

"Mother, do my hair." Vanessa spoke abruptly, handing her the brush. The child was so willful, as Brack was willful. But there was a softness in Vanessa's nature, too, a loving that sometimes expressed itself with small arms flung about Maybelle's neck and a cry, "Oh, Mummy, Mummy, hold me tight. Never let me go!" Maybelle brushed the flowing red hair of her daughter and wondered what would it have been like to have lived a normal life.

Because of her own dislike of all things Stewart—a dreadful hangover from those awful scenes with her father, the dictatorial Isaiah, so many years ago—Maybelle had deliberately infected Brack against his own kin. At times, she wished that she could be a Catholic and go to confession, to sit in the darkness of the confessional booth and whisper to a stranger, "Father, I have sinned. I have poisoned the mind of my son while he was growing up, against the Stewarts and their kind. I did it deliberately and with malice, Father, because I had been so often hurt and rejected at home, because they said I was bad. Am I bad, Father? Am I beyond redemption?"

"Ouch! Mother, you're brushing too hard," Vanessa scolded her. "You're hurting Vanessa!"

Maybelle swept the child into her arms and hugged her passionately, hugged her with an inexplicable ache in her heart, hugged her and wished that she would never have to let her go. "Oh, Vanessa, I love you. I love you, I love you, I love you!"

Three weeks later, the Golden House burned to the ground.

It began in the evening at a livery stable half a block away. A random spark from a blacksmith's forge landed on a pile of dry wood shavings. The shavings burst into bright flame. Before anyone noticed, the fire had spread up the tinder-dry walls of the stable. By the time the blacksmith himself ran to ring the firebell, the walls and roof of the stable were engulfed and flames billowed on a stiff breeze to neighboring wooden structures. Fire was the nemesis of the town. Fires occurred so frequently that senses were keyed to the whiff of smoke and the lick of flame. For Maybelle, the smoke was enough. She dashed through the Golden House shouting, "Fire! Fire! Get out, ladies and gentlemen! Everybody out!" They stumbled from bedrooms and parlors, in various stages of undress, clutching blankets. There were patrons who had only enough time to grab their boots and a few who jumped from windows stark naked.

Outside, a drunken crowd gathered to watch the spectacle. The outpouring of people from the Golden House was a source of great sport and raucous laughter. Maybelle shouted for a bucket brigade. "Help us, you damn fools!" But there were not enough buckets, the heat drove them quickly back, and none of the bystanders responded to her pleas.

"Let 'er burn!" shouted a drunken miner. He tipped a half-empty bottle and drained it in a few gulps. "Let the whole goddamn town burn! Ain't nothin' but a hellhole anyhow."

Maybelle stared at the drunken man and then at the flames licking the walls of the Golden House. One of her girls, Linda Sue, patted her consolingly on the arm. Maybelle shrugged. "We couldn't have saved it anyway." During the next three hours, eighteen buildings, shacks and tent dwellings were reduced to ashes.

As morning light sifted over the hills and fog rolled in off the bay, she picked disconsolately through the debris. The prostitutes gathered in a miserable clutch, watching in disbelief. Someone sobbed.

"What'll we do now, Maybelle?"

She sighed, kicking over the fire-blackened remains of an iron bedpost. "Damned if I know, girls. I'll just have to see if I've got any friends left." Later in the day, it became obvious that moneylenders—like the bystanders the night before—were not eager to help. Too much had been lost, too fast. Besides, respectable money did not rush to invest in a whorehouse. Maybelle already had sold off a number of real estate parcels to finance the venture; the only piece of ground still in her possession was the one on which the Golden House had stood. A banker offered to buy, but at half the going price of neighbors on either side. Maybelle was incensed. "That's ridiculous, George, and you know it." The banker replied with an oily smile. Finally, she accepted the price.

That was the week that Charlie Prime came back. The old miner rode in on a spavined mule, more bones than flesh, and found the tent in which Maybelle and several of her prostitutes had taken refuge. He croaked her name and slid off the back of the mule into the dust. Charlie Prime was a sweat-stained apparition, his clothes in tatters, gray whiskers covering his face. He stank of dysentery.

"Oh, Jesus Christ, not him!" Linda Sue wrinkled her nose in disgust. "Nothing turns up like a bad penny."

Maybelle rushed from the tent. "Help him," she said. "Get some water. He needs water."

"It ain't water he needs, it's whiskey."

Maybelle knelt at Charlie's side. Someone brought water and a cloth and she bathed the grizzled face. He watched her with sunken, rheumy eyes.

"I thought I wouldn't make it, partner," he said.

"Of course you'll make it, Charlie. A tough old bird like you will always make it." She forced a sip of water between his lips. The mouth of the miner was dry and stank of rotting teeth. "All you need's a little cleaning up, and you'll be fit as a fiddle."

"Not this time, Maybelle. I ain't gonna make it this time, and that's for sure. I just had to get back here, though, to tell you what I got."

"That can wait." Maybelle ordered three of the women to help her carry Charlie into the tent. Muttered objections stilled as her anger flashed. They dragged him inside and flopped him across a cot. "All right," Maybelle said. "Let's get some soup into him. You there, Barbara. Stoke up that fire outside and warm some soup."

And so Charlie Prime was fed. Then they cleaned him, cutting off the soiled, rotting clothing and bathing the ravaged body from a tub. Finally Maybelle rummaged in her one remaining suitcase, found a bottle of liquor and gave him a drink. As he took a swig, gratitude spread over his face. "You're a fine woman, Maybelle, and that's a fact. By God, you're an angel."

"Hush, Charlie. Get some rest."

He shook his head. "No time. No time to rest now. Listen to me; I've got to tell you something." His hand clutched at her sleeve and drew her down. His eyes flicked suspiciously toward the three other women within earshot. "Tell 'em to step outside. I got something private to say."

"Charlie, it's no—"

"Tell 'em to step outside."

Maybelle nodded to the women, who sullenly complied. When they were gone, Charlie Prime gave a soft, dry chuckle. His voice had dropped to a croaking whisper and there was a rattle in his throat. His breath smashed at her in waves of putrefaction. "Maybelle, I..." He coughed lightly. A line of reddish spittle drooled from his mouth into the whiskers. "I...I struck it rich."

Maybelle nodded. How many of them were like this? They suffered unbelievably in those hills in quest of a dream. They toiled and starved and lost their minds, each thinking he was within reach of the precious metal, the spellbinding yellow gold that would end forever the drudgery and somehow, by an alchemy of the mind and spirit, make life worth living. She had seen them come and go, addled by gold fever, ravaged by disease, babbling mindlessly about the great strike. Gold.

"You get some sleep," she said.

"No. Listen. I'm serious. I mean it. A strike. I ain't whispered to a soul, not a soul. I buried my stash up there rather than to risk bringin' it out. They think it's a tailed-out claim, not worth fooling with. If anybody passed by, I said as much. But, listen, it ain't a tailed-out claim. It's pure gold, gold by the handfuls, gold imbedded in the rock on dry diggings..."

Painfully, persistently, he talked. He had gotten the word the previous year from a Yuma Indian. The Indian laughed bitterly, hating the whites. He trusted Charlie Prime, as all of the tribe did, regarding the old drifter almost as one of his own. What greedy fools the whites were, swarming like locusts in these treacherous hills after yellow gold. And what a huge joke that a wondrous strike lay so close to the surface, for in Indian legend it was said that the vein of the mother lode itself surfaced here on this spot, in a dry gully above the Tuolumne River.

"I've got the proof. I brought it with me, Miss Maybelle. You'll find it in the saddlebag strapped to that mule of mine. Listen, it's yours. I never forgot how you treated me. When I needed a grubstake, nobody else paid me any mind. They told me to get away. 'Get away, Charlie Prime. You draw flies.' But you didn't do that. You fed me in your cafe, remember? You brought me a drink of whiskey and gave me four hundred dollars. Well, I told you then that we was partners. I wrote it up, all neat and proper, didn't I? Neat and proper. Yes, indeed." The voice paused. The old man seemed to be strengthening. The rheumy eyes cleared and his face lifted. He had been speaking in a rush, however, as if to get it all said, as if time were running out. When she started to speak, he placed a finger to his lips. "I ain't got nobody, Maybelle. Not a soul to mourn my passing. So it's all yours, partner. The whole damned mine is yours, and everything I took from it. You'll find it... find it..." He coughed again. He raised one hand, pointing a finger frantically at his breast pocket. "You'll... find.... it..."

The words stopped. The eyes glazed. The face froze. The breath ceased.

Charlie Prime was dead.

From the breast pocket she drew out a rumpled map marking a gold claim on the Tuolumne River. An infinite weariness came over her. It was not fair. A man should have a better life than that, and die in better circumstances. And for what purpose had he died? To pursue a fool's dream, to draw a ridiculous map in pencil that one could barely read, and to carry to the end a delusion of gold. She wadded up the paper and stuck it into her apron pocket. Slowly she rose from beside the cot and walked out into the waning afternoon. Sunlight streamed over the bay, laying a carpet of diamonds along its sweep. Sea birds wheeled and quarreled. The sky was a fine milky blue, in contrast to the tedium of the town with its shacks and tents and outdoor cookstoves, its trundling wagons and horse dung fouling the dirt streets. Perhaps she was suffering from delusions, too. Her delusion was that there was more to San Francisco than met the eye, that this was the city of promise for Maybelle Stewart. She believed that San Francisco was more than what some called it, a cesspool of thieves and murderers and drunks. San Francisco had to be more than that. And California itself now battled for statehood and soon would join the rest of the nation; of this she was convinced.

Maybelle sat down on a stump, and her mind turned to thoughts of Vanessa. The child was being kept by Mrs. Miller, whose house she could see at the foot of Telegraph Hill. Soon she would walk over there and see Vanessa, and do her hair.

"What d'you want me to do with this mule, Maybelle?" It was Crystal Lee speaking. She was the eldest of the prostitutes, an angular woman of thirty who had been one of the survivors of the wagon train years before. "He's on his last legs, looks like. I never seen a more woebegone critter in my life, except maybe his master."

"Take him over to the stable, Crystal. Tell Roy to feed him and rub him down. I'll settle up later."

"Might as well throw this away, then," Crystal removed a sweatstained saddlebag from the swayed back of the mule. The ancient leather was dried out and partially rotted; from a distance it had no shape at all. "Old Charlie ain't going to need it no more."

"No," Maybelle sighed, "Charlie won't be needing it."

Crystal Lee tossed the saddlebag so that it landed at Maybelle's feet. Without really knowing why, Maybelle tugged at the rusted buckle. The strap broke and the saddlebag fell open.

Two nuggets spilled out into the dust. Maybelle snatched them up and looked closely. They were heavy. They were gold. And—she caught her breath—each nugget was as big as her thumb!

"Crystal! Hurry up with that mule. Then I want you to

round up the older girls, right away. Tell them to come as quick as they can. I want Ruby and Pearl, Mary Beth, Linda Sue, Penelope and Sissy. Find every one, even if you've got to flush 'em out of somebody's bed. We've got work to do!"

"Yes, ma'am. But what on earth for?"

Maybelle smiled. "First, we're going to give our partner Charlie Prime a Christian burial. And then we're going into the hills and dig for gold!"

A drier, more inhospitable chunk of real estate she had never seen. Charlie Prime's dig was a large shelf gouged from the side of a thicketed hill one hundred yards above the river. Here, in some ancient times, another stream had meandered down from the heights in wet weather, creating a dry wash of granite boulders and slabs; the whole area was overlain with stones ranging from the size of fists to the size of pumpkins. Even walking on this moonscape was perilous, much less mining it. The only evidence that Charlie Prime had ever been there was a few rotting timbers for a lean-to and some meager excavations at the base of the hill.

Word of the coming of the women to mine a claim spread like brushfire through the rugged hills, so that by the time Maybelle led her seven girls up the last five miles of river valley they were followed by a whistling, catcalling mob of miners. "Hey, where ya going, honey?"

"Lost yer way, little girls?"

"You can come to my digs anytime. I got the tools. Haw, haw, haw."

"I like a redhead, no matter what color it is."

Prodding three pack mules laden with supplies, Maybelle came at last to the shelf, rechecked her map, peered up that forbidding slope and announced, "That's it." Some of the men offered to whip the balky animals up the slope but Maybelle firmly declined and the women did this chore themselves. A crowd started to follow them up. Maybelle unslung a Sharps rifle from her pack and loudly instructed her group, "See that your pistols are loaded." The onlookers backed down and joined the swelling mob that had settled along the riverbank. The women unpacked tools, equipment, and food, set up a single large tent and spelled each other at guard duty. It was clearly an impasse and the sport began to wane. By the third morning most of the men had cleared out except for a few

drunken diehards squatting along the river in the heat and
the flies. By the fourth day they, too, were gone. Maybelle
descended to make a circuit of the area and surrounding
thickets. Then she climbed the slope again.

"All right, ladies. To work!"

They began with a meticulous, stone-by-stone search of the
claim. If Charlie Prime's find had been so rich, Maybelle
reasoned, then surely he had stashed gold somewhere. But
after inspecting every foot of the site, except for a foul hole
which Charlie had used for a latrine, they found no evidence
of a hiding place. Maybelle ordered the latrine filled with
dirt. The old miner had toiled, however; this was obvious
from the sheer amount of rock and dirt that had been moved.
Much of the hard work was concentrated around the base of
the hill, where the shelf joined the downward slope. It was
here that Maybelle decided they would begin their efforts.

One had to adjust work to the climate in these hills.
They were in the hottest part of late summer now and the
sun rose over the rim of the Sierras like the great orange
mouth of a celestial furnace, blasting them mercilessly at
midday. The only tolerable coolness came in the mornings and
the late afternoons. Even then, flies and bees and assorted
pests assailed them. Their rugged male clothing—Maybelle
had insisted that her diggers wear trousers, high-topped
boots, long-sleeved shirts and hats with wide brims—soon
were malodorous from constant saturation with sweat.

From the first day, the toil was accompanied by groans
and lamentations. It was brutal work: Three women dislodged
stones, dug up the hard-baked soil and shoveled it into
buckets; three others carried the buckets down the slope to
the water's edge and dumped them into a wooden and metal
rocker; and two women constantly worked the rocker device
as the water flowed through, searching the soil residue for
glints of flaked gold on the riffle bars at the bottom of the
sluice. At evening of the first day, Maybelle's bones and
muscles hurt in ways that she never knew possible. Her
hands, though gloved all day, were blistered and bleeding.
Her feet in the heavy work boots were each a solid ache. The
others shared the miseries, usually with loud vocal protest.

"Maybelle, my back. I think my back's broken. And this
arm, I can't move it. I absolutely hurt all over, and I don't
know where I hurt worse." This was Sissy, a pretty blonde
with a little-girl voice who was always a favorite among the

men. "And just look at my nails! Maybelle, they're . . . they're ghastly!"

"Jesus," groaned Ruby. She was a strapping brunette with an hourglass figure even in her miner's clothes. "I'm going to lie down here and die."

Maybelle listened gravely. "You'll get used to it, girls. I want to remind you that today this whole crowd put in two hours of labor. Two hours! I think we moved about six bushels of dirt for a few paltry flakes of gold that you could put under your thumbnail. A real miner has got to move more dirt than that to make wages. Three men should work eighty to a hundred pails of it in a day, from diggings to wash. And the most they might make is five dollars to fifteen dollars a man."

"How do we know we'll find anything at all?"

"We don't."

"That Charlie Prime, damned old coot, gave you a line of goods, Maybelle. This is the silliest caper I've ever been on, and I've been on a few."

"Maybe. Maybe not. You can leave anytime you like. Nobody's holding you here, Ruby."

Ruby pondered, staring into the flickering fire. Somewhere a coyote howled. Night creatures stirred in the thickets. Up from the river came the sound of chuckling water. Somebody slapped at a mosquito and cursed. Ruby shrugged, grimaced from a shoulder ache and offered a conciliatory smile. "Oh, hell, I'll stick. I don't know no better anyhow. Nobody ever said we was smart. If we was smart, we wouldn't be whores."

"With any kind of luck maybe you can retire."

Someone snickered. "Ruby won't want to retire."

Laughter rippled around the campfire. It was an intimate, musical sound. Never before has there been the laughter of women in this ungodly place, Maybelle thought. At last they spread their blankets for sleep, each knowing she would take a turn on guard duty with the rifle before morning. As the fire died, Maybelle lay staring up at a canopy of stars blazing across the heavens. Old Charlie, she realized, might have been a muttering lunatic after all, but even if that were so, somehow this was worth it.

After that, the days passed in unrelieved toil. Picks and shovels tore at the stony earth. Down the hill and up the hill went the bucket bearers. There was a constant sound of gravel washing in the rocker. They found gold, sure enough, but only in miniscule quantities, in flakes and dust. Occasion-

ally a few male miners passed by, heading for diggings upstream or simply drawn by curiosity from all the talk that
went on in the roaring camps. The Sharps rifle quickly
discouraged them.

Maybelle and Sissy made a trip for supplies to the nearest
camp, Dutch Bar, nearly five miles away. They bought pick-
led pork, coffee, potatoes, dried beans, hardtack, and flapjack
flour, all at outrageous prices. In a hot, flyblown tent, the
shrewd storekeeper sold cheese and raisins at a dollar and
fifty cents a pound, payable in currency or gold dust, and
dried apples for a dollar. Miners rented a broad axe or a
crosscut saw for two dollars a day. There were six hundred
diggers in the region of Dutch Bar, he told the women.
"They're taking out fifty dollars' worth of gold apiece per day."
The gambling tent did a brisk business as bored miners found
their way to the tables at nightfall for monte and draw poker.
The talk, incessantly, was of gold. "Big strike on the Sonora, I
hear tell. They're taking pound dirt. But it's too late now.
There's three thousand miners camped along the gulch."

Maybelle and Sissy were a sensation at Dutch Bar. Men
flocked around them and followed wherever they went.
Surprisingly, the reaction was respectful, the manners subdued. One grizzled miner, swigging at a whiskey bottle,
drawled, "Law, I ain't seen a woman in so long! You're angels
from heaven, Missies, and that's the truth." Among these
men, Maybelle saw many signs of illness. Dysentery was a
scourge of the mining camps, and left its weakened sufferers
sprawling in tents or under brushy lean-tos. There was a
heavy odor of human refuse from untended waste pits.

Again, their return downstream was followed by its male
entourage; again, a few lingered for a day or two, hoping—to
no avail—to be favored with the company of a woman. By
now, the girls themselves were restless and felt the need for
entertainment. There were noisy complaints. Maybelle held
firm. "I've got one rule that you all understood from the
beginning. No men. Bring men into this camp and you're
asking for trouble. If you want a man, then you're no longer
in the dig. Is that understood?" Grudgingly, they complied.

The toil resumed. Blisters broke and bled, broke and bled
again, and finally turned to calluses. Muscles hardened and
no longer ached. Shoe leather began to wear out, buttons
came off and sunbleached clothing began to fray. Only occasionally did the hard earth give up a tiny store of what they

sought; but invariably, a slightly more generous find in the rocker box—flakes of placer gold, borne from some point farther up the ancient dry gulch—was a cause of excitement. But the yield tailed out, always, and spirits sank.

Finally, the quarrels began. At first, it was a flash of tempers between Ruby and Sissy over a coffee cup. Then Mary Beth and Pearl started throwing clods at each other in an argument over whose turn it was to carry the pails. The heat, the labor, the sweat, the mosquitoes and snakes and flies assailed them day after day. In five weeks of hard labor, they had worked in pockets across the entire shelf without success. Charlie Prime's gold, if there was any, eluded and mocked them. Maybelle even began to wonder if the fine nuggets tumbling out of his saddlebag had been a trick of her own imagination.

"There's no telling where that old fart picked 'em up," Ruby grumbled. "Probably stole 'em off a drunk."

And then the rains began.

It was too much. For days the cloud masses had built over the foothills only to dissipate by evening. The clouds were tantalizing at first, a welcome relief from the broiling heat. And then one day they broke at last. As the first shower pelted down, the women threw aside their picks and shovels and turned their faces gratefully to the sky, mouths open. The shower passed. A drizzle set in. It drizzled all that day and all night, and the next day and the next night. And when the drizzle stopped, there was only scattered sunlight and not enough to dry them out. The clothing was wet and stinking, the tent soaked, the bedding soggy and cold.

Mary Beth was the first to get sick. She developed a fever and runny nose and diarrhea. One morning she could not get up. She lay in her damp blankets for days in misery. And then Pearl became ill, and Ruby. The others could not work in the rains, for from the first shower the slope down to the river had turned to mud. By now the entire camp was mud and loose rock. And when Mary Beth's condition did not improve, Maybelle had to admit to herself that they had reached the limit.

"I'm sorry, girls," she told them that evening as the rain drummed down on the tent. "I'm sorry I brought you out here on this fool's errand. You've all worked like hell with little to show for it. We should have stayed in San Francisco."

"What kind of wages have we taken?" someone asked.

Maybelle drew out the pouch containing their small hoard of gold dust. "It figures out to about two dollars a day."

"Two dollars a day."

No one spoke after that.

The rain stopped just before daybreak. For the first time in a week the sun came up clear and fine over the Sierras. Birds flashed in the trees and the wet land was clean and fresh. With lifting spirits, Maybelle and her group made ready to break camp. Pearl, Linda Sue and Ruby had decided to go into the mining camps where there was ready money to be made. Sissy, Mary Beth, Penelope and Crystal said they would accompany Maybelle back to San Francisco.

As they prepared to take down the tent, Sissy came to Maybelle with a puzzled look on her face. The little blonde was bronzed by the sun; her nails were cracked and short, her hands toughened. "There's something funny happening to the ground back there," Sissy said. "Come and take a look."

They went to Charlie Prime's old latrine. The evil-smelling hole had been filled with dirt since their first day of making the campsite tolerable. Maybelle had forgotten it was even there. But now the hole was back, enlarged to the size of a small crater. Rainwater had soaked the dirt fill and washed it down into an opening which led to an underground outlet. The stench also was gone.

"Somebody could break a leg, stumbling into that thing," Maybelle grumbled.

"Look down inside."

"I don't want to look down inside. Phew!"

"Go on, Maybelle. Take a look."

Maybelle looked. A rotting square of board jutted at an angle in the hole, a false bottom that was dislodged. Her senses quickened. "That shrewd old bastard." The loose board had covered a small chamber, now partially filled with loose stones. Wedged into the stones was what appeared to be the top of a large leather sack.

"What is it, Maybelle?"

"I don't know. I don't even dare to think. But we'll find out. Give me your hand."

Grasping Sissy's hand for support, Maybelle straddled the muddy opening and worked her way down. Bending and reaching, she grasped the top of the sack and pulled. The sack was wet and surprisingly heavy. It slipped from her

grasp. She worked it free of the stones. By now, Ruby and
Pearl had joined them. They managed to bring up the sack,
dripping muck. Maybelle came out of the hole breathing
hard. The others stepped back. Maybelle drew her sheath
knife and sliced open the neck of the sack.

"Jesus . . ."

A sunbeam stabbed down. The gold flashed and gleamed.
The sack was filled with it—nuggets, stones and chips. Some
pieces were half the size of a man's fist. Where the sack had
been lodged there now yawned a hole big enough for a miner
to wriggle into; a hole partially covered with planking and
rude timbers, with a channel leading off into the hill itself.
Even from above, Maybelle could see that part of the channel
wall was solid rock, cut through by the implements of man.
In spots, the rock bore a fine yellow glitter.

She sat down heavily in the dirt beside Charlie Prime's
gold mine and burst into tears.

"We're rich, girls, We're rich! Goddamnit, we're rich!"

Captain Francis Drake Stewart did not like the look of the
weather. Pensively he stalked the afterdeck of the clipper
ship *Typhoon*, frowning at the sky to the south. Dark cloud
masses piled there, blotting out the sun. Already the day had
turned a slate gray and a stiffening wind brought rising seas
and flying scud. The restless Atlantic was gathering its power
in worsening swells capped with gray froth. He fastened his
greatcoat more closely against the chill.

"Mr. Cochrane, see to the fore-topgallant. We've got a blow
ahead, I fear."

"She's fixed, sir. The rent's been sewn. We did the work on
the yards."

Damn, he should have noticed. Of course, the repair had
been made. He had become too preoccupied of late. Cochrane
did not seem to notice, but that was the man's way. The burly
mate stood at his elbow awaiting command, the big face
bronzed and honest. They had sailed together long and far,
from China to the Arctic seas, to Europe and around the
Horn. They communicated as if by instinct. Drake remembered
the early days, when Cochrane was surly and resented taking
commands from a black skipper. But that had been washed
clean, washed away under the pressures and crises of the
open sea, washed away in storm and wind, and on those wild

races to San Francisco which set new speed records for the
Typhoon. Now the two men, captain and mate, seemed often
to think as one.

He shook his head. Enough reflection. They were two days
out of Rio, beating down that rugged coast with the pretty
harbor of Santa Catarina beckoning. In the shelter of Santa
Catarina's crescent bowl and surrounding hills, *Typhoon* could
ride out a blow in peace and safety, taking on more supplies
of wild fruit and berries to relieve the tedium of shipboard
diet. But already they'd spent three days in Rio, with its
lovely beat and fiery grog and hot Indian women, and time
was passing them by. At this rate they would surely not make
California in the promised ninety days, if they made it at all.
Cochrane was eyeing him expectantly. Drake put him off a
moment more. "All cargo stowed and secure?"

"Aye, captain. Stowed and secure."

"And"—the handsome face of Francis Drake mirrored a
flicker of distaste—"the passengers?"

"Stowed and secure, sir." Cochrane indulged himself a
fleeting smile. "Including the lady."

"Very well, then. We'll make straight for the Horn."

Cochrane's head bobbed approvingly. "The Horn it is,
sir."

For the first time, the *Typhoon* carried passengers at sea. It
was almost too much, for the clipper ship was built for speed
and cargo, not passengers. She was a knife-blade of a hull
rushing beneath a cloud of sail. Crews hated the clippers, for
they were wet and miserable belowdecks and always demanding that men swarm aloft in the foulest blows. "Stinking blood
boats," grumbled old salts. But to the mind of Francis Drake,
the *Typhoon* was something more, a living thing of breathtaking beauty that stirred a passion in him the likes of which no
woman had ever stirred. In every port of the world the
crowds invariably flocked to stand and stare at the majesty of
this ship. In a score of languages, he knew, they jabbered
about *Typhoon*'s mulatto skipper, the "nigger of the clippers,"
a driven man.

Well, his father had made it possible. Searching the restless gray horizon with a spyglass, Drake's mind returned
again to the memory of Ward Stewart. He shut his eyes
tightly, opened them again. He needed to forget. Captain
Stewart had made his own life and taken it in his own way, at
his own time, with a pistol at the temple. So be it. Age and

infirmity had stripped him of pride and prison taken away his last dignity, so why not the bullet in the brain?

"Captain, will the weather turn foul?"

The voice was languid and warm. He turned quickly from the rail. She mounted the afterdeck followed by the fat black slave woman who was her maid. Francis Drake felt keenly the pale blue eyes searching him from an oval face framed in shining black hair. She wore a long blue cloak with a fur-trimmed hood, thrown back; her hair blew in the wind. She stood by the railing, as if to take her bearings.

"We're in for a blow, but nothing too violent, ma'am."

"You're not stopping at Santa Catarina?"

"No. We're losing time."

The perfectly formed eyebrows arched, questioning but amused. "Time, captain? Are we in that much of a hurry?"

"Time is money, ma'am. It's what gives the clipper its edge. We don't just sail around the Horn, we race her. Ninety days out of Boston, maybe less. Compared to six months on the usual scow. But then, you know that already. That's why you booked passage."

Her full lips pursed. "True."

He was uncomfortable with the woman on deck, and wondered why. Not many women made Francis Drake uncomfortable. The fact that she had invaded his most intimate world, the *Typhoon* itself, certainly had something to do with it. But there was more. She was Elizabeth Chares, the wildly beautiful daughter of Mason Chares from Charleston, and that also had something to do with it. Chares had made his fortune in cotton and slaves. Her pale blue eyes seemed to look at a man with a mixed expression of excitement and amused speculation, as if he were a potential piece of property. Oh, well. She was but one of five passengers, for which he had been paid two thousand dollars a head. And the voyage would not last forever.

"Everybody," he said, "wants to go to California. Damned if I know why."

"It's for the adventure, Captain." Smiling again, tossing her hair, she walked across the afterdeck and stood beside him, her sleeve just brushing his arm. "It's the most exciting thing that has ever happened. Imagine, Captain. Gold." She spoke with a sultry Southern accent, and he wondered fleetingly if perhaps a drop of black blood ran in her veins. Only a drop. He chuckled.

"Do you find that amusing, Captain? The hunger for gold?"

"Um. Well, I suppose so. But most of these people rushing to California ain't going to find it, Miss Chares. Most of them are going to go out there, become sick, disillusioned and broke and come back with nothing to show for it—if they come back at all. Oh, sure, there's gold to be taken. There was a vessel, the Lexington, back in the harbor at Rio. She was loaded with three hundred thousand dollars in gold taken from the placer mines in the Sierra Nevada mountains. Occasionally you hear of a rich strike, worth thirty thousand dollars or fifty thousand dollars, even more. But these are exceptions, and often gross exaggerations. They're fed by the press to the suckers back east. Do y'know why? To generate people, Miss Chares. People mean money. If anybody stands to strike it rich, it's the merchants, the land speculators, even sea captains like me."

He was tempted to go into detail. The stakes were high for this voyage. It would recoup his finances nicely. The Typhoon carried far more profitable cargo than five passengers. Packed into the holds was eighty-five thousand dollars' worth of goods, from nails and flour to parts for steam engines. To acquire it all, he had spent every dime he could beg or borrow. But in California, a bottle of liquor sold for forty dollars and a pack of playing cards for five. The Typhoon's cargo would net him two hundred and seventy-five thousand dollars. But why bore the lady with such details?

Francis Drake offered a wry grin. "Gold strike, Miss Chares? The gold strike is a myth."

She pouted. "I say it doesn't matter. Fact or fancy, what's the difference? The point is, it's exciting and it's fun." She turned and looked him full in the face. The blue eyes glowed. "Don't you like to have fun, Captain?"

There it was again, bold and nakedly open and unmistakable. Drake's stomach tightened and he felt a sudden weakness in his loins. Quickly he looked to the horizon to bring his thoughts in order. Behind Elizabeth Chares, the black maid glared at him with eyes full of menace. Old gal, he thought, you ain't going to protect the virtue of this mistress.

"Miss Chares, do you know how big this gold rush is getting to be? Do you have any idea? There's people by the tens of thousands going west by the wagon trains, at the speed of a walking mule or oxen. This is March. In another two months, those wagons will be a line running from St.

Joseph, Missouri, clear to Sacramento. And there'll be a dead body for every mile of the way. There's nearly fifty thousand more going by way of the Isthmus of Panama; and a lot of those folks will come down with malaria or cholera in the jungle and never see California."

"That's very true, Captain Stewart." Elizabeth Chares took on a new tone, at once intense and invigorated. "But think of it! All those people are leaving behind the drabness, the routine of their lives and striking out on new adventure. They're not accustomed to travel as you are. Most of them, after all, are shopkeepers, small merchants, businessmen. Why even my father..." she hesitated and bit at her lower lip.

"Yes?"

"I was going to say that even my father spoke of what a lark it would be to pick up, leave behind the cares of business and politics and go to California."

"Just why are you going to California, Miss Chares? There's only a handful of women in the whole town of San Francisco. In the entire state, there's probably twenty men for every woman. It's a hard place for a woman, California."

She laughed. "Captain, I'm going to California simply to get a little different slant on life than one gets in Charleston society. I'm going because I want to, and because it's there. And I honestly can't think of better reasons than that, can you?"

He smiled. Now it was his turn to look her fully in the eyes. The eyes had a glint of defiance that he found fascinating. And the blue, he noticed for the first time, was flecked with green. "No," he said. "I can't think of any better reasons than that." The eyes widened, locked into his, and suddenly softened. The face was very near, intensely feminine. Her glance faltered and fell away. It was as if, for a fleeting instant, proud Elizabeth Chares had felt herself in some strange new depth.

"I must go to my cabin now," she whispered.

He watched her move away, trailed by the broad black presence of the slave woman.

Francis Drake Stewart felt a powerful hunger.

Elizabeth Chares did not emerge again from her cabin for three days. They were arduous days for *Typhoon* and her crew, as the storm rose to gale force out of the southern Atlantic, threatening to drive them into the rocky shore of

Argentina itself. In making his eastward tack to clear the
headlands, Drake had not reckoned on this heavy a blow. And
so his seamen toiled endlessly in the yards, reefing, clewing,
bending, and hauling, as the clipper and her captain took
advantage of every shift in wind.

"Loose your fore-topsails, Mr. Cochrane!"

"Fore-topsails loosing, sir. Loose fore-topsails! Lively now,
lads."

"We'll bring her about now. Make our dash to the Horn.
Steady as she goes!"

"Steady as she goes, sir!"

The sea came in massive, rolling combers, each more
mountainous than before. On such a devil's tide, *Typhoon*
labored in deep troughs and rose to giddying heights, like a
leaf on a maelstrom. Seas raged and crashed, and the wind
ripped out of the southwest to slash their faces with flying
sleet and freezing spray. Belowdecks, all was chaos and
misery, cold food and cold, sodden bodies. The three male
passengers—a Boston banker, a French aristocrat and a shipping magnate from Philadelphia—rolled helplessly in their
bunks, engulfed in waves of seasickness.

"Reef topgallants! Stand to the main brace! All hands aloft!"

"We're under too much sail, sir. I fear she'll broach!"

Francis Drake felt the deck under his feet, felt each slide
and twist of *Typhoon*, knew the state of her from each
shudder and groan of timber. It was as sensitive a communication between ship and master as could be had between
living things. Even Cochrane was not lord and master. The
mate's warning sifted through his mind and for the moment
was ignored.

"Steady as she goes, Mr. Cochrane!"

"Steady as she goes, Captain."

And at last they came through and emerged into the calm
Pacific. Francis Drake ordered a general cleaning and sprucing
up of the *Typhoon*. Oil lamps were lit again and from the
galley there came the odors of cooking. A school of whales
emerged off the port bow and escorted the ship for an entire
day, blowing and rolling. The sun at last rose in peaceful
splendor, drying sails and clothing and lifting spirits. Sea
birds frolicked in the morning light, and Francis Drake felt at
peace with himself.

"Good morning, Captain." She was pale and her face
seemed thinner. She wore a coat of powder blue and carried a

fur muff. The slave woman was not with her this time. "It is a lovely morning indeed."

"Yes, ma'am. The worst of it is behind us. It should be clear sailing from now on." He smiled, warmed by her presence. Sunlight played upon the raven hair, accentuating the softness of her face. He had never seen anything so beautiful. "I hope you didn't suffer unduly from the storm, but that's Cape Horn. Now you're a veteran."

Elizabeth Chares leaned her elbows on the mahogany railing beside him, her shoulder brushing his. "Suffer, Captain? I've never been more miserable in my life. I think I would have jumped overboard and ended it all, if I could have gotten out of my bunk. I'm just glad it's over, that's all." The blue eyes found his. "I understand that you never left the deck the whole time."

"The captain is always on deck in a storm. Sometimes you have to lash yourself into a deck chair, so as not to be swept overboard. This blow wasn't that bad."

"I see." She looked out across the sparkling water. Sunlight gave it the sheen of diamonds on blue velvet. Francis Drake relished being able to share it with her. Then he realized that her manner toward him had undergone a marked change. Gone was the flirty, supercilious mood of before. Careful, he thought. "How long have you been at sea, Captain?" she asked.

"All my life. I've never known anything else. I was aboard one of my grandfather's fishing boats before I was twelve. He was a Cape Cod man."

"He owned fishing boats?"

"Yes. Several of them." Francis Drake chuckled. "I know what you're thinking. You're thinking that a black man is unlikely to be owning boats, and that's true. My grandfather was a white man. My father, Captain Ward Stewart, was his son. Ward Stewart was commander of a fighting frigate in the War of 1812, and later a *Black Ball* packet, running passengers and mail to England."

She stood silently, listening. Instinct told him that her interest was genuine. And so he found himself talking, as he had rarely talked to anyone before. He talked of his father, Ward Stewart, who killed a man in Boston over a woman and fled to the West Indies. He told her of how Ward had become captain of an African slave ship, hauling cargos of misery across the Atlantic to the Caribbean.

"I was born in Jamaica. My mother arrived in one of my father's slave ships. He left her well cared for, and took me to Cape Cod. My grandfather was dead by then, but his employees kept the fleet going. Father instructed them to prepare me for the sea. And if I had the mettle for command, I was to be given a ship of my own at the age of twenty-one. I was given a brig."

Elizabeth Chares turned her back to the rail. He noticed the swell of high firm breasts beneath the coat. She looked up at the great cloud of canvas. The full lips parted and the neck formed a graceful white curve in the sunlight. "This is no brig."

Francis Drake smiled. "I did well on the China trade. That's where I saw my first clipper ship. To own one became my dream."

"And your father? What happened to him?"

"He went to prison, finally. I used this ship to earn the money to buy his freedom. I owed my father everything, you see, and there was no way to repay the debt." He swallowed. He felt the weight of it all creeping over him, the nagging depression that he could neither fathom nor conquer. "But my father put a pistol to his head and pulled the trigger. He felt . . . he felt that his life was a failure of his own making, and I couldn't seem to convince him otherwise."

She was looking at him closely. "You loved your father?"

Francis Drake shrugged. "I think so. He was good to me. He could have left me in Jamaica. Did I feel love or gratitude? How do we know the difference?"

"Yes," she breathed. "How indeed?"

That night, for the first time since the storm, he fell gratefully into his bunk and slept deeply. Sometime after midnight, a sound penetrated his senses that was out of phase with the groanings of timber and wash of the sea. His eyes snapped open, staring into the darkness of the cabin. There it was again, a whisper of clothing being removed. The room had an odor of sweet scent. He rose up. "Who's there?" Out of the darkness, she placed her fingers lightly to his lips.

Elizabeth Chares slipped into the bunk beside him. She was naked and shivering. The full mouth came to his. Her kiss was a wet fire, and her tongue darted into the depths of his consciousness. Her hand found the swelling mass of him. Flinging the covers aside, he caressed her loosening thighs.

The hugeness of him startled her. "Oh, my word!" she gasped. A spasm of delight coursed through her body.

He found the hot wet tightness and entered it. In the massive, thrusting joy of it, he was only half-aware of her animallike cries. He exploded into her. And the night came flowing down.

Afternoon sunlight filtered through the great bay windows, its beams striking the inset prisms and breaking into cascades of rainbow colors. Maybelle found the effect enchanting, especially at this hour of the day. Finishing her tea, she ordered the butler to clear away the things and strolled to the window. She wore a wine-colored gown with white lace trim at the bodice and a dark velvet choker. The choker was caught with a diamond brooch. Her hair was upswept for the afternoon, a style that she found cooler. It was interesting, now, to try different hair styles.

"Will that be all, madam?"

"Yes, Herndon. Thank you."

The butler withdrew, bearing his tray.

She had always wanted a bay window. Strange, the things that fulfill our desires. She had also wanted a house on a hill with a view of water. Now she had both. Or, more appropriately, all three. The bay window was a gigantic affair, thrice the width of an ordinary window and half again as tall, occupying most of the southwest wall of the main parlor. And the new house—although Maybelle found it difficult to call such an elaborate, eighty-room structure a house—had been constructed to her specifications near the top of Nob Hill. It commanded, of course, a magnificent sweep of the bay itself; so stunning was the view, indeed, that the bay in all its moods became subtly a part of Maybelle's life. From here she could keep watch on the swift and often dramatic changes of weather, the constant interplay of sunlight and fog, and the shipping. Ah, the shipping! Once, only a handful of vessels, generally small and hard-used by the sea, dropped anchor in San Francisco. Now, on any given day the harbor was crowded with every type of ship from those curious sidewheel steamers lumbering up from the coast of Panama to junklike sailing craft from China, packed to the gunwales with Celestials brought over by brokers to toil in Gum San, the Golden

Mountain. The Chinese had spread into the gold fields like a
yellow horde, attacking with picks and shovels and seemingly
boundless energy the tailings of gold mines which white men
had considered worked out. One saw great schooners as well,
bringing loads of trade goods and even lumber around the
Horn. There were barks and brigs and converted whalers.
Indeed, anything that would float seemed bound for San
Francisco.

As her eye drifted over the great bay and its shipping, she
caught her breath. Standing well offshore, but still under full
sail, was a white cloud of canvas gleaming in the setting sun.
A clipper ship! Was a more beautiful vessel ever created by
the mind and hand of man? Maybelle moved to the telescope,
rising from its steel tripod, and focused on the bow of the
lovely vessel. She read the word *Typhoon*. A fitting name for
a magnificent ship.

"Begging your pardon, madam"—Herndon gave a polite
and disapproving cough— "but there is a Mister Hatfield
here to see you."

"Show him in."

"Maybelle!" David Hatfield swept into the room with a
smile displaying rows of even white teeth. He wore a suit of
dove gray trimmed in black velvet. The gambler had visibly
prospered in the gold camps. Maybelle also found his various
talents useful and paid him well for little chores. With
Hatfield's help, in fact, she had brought in a hundred new
girls to work the mining camps. A dozen more were kept
here in San Francisco to staff her new combined restaurant
and pleasure house, the popular Nocturne II on Portsmouth
Square. The establishment was complete with Parisian chef
and a string quartet. "You're looking well, Maybelle. Yes,
you're looking well indeed."

"Of course, David. I always look well."

"Yes, and now that you're rich, you look even better."

"So it seems. Pour yourself a drink and tell me what
success you've had. Did you find him?"

Hatfield moved to the sideboard, poured two fingers of
bourbon into a crystal whiskey glass and downed it at a gulp.
"I found him," he said.

"Where?"

"Up in the gold fields, of course. A little claim near
Hangtown. He was there with about a dozen other Celestials,
working like a dog. Damn, those people can work."

"And . . . ?"

"And"—the gambler deliberately fished for a fresh cigar, snipped the butt, thumbed fire from a wooden match and filled the air with blue smoke—"I brought him with me. He's outside with the interpreter now."

"You're sure it's the same young man, the one they call Shingling?"

"It's the same."

"Well?"

"Well, what?"

"Well, damn it, bring him in!"

Hatfield smirked, went to the mahogany double doors leading to an anteroom, opened them with a flourish and said, "Please. Come in."

Shingling entered hesitantly, wide-eyed at the wonders of this rich house, padding across the carpet in old felt boots, sweat-stained cotton trousers and a blue cotton jacket. Clutching a conical straw hat, he gave off odors of sweat and earth which Maybelle found instantly familiar. He was a stocky young man in his early to middle twenties—how could anyone tell their ages?—and his awe was clearly tinged with fear. He was accompanied, at a distance so as to avoid contact and soilage, by a young Chinese prostitute from Nocturne II. Her name was Lotus.

"Welcome to my house, Shingling," Maybelle said. As Lotus translated into the Cantonese dialect, Shingling made a quick bow. His forehead glistened with nervous sweat. "Do you remember me? I'm the woman you jerked out of the path of the runaway team. You saved me from serious injury and maybe even death, and I'm grateful."

There followed a lengthy translation, during which Shingling's expression slowly changed from wariness to recognition. He bowed again and rattled something in Chinese.

"What does he say?"

"He say he very glad white lady is okay," Lotus said. "He only happen to be there and do what anybody would do. It is nothing. Can he go now?"

The quick laughter from both Maybelle and David Hatfield clearly puzzled the man. Shingling offered an apologetic smile and again spoke to Lotus, who also was amused.

"He say he sorry to be funny. He no mean to be funny, but can't think of right things to say. He never been in house like this one, so big and so grand. He very nervous."

Maybelle rang for Herndon and ordered more tea. There was a silence as it was served. "Well, Shingling, I can't blame you for being nervous. I'd be nervous, too, if this house belonged to somebody else and I was a guest for the first time. I must apologize for having such a big, showy house, because actually I'm a humble person like yourself. But you see, Shingling, I struck it rich in the gold fields. That is, a partner of mine struck it rich and left me a whole damned gold mine, all my own. I guess I'm the richest woman in California. And if you think that's strange, just listen to this. I also own a whole string of pleasure houses. That's my profession, see. My name is Maybelle Stewart, and I'm a whore. Herndon here don't like for me to talk that way; it embarrasses him. But when you're as rich as I am, you can say any damned thing you please and folks'll listen, even snooty butlers. Isn't that true, Shingling?"

As Lotus stumbled and halted with the translation, Shingling's face took on a wide smile. As Maybelle's last words came through, he nodded vigorously and chuckled.

"Yep. I'm friends now with the new territorial governor— he was here at the mansion for dinner just the other night— and very brainy fellows like Mr. Audubon, who paints pictures of birds, and lots of politicians, merchants, bankers. Wealth, you see, is a great leveler. And that means that we can be friends too, even though I've got it and you haven't got it—at least, not yet. Do you think we can be friends, Shingling?"

Again the smile, the nod.

"What I brought you here for was to give you a reward for pulling me out of the way of those runaway horses. I don't want to give you too much reward, so's it would corrupt you; and I don't want to make it too little, so's it might offend you. But from what I've found out about you Celestials, you've come to this country on credit, through a broker in Canton, to mine the gold. Somebody said there's ten thousand of you here already and more on the way. And you've got a family somewhere back in China to feed, and that's where your money goes. Am I right so far?"

Maybelle was right.

"Good. Therefore, I've made out a bank draft in the amount of one hundred thousand dollars, with instructions to open an account in your name. And I figure that ought to set you up for life."

She was pleased with herself. Actually, her intention had been to make the gift less than that, around fifty thousand. But the young man was appealing, and in the rush of her own rhetoric Maybelle's generosity had expanded. Even David Hatfield looked at her in surprise, and Lotus was so flustered that she had even more difficulty translating. It took numerous repeats and false starts to get the message through. And when Shingling finally understood, he gave the matter a moment of quiet thought before making his reply. The eyes of Lotus, the translater, widened in astonishment at his words. There was a flurry of Chinese back and forth between them before she passed it on.

"Shingling, he say he very grateful for so generous an offer, but he could not possibly accept. He done nothing to earn such a sum of money, and he don't believe in taking money not earned. I think he afraid it also might bring bad luck. Anyhow, that's what he say."

It was Maybelle's turn to be astonished. As Shingling bowed and smiled, she stared at him in disbelief. "You're turning down one hundred thousand dollars?" She looked at Lotus and then at Hatfield and then back to Shingling. "That's a fortune, and you're turning it down?"

Shingling acknowledged that, yes, he was turning it down. But he offered profuse apologies and hoped the lady would not be offended. He was an unworthy person, a simple farmer, and knew nothing of manners. Please forgive...

"All right, all right. I forgive you."

Perplexed, Maybelle went to the bay window and stared down at the harbor. The great clipper ship was taking in sail and preparing to drop anchor. What to do about this strange Chinaman? As she pondered, the others stood in polite silence. Finally, Shingling again spoke in rapid-fire Chinese. When he had finished, Lotus said to Maybelle: "Ma'am, there is something."

Hah, she thought. Every man has his price. Even for the wily Oriental, there is always something.

"What is it?"

"Shingling, he say he like very much to learn English."

Immediately, the cynicism of her previous thought struck Maybelle like a blow. She turned back to them. He bowed and clutched his hat more tightly. "English?" she said.

"He like to learn to read and write English language, like I do. He say in this way, he can get better job, work, make money, be somebody." Lotus's manner had suddenly softened toward Shingling. She spoke more warmly, a gentle advocate trying to make Maybelle understand. "He never went to school. There was no school in his village and he worked the fields with his father. So he is not able to read and write, and is ignorant of life. Could you help him learn to read and write?"

Maybelle walked to Shingling and took his hand in hers. It was a hand of iron, hardened by a lifetime of toil. She squeezed the hand and felt a strange exuberance out of all proportion to such a simple request. "You're damned right he'll learn. And Lotus, I'll even pay you extra to teach him. Would you do that for me?"

"Yes, madam. I'll do that."

Shingling spoke again. Lotus frowned, and then translated. "But first, he got to go back to his companions at the mine. He gave his word to work this season until the rains begin. Then, when can't dig no more, he come to San Francisco with his wages to learn English."

Maybelle sighed. "All right, then. It's agreed."

Shingling made his goodbyes. As he and Lotus went out, Maybelle looked into the bemused face of David Hatfield. The gambler lifted an eyebrow. "Maybelle, I'll never understand you."

"Sometimes I don't understand myself." She smiled. "But no matter. Come to the window with me, Hatfield. I want to show you something." She pointed to the clipper ship, now riding at anchor in the harbor. "See that beautiful ship down there? She's called the *Typhoon*. I seem to recall her being in this harbor before. I want you to go down there, give the captain my card and invite him to join us for dinner tomorrow night at the Nocturne."

"But you don't even know who he is."

"It doesn't matter." Maybelle Stewart's eyes flashed. "A man in command of a vessel like that is bound to be interesting."

VIII

They left their lodgings and hailed a hansom cab into the city. Twilight descended, intensified by a mist rising from the Potomac. The air was damp from a late afternoon shower. Thaddeus Stewart could hardly contain his excitement. He started to speak of it as the cab hurried through the gathering evening, but then abstained. His friend Ted Judah had fallen into one of those periodic silences. Thaddeus let himself be content to rock along with his private thoughts, accepting the other's moody ways. Judah was a railroader, after all, and not a social creature. His passion was trains, not drawing rooms. Beyond the world of locomotive and high rail the grave young man was out of his element. Besides, Ted Judah again had been obliged to leave his bride, Anna, back in Buffalo, this time so that he and Thaddeus could come to Washington, D.C. It was enough to make any young husband morose. And so Thaddeus let himself be lulled by the sounds of horses' hooves and carriage wheels on damp pavement.

Gaslights were coming on, reflecting in yellow pools of rainwater. An occasional puddle splashed into widening ripples of light. He drew a cigar from his pocket, struck a match and cupped the flame. The face in the glow was full and heavily masculine now, bronzed from weather and accented by a black mustache. The hands, like the matured body of the man himself, were thickset and powerful. The whole gave an effect of quiet strength to which women invariably responded.

Thaddeus blew cigar smoke and reflected pleasurably on the evening ahead. The shrewd Asa Whitney was still trying to sell his dream, and he needed train men. Not just politicians and tycoons, but young, eager men who were engaged in the technical business of building railroads. And so the merchant's invitation, tapped out over the new telegraph wires, had found Thaddeus and Ted in Buffalo. Well, they reasoned, why not? Ted Judah, for all his misgivings, knew that great events were fashioned and given thrust in Washington, not the wild gorges of the Niagara. And thus he had announced to an incredulous Anna, "Thaddeus and I are going to Washington. Back in a couple of weeks." That was that; and they had boarded the train for this strange journey.

Thaddeus chuckled, rousing Ted Judah from his reverie. "What is it?" the engineer asked.

"Nothing."

In the two years since taking his engineering degree in Philadelphia, life had unfolded for Thaddeus. But the best stroke of luck had been his friendship with this moody railroad construction man. They had met in the Philadelphia locomotive shops of George Barrett and taken an instant liking to each other. Judah was several years older than Thaddeus but quickly recognized a kindred spirit. It was he who secured for Thaddeus a job with a surveying crew on the new Niagara Gorge Railroad, for which Judah was working as location engineer. Together they labored through the wild reaches of the Niagara Falls canyon, plotting the route of a railroad that would link the ship piers of Lake Erie and Lake Ontario. Thaddeus remembered one day the tireless Judah bracing the tripod in that stony gorge, drenched in flying spray and buffeted by wind, suddenly shouting over the tumult, "Stewart, nothing is built at all—not a tie laid nor a spike driven—until one man with a dream in his head sights through the glass and plots a route." Under Ted Judah's guidance, Thaddeus advanced from chainman to surveyor to assistant engineer. And Thaddeus had been present for his friend's wedding to the beautiful Anna Pierce, of the wealthy New England family. As the life of the newlywed took on a dramatically new dimension, Thaddeus felt within himself a powerful longing to find that kind of happiness. It was almost a physical pain to bask in the light of Judah's bliss.

"Ted," he said abruptly, "I envy you."

"Huh?" Judah blinked owlishly in the dusk. "I'm sorry, Thad. I was thinking."

"I know what you were thinking about. And I don't blame you. I've often wondered what it would be like to be married."

Judah laughed. "Well, it doesn't sit well with everybody. You've got to have the right person. But, Thaddeus, there's nothing stopping you."

"True. But to get married, one must have a fiance."

"Thad Stewart, if ever any man had his pick, it's you. I've never known a fellow with so much fatal charm. Sometimes I think even Anna finds you fetching. As for prospects, Ruth Barrett is the most sought-after beauty in Philadelphia, and she's crazy about you. Why not Ruth, Thad?"

Thaddeus sighed and tossed his cigar out the window. Why not Ruth, indeed? He was a fool. Even his friend George Barrett, her father, had made oblique suggestions. And Ruth, in her headstrong way, had informed him bluntly that she loved him and would have no other man. At the next moment, of course, she was accepting party invitations from any one of the dozens of Philadelphia bachelors who courted her relentlessly. She manipulated them all like puppets and delighted in her adoring retinue. Thaddeus suspected that Ruth played at life as a game, and that even her crush on him was a game. Was she fascinated simply because he seemed distant and unattainable? The thought occasionally crossed his mind. But each time it did, the awareness of Marguerite overcame him with its bittersweet power and nothing else mattered. Marguerite. She was in Washington, too, visiting friends. What a remarkable coincidence. And he must see her somehow, if only briefly. Her letters lately had seemed somewhat strained. Yes, he would do that very thing while the opportunity presented itself. He would see Marguerite. His spirits lifted again.

It was fully dark by the time they turned down Pennsylvania Avenue. The streets teemed with carriages, horses, and pedestrians. "What an odd town for a nation's capital," he said.

"You can have my share of Washington, old boy," muttered Ted Judah.

"The place is always under construction, always in flux. One wonders if the streets will ever be paved. In summer it is heat and dust; in winter, cold and mud."

Thieves and footpads, he brooded, were everywhere. Thaddeus had taken to carrying a derringer pistol in his pocket whenever he went out. And the city was a hotbed of intrigue. Men engaged in fistfights and duels over the issue of slavery. Over all, the mists of the Potomac lay their moist patina of humidity, discomfort and strange miasmas. There were those who insisted that the night airs of Washington were poisonous. Even President Zachary Taylor had died in the

White House. Of the cholera, they said. And Millard Fillmore had taken his place.

"Here we are." The cab turned into the curved driveway of a graystone mansion on K Street. Wheels crunched gravel. White-gloved servants hurried out to open the doors of arriving carriages and let down the steps for Asa Whitney's guests. The scene was bathed in lamplight as elegantly dressed men and women moved from the carriages up broad stone steps into the foyer. Several women turned to stare at Thaddeus as he and Ted Judah alighted from the hansom cab and mounted the steps. "See what I mean, lad?" Judah murmured.

Impressions fleeted around Thaddeus. Warm lights and reflected glass. The scented crowd. Bubbling conversation. An odor of fresh flowers. They gave their cloaks and top hats to a servant, drifted with the crowd through the foyer and into a grand parlor ablaze in lamplight. From a corner dais a string trio played Mozart. There were glimpses of potted palms, a clink of glasses, a sense of restrained gaiety.

"Thaddeus, my boy. How nice to see you again!" Asa Whitney emerged from a crowd, ebullient, advancing with both hands extended. "And Ted Judah! I'm so pleased that you could come." Then he was steering them both lightly by the arms through a glittering assemblage of Washington society. Thaddeus looked into noncommittal smiles, smiled back, bowed, shook hands. Half-familiar faces swam past him as Asa Whitney made introductions—the Secretary of State, the Vice-President, congressmen, senators.

"Asa, dear, who are these positively divine young men?" The woman came into their midst on a swirl of yellow silk and flashing diamonds, extending to Thaddeus a white-gloved hand, beaming a practiced smile under a polite arching of aging eyebrows. She was beyond fifty and stood over six feet tall.

"Gentlemen, Mrs. Marvella Clive, the Washington hostess." The merchant offered a conspiratorial wink. "Marvella opens all doors and knows where the bones are buried."

"You devil, Asa." A giggle. A flash of jewels. A shrewd appraisal with violet eyes. "Don't tell me. You're Thaddeus Stewart. I've heard so much about you. The Pittsburgh Stewarts are quite famous, you know. I was once acquainted with your Uncle Nathan in New York. Lovely man. Too bad he had to leave us under the wheels of a train." Marvella shrugged, as if to say that life had its tragedies which we must

all endure. "And you would be Theodore Judah." She extended her hand again. Judah, flustered, seemed undecided
whether to kiss it or to shake it. Gravely, he shook it. "I adore
railroad men. If I were only thirty years younger."

"Your youth is eternal, my pet," Whitney murmured.

"Yes. Permit me." From behind her, she drew a stoutish
man with an impressive girth, a beak of a nose, unruly gray
hair and a jutting jaw. "Gentlemen, may I introduce Senator
Thomas Hart Benton? Senator Benton is . . . well, I don't have
to tell you who Senator Benton is."

"Not hardly," Whitney said coolly.

"Stewart, eh? Any relation to Stephen Stewart, in St.
Louis?" Benton's voice boomed, as if he were making a
speech.

"My uncle, sir."

"Delighted. Known Stephen for years. He was with Lewis
and Clark." Benton turned to Whitney. "The lad's uncle was
with Lewis and Clark. Fine man, Stephen. Good stock. Stout
fellow. Building an empire for himself in St. Louis and St. Joe.
Most beautiful wife you have ever seen. Catherine. Hell of a
woman." The eyes of the Missouri senator narrowed, locking
on those of Thaddeus. The personality was sheer power,
Thaddeus thought; no wonder the old man was a wheelhorse
of Congress. "Know an aunt of yours, too, although I daresay
the family would just as soon she weren't related. Maybelle."

Thaddeus grinned. "I hear she's a hell of a woman too, sir."

"That she is, boy. That she is. Richest woman in California
now, did you know that? Damned if Maybelle didn't strike
gold."

"I didn't know that."

"Best to keep up with your kin, boy. Blood's thicker than
water."

Asa Whitney was at their elbows again. They moved from
group to group. Talk ebbed and flowed. But it was talk that
fascinated Thaddeus, talk of capitol cloakrooms and political
maneuver, talk of Free Soil and slavery, talk of railroads.

"It's ridiculous. Damned ridiculous, sir. The War Department wants a survey of five routes to California. Five! My
God, don't those fools know that the only logical route is the
southern route. Take off from Memphis, sir, and make a
beeline for California. That's the only way."

"Don't let Tom Benton hear you say that. He can't see
anything but the middle route from St. Louis."

"Hell, that's because he owns St. Louis."

"I hear he's sending Frémont out to survey the Buffalo Trail."

"We don't need any of those routes, sir. The railroad will leave the land despoiled. Look what it's doing to this nation already. It's changing the way we live, and I say such rapid change is dangerous. The land will be ruined. It'll be a desert in the west where only buzzards shall feed upon carrion left by the iron monster. Mark my words."

"There'll be no compromise on the northern and southern routes. None. As John Calhoun said, 'We're not one nation, but two.'"

"I still say Asa Whitney had the best idea of the lot, taking off from Michigan and running the line to northern California. If Benton hadn't beaten him down so bitterly in the Senate, Whitney's plan might have won out. His idea for a federal land grant started the ball rolling, anyway."

"There's bitterness between Whitney and Benton."

"Then why's Benton here? And Jeff Davis, I saw him in the crowd somewhere. And Senator Andrew Butler of South Carolina. Butler doesn't want any federal land gift to the young western territories, period."

"They're all opportunists. They couldn't pass up this party. Politics makes strange bedfellows."

And if it wasn't railroads, it was California.

"Flash in the pan, I say. There's nothing out there worth keeping."

"Fiddlesticks! Do you call fifty million a year in gold a flash in the pan? It's a great state, California. A great state!"

Thaddeus smiled. In his pocket he carried his latest letter from Uncle Stephen, postmarked St. Joseph, Missouri, 1852. He had almost committed the letter to memory. "Thaddeus, it's a torrent out here. Unbelievable! We've got twenty Stewart steamboats a day disgorging people at St. Joseph, and they're all heading for the gold fields. By the end of May, fifty thousand had already passed through Fort Kearny. There's almost a solid line of wagons on the trail to California. I hear San Francisco's a sprawling town, all tents and shacks and dust, miles of new streets up and down the hills. They've got Yankees and Southerners, Mexicans, Chileans, Europeans, Australians from the penal colonies—a bad lot, those. Two hundred prostitutes came from Sydney by boat. There's Frenchmen, and Chinese galore. St. Louis and Independence are swarming, too. We're building steamboats as fast as we can, and I'm negotiating for a mail contract to open a stage line to Salt Lake City. Catherine sends her love. Stephen."

As he and Ted Judah detached themselves from yet another group (Good Lord, he thought, Whitney must have three hundred people here!), Thaddeus moved back toward the front part of the parlor. Still more guests were arriving. From his height, he could see over most of the heads. His eye caught a glimpse of golden hair which seemed disturbingly familiar. Ths woman's back was to him, and she stood beside a tall, uniformed Army colonel of cavalry. He started to move toward her, but was distracted again.

"Mr. Stewart, I believe." A short, handsome man addressed him. He had piercing black eyes, a neatly combed dark beard and mustache and wore several small medals pinned to the lapel of his elegant tuxedo. The medals glistened in the light, "Colonel John C. Frémont, sir."

Thaddeus was astonished. The famous pathfinder of the West barely came up to his shoulder. Frémont had impeccable manners and spoke with an accent that was slightly French and slightly southern. "I believe you spoke with my father-in-law, Senator Benton?" said Frémont.

"Yes. A most impressive man, Senator Benton."

"Thank you. And he was also impressed by you. I share the sentiment, having spent a good deal of time in the country first explored by your uncle and his companions."

There it was again, of course. Lewis and Clark. It always surprised Thaddeus to hear that Uncle Stephen was a national hero of sorts, simply for having been on the expedition.

Frémont, an engaging conversationalist, made small talk with Thaddeus and Judah. He mentioned that he was planning a fifth expedition into the West, this time to find the best route for the transcontinental railroad. He asked offhandedly if Thaddeus or Judah had a preference for any of the routes. The fact that they did not seemed to please Frémont. "Perhaps, Mr. Stewart, you'd like to join my group?" It was said lightly and quickly passed on. Frémont then introduced them to another railroader, an older, stocky man with the rugged manner of a construction boss. His name was Roswell B. Mason, and he was chief engineer for the new Illinois Central project, building seven hundred miles of railroad across the prairie. Frémont withdrew, leaving them in earnest talk with

Mason. The engineer seemed uncomfortable in a social setting and eager to talk with men of his own kind. "I've heard
of you, Ted Judah," he said. "You're making a name for
yourself up there in New York. There's not that many good
construction engineers around."

Ted Judah blushed with pleasure. "It's exciting work, Mr.
Mason. But then, I don't have to tell you that."

For the first time, Roswell Mason smiled. "There's more
than ten thousand miles of railroad in this country already,
gentlemen, and more track being laid every day. Out there in
Illinois, the settlers are pouring in to break ground with the
plow. They're raising wheat and corn and hogs. We've got
nearly a million people in Illinois, and thirty-five thousand in
Chicago. That's going to be a natural market when our
railroad is completed. We're building over seven hundred
miles of track, from the town of Cairo on the Mississippi up
to the northwest corner of the state, west of Galena. Another
spur line will run from about the middle of the state to
Chicago. It's going to make huge difference. Today, it costs a
farmer thirty cents to ship a bushel of grain by steamboat. By
train it'll cost him twelve cents. And wherever we lay track,
gentlemen, this country shrinks. It still takes a week to travel
by rail and steamboat from New York to St. Louis. When the
last rail is spiked down, you'll cover the distance in two days!"

Thaddeus's attention wavered. Some instinct pulled his
thoughts back to the golden-haired woman. Excusing himself,
he worked his way through the crowd, hoping for another
glimpse of her. Surely it was too much of a coincidence even
to consider. But still . . .

And then he saw her. The golden hair appeared in a
convivial group of young people. She was laughing, head
flung back and blue eyes filled with merriment. And then the
eyes saw him and the laughter stopped. Astonishment flooded her face.

"Marguerite!"

Faces turned to him. Mouths opened in surprise. Clumsily
he pushed toward her, stumbling over someone's feet. "Well,"
a woman gasped, "the very idea!"

And then she was near, and he grasped her hands in his.
"Marguerite, what a surprise. How are you? What are you
doing here?" He was speaking in a rush. Her face flooded
with warmth, her expression startled and joyful and—what
was it, lurking there behind the eyes?—perplexed. She turned

to the Army colonel and said something. He was a tall, ruddy faced man with rust-colored hair and freckles. Thaddeus heard her say, "My cousin." She said it quite distinctly, with emphasis. The colonel nodded, smiled, extended his white-gloved hand to Thaddeus.

He was ecstatic and voluble. Marguerite's friends stood back, smiling self-consciously. Thaddeus realized he had intruded, and stammered apologies.

She smiled reassuringly. "Let me introduce you."

Names and faces passed without meaning. Someone said, "Stewart? Your cousin?" This was a tall brunette. She took Thaddeus's hand and held it in a lingering grasp. Her eyes were bold. But he only half-noticed. He turned from her, so happy to see Marguerite.

They whispered behind him, "Cousins. Her first cousin."

Dinner was announced. They moved together into a great dining hall ablaze with candlelight. Asa Whitney had done this party in the grand manner. There were three huge tables with place cards, and liveried waiters to assist the guests. "Mr. Stewart? This way, please." Disappointed at being separated from Marguerite, he followed the man's broad back. He was seated beside Ted Judah, with Senator Benton, Frémont and Mason nearby. He looked for Marguerite, but she was at another table and apparently did not see him. She sat beside the tall colonel.

Thaddeus only half-listened to the table conversation. Senator Benton and Roswell Mason talked more of the Illinois Central Railroad. "Mr. Mason, your railroad proves the validity of the federal land grant as a means of extending our national rail system," Benton was saying. "Twenty-five million dollars in credit, secured by two million acres of government land in alternate sections. And as I understand it, the Illinois Central acquires its title to the land as work advances. Excellent. What do you think of that, Mr. Stewart?... Mr. Stewart?... Thaddeus?"

"Eh? How's that, Senator? Sorry, I was just..."

"She is lovely, isn't she. Your cousin, Mr. Stewart?"

"My first cousin, yes."

"Too bad."

"We were saying, Mr. Stewart, that the land grant system is working well as a means of financing the Illinois Central, and it's bound to be equally effective for the transcontinental railroad. Especially if it takes off from St. Louis."

"This sectional bickering has certainly thrown a wrench into things, Senator," said Mason. The engineer spoke from the neutrality of a technical man, detached from partisan politics.

Benton ignored the comment. "Colonel Frémont has assured me, gentlemen, that the Buffalo Trail is the most realistic all-weather route. Isn't that so, Colonel?"

"Absolutely, Senator," Frémont said.

"And to prove his point, he intends to take an expedition over the route this very winter."

A murmur of surprise passed among the listeners around the table. Thaddeus heard someone say, "In winter? He had a disaster the last time out." The remark brought a flush to Senator Benton's face and he started to seek out the speaker. Frémont restrained his father-in-law with a wave of his hand.

"That's correct. I say the Buffalo Trail will provide an all-weather route along the thirty-eighth parallel. It is true that my last expedition was a disaster. Everyone knows that. I deeply, deeply mourn the eleven brave men who died in our mutual effort to explore the great mountain range of the Rockies." Frémont paused. The effect was electric. Suddenly the entire dining hall had fallen silent. Thaddeus felt the impact not only of Frémont's speech, but more profoundly of three hundred people caught in his spell. Now, his voice dropped to a hoarse whisper. "I would undo it all, if I could." He glanced at Thaddeus, smiled quickly and picked up his fork. The room seemed to exhale. Gradually, conversation resumed.

The spell of Frémont's words hung over the crowd during the remainder of dinner. Even afterward the mood was subdued. As the women retired to the parlor, men drifted to the billiard room for cigars and brandy. Talk filtered around Thaddeus. Asa Whitney caught his arm. "Didn't know your family was so thick with Senator Benton."

"Neither did I."

"He ain't a senator no more, actually, but no matter."

"Not a senator?"

"Fiesty old man, a Free-Soiler to the core. His anti-slavery stand for Missouri cost him his Senate seat last year. So he turned around and got himself elected to the House. He refuses to be silenced, says slavery must be opposed by every constitutional means."

Thaddeus nodded, only half-listening. Finally he withdrew

from Whitney and left the billiard room. He found Marguerite in the foyer, chatting with Marvella Clive. After perfunctory small talk, Mrs. Clive left them alone.

"How delightful it is to see you this evening, Marguerite," he said. "I've missed you so."

"Yes, it is delightful." She seemed reserved and ill at ease. "I'm glad you had a chance to meet Peter Heflin. We've often talked of you."

"Peter Heflin?" Again, the stab of jealousy. "You didn't mention him in your letters. Have you been friends for long?"

"Didn't I mention him? I'm sorry. Peter is from South Carolina. He's a protégé of Senator Butler, who appointed him to West Point some years ago. He's had a meteoric rise in the Army. We met at Marvella Clive's. She is such a dear."

"She was a friend of your father."

"Yes. She was taken with Father. He was quite the handsome rake of New York in those days." Marguerite paused. "I've had people tell me that you favor Father. He and Uncle Stephen both had the Stewart good looks, as you do. Did you know that?"

"That I look like him? No." Thaddeus chuckled. "But then, that would be a nice compliment, wouldn't it?"

He thought, why are we skirting around the edges of things like this? What's wrong with us? He wanted to speak of her letters, and how infrequent they had been lately. He wanted to ask her if anything was wrong. But he did not.

Marguerite turned away from him and walked to the window. It looked out onto a small patio and garden, bathed in gaslight. From the other rooms, Thaddeus heard the murmur of the crowd. The string trio was playing again.

"I'm staying at Marvella's home," Marguerite said.

"I see."

She faced him again. The blue eyes were troubled.

"Thaddeus, I . . . I don't exactly know how to tell you this. I had to say it in person. I couldn't just write it in a letter. That seemed so cold and impersonal."

"Tell me what?"

"Peter and I . . . That is, Colonel Heflin and I are engaged to be married."

There it was. It fell between them and remained on a gulf of silence. Thaddeus knew that he should say something. He looked at her dumbly. His mind seemed to expect something further from her, a qualification of the statement, such as, "Colonel Heflin and I are engaged to be married, but..." There was no qualification, however; only the fact. For one instant the blue eyes were looking beseechingly into his, as if in search of approval. And then they turned away, no longer able to see his face and accept the hurt that kindled there.

Thaddeus became conscious of the quiet surrounding them. It was as if they stood in a pocket of time and space, facing each other. A grandfather clock ticked in the corner, measuring off the seconds. The sound seemed to monitor the beating of his pulse.

"Engaged?" he said.

It had to happen sooner or later. He had always known it would have to happen. Anything else was fantasy. He had been living in a dream world. But how unprepared he'd been, how naive!

"Yes. We will marry in September. Peter will be assigned to headquarters duty in Washington, and this is where we will make our home. I... I want you to visit us often."

"Engaged," he said.

"Please give me your blessing, Thaddeus. It means so much to me. We must not lose our friendship. Our friendship is so special. Do you understand?"

"Of course," he said.

The silence came again. The blue eyes searched his and for an instant seemed to well with tears. A trick of the light, he told himself, nothing more. There was nothing else to say. And so he turned and walked back into the billiard room. He did not see her take the handkerchief from her evening purse and go back to the window, pressing it to her eyes.

Two days later, Thaddeus arrived at an apartment in Washington and sounded the brass door knocker. A servant ushered him into the presence of the small, handsome man with the snapping black eyes. They chatted amiably for a few minutes.

"Captain Frémont, were you sincere in inviting me to join your expedition to the West this winter?"

"Yes, Mr. Stewart. Quite sincere."

"Good. I shall be delighted to accept."

Frémont poured two glasses of whiskey and they drank a toast.

* * *

Lightning flickered from a cloud bank massed over the eastern prairie. There was a muttering of thunder, but without rain. The flashes came again, jagged tongues splitting the rolling black shapes. Below, the parched grasses made varicolored ripples in the breeze. It was the timeless rhythm of the raw land, the vast emptiness of the plains in a silence broken only by the howling coyote and moaning wind. At last a great vertical bolt stood against the clouds, fed by some infinite surge of power. The lightning struck the ground with a mighty report that went echoing over reaches of land and sky. Smoke puffed in the dry grass and flame licked greedily upward, growing and moving with the wind. All that day dark smoke plumed in the prairie sky and at night the flame lay its fiery line across the horizon, first moving southward and then shifting to the southwest. By the second day, the conflagration had swept across a hundred-mile front of prairie at the speed of a walking horse.

But it was still fifty miles to the east of where Thaddeus rode. He had noticed the smoke pall the afternoon before, but dismissed it from his mind. He was more intent on the hunt.

"Easy, boy." He sat on the Appaloosa lightly, giving rein. "Easy does it." Drawing the Sharps rifle from its sheath, he followed the game trail toward a small wooded patch on a distant rise. He was unprepared for the covey. It burst from the grass with no explosion of feathers. He swung to his left, tracking the sound, and saw them against the slate-gray sky. Dark fluttering shapes were rising in a tight flock and turning as they flew. The Sharps came up instantly. His eye picked a single shape. Dropping the bridle, he snapped the stock to his cheek, bead-tracked the bird, giving it lead, and fired the shot with a fluid trigger squeeze. The shape faltered, dropped in a shallow curve and plummeted into the grass. Grabbing the bridle, he rode hard to the spot and came off the pony at the run. But the bird had not flopped into the obscurity of the grass; it lay still, a clean kill, bleeding from the breast. Thaddeus plucked up his game and secured it by a leather thong to his saddle. His heart hammered with the elation of the deed. Mounting again, he turned the pony back toward camp.

It was an hour's ride. As usual, he was surprised at having come so far. They were camped on the Saline fork of the Kansas River. Prairie wind rustled the tent flaps. But it was

not like coming home. Nobody stood peering as he approached;
there was no welcoming halloo. He descended into the gully
by the river and slid off the pony, bringing rifle and game.
The camp was quiet. There were eighteen others in the
party thus far, including ten Delaware Indians and two Mexicans.
Most of the men were out hunting, but a few remained
tending the horses and mules and mending gear. Thaddeus
glanced expectantly toward the big white tent which would
be Frémont's, but it remained empty. A figure stood by the
low cookfire, inspecting an instrument. Thaddeus recognized
the daguerreotypist, Carvalho. "He hasn't arrived yet?" he
said.

Carvalho shrugged. "Not yet. We got word while you were
gone. The pathfinder has been sick. He will be here this
afternoon."

"Good."

"You hunted well?"

"Some quail, two fat pheasant."

"We shall add them to the pot." The man turned away,
intent on his equipment.

Frémont came at sundown, riding a big bay horse and
accompanied by two more white men. He slid wearily out of
the saddle and exchanged perfunctory greetings. The pathfinder was not well. "A touch of the grippe," he announced,
and vanished into his tent.

The other men were young, a lieutenant of the army
engineers and an acquaintance of Frémont's whose name was
Brown. The lieutenant, a fresh-faced, outgoing fellow, introduced himself to Thaddeus as Herbert Willoughby. They
agreed immediately to share a tent. As the sun went down in
a smear of orange, they lit after-supper cigars and lounged by
the fire, resting against their saddles. Thaddeus's sense of
isolation, so oppressive in the four days since he had come to
the camp, began to lessen. "He's feeling rotten," Willoughby
said. "I'm surprised that we shall go at all, at least not for
another week. But he insists on moving out in two days. A
determined man, Frémont. No wonder he's a legend in his
time."

They talked of their individual backgrounds, schooling,
interests. Willoughby was amused by Thaddeus's passion for
railroads. His own interests did not go far beyond the Army.
He was a West Pointer, the son of a New Jersey confectioner,
and had been assigned by the Army to accompany this

expedition in order to give it at least a semblance of military involvement. "With five transcontinental railroad routes being argued, everybody is jealous of everybody else."

Thaddeus sighed. "This sectionalism is going to tear the country to pieces. I suppose you've heard of the violence in the Missouri and Kansas territories. Much blood is being spilt over slavery."

Willoughby drew on his cigar and the glow bathed his youthful features. "It's all foreign to me. I've never been in the South. I can't get used to the idea of one man owning another. It is alien to everything I've been taught. But the Army is a huge mixed bag of Northerners, Southerners and God knows what else. Southerners, at least the one's I've encountered, burn on a short fuse. They're very defensive."

The image of Peter Heflin came to Thaddeus's mind. Tall, rusty-haired, freckled Peter Heflin. He had not even had an opportunity to talk with the man, so hurriedly had he left Washington. And he had made no attempt to correspond with Marguerite. Of what earthly use was that now? The thought of her still put an ache in his heart that he could neither comprehend nor justify. He thought, And why shouldn't she be engaged to marry?

They turned in early. He slept fitfully, troubled by dreams of Marguerite. It was still dark when someone shook him roughly by the shoulder. He swam out of the fog of sleep.

"Hnnnnh?"

"Wake up, Stewart! Quickly, man, wake up!" The urgent voice of Herbert Willoughby came from the darkness of the tent.

"What is it? What's wrong?"

"Get your clothes on. Strike the tent. We're hauling our butts out of here."

"Strike the tent?"

"Prairie fire! Come on, roll out. Move!"

Blindly, he groped for clothes and boots. There was a rush of tugging and pulling. Instinctively he grasped the rifle, threw things into his pack, stumbled out into the open air clutching at belongings, his mind still fogged.

The odor struck him first, an acrid stench of burning grass and smoke. He coughed, blinked, focused his eyes. Men were running about, tents falling, horses stamping excitedly. From the chaos a voice bellowed, "Hurry, you men. Grab your animals. To the south! Move!"

"Here, Stewart!" It was Willoughby again, thrusting blankets into his already laden arms, shoving him along toward the makeshift corral where horses and mules were tethered to staked-down ropes. And then, over the rim of the gully, he saw the fire. The flames boiled in a solid wall, higher than he had ever seen, dwarfing a man on horseback. Fed by tinder-dry grass and a gusting wind, the prairie fire crackled and roared, hurling light in lurid shapes.

"What about the tent, Willoughby?"

"No time for the tent. Run, man, for the animals. Run for your life!"

The Appaloosa jerked frantically at its tether, eyes crazed with fear. Thaddeus spoke soothingly to the animal. His voice had a calming effect. Quickly he lashed his belongings to two pack mules, tethered them together, then freed and mounted the pony. Clutching the mules' bridles, he trotted out of the draw, sweating from the heat at his back. Glancing behind, he saw tents burst into flame as the wall of fire swept over the abandoned campsite.

"Ride, man!" A horseman loomed beside him. It was Frémont. The pathfinder lashed at the flanks of Thaddeus's Appaloosa and wheeled away, harrying his men. In the wild flight, the leader seemed to be everywhere, whipping and shouting, prodding and cursing. Thaddeus urged the pony to a gallop, charging over the dark grasslands as if in a futile effort to catch his own bounding shadow. Around him, the running hooves of horses and mules pounded through the heavy dry grass. In ten minutes they slackened speed and the riders began to seek out their friends, some pausing to look back at the inferno they had so narrowly escaped. Then they settled into a steady southward trek, each mile of progress widening their distance from the fire. By daybreak they were strung out over the prairie and the fire wall was a tiny bright line of orange far behind, flickering beneath billows of smoke. Still Frémont urged them on, permitting only one brief rest stop. They rode all that day and did not make camp until sunset.

"Near miss, that one. We'd have been cooked for sure." Herbert Willoughby dropped wearily into the dirt, balancing a plate of hot beans. "If Frémont hadn't given warning—"

"Frémont? I thought we had a sentry out."

"We did. The man went to sleep. Frémont woke up. He's got a sixth sense for danger, they say. Sleeps like a cat."

When they had eaten, the men were summoned for a meeting at the campfire. As usual, the Indians and the Mexicans clustered in their own ethnic groups. When all had gathered, Frémont strode into the light of the fire. Despite his short stature, the man's bearing gave an impression of height. Again Thaddeus sensed the inner power and magnetism of one completely confident in his leadership.

"This is a very serious matter," Frémont began. The eyes snapped in the firelight. "Because of one man's inattention to duty back there, we could have had a disaster." He spoke in English, then quickly repeated the same thing in Spanish and the Delaware tongue. They would be spending months together on this expedition, he said. They would encounter dangers and hardships ahead. Nature gave no quarter and did not tolerate lack of discipline. Their lives depended on each other's vigilance. Hereafter there would always be an armed sentry keeping watch, and any man who fell asleep or failed in his duty would be banished from the expedition. Banishment, in the wilds to which they were headed in the middle of winter, was virtually a sentence of death. "Am I understood?" he said. There was a muttering of assent. "Do I make myself clear?" He had made himself very clear. "Are there any questions?" There were none. "Very well. I have one other unhappy announcement to make at this time. I've received word that Captain Gunnison, the leader of one of the five railroad survey teams, and seven of his men have been killed by Ute Indians near Sevier Lake." With that, Frémont turned away from them and strode back to the solitude of his tent.

The trek continued southward until they reached the Arkansas River; then they bore to the west, following its flow. Days of riding left Thaddeus painfully saddle-sore until his body toughened to the rigors of the trail. Frémont always rode ahead, usually alone. By the end of November they were across the Arkansas River and passing their final civilized outpost, Bent's Fort. The weather grew colder as they finally turned up the Huerfano River in hilly country thick with grass and pine. By now Thaddeus had made friends with several of the others, notably the daguerreotypist Carvalho, whose admiration for Frémont was boundless. As they rose past the looming presence of a butte overlooking the turgid Huerfano, Carvalho exclaimed, "They ought to put a statue of him right up there. He should be astride a horse and pointing to California, the land to which he blazed the trail."

Thaddeus had little direct contact with Frémont. While the leader was always in view on the trail, and could be heard giving commands or conversing with two of the older Americans who had accompanied his previous expeditions, there existed a distinct separation between him and the rest of the party. The effect of this was to heighten the pathfinder's image of authority. It was most notable with the Indians, few of whom dared approach him. Even Willoughby was impressed. "I'll say this for him, the man's got a real knack for command." Thaddeus was somewhat surprised when an old trail hand, Bo Williams, came to him one evening after supper and announced, "Colonel Frémont wants to see you, Stewart."

Frémont sat in his tent at a camp table, studying maps by the light of an oil lantern. He motioned Thaddeus to a canvas stool and continued his perusal in silence. Finally he turned around and lit a small cigar. "Well, Stewart, are you enjoying the journey so far?"

"It's beyond anything I'd imagined, Colonel. Every day there's some fantastic new sight to see. I think I'm beginning to understand why you've come so often into the West."

"It's a big land, Stewart." The dark eyes studied the glowing tip of the cigar. "Folks back east don't realize how big and how magnificent. A land like this gets into a man's blood. The earth, the sky, the sunsets. And when he hits the mountains . . ." He paused, seeming to ponder some deep reach of memory. "Well, you'll see what I mean."

"The mountains?" Thaddeus said. For days, they had marched toward the rising immensity of land. From atop his pony, he had watched the mountains gradually develop from a great blue smudge on the horizon to jutting foothills and distant peaks. There was a majesty about them, when seen from the plain, that seemed to intensify everything: the silence, the vastness of sky, the minuteness of men on horseback. He felt himself shrinking in significance as they drew ever nearer. And now they were camped at the foot of the first rocky slope. The trek, he sensed, was about to begin in earnest. "Next to these, the Allegheny Mountains of my boyhood are mounds."

"You grew up around Pittsburgh, didn't you?"

"I was raised by my Uncle Stephen, in my grandfather's home."

"I suppose you know, then, that the first locomotive has arrived in Pittsburgh. Your hometown is on the railroad now."

"Yes, I knew that. It's very exciting."

"I share your feelings about railroads, Stewart. In fact, I knew quite a bit about Thaddeus Stewart before we met. Asa Whitney thinks highly of you. So my invitation to join us wasn't an idle whim. I needed somebody who could look at these mountains with the eye of a railroad man; someone who at the same time wasn't so wedded to a specific route as to cloud his judgment and youthful enthusiasm. Do you know what I mean?"

"I think so."

"We've come into a whole new era of exploration, Stewart, one that puts a premium on individuals with technical abilities. In the early days, people like Lewis and Clark, Zebulon Pike, and others could afford to be scientific novices, brilliant amateurs in geographical field work. But they weren't exploring with the objective of building railroads, railroads that will bridge and tunnel through these mountains, railroads that will span the continent from sea to sea and reduce this two-thousand-mile journey from five months of pain and death to two days in a chaircar. But to do that, to build those railroads and bring the dream to reality, we've got to be more than adventurers, more than seekers of excitement and glory. This is the work of the expert, the topographical surveyor, the geologist alert for hidden springs and faults, the intent observer of the scientific fact. Our surveys must be sure and meticulous, our maps unerring, our instincts sure."

Thaddeus was inspired. This, he sensed, was the essence of it. And if nothing else came of this trip into the West, if no certain route was actually charted by their expedition, then the sheer power of Frémont alone would be enough. The experience of seeing the man in action would justify Thaddeus's involvement.

Frémont looked at his maps again and beckoned for Thaddeus to join him. His fingers traced lines and contours of mountain topography. "It is now the second day of December. We will move into the mountains here and then make our way to the divide here. It lies between the Huerfano and the Rio Grande rivers. I am convinced that the thirty-eighth parallel provides the best route for the railroad in all weather. Our purpose is to test out this theory in the snow season. If all goes well and God is with us, we'll be here"—the finger swept westward into the uncharted blankness of the map— "in January. And at about that location in the Utah territory, we will be at the summit of the Rocky Mountains. This is a trail that we partially blazed in eighteen forty-eight."

"But I understand that you encountered very heavy snows in that expedition. In fact the severe weather was one of the reasons that . . ." Thaddeus caught himself. The black eyes turned upon him with an intensity he had not seen before. The face of the pathfinder seemed to darken, almost as if from some inner rage; but he could not be certain of that. "Well . . . that you had difficulty," he said lamely.

Frémont did not respond. He stared at the map and clenched his fists until the knuckles were white. The intensity of the man remained for several minutes, as if he were fighting to keep himself under control. At last it eased. Frémont said hoarsely, "That will be all, Stewart."

Thaddeus nodded and withdrew, stepping gratefully back into cold, open air. An hour later he lay in blankets with his head on his saddle, staring up at the cold, impartial stars. He had described the scene to Willoughby, who still sat by the fire deep in thought. "Eleven men died on that last trek through these mountains," Willoughby said. "They froze and they starved. And among those who survived there was a strong suspicion of cannibalism. Did you know that, Stewart?"

"Not really. I hadn't searched out the details."

"There were some nasty versions of the thing afterward, including allegations that Frémont abandoned his men in the wilds to save his own skin. Others argue that he had to split the party in order to move fast and get help; that if he hadn't done that, they all might have died. Anyhow, there are a lot of unanswered questions about this man. Some people, like Carvalho and old Bo Williams and those Delaware Indians, would gladly lay down and die for him. And then there are others . . ."

Willoughby's voice trailed off. Thaddeus looked up at the blaze of stars and thought of the uncharted wildernesses that lie within the minds of men. Abruptly, a shooting star streaked across his line of sight, moving from east to west.

A good omen? Or bad?

Day after day now, they breakfasted and were in the saddles at daybreak, moving west over rough country that progressively grew higher. Horses and men panted in the thin, cold air. Men complained of headaches and nausea as their systems adjusted to the increasing altitude. Only the mules seemed unaffected, plodding in head-to-tail file be-

neath their packloads, small hooves picking daintily over
roughening stones. Thaddeus rocked along in the saddle,
enthralled by the scenic wonders unfolding before his eyes.
The air was so clear that from the heights one could turn and
look backward and see for a hundred miles. Every detail of
tree and shrub, outcropping and distant peak stood out with
stunning clarity. The pine trees and sweeping meadows gave
way to stunted thickets, the thickets to grassless slopes and
loose rock.

A warning rippled back from man to man along the file.
"Injuns ahead. Watch your animals." None appeared. But
Thaddeus could not shake the eerie feeling of being watched.

On they pushed into ever wilder country. The map became
a blank. The weather grew colder, with frequent snow flurries
and ice crusting in the streams. Supplies of dried corn for the
animals ran low. Hunting parties were detailed to replenish
the expedition's meat, but game proved scarce and time after
time hunters returned empty-handed. They dipped into their
emergency rations of pemmican, the dried meat mixed with
suet, seasoned, and rolled into sacks of animal skin. As the
cold and discomfort worsened, Frémont became more and
more remote, vanishing into his tent at the end of each day's
trek and not emerging again until after dark. At night he
seemed to be constantly awake, prowling the camp, checking
the guards. Men whose rifles became soiled or who allowed
snow accidentally to invade their gun barrels were made to
walk the next day's trek while the others rode. It amazed
Thaddeus that not a man protested, but took his punishment
solely on the strength of John C. Frémont's command.

"There's them what call him a tyrant," Bo Williams, a
grizzled mountain of a man, mused one evening at supper.
He spat into the campfire. "But it ain't to my face that they
says it."

Now only Bo Williams approached the nearly sacred environs of Frémont's tent, and he, only when summoned. Among
the others there was a growing sense that the pathfinder's
solitude must be preserved at all costs, that somehow their
survival depended on his being regarded as larger than life.

The north wind moaned over the vast emptiness of the
Uncompahgre Peak. Thaddeus had never seen such a desolate winterscape. It brought them into the startling panorama
of the Grand River, where they made early camp. Orders
came down to check all weapons and be extra vigilant. As

every eye scanned the rugged terrain, Thaddeus whispered to Willoughby, "Are we expecting company?"

"There's a party of Utes out there, coming in. They're well armed—"

He did not finish the sentence. A whoop keened out of the gorge. "*Yieee yiyiyiyi!*" The Indians came at a full gallop, brandishing rifles, spears and arrow-filled bows. Thaddeus raised his Sharps rifle, remembering the recent fate of the Gunnison party. There were sixty warriors, all whooping and circling the camp in a cloud of dust. Abruptly, one of the leaders raised his arm and the tumult stilled.

"Ugly devils, ain't they?" Willoughby said.

"I'd say so."

"Don't shoot until you're told."

Thaddeus grunted acknowledgment.

The Utes had come to barter. Loudly, shaking his rifle, the leader demanded payment in rifles and ammunition for allowing the expedition to hunt on Ute lands. Frémont had made it an inflexible rule never to supply Indians with weapons in barter. And despite the furor at the campsite, the pathfinder remained hidden away in his tent as usual. Bo Williams and one of the Delaware Indians carried messages back and forth. No, came the reply, the Great Captain would not meet the demands of the Utes. He regarded the Utes as clamorous old women for bursting so rudely upon the expedition.

"My God," Thaddeus whispered, "they'll massacre us all."

Bo Williams overheard him on his way back to Frémont's tent. "They ain't got no ammunition, boy," he muttered. "If they did, you'd be fightin' for your scalp already. Cap'n knows what he's doing. Their powder horns is empty and so's their cartridge pouches. And force is the only language they respect."

It was true. After more noisy bluster and threatening gestures, the Utes withdrew to camp in a draw several hundred yards away. From Frémont's tent came orders to hobble the horses and mules in the center of the camp and maintain a defense perimeter all around. No man slept that night. The following morning, the Indians broke camp and rode away.

The expedition pushed on.

The weather worsened. The terrain became increasingly difficult. Hunger began to stalk them. Two weeks after the incident with the Utes, they killed and slaughtered the first of their horses for food, sliced the red meat and packed it in skins.

The meat of the first horse was consumed; then, a second horse was slaughtered; then, a mule. It was surprising how rapidly twenty-two men could put away food, even on half-rations. Thaddeus began to experience a gnawing in his belly and a lassitude totally strange to anything he had known before. Hunger was at first a sharp consciousness of insufficiency. But then the edge tended to wear away, as day followed day on short supply, and the body began to burn away its own excess fat and muscle tissue. His clothing enlarged in proportion to his body, the buckskin shirt and trousers hanging on his lank frame. The men had long since stopped shaving, since beards provided protection and warmth to the face and neck. But now the beards were ragged, matted growths on hollow faces. A hand mirror reflected to Thaddeus a face he barely recognized as his own, the eyes glowing back at him from hollow sockets, the cheekbones jutting even with the heavy black beard, the nose thinning and sharpening. Loss of body weight sapped his energy and made his body more sensitive to cold.

They continued their march westward beyond the Grand River to the Green River in Utah territory, and then beyond the Green into a devil's warren of snow swept peaks, canyons, gorges, defiles, steep slopes, and yawning valleys. The suffering of the train was compounded by increasing exhaustion. They slogged through patches of waist-deep snow, fought for balance along narrow icy ledges, pressed on despite dizzy spells and nausea and pain. Each animal destroyed meant one less bearer of equipment and supplies. Anything of weight that could be discarded was: camp stools and extra cookpots, tents and spare harnesses, pick axes and utensils.

Since they had first plunged into the mountains, Thaddeus had kept his own daily log of landmarks, distances covered, positional sightings by the stars and distant peaks. He applied basic surveying techniques learned at the university and from Ted Judah in the Niagara Gorge. He calculated the degree of the slopes they climbed and descended. He made notes on the general terrain and its suitability for bridging, excavating or tunneling for a railroad grade. Despite the ordeal they now suffered, he continued his stops for sightings and made nightly scribblings by the light of a sperm oil candle.

On the twentieth of January, the Appaloosa was killed. Thaddeus did not partake of the evening meal.

Now there were no longer enough mounts even for doubling riders, and so Frémont ordered that all should walk except one man, Oliver Fuller. An assistant engineer from St. Louis, Fuller suffered from fever and chills and had been unable to keep anything on his stomach for days. There were whispers among the Delaware that he had the stamp of death upon him. Fuller rode through the wind-driven snow, clutching the horn of the saddle. The others labored on foot through drifts along the ever ascending slope with Frémont still in the lead. Ahead and on all sides, the mountains loomed in Olympian snow-shrouded silence.

On the evening of the fifth of February, Frémont again summoned Thaddeus to his presence. The tent of the pathfinder had become a ragged remnant. Frémont himself was a gaunt figure of starvation and profound weariness. The dark eyes had lost their luster and the emaciated body was engulfed in clothing. Frémont's voice rasped.

"Stewart, you've been charting our position?"

"Yes, sir. As best I could."

"Let me see your map."

"It's rough, sir." Thaddeus uncased the tattered sheets so laboriously compiled, marked by degrees of longitude and latitude based on his star fixes. He spread the map and pointed to a spot. "I reckon we're right about here, Colonel."

Frémont nodded and drew out his own map, now painstakingly filled in along the route they had taken. From it, Thaddeus could see that they had crossed a vast uncharted area of the Utah country. Ahead, approximately three day's march at their present slow rate of progress, Fremont had penciled an X. "Not bad, Stewart. Not bad at all. I put us at about the same general location, give or take a few miles."

"Thank you, sir."

"Wherever you go on the face of the earth, and under whatever circumstances, the stars are in their courses, eh?" The pathfinder chuckled. "Wondrous thing, the order of nature. Never seen it to fail." He produced a ruler, lay it between their present position and the X and drew a pencil line. He lay a compass on the line and read the results, one point north of due west. "Yes, that ought to do it. Yes, indeed. Thank you, Stewart."

Puzzled, Thaddeus folded his map and returned it to its

skin pouch. His mind swirled with questions, and the main ones had to do with survival. Would they survive? Or were they doomed to an even worse fate than the expedition of eighteen forty-eight? He started to speak, but Frémont impatiently waved him silent.

"Stewart, what are the men saying now? Precisely what is their state of mind?"

"They are wondering if we're going to make it, sir. They're beginning to lose heart."

"I see. And the sick man, Fuller, how is he?"

"The Indians say Fuller's dying."

Frémont sank into thought. The compass lay on the map, its metal reflecting candle glow. The pathfinder himself was a starving man, losing strength by the day. He sighed. "Three more days, Stewart, and we reach the place I've marked on the map. Do you know what that place is?"

"No, sir."

"It's our salvation, Stewart. It's a little Mormon town called Parowan. A hamlet, really, only forty rods square and containing four hundred souls. We'll make it, Stewart. And Fuller will make it, too. I want you to spread the word. You're a young man, and they'll listen to you. Bo Williams is an old hand, and has been with me a long time. I'm afraid they won't as readily believe him. But you... Well, the men respect you, Stewart. They respect you, and they will listen to your word. I want you to tell them, tell them that you've talked with me and I say we'll be at Parowan in three days." The eyes glittered from their sockets. A bony hand clutched at his arm. "I want you to tell them, Stewart."

Thaddeus nodded. He left Frémont's tent. He went to the campfire where the others were gathered. He told them as convincingly as he could what the pathfinder had said. They shook their heads and grumbled among themselves.

Bo Williams spat tobacco juice into the fire. "Only one man alive could pull off a thing like that," he said.

"Who's that?"

"John C. Frémont."

Two days later, as they struggled up yet another snow-filled draw in the waning afternoon, with an icy wind blasting their faces and the mules groaning in misery, the engineer Fuller fell off his horse into the snow and died.

Twenty-four hours after that, they crested a saddle between two mountains and looked down into the hamlet of

Parowan. Thaddeus saw smoke rising from a half-buried
chimney, heard a dog bark and smelled the unbelievably
savory odor of food cooking. Another dog barked, and another, as the struggling, ragged men of the expedition staggered
and tumbled down the slope. Doors opened. Men emerged
from the shacks and houses. Someone shouted. The men of
Parowan began to make their way toward the newcomers.
Someone cried out near Thaddeus. "Thank God! Thank the
Lord! We are delivered!" He turned and saw Bo Williams
stumbling forward, tears pouring down his grizzled cheeks.
They were delivered, but not intact. The body of Oliver
Fuller was already freezing.

Parowan, Utah, was a miracle. The kindly Mormons took
them into their homes, fed them, provided warm water tubs
for bathing, gave them real beds in which to sleep. Thaddeus
was so exhausted he did not even catch the name of his hosts.
After an incredibly tasty dinner of lentil soup and hardtack,
he collapsed onto a cot and slept for fourteen hours. When he
awoke, a gentle giant of a man with a full gray beard sat on
the edge of the cot and looked down at him.

"Mr. Stewart?"

"Yes."

"My name is John Boniface. I am one of the elders of this
community . . ."

The truth of it was, John Colby Stewart feared Jesse
Brennan, feared him more than he feared a rattlesnake,
feared him with that special gut-wrenching fear that turned
his mind to jelly and gave him nausea. Now they rode in the
cold mist of the river valley, the horses blowing and picking
their way through canebrake, and John Colby could see the
bulky slouched figure of the outlaw just ahead and wished he
could kill him. Brennan rode in the slope-shouldered, loose
style of one long worn to the saddle. Jesse Brennan could
murder a man or rape a woman without qualm; he had the
mean, brooding look of a stray dog, and he ruled these men
with the sure hand of the tyrant. Long ago, John Colby had
heard somewhere that evil begets evil, and it was true
enough. In their six weeks of roaming out of Pittsburgh down
the riverbank to Louisville, and then striking southward
through Kentucky, there had developed among each of them

a callous indifference to human life. And now they were riding into a village, the name of which he didn't even know, to hang a man because Jesse Brennan said so.

John Colby turned in the saddle and looked back at the boy, Jeremiah Peace. He was pale, bone-thin and not a day over fifteen. They had picked him up at place called Bardstown, an orphan with no home. And after that, in a drunken rage Jesse Brennan had slaked his lust on him for the lack of a woman. The other ten of them had sat in silence around the fire, not speaking a word and not lifting a finger, while the boy cried and whimpered in Brennan's lean-to in the woods. When John Colby had looked in alarm at Drake, the old hand, Drake had simply spat tobacco juice into the fire and muttered. "You jest be glad it ain't you." That had happened three weeks ago, and Jeremiah Peace was still with them, so under the spell of Brennan that he would not even take a chance to escape.

"How are you doing, boy?" John Colby said.

Jeremiah Peace rocked along on the half-blind nag he'd been provided and did not reply. His eyes stared back at John Colby from dark shells, seemingly devoid of life.

Evil begets evil, John Colby thought. Abruptly he remembered, and turned the phrase again in his mind. "Evil begets evil." He could visualize the face of old Bigelow, the schoolmaster, and his thin lips saying it out loud. "Evil begets evil, Mr. Stewart. I'd suggest you remember that." Old Bigelow had been an angular figure in black, forever rapping students on the knuckles with his long ruler, forever carping, spouting homilies and reminding John Colby of his cousin Thaddeus. "Now, when Thaddeus Stewart was in this school..." Thaddeus. John Colby's mood darkened even more, and his hatred of Thaddeus overcame even the loathing of where he was and with whom and what they were on their way to do. Always it was Thaddeus, the smarter, the better bred, the more respected; Thaddeus, the model of deportment and the apple of his Uncle Stephen's eye. Well, John Colby had fixed old Bigelow at last. He had loosened the shoes of the schoolmaster's ancient horse and stuck a nail under the saddle. Then he had watched while the teacher mounted, watched the beast buck and rear, and laughed when the hated black-garbed figure was catapulted from the nag's back into a horse trough, breaking his neck. No one ever knew, of course, and schoolmaster Bigelow never rapped another knuckle or taught a day of school again. He was left a half-paralyzed shell, dragging his left foot along while his useless left arm flopped in the wind. John Colby chuckled to himself. Evil begets evil.

Well, he himself had become a drifter, a river rat, and a petty thief. So be it. He had looked into the half-masked face of his father, Stephen Stewart, and finally let all the bile pour from his tormented self. "You want me to be like Thaddeus, follow in Thaddeus's footsteps! But I'm not Thaddeus. I'm me, John Colby, your son! I am myself."

Now, riding this stolen, swaybacked mare along the river-bank in the misty damp, his coat and hat sopped through and the dread eating at his vitals, he saw his father's face in memory, saw the uplifted cane quivering in rage and ready to strike, heard the sharp outcry of his mother at the door: "No, Stephen!" He had left them, then. He had shagged downriver, and finally fallen in with this lot.

The column stopped. From in front, the burly man peered back through the murk. "Who is that? Who shouted like that? Was that you, Stewart?"

"I'm sorry, Jesse. I just wondered when we were going to stop, that's all. I didn't mean to be loud." He felt his face flush hotly, felt the piglike eyes boring into him from beneath the wide brim of the hat.

"It ain't nothin', Jesse," one of the other men said.

The bulky figure rode on.

They camped in a hollow in the edge of town. It had started raining again and there was no dry wood to be found. John Colby's job was to make fire, and he hated wet wood. He roamed for a quarter of a mile along the high ground before he found an overhanging ledge of rock and, beneath it, a fallen tree shattered by lightning. He took the pieces back to the camp and finally got the fire going while Brennan squatted in the shelter of a canvas lean-to, oiling and cleaning the great horse pistols he carried stuck in the belted top of his pants. Brennan also kept a pocket pistol and a rifle within reach, and a bowie knife in his boot. John Colby had seen him hurl the knife at a settler with such force that it drove through the man's body and pinioned him to a tree, where he slowly died. Then, casually, Brennan had ravished the man's wife before slitting her throat. John Colby shivered as the flames licked higher.

They ate voraciously of fried fatback, beans and stale bread. John Colby mopped the last of the beans from his tin plate and wished for more. He noticed that the boy Jeremiah Peace had barely touched his food.

"You going to eat them beans, Peace?"

The boy stirred, seemingly from deep reverie. "No, you take them. I ain't hungry."

"You best eat, boy." From the lean-to, the pig eyes glittered in the firelight. "Got to keep up your strength." John Colby looked away, heard Brennan getting to his feet, heard the heavy boots start down the slope toward them.

"All right, I'll eat," Peace said. He picked up the plate. The boots stopped walking. There was a brief silence, and then John Colby heard the sound of Brennan urinating where he stood. The outlaw belched, broke wind, returned to the lean-to.

Jeremiah Peace murmured something. John Colby thought he had heard the words but was not really sure.

"What was that you said, Peace?"

"Nothing. I didn't say nothing."

John Colby did not pursue the question. He knew. He had heard the boy saying to himself, "The Lord is my shepherd, I shall not want . . ."

Under stress, there is some inner chemical that speeds a man's blood, disturbs his rest and yet gives him reserve energy in abundance. And so it was the following morning. Drake, the old hand, kicked and shouted them from their blankets at dawn. "Drop yer cocks and grab yer socks! Get a move on, you shits." John Colby came to his feet, rubbing sleep from his eyes and feeling the roughness of three-day-old whiskers. They ate more fatback and beans, washed them down with boiled coffee, and mounted in the gray light of another cheerless day. As Brennan took the lead, they rode out of the hollow and into the dreary little town. It was a place of sagging false-front buildings with dirt-smeared windows peering out onto muddy streets. The whole town was about five blocks long, with a steepled church at each end.

Brennan positioned two men with rifles at each end of the street; the others formed a loose phalanx around him. The outlaw advanced upon a small stone house with a broad front porch. He and Drake dismounted, ascended the porch and banged loudly on the door. Several dogs started barking and a

window flew up next door. "What's that racket? Who is it?"
But then the neighbor saw the look of the men creating the
disturbance and quickly shut his window again.

There was a sound of bolts sliding free inside the heavy
front door of the house. The door opened and a dark,
gray-haired man stood there blinking. He wore long under-
wear and his feet were bare. "Huh?"

Drake grabbed him by the throat and threw him down.
Inside the house, a woman screamed and a child began to
cry. Drake and Brennan each grabbed a bare foot and dragged
the man across the floor and down to the mud street, his head
banging on each step. Only when he came into the light did
John Colby see that the man was a light-skinned Negro.

"Oh, my God, no!" It was the woman. She burst from the
house in a furious rush. She appeared to be in her late forties
and was white. "Don't hurt him, Jesse. Please don't hurt
him!"

"You shut up, Mercy. Did you think I wouldn't find you?
Livin' here like a common whore with this . . . this darkie man
friend of yore'n. No sister of mine is goin' to carry on such as
that." Brennan slapped her savagely across the face, knocking
her back against the porch. Two other men grabbed the
squirming captive and quickly bound his wrists with rope.

John Colby watched in horror. His mouth was dry. He
seemed unable to move. He sat still on his horse, as did
Jeremiah Peace. Brennan looked toward them and drew one
of the horse pistols. "Do you git off them horses, or do I
shoot you off?" They jumped off the horses.

"Oh, Lord! Oh, save me, Lord!" the man screamed. Drake
struck him with a pistol butt, but the man only thrashed and
screamed the louder. So they dragged him through the mud
to a gnarled oak tree. Someone uncoiled a rope and lofted it
over a low, drooping limb. The woman was screaming again.
John Colby looked up and down the street, thinking that
surely the townsfolk would come out from their houses. But
nobody came. The houses were silent, the mud street empty.
Only the soft rise of blue smoke from chimneys gave evidence of life at all.

It took three men to hoist the struggling Negro onto a
horse—John Colby's swaybacked mare—while a fourth man
dropped a hangman's loop around his neck and jerked it
tight. As the loop was secured, the man ceased his struggling
and shouting and sat silently, looking toward the sky. His lips

moved wordlessly. A heavy stillness settled over the street, broken only by the woman's sobs by the porch. "Don't kill him, Jesse. Please don't kill him. He never done no harm, and he's been good to me. Please..."

Brennan ignored her, strode to John Colby and stood confronting him, flicking a small horsewhip against his boot. "What's the matter, Stewart? You look pale as death. You ain't got the stomach for this, is that it? Well, boy, we'll fix that in a hurry. What you need's a little experience." He grabbed John Colby's arm, twisted his hand open and slapped the handle of the whip into it. "You're goin' to do the honors, fellow."

"D-Do the honors?"

"You're goin' to kill yourself a nigger."

John Colby's stomach knotted. Sweat glazed his face. Feeling the weight of the whip in his hand, he walked to the swaybacked mare and looked up into the face of the doomed man. The Negro looked down at him with no expression. John Colby's mind was in a turmoil. How could this happen? What was he doing here? And yet here he was, and suddenly his own fate was bound inextricably with that of this man whom he didn't even know. For no reason at all, it seemed terribly important for the deed not to be totally callous; he should know at least something about this Negro, some scrap of information. He heard himself saying, "What is your name?"

The Negro's eyes blinked. An expression of surprise flicked over his face. "My name?"

"Your name. What is your name."

"My name is Cotton Mayhew."

"How old are you, Cotton Mayhew?"

"I don't know. I never learned. But I ain't fifty yet, I'm sure of that. Is you... is you going to send me to Glory?"

"Yes."

"Oooh, Lord!"

"Get on with it," Jesse Brennan snapped.

John Colby lifted the whip. The swaybacked mare, suddenly restless, shifted her feet. The Negro swayed in the saddle, his face the color of brown ashes, and shut his eyes tight.

"Do it!" Brennan said.

"Forgive me, Cotton Mayhew," John Colby said. And he brought down the whip on the mare's flank, hard.

Whack!

With a shrill whinny, the horse bolted forward. A gasp

came from the throat of the Negro and was cut off. The body
dragged from the saddle, legs flailing. He seemed to contort
at the waist, jerking upward against his own weight in a
wrenching spasm. The eyes bulged from their sockets, the
face contorted, the neck snapped, the legs ceased their
thrashing, the body swung, the rope creaked softly, the toes
twitched . . . twitched . . . twitched . . .

John Colby doubled over and vomited.

The mare whinnied again, shrilly, and her hoofbeats went
thundering away down the muddy street.

The men stood in a loose cluster, looking up at the figure
swaying in the breeze, silently avoiding each other's eyes. In
the unexpected hush of death, there was only the sound of
the woman sobbing by the porch.

They rode out of the town without speaking and not
looking back, the bulky, slope-shouldered Jesse Brennan in
the lead. Not until that evening, when there was distance
behind them and a campfire roaring by the river and men
could wash away the memory of it by swigging down fiery
whiskey, did speech return.

"How come nobody showed his face in that town?" one of
the men asked. "Ain't they got no law, no constable? It was
spooky. Not a soul come out of them houses."

Drake wiped the neck of a bottle and took a long swallow,
his Adam's apple bobbing in the firelight. He put the bottle
down and said, "They ain't got no law. That's a nigger town.
Ain't nobody in that town but niggers."

"Except for one white woman," another voice said.

Drake's eyes flicked nervously to the lean-to, some distance up the slope. Jesse Brennan had summoned Jeremiah
Peace to the lean-to and sat drinking while the boy, shivering
and weeping, awaited his next ordeal.

"That's right," Drake said, "except for one white woman."

Two days later, John Colby left the Brennan gang and made
his way north. He rode hard, haunted by the memory of a
body swaying in the breeze, haunted by old Bigelow's words:
Evil begets evil.

IX

Dinner was a bore. But then it was always so. Francesca despised the forced pleasantries, the banalities. A necessity, however; business did make its unique demands.

"Lovely party, Francesca."

"Thank you, Browne. Charming."

"I think we have an excellent opportunity to secure the Birdwell contract. He seems more amenable to shipping by water. Family tradition, and all that."

"Is he signed?"

"Uh, not yet."

"Sign him, Browne."

"The cost, Francesca. It is still a trifle steep, compared to rail."

"Fiddlesticks."

She sighed, fluttering her fan. The evening was warm, and her underthings beneath the formal gown were uncomfortable. Down the glittering table, the faces of the guests turned toward her and smiled their bland smiles. Like cardboard cutouts, she thought, all in a row. But then they all worked for Stewart Company, or were jobbers and shippers and their wives. Francesca knew what they said behind her back, and relished the random whispers.

"Tough businesswoman."

"Right you are, Jack."

"Thinks like a man."

"Runs a tight ship."

"Pity she's still not married."

The latter nettled her somewhat. It was one thing to be the queen of New York's inland shipping commerce, but quite another to know they were so aware of her loneness. She thought of it that way during long evenings of isolation in this

165

great house with no one about but the butler and the maid.
Alone, but not lonely. Francesca Stewart lived with pride,
and could do without the rest of them. She was her father's
daughter.

"Who is that man at the foot of the table, Browne, the one
in the checkered vest seated beside Minerva Carp?"

"That's her son, Poindexter. Lawyer."

"Odd, I didn't meet him earlier."

"Quiet chap. Reserved, they say. Attentive to his mother."

"And his wife, where is she?"

"Bachelor."

"Thank you, Browne."

Talk was a spirited murmur, punctuated by sounds of
cutlery and the pouring of wine. For years Francesca had not
permitted spirits at table, but lately had decided it was better
to serve wine than to be considered a prudish hostess. People
did seem to relax and have a better time with drinks,
although she did not personally indulge and disapproved of
women who did.

The table talk became louder and more boisterous. Claude
Matting, the banker, carried on a lively discussion with the
owner of a stevedoring company. Matting's face was flushed.

". . . link this great land coast to coast, and that'll be a
wonderful thing. Wonderful thing, I say. You'll ship goods,
riverboat and rail, at a fraction of the cost. There's very
strong sentiment in the Congress for the transcontinental
railroad. Very strong. It's just a matter of picking a route,
that's all. Picking a route."

"Claude, it's not a certainty."

"Nonsense, my man. Look at Chicago. The town's booming
there in northern Illinois. Who'd have thought it? Chicago
was a lake and canal terminal until now. And look at what's
happening. It's become a railroad center, biggest in the Middle West. You got the Chicago and Rock Island, the Michigan
Southern—Sam Reed was location engineer for the Michigan
Southern, Francesca; used to work for your dad building the
Erie Canal—and the Illinois Central. In a few years I look for
a dozen more railroads to come into Chicago, direct from
Cleveland, Pittsburgh, St. Louis, Milwaukee—"

Francesca's eyes flashed. "My father believed in steamboats and canals. Waterways opened this country and waterways are still the backbone of commerce."

"Francesca, I'm not disputing that. There'll always be

water shipping. Some bulk cargos—coal, crushed stone, iron ore—naturally move cheaper in certain areas by water. The Great Lakes are natural waterways, and the Erie and Ohio canals connect up to the inland river systems. But rail, that's the wave of the future. Fortunes are being made in rail, right now. I think you ought to get in on it, Francesca, instead of fighting progress. Why, you've got a couple of nephews already involved. That young Thaddeus Stewart, I hear, made a fine divisional engineer on the Illinois Central. Then there's that young financial whiz right here in New York, Brack Stewart."

"Brack?"

"Right. The son of your cousin Maybelle from out in San Francisco. I've had some bank dealings with him. The lad's sharp as a tack. Sharp as a tack. Got his eye on railroads. Sees a bonanza there."

Francesca felt her irritation rising. Matting was a damn fool when he drank. Now he sat at her own table spouting ludicrous claptrap. But she couldn't antagonize the man. Deliberately she turned to a man at her left and asked, "Do you think John Brown was mad?" The question, of course, provoked a noisy babble. The antislavery insurrection and hanging of the zealot Brown was on everybody's mind. It inspired more talk even than the much ballyhooed political debates between Illinois Senator Stephen Douglas and his losing challenger for the seat, the lawyer Abraham Lincoln. The subject of railroads was quickly overwhelmed.

Claude Matting raised his glass to Francesca. "Touché," he murmured.

When dinner ended, Francesca led her guests to the parlor. The mood subdued once more. She sought out Minerva Carp. The widow, an ample-bosomed socialite with a glint of challenge in her eye, stood with her son. Poindexter Carp was a pudgy man with soft eyes and thinning hair. He seemed ill at ease. Francesca ignored him and extended her hand to the widow. "So delighted you could come to my little party, Minerva. I hope you found the food and company to your liking."

"Delightful, Francesca. And may I say how splendidly you do entertain." The woman was stout, with an imperious gaze and firm handshake. Her gown was tastefully simple, and she wore a single strand of beads. "Miss Stewart, have you met my son Poindexter?"

Francesca seemed to notice Carp for the first time. She gave him her best smile. She shook his hand and found it soft and damp. She gave it an extra squeeze of greeting. There was no palpable response. "Mr. Carp." She offered a girlish curtsy.

"Um, Mrs., um, Stewart."

"Miss Stewart." She fluttered her fan. "Dear me."

The rest of the chat was perfunctory. Francesca returned the steady gaze of Minerva Carp in kind, spoke no more to her dullard of a son and found in wordless woman-to-woman communication a kindred spirit. They parted with Francesca's warm invitation to tea the following Thursday and Minerva Carp's vigorous acceptance. Within the half hour, mother and son departed with the other guests, in a hansom cab.

Two days later, in her office overlooking the Hudson River waterfront, Francesca heard a preliminary report from Blake Plumwether, her male secretary and general factotum. He read rapidly from a notebook, peering through steel-rimmed spectacles. "Minerva Carp, age fifty-five, widow of Robert Carp. He was in the mercantile business and left her moderately well-fixed, but bank records indicate her finances are no longer secure. Bad investments. The son Poindexter, age thirty-five, is unmarried and has a modest practice as an attorney-at-law. He lives at home with his mother and appears to be devoted to her. He seems to lack social connections or strong interest in females, though on occasion he patronizes ladies of the evening. Carp was engaged to marry some years ago, but his mother became quite ill and the engagement was broken off. There was no breach-of-promise suit, so I assume the break was amicable."

Francesca stood at the window, absorbing Plumwether's report. On the river, the morning packet to Albany moved away from the wharf. It was a sturdy white vessel with the name *The Stewart Company* prominently displayed between thin smokestacks. The deck cargo appeared to be untidily stowed. She made a mental note to have the deficiency corrected.

"And his health?" she asked.

Plumwether scanned the notes, muttering softly to himself. The habit irritated Francesca, but she kept silent. He replied, "The family physician says that aside from a mild touch of gout, Mr. Carp's health is good."

"Thank you, Plumwether. That will be all."

Minerva Carp arrived promptly for tea on Thursday and was ushered into the sunroom. Actually this was a glassed-in addition to the back of the mansion, shaded by awnings and commanding a marvelous view of the broad, sloped yard, the massive family crypt with its separate garden, and the slate-still river. Francesca had had the sunroom built to her own plan, furnished in a patio motif with numerous potted palms. Massed small-paned windows opened to admit the breeze from the river. The air at this time of summer was cooled by stately elms and maples surrounding the estate.

"What a lovely view," Minerva Carp murmured. "And that structure near the river, is that the famous Stewart crypt?"

"Yes. My father built that crypt for my mother." Francesca busied herself with the tea things. She steeped and brewed in the English manner, and preferred to do it herself. The serving maid brought small wedge-shaped cookies on a crystal tray. "Mother died in the cholera epidemic of eighteen thirty-two at Syracuse. Father was building the Erie Canal at the time. He adored my mother. He never got over it." Her face softened in the afternoon light. Minerva Carp's eyes widened slightly. The wistful expression erased momentarily the hard edges of Francesca Stewart's features and made them almost beautiful. "He believed that they would be together again in the hereafter, and even hired a spiritualist to try to communicate with her spirit. I don't think he had any success. He wanted her tomb to be the finest in America, and I suppose it is. That's all imported Italian marble. He brought the stonecutters from Italy. He would sit for hours on that bench down there under the great elm tree. I lived here with him, you know. My sister..."

Minerva Carp sensed an opening and deftly probed it. "I know what you mean." She sighed. "Some young people lack proper devotion to their parents." She put down her cup and hurried on. "And I do sympathize with how your father must have grieved. Poor man. He was so famous, so brilliant and yet so—how shall I put it?"

"Loyal," Francesca said. "My father was loyal."

"That's it. Loyal."

It was a mutual touching by words, no more. Minerva Carp knew that she had done well. They passed from it quickly to speak of the humidity, the lovely party, Francesca's gown ("May I say how much I admire your taste in clothes?" Minerva purred. "So subtle, so balanced, and yet not slavish to fashion.") and the enormity of this graystone mansion, Blossom Hill.

To her own surprise, Francesca found herself enjoying the chatty conversation of this older woman. Minerva Carp's fortunes might indeed be turning for the worse, but she made no mention of that and bore herself with dignity. Regardless of the actual relationship with her husband during his lifetime—Plumwether's report noted that he had been a stuffy man, pedantic and humorless—she sanctified his memory. There was no talk of the hard lot of the widow in today's world, for which Francesca was grateful.

Francesca decided to come to the point.

"Your son Poindexter seems such a pleasant man."

"Pleasant? Perhaps so. But inclined to be rather dull, I fear." Minerva Carp's face lifted in an engaging smile. "Nonetheless, he is loyal to me and I appreciate that enormously. He does have his good points."

"His law practice, does it thrive?"

"Dear me, no. Poindexter's problem is that he lacks the spunk to succeed. He is just not aggressive, no get-up-and-go." She gave Francesca a meaningful glance. "I think it takes the right woman to prod a man to succeed, don't you? In his case, the right woman simply has not come along. And I don't mind telling you, he is thirty-five years old and life is passing him by."

Francesca sighed. "Yes. We all have our needs, don't we?"

"Life's plums are not plucked by those who won't reach."

"Minerva . . . may I call you Minerva?"

"Please."

"As you know, I'm a woman in business. I've carried on my father's enterprise, expanded and shaped it, tried to give it vigor. In this respect, I am unlike my sister Marguerite, who has chosen to marry an Army colonel and now lives in Washington. Be that as it may, she retains her share of our family holdings, even though she does not choose to contribute to their earnings." Francesca rose from the settee and strolled to the windows. From old habit, she preferred to speak on her feet. "Marguerite and I are sisters, but blood is not always thicker than water. I want to think that we love each other, but I'm not certain of that. Do you get my meaning?"

"Absolutely, my dear."

"What it boils down to is this: I am a woman alone, doing

competitive business in a world dominated by males. It is a man's world out there, whether or not they deserve it. Someday that may change. But this is eighteen fifty-eight. I had to fight to win what was properly mine. Because I'm a woman, those who controlled my father's business considered me unfit to be president and chief executive officer of a commercial enterprise of Hudson River steamships, freight warehouses and canal packet boats. We barge freight over a half-dozen canals, ranging north to Canada and west to Chicago."

"A marvelous enterprise."

"Perhaps. And there are those, as I'm sure you've perceived, who look askance and wonder why I've not yet chosen to marry. I don't have to tell you that a woman controlling a business of this magnitude is not lacking in opportunity. I could have gone down the aisle long ago, Minerva." She turned from the window, eyes flashing. "But why the hell should I? Why should I hand all this"—her hand made a sweeping gesture, encompassing the sunroom, the mansion, the tree-shaded grounds, the river and beyond—"to some man, just because he was born with a pair of balls?"

Minerva Carp's eyebrows lifted. A faint smile touched her mouth. She sat primly erect in her chair and said nothing.

"I am, however, a businesswoman. It would behoove me, as a businesswoman, to have a husband with whom I could be identified. There are many things to be done, and a woman alone is at a distinct disadvantage as she attempts to achieve them. Today, for example, decisions affecting our lives are made in Washington, notably in Congress. Decisions also are made routinely at the ballot box. But the door to the political process is marked 'Men only.' It is closed to women. We don't even have the right to vote!"

"Surely you're not suggesting . . ."

"That women should have the right to vote? Of course, I'm suggesting it. I'm saying it. But I'm one voice shouting down the rain barrel, and even I don't say it in public. Besides, the time is not right. The nation is already too split over slavery to be saddled with women's rights as well. One right at a time is about all we can stand to dispute at the moment. And believe me, Minerva, the slavery issue will plunge us into war. Before this is resolved, we'll have a bloodbath that will make the Revolution look like a back-alley brawl."

"I've never heard a woman speak of these things before. It

isn't our province to speak of such things." The face of
Minerva Carp seemed to contort as her mind groped for a
logic that was not there. There was almost a guilt upon
Minerva, to think that Francesca—or any woman—would
dare to intrude in areas so restricted to the world of men.

For a moment, Francesca felt pity for this woman, who for
all her apparent strength of character remained locked into
traditional femininity. "Don't let it trouble you too much right
now," she said gently. "Besides, that isn't the point. The point
is, I've got a business proposition for you, and it might be to
our mutual advantage."

Mrs. Carp nodded. "Yes, it might at that."

"I believe that your son Poindexter has unique characteris-
tics. Frankly, I find them quite attractive."

"My intuition told me as much."

"I propose a business arrangement, a contract between
Poindexter and me. A marriage, but in civil ceremony and
subject to cancellation by either party on demand. In return,
you shall have ample financial reward and your money problems will be stabilized."

"My money problems?" Dismay flooded Minerva Carp's
face. "How did you know?"

"It doesn't matter, Minerva. These things are impossible to
keep secret. I have my information. Your financial condition
is, to put it mildly, precarious. You're in danger of losing your
home. Your bank account is in dreadful shape."

Minerva Carp bit at her lip. Francesca stopped speaking
and waited in silence. At last, the widow's face brightened.
"Just think of it. I'm to have a daughter-in-law!"

Francesca smiled. "More tea?"

The wooing of Poindexter Carp was quick to kindle and did
not escape the notice of New York society. Almost overnight,
the once standoffish Francesca Stewart was seen at various
functions in the company of Minerva Carp and her bachelor
son. The sudden rush of activity took them to museums, and
galleries, plays, concerts, openings and, of course, to private
parties which Francesca had avoided in the past. Hostesses
alert to opportunity vied with each other to invite them. The
presence of Francesca Stewart was a feather in one's cap. It
was more than Francesca's wealth, which of itself was enormous; there was the very mystique of Stewart involvement.
She was the daughter of Nathan Stewart, who had been
associated with Robert Fulton in developing the commercial

steamship and with De Witt Clinton in construction of the
Erie Canal. Nathan Stewart was a man who himself had set
tongues to wagging with his love affairs and, finally, his
marriage to Yvette Marchand, the stunning French ward of
the blue-blooded Livingston family. While all this was now
decades in the past, society rarely forgot. Stewart credentials
were impeccable. Besides, it all made for lovely gossip and
speculation, livening an otherwise dull social season.

"You know, I never before thought of Francesca as being
especially attractive, did you? Not unattractive, mind you—
heavens, with all that wealth—but, you know, plain."

"Plain."

"Precisely. I felt that she was plain. But now, my dear,
those new gowns are stunning. She orders them from Paris,
you know. And her hair, it has a rather nice luster, wouldn't
you say? She had something done to soften her face, especially around the eyes."

"Do you suspect she's using rouge?"

"I wouldn't be at all surprised."

"She is taller than Poindexter, but I don't suppose that
really matters."

"What a coup for Minerva, eh? Poor dear, just hanging on,
they say."

"Certainly his future would be secure, if . . ."

"If what?"

"Do you really think they will . . . ?"

Francesca found herself relishing the new role. It had begun
for her as a purely tactical venture, a pretext for injecting
herself directly into the life of Poindexter Carp. The plan was
that of Minerva Carp herself, who knew that her son could be
relied upon as the dutiful escort for his mother and her
unattached female friends. Ordinarily these were older wom-
en, widows prudently chosen by Minerva for their stability
and maturity. Never before did Minerva even tolerate the
idea of Poindexter marrying. He was too unassuming, too
dependent, and no woman could rise to her standards. And
so the relationship between mother and son had developed
into strong friendship and mutual dependency. She knew that
he was drawn occasionally to ladies of the evening; she
strongly disapproved, but could not bring herself to acknowledge openly that Poindexter could succumb to such base
appetites. The very thought of it caused her to shudder.
However, she was not above using the knowledge—deftly

hinting at it—to cause him discomfort. Minerva also knew that the delicate nature of her health could bring Poindexter around. Indeed, her sudden attack of migraine headaches had broken up his only serious attempt to stray—the engagement to that storekeeper's daughter some years ago. Now, of course, it was all coming to fruition. Minerva Carp was positively ecstatic, and shared Francesca's own rising excitement as the friendship of the three of them ripened.

In due time, Minerva was stricken with a headache on an evening in which they had planned to go out, and announced that she would remain at home.

"I'll stay with you, Mother," Poindexter said.

"No, no, my dear. You must pick up Francesca. She is expecting us. She would be so disappointed. You two go ahead and have a good time."

Thus, Poindexter Carp and Francesca Stewart began to appear more and more often without the company of his mother. They attended the Harvest Ball and the Autumn Beaux Arts. They were seen at Mrs. Cornelius Bryant's annual pre-Thanksgiving soiree and were together at a number of parties during the Christmas season. As January closed in over the city with snow and ice and weeks of gray, cheerless days and freezing nights, speculation about the most prominent new twosome in New York warmed the hearts of matronly matchmakers.

He was attentive and presentable. His manners were quite good. Behind the blandness, Francesca sensed a keen intelligence. To her surprise, he read widely and well and kept abreast of political affairs. He was not without friends, some of them in high places. He played whist with exceptional skill and was at ease on the dance floor. He was an easy companion. If he recognized that he was being maneuvered toward marriage with Francesca Stewart and that his mother was part of the conspiracy, Poindexter Carp made no acknowledgment of it. He was, after all, devoted to his mother—a matter of temperament and conditioning—and this was his most pronounced weakness. To Francesca's practical mind, such devotion was a mixed blessing. It took from Poindexter the independence and strength of character she admired in a man, and without which she could not love him; and yet this powerful constraint upon his life provided her with her own opportunity. She did regard Poindexter as an opportunity—a bright but malleable man who could be shaped and motivated by a clever woman. He was a piece of living clay, as it were, awaiting the molding of the artist's hands.

"Poindexter, my dear, I can't remember what life was like before I met you and your mother. She is such a dear. And I must confess, you both have brought so much pleasure into my life."

The mood was subtle. Francesca carefully picked her words and tone of voice to match that subtlety. They sat in the east parlor of her house, which she had converted into a library. A fire danced in the grate beneath a massive stone chimney that her father had built. It was snowing again. Outside, gaslights made pools of light in the soft whiteness of the earth, and reflected thick falling snowflakes. Again, Minerva Carp had been unwell and Poindexter had come alone. Artfully, Francesca had suggested that they change their plans about going out. And so they had dined together by candlelight while Poindexter enjoyed a fine Bordeaux wine. Now, as they shared the settee and the fire, Francesca poured brandy for him, leaning across and brushing her breast against his arm.

He was not a handsome man. His hair was thin, his face a bit too round, his skin colorless and given to easy perspiring. She did not love him. But that, Francesca reasoned, made it even better. But could she arouse feelings in him? They talked of art. They talked of the string quartet they had heard last week. The flush of brandy was upon him and he laughed overly much. She laughed with him and slipped her hand under his arm.

"We're being naughty," she said.

"Well, so we are. Delightful. Delightful," he said. "And I must say, the roast was fantastic. I don't know when I've had better."

"You're not sorry that we stayed home?"

"Not at all." He chuckled, sipped brandy, cleared his throat. "Not at all."

She placed her hand upon his thigh. It seemed a thoughtless gesture, not intended for intimacy. They chatted on. Then she hesitated. "My word."

She drew her hand away. "I had my hand on your . . . on your limb. What must you think of me?"

His eyes blinked. His mouth worked. He drew a handkerchief and dabbed at his forehead. "Really?" he said. "I, um, thought nothing of it, nothing at all. Really . . ."

"No, you must think I'm terrible, like one of those . . . those tarts I've heard about. A woman must control her desires, don't you think? It is unseemly for a female to desire."

"Yes. Well, I . . . that is . . ."

"It's just that I feel so close to you, Poindexter. Isn't that a terrible thing to say? I have . . . I have impulses when I'm near you." Her eyes caught his and held them. She saw the shyness there, the indecision. Damn! She got to her feet, walked around the room. "I feel that I am betraying your mother's confidence in me. She is such a dear friend."

"Mother loves you very much. She said so."

"And I love her, Poindexter. But the difficulty is that I also . . ." She caught herself.

"What?"

"Nothing. Never mind."

She stood at the fireplace, looking into the flames. The low light was deliberate, accentuating the dark softness of her eyes. She had done them in a new shadow makeup, just a hint of it, to make them seem larger. She wore her hair in an upsweep, framing her face and reducing the hardness of her features. She heard him get up from the settee and approach her from behind. "Francesca?" he said. "My dear."

"I feel badly about this, Poindexter," she said.

"Don't. It's human to want." His hands came to her waist, lightly as birds settling and ready to fly. She could hear his breathing. He was standing directly behind her now, and very gradually she drew back from the fireplace, so that her body was touching his. He said: "Francesca?" She turned then and drew him to her. The kiss was moist, brief and their lips not fully met. But it was enough. He was groping for her, breathing hard. The hardness was at his groin, pressing against her, and she sighed. It was not unpleasant, and despite herself Francesca felt unexpected stirrings.

"Francesca." His hand touched her breast.

Gently, she pushed him away. "Please, Poindexter. You're making me weak."

"Francesca."

"Not here, darling. Not now. I'm a respectable woman. We must not . . ." But deliberately, she put her hand down to his hardness and squeezed it. He groaned, clumsily tried again to kiss her, found her suddenly cold and unyielding, was flustered. She drew away from him, went to the closet, found his coat and hat. "Now, really, you must be good. Whatever possessed you, Poindexter?" She reached for the bell cord and rang for the butler. "It has been a lovely evening. Now you must go home."

Five minutes later Poindexter Carp was in his carriage, pulling away down the snowy drive. Francesca stood at the window, waving until he vanished from sight. She went up the stairs smiling to herself, undressed for bed and blew out the lamp.

The house settled into its familiar silences and the cold of the night deepened, but she could not sleep. Her mind kept drifting back to the feel of his excitement in her hand. A tremor passed through her body.

Six weeks later, Minerva Carp sent out cards announcing the engagement of her son, Poindexter Carp, Esq., and Miss Francesca Marchand Stewart of Blossom Hill. Excitement gripped New York society. As spring arrived, parties and receptions for the couple took place at a heady pace. It all culminated in the wedding on the third of June in the Community Chapel on Fifth Avenue. And then they were off in a shower of rice for a honeymoon voyage by steamer up the Hudson to the Erie Canal, westward by packet boat to Lake Erie, and then a leisurely cruise of the Great Lakes to Chicago.

The bride, it was said, refused to take the train.

Upon their return, Poindexter Carp's law practice unexpectedly began to expand and take on importance. There were those clients drawn to him for legal advice simply because he was the husband of Francesca Stewart Carp. But others shrewdly deduced that Poindexter Carp in the future might become a man to reckon with. The Hudson River mansion also took on a new life, drawing dinner guests from a wide spectrum of city and state leadership. Old political loyalties, going back to the years of Nathan Stewart's considerable efforts as a wheeler-dealer on behalf of the Erie Canal, were freshened and rekindled by Francesca. Poindexter himself turned up at more and more public functions. His public speaking ability, never one of his strengths, began to improve and take on character. What his listeners did not know was that night after night in the library of the mansion, Poindexter Carp rehearsed speeches written by Blake Plumwether at Francesca's instructions. Standing before a full-length mirror, with Francesca and his mother to monitor and critique, he repeated the bold cadences and high-flown political rhetoric. A speech instructor arrived twice a week to drill him in diction. ("Now then, Mr. Carp, repeat after me: How now brown cow. It isn't precisely what you say, but how you say it that matters.") A tailor came to redesign his wardrobe. From Washington there arrived a senior Congressional aide to do nothing but discuss current national events and the inside realities of Capitol cloakrooms. He developed a philosophy that was basically conservative, pro-business, and moderate on slavery, though Francesca found in him irritating tendencies toward populism. On the subject of expansionism, it was understood that Poindexter Carp would endorse and share his wife's most ardent and unyielding position: absolute opposition to giving away federal lands for the purpose of financing construction of railroads.

"The railroad barons will pick our pockets if we let them," Francesca declared. "They will plunder our most vital natural resource, land, and will turn the people's heritage into their greedy profit. We must resist this possibility wherever it arises, and especially the most diabolical plunder of all, the transcontinental railroad."

It went on for eighteen months. For eighteen months, Poindexter Carp was groomed, rehearsed, prodded and praised. His sense of self-esteem, never significant before, began to thrive. Francesca saw to it that he was recognized by important people, interviewed by the journals and invited to all the proper functions, with her by his side.

At last, one evening at dinner with Minerva Carp, Francesca sprang her little surprise on Poindexter. "My dear, I've had delightful political discussions with the governor and several Tammany people this week. They feel that the time is ripe and the man is ready. They asked me to find out how you feel about it. Naturally, I was thrilled and proud."

"My word, Francesca," Minerva Carp said brightly, "whatever are you talking about?"

"It's Poindexter, Mother. They're all just wild about Poindexter. A dynamic new presence in politics, they call him. They want Poindexter to run for the United States Senate!"

Poindexter Carp choked on his soup.

X

The morning was a misty gray wash at his window. Brack Stewart studied the gathering light from his bed. He had awakened gradually, luxuriously, and then lay in the quiet, letting his mind absorb impressions. The female body beside him was a soft presence, breathing quietly in sleep. He was only partially conscious of her, and more as a rhythmic entity than a living creature. Her name, he recalled, was Evelyn Grand and she was an actress. Her behavior in bed was as wild as Brack's fantasies had been when he first saw her on the stage. That was gratifying. One never knew what a new seduction would bring. The thought was making him harden again.

He concentrated his mind upon himself. It was a matter of habit. Brack Stewart rarely thought beyond himself, a fact which seemed to contribute to his remarkable career success. He focused now upon his organic system: heartbeat, blood flow, breathing, sexual awakening. He imagined himself looking about inside muscle and viscera, lungs, testicles. Here I am. This is me. Brack Stewart. At the same time, he was conscious of his surroundings as they related to him. The bachelor apartment was one of his pleasures, a place of good woods and carpets, brass fixtures, crystal decanters (he did not care for alcohol but saw that visitors were amply supplied), subdued elegance and objets d'art. His windows commanded a superb view of the busy New York harbor. The whole never failed to impress those who came to share his nights.

He smiled, thinking of the variety of experiences that had come to this bed. Gradually the part of him which did not think and reason took charge, as he'd known it would. The outward conscious mind ceased its drifting and turned in-

179

ward. The familiar lust filled his senses. He pushed off the
covers and looked down at himself. Stand there, proud devil,
he thought. Slowly, he moved his bare left foot under the
sheet until it touched hers. Slowly, his entire left leg closed
against the satin warmth of her leg and thigh. Slowly, he drew
down the covers to expose the pearly nudeness of her.
Instinctively, she curled her body against the light and air,
turning her back to him. He moved against her and slipped
his fullness gently between her thighs. She murmured in her
gradual awakening, sighed, responded to his undulations.
Her hair was a mass of soft brown on the pillow, faintly
scented. Her jawline and throat and breasts glowed in the
gray light, unblemished and perfectly formed.

"Good morning," he whispered.

She smiled and turned to him. She stretched deliberately,
exciting him more. Her eyes flickered open. They were violet
and thickly-lashed. The mouth smiled, full-lipped and warm.
His hand touched her breast, lightly stroked the swelling
brown nipples. His mouth sought her throat.

"Brack," she said.

"I woke up wanting you."

"Darling, my goodness..."

"What?"

"That goes all through me."

"Here?"

"There. Yes, darling, there."

Afterwards, they lay entwined. The quiet was intense. He
sensed his heartbeat subsiding. The gray light warmed at the
window. Rising on one elbow, he looked out. The mist had
broken; the harbor came into view. Sunlight appeared, lighting the stern of a steamship chugging out from the Battery
beneath an escort of circling seabirds.

"I will leave you now," he said.

He bathed, shaved, dressed in a black suit, freshly starched
linen, and soft black boots buffed to a high polish. He
brushed his long black hair straight back, mindful of the
sheen of its natural waves. The mirror reflected delicate
features and piercing brown eyes. The nose was almost too
perfect in its symmetry. The smile was a flash of even white
teeth, and he used it more often for effect than feeling. ("A
cruel smile," somebody had called it. "You have a cruel smile,
Brack, and it's breaking a thousand hearts.") So be it. He put
away the matched set of silver-backed hair brushes, donned a

new beaver hat of pearl gray, let himself out of the apartment
by the front door and bounced down the steps, whistling.

The morning was fine, the streets of New York were
already crowded with horse-drawn carriages and hansom
cabs. He strode up Fifth Avenue with a spring in his step and
life surging from each fiber and pore. He delighted in the
vigor of it, was enthralled by his own sense of well-being.
Around him, the city flourished. There were new buildings
everywhere, buildings with imposing facades and delicate
stonework—nymphs and cherubs were in fashion, which he
considered tasteless. He saw the morning alive with pedestrians, carriages, pushcarts, cyclists. He heard the cacophony of
city noises—horses' hooves, carriage wheels, jingling bells,
pianofortes, violin strings squeaking from upstairs windows
and a singer doing scales, hammering hammers and rasping
saws, the whistles of constables, cries of street vendors and
the hoot of distant steamship horns.

A letter had come from his mother last week. "Come to
San Francisco," she wrote. "You'll love it here, Brack. We're
swarming with newcomers. The town is booming. There are
fortunes to be made at every hand." The letter had taken six
weeks to reach New York. San Francisco, indeed! The thought
gave him a cynical smile. Imagine giving up all this to go off
to some shantytown in the West to do business with miners
and rogues and thieves. Oh, he knew San Francisco all right.
Everybody did. It was a wild and uncivilized place, swarming
with human flotsam, where his mother lived in a tacky
eighty-room mansion on Nob Hill counting her gold and
presiding over the biggest string of whorehouses in the West,
or perhaps even the world. She was Maybelle Stewart, the
Bordello Queen of San Francisco. And he, Brack Stewart,
Harvard, summa cum laude, had embarked upon a bright
career in the heady world of high finance in New York. In
certain inner sanctums of wealth, it was whispered, Brack
Stewart already was being quietly watched with great expec-
tations. He was supposed to chuck all this and go West? Not
hardly, Mother dear.

"Good morning, Stewart." The speaker was Cyrus Pound, a
pale, hawk-faced former schoolmate at Harvard now trading
on the Exchange. The man was colorless but moderately
successful. "Bullion is up, I hear. Are ye buying or selling?"

"Sitting it out, Pound. If war comes, there'll be richer
pickings in arms, wouldn't you say?"

"And if it doesn't?"

"If it doesn't, I'll opt for land."

"Not bullion, then?"

"Not hardly."

He left Pound glumly shaking his head. Why ask a question, he thought, if you only want to hear one answer?

Well, he would have to visit his mother, he supposed. The old girl was not getting any younger and they hadn't seen each other since his middle teens. She'd packed her girls in wagons and gone overland from St. Louis to California, leaving Brack in the care of friends of the powerful Senator Thomas Hart Benton. And it was these guardians who'd gotten him into Harvard. Maybelle Stewart had always provided funds somehow, even in the worst of times. He disliked thinking about that, knowing his sustenance was the fruit of his mother's occupation. He was not alone in this discomfort. His sister Vanessa, writing from finishing school in Paris, had confessed in a letter, "How I dread going home to San Francisco! If only mother would give up this dreadful business of dealing in whores. Out of sheer mortification, I can't ever invite my friends to visit my home." His sister had grown into a beauty, he had been told. Well, that was one bright spot. The boyhood memory of Maybelle's constant lectures about the Stewarts, and what sons of bitches they were, gave him a less-than-enthusiastic sense of family identity. Not that family attachments mattered all that much; hell, he really cared for no one and avoided strong personal relationships anyway. It was his nature, he reckoned. And besides, there was real strength in detachment.

He arrived at the handsome brick and marble building housing the offices of Hagen & Watts, Financiers. It was so designated by a single brass plate gleaming beside the ornate double doors. He took the granite steps two at a time and pushed into the cool main lobby with its veined marble floors, sculpted ceilings, and echoes.

"Good morning, Mr. Stewart," a male receptionist called. "They are gathering in the boardroom just now."

"Thank you, Harrison."

He moved quickly up broad, carpeted stairs, letting his mind play upon the immediate task at hand: the taking of the Nolichuckey and Southern Railroad. If all went as planned, this would turn out to be a profitable morning indeed.

It was vital to communicate in business. But it was equally

vital, Brack Stewart had long since deduced, to anticipate. This was an instinctive thing, not to be learned from whole libraries of economics and finance. The knack had vaulted him, not yet thirty years old and a scant five years out of Harvard, into his position as an associate with the firm of Hagen & Watts. His exact function, however, was kept deliberately vague.

Shrewd McRoberts Hagen, a Scottish immigrant arriving penniless in New York, had amassed a fortune in various banking and lending enterprises. He knew from experience that a bright young man commanded greater leverage as a factotum. In commerce, as in politics, it was beneficial to keep one's true power masked. At the same time, young Stewart was paid extremely well. Hagen recognized, after all, that such a combination of mind and personality was rare. Stewart was worth many times his wages in profits generated to the company. McRoberts Hagen was a cold and manipulative person, canny in the ways of power. But he recognized in Brack Stewart something more, a mercilessness which he once expressed to an intimate. "The lad is utterly ruthless. He is without pity. He will go far."

The morning staff meeting was ritualistic. A half-dozen officials of the firm, including Brack, stood beside their high-backed chairs awaiting the arrival of the chairman. Hagen always walked into the boardroom at three minutes past nine o'clock, on the dot. "Punctuality, gentlemen," he was fond of reciting, "is natural to the ordered mind." It went without saying that there was no place in Hagen & Watts for the disordered mind. Hagen was a huge man, given to gastronomic excess, yet he was fastidious in dress, carefully groomed. To accommodate his girth an extra wide, overstuffed chair had been built; to avoid its being conspicuous, all the other chairs were designed to the same dimensions. The face of McRoberts Hagen matched the body, fleshy and florid; it was dominated by a great red nose, but the eyes that peered from the mass of flesh resembled twin chips of pale blue steel.

"Gentlemen." The bulk emerged, advanced, found its chair, descended. A hand waved. "Please." They all sat. The ritual had begun. McRoberts Hagen looked expectantly at the secretary-treasurer, a pale, nervous man named Whorter. Whorter read in a rapid monotone the morning's agenda and the minutes of yesterday's meeting. Discussion moved swiftly from item to item: a convertible debenture to be issued, a

heavily watered common stock to be monitored, a bank in
New Jersey to be audited for possible pilferage of accounts.

At last they came to the matter of the Nolichuckey and
Southern Railroad. McRoberts Hagen nodded to an aide.
"Bring in Mr. Damion." There was an intake of breath around
the table, a sudden leaning forward in the chairs.

"Damion? Here?" The speaker was Harrigan, the vice-
president for accounts. "But I thought . . ."

A pudgy finger silenced him. "All in due time." The pale
eyes flicked to Brack Stewart, who acknowledged with a faint
nod.

The man who entered the boardroom was older, gray,
balding. His linen was frayed. His hands were restless, large,
callused. The hands, Brack thought, of a working man. His
black suit, though of good quality, was old and in need of a
press. He stood at the foot of the conference table, peering
down it through heavy spectacles that greatly enlarged his
eyes. "Mr. Hagen," the man said. His Adam's apple bobbed
nervously.

Hagen nodded but did not speak. It was the vice-president
for accounts who spoke. Harrigan rattled a sheaf of papers
and cleared his throat. "This is Mr. Harry Damion. Mr.
Damion is president and principal shareholder of the
Nolichuckey and Southern Railroad. The line runs exactly
eighty-three miles in Illinois. Mortgages of the Nolichuckey
and Southern are held by one of our subsidiary bonding
companies, which we recently acquired. Mr. Damion's accounts are in arrears as a result of competition from the new
Illinois Central line, running the length of the state on a
primary system of seven hundred and five miles from Cairo
to Chicago and Galena." The vice-president for accounts
hesitated, exchanged glances with Damion, then resumed his
report. "Mr. Damion is asking for an extension of his mortgages, which includes rights-of-way for the line, trackage, and
rolling stock. A portion of the debt is unsecured, and based
largely on his personal friendship with the late owner of our
subsidiary financing company. We have looked into this arrangement and Mr. Damion's character and personal references. The Nolichuckey and Southern is a small, private
venture, one of countless such railroads now operating across
the country. It was originally constructed on speculation that
one of the towns it serves would become a staging area for
westward expansion and a terminal for the Illinois Central.

This did not occur. However, the region has great potential for grain and livestock production and with additional financing Mr. Damion could extend his track another fifty miles to link up with the Illinois Central. This we believe, would assure financial success of the line, and there are strong indications that a federal grant of land could be obtained over the fifty-mile distance to secure the additional funding as well as the future financial strength of the Nolichuckey and Southern itself." The vice-president for accounts put aside his report and looked expectantly at Hagen.

"And what is your recommendation?" the chairman asked.

"We recommend approval, sir." The eyes of the vice-president darted around the table. A sheen of perspiration stood on his upper lip. "Mr. Damion's references as to character and integrity are of the highest."

McRoberts Hagen smiled. "Yes, well, we are certain of that. Mr. Damion is not unknown to me, and I have the highest regard for his, ah, integrity." The heavy face lifted in a smile at the railroad man. Damion smiled back dubiously, and shifted his weight from foot to foot. Hagen's smile faded. "Unfortunately, integrity is not the only element to which we must address ourselves. Hagen and Watts is accountable to its own shareholders as well. Because of the risk factor in this proposal, I have asked Mr. Stewart to look into it for us. Mr. Stewart?"

The vice-president for accounts seemed to pale.

Brack Stewart focused his attention upon McRoberts Hagen, looking at neither Damion nor the vice-president. He spoke rapidly and without notes.

"At your suggestion, Mr. Chairman, I have undertaken a study of the Nolichuckey and Southern situation and sent staff men to the field for on-site inspection. In essence, the vice-president for accounts is correct on several points, and I so stipulate to everything he has said thus far." Brack smiled inwardly sensing Harrigan's relaxation. The man was a rival and their dislike mutually felt. "However,"—he paused for effect, pleasurably aware that the room was now utterly quiet—"there are, as you suggest, Mr. Chairman, other factors that we must consider. Trackage and rolling stock of the Nolichuckey and Southern are aging and in disrepair. This suggests that the actual percentage of unsecured debt is considerably greater than that implied by the vice-president for accounts. Additionally, we shall have to anticipate replacement and repair costs in order to bring equipment up to standards. Cash flow of the line is also considerably below acceptable levels for further financing, and even below acceptable levels for extending the existing mortgages. Finally, the political climate of the nation includes a very real prospect of armed conflict in the near future and rising resistance in Congress to railroad land grants—I refer you to the maiden speech of our own new senator from New York, the honorable Poindexter Carp, as a case in point—gives us no assurance whatsoever that a land grant could be obtained."

"That's poppycock, sir!" The face of Harry Damion mottled in anger. The magnified eyes glared through their spectacles. The big hands opened and closed in frustration. "The future of the Nolichuckey and Southern is excellent, absolutely excellent. Settlers are pouring into Illinois. We are increasing our revenue miles every day. I have figures to prove—"

"In light of these considerations, Mr. Chairman—"

"Listen to me. Please, listen!"

McRoberts Hagen waved Brack to silence. The blue eyes fixed upon the offended railroader. "Mr. Damion, this is a report. Surely you'll give us the courtesy of discussing a matter of such importance to our company."

"But that young man is giving you a warped picture of our situation. It isn't that way at all."

"Do you deny that your equipment is in need of repairs and that the cash flow of your company is below par? Do you deny this, Mr. Damion?"

"Well, no. It's true enough, as far as it goes. But in a very short time, we're going to be turning around. We'll show a profit on the Nolichuckey and Southern, I promise you that. As for the land grant, it's virtually assured. I've had promises from Senator Stephen Douglas and the former Illinois congressman, Mr. Abraham Lincoln, and even a pledge of support from the Illinois Central folks themselves."

"And where are these Illinois Central folks, Mr. Damion? Why aren't they here with you today?"

"Well, I didn't think I'd need them. They're busy men. How could I ask them to come all this way, just to speak for a pip-squeak railroad like mine? But I assure you, gentlemen—"

"Please proceed, Mr. Stewart."

"As I was saying, Mr. Chairman, in light of these considerations, I can only recommend that we foreclose on the Nolichuckey and Southern Railroad and either attempt to negotiate its sale or take actual control ourselves to put it on a sound financial footing."

"No. No, you can't do that! Give me some time, gentlemen. I beseech you, give me some time. I'll renegotiate my financing, pay off my debt to you and meet the obligation in that way. Surely you'll let me do that. I'm certain to get all the financing I need."

"I'm sorry, Mr. Damion, but the terms of your obligation are quite specific and you have failed to meet them. Hagen and Watts holds a responsible position in the financial world, sir. We honor our obligations and expect others to do the same. I'm sorry."

"Listen, you still don't understand, Mr. Hagen. I've got my lifeblood poured into this railroad. It's been my dream. I helped to build it with these hands. I can even run a locomotive, if it comes to that. My three sons have worked along with me to create the Nolichuckey and Southern and make it a success. We've put our stake in ourselves and in Illinois. I have faith in this country, Mr. Hagen, faith in its people and its energy. There are matters that go beyond cold statistics and supposition here. America is built on a firmer foundation; it's built on humanity, faith in God and faith in people. Damn it, man, I've never tried to cheat anybody, always paid every last nickel that I could pay, practically beggared myself to meet as much of our obligation as I possibly could. I never attempted to compromise your faith in me by issuing watered stock or hiding assets or any of those things. Look, I won't even buy a new suit of clothes."

"That's all very commendable, Mr. Damion. But it isn't business."

"That railroad is my whole life. I've given it everything I could beg, borrow or steal. If I can have that much faith in its future, why can't you have a little faith in me?"

"I'm sorry, Mr. Damion." The face of McRoberts Hagen had grown cold, his manner abrupt. Clearly, the matter was resolved. Turning to Brack Stewart, he said, "We shall foreclose on the property, Mr. Stewart. See to the details, will you?"

"Certainly, sir."

Harry Damion, ashen-faced, almost collapsed and had to have support to remain on his feet. He glared at Brack Stewart, the eyes huge and swimming behind their powerful glasses. He was having difficulty breathing. "Young man," he

said, "you have just plundered for yourself a railroad which, I
don't doubt for a minute, will produce untold millions in
profits. I suspect that you have a golden future in the world
of high finance. But your immortal soul, sir, will burn in
hell!" He turned and walked out of the boardroom. The door
closed softly behind him. Most of the staff members of Hagen
and Watts stared in silence at the mahogany tabletop, avoiding
each other's eyes.

McRoberts Hagen said: "Next order of business."

Two weeks later, the body of Harry Damion was found
floating in the East River. But already, Brack Stewart had
quietly affirmed that a land grant for the Nolichuckey and
Southern would be passed immediately in Congress, not only
to close the fifty-mile gap to the Illinois Central but also to
extend the line for one hundred miles beyond its present
terminus. The immediate value of the land grant, which
Hagen & Watts would use as collateral to lend construction
money to itself at its own rate of interest was nine million
dollars. Brack Stewart's share of this windfall, to be extracted
on a commission basis prearranged with McRoberts Hagen
before the board meeting, would make him a millionaire.
Thus, his first venture into railroading was reaping handsome
rewards. And what golden future treasuries still waited to be
unlocked! But the next time, he did not intend to share with
McRoberts Hagen or anyone.

Exhilarated by the news from Washington, he dined alone
in the sumptuous privacy of his club. He took a brisk fencing
lesson and was bathed, shaved and massaged. He dressed
carefully in a suit of dark velvet tailored for snugness, put on a
fresh shirt and tie, and a broad-brimmed hat. He splashed on
a sweet cologne and completed his attire with a boutonniere
for the lapel and a silver-headed walking stick, heavily weight-
ed for use in case of attack. By nine o'clock, as gaslights
glowed along city streets, he was in a hansom cab, riding into
a neighborhood of dimly lit cafes, from which there came
sounds of boisterous music and laughter. Tipping the cabbie
to wait, he went into a cafe and made his way through the
smoky gloom to a solitary table in the rear. As his vision
adjusted, he was aware of the eyes watching from the crowd.
Casually he looked about, briefly caught several glances, gave
no response. At last, from another table he found the eyes
that he fancied. They were green eyes from the delicate face
of a slender young man with very blond hair. Brack drank a

small glass of sweet wine and waited. Presently, the young
man left the table and came to him. "Have we met?"

Brack Stewart smiled. "I think not. But it certainly can be
arranged."

"Shall I sit down with you?"

"Yes. And I'll order you a drink."

The blond youth slipped into a chair. Brack saw that his
skin was very white, very soft.. The lashes of the green eyes
were so long that they seemed almost artifical. "I'd like a
drink," the young man said.

"Good." Brack Stewart slowly unwrapped a cigar. There
was a pressure in his groin. His hands were trembling. "I have
a cab waiting outside."

It was going to be an interesting evening.

XI

The steamship *Panama* labored through a running sea, side-
wheels thrashing white froth. She was a stubby, ugly craft
serving a curious shuttle service from the steamy jungle
crossing northward along the Pacific coasts of Central America,
Mexico and California to San Francisco. En route, she bore
the hopes, schemes and disappointments of a restless tide of
humanity bound to and from that frontier of adventure, the
West Coast. Upon her decks there clustered a mingled host
of soldiers, thieves, freebooters, opportunists, intellectuals,
gunfighters, aliens, whores, schoolmarms, wives coming to
join husbands, husbands in flight from wives, clerks, store-
keepers, murderers and main-chancers. Half that motley
assemblage was usually seasick, so that by the time she
turned into the great bay of the Golden Gate, the wind
whipping her funnelsmoke into a looping black plume, the
Panama reeked of unwashed bodies, vomit and cheap whisky.

Vanessa stood by the professor at the railing, staring land-
ward at the familiar humps of smoky blue hills. In the

crescent of the shore, that dreary jumble of buildings and shacks, tents and tumult which was San Francisco had grown alarmingly in her four-year absence. Now it spread up and over the bare hills, reminding her of some great creeping trash pile. "Well, there it is, Monsieur Ligon." She spoke in French. "Feast your eyes on San Francisco."

The old man stroked his white whiskers and nodded, eyes crinkling. "I have seen more beautiful towns, it's true. But any place that produces one as lovely as you cannot be all bad."

"Give it time." She smiled ruefully. "It'll grow on you."

Four years, she thought. Four years, and now back to this. Strange how the dread had grown in her mind. After Paris, London, Berlin, Florence and Rome, to return to San Francisco was a cruel joke. She remembered her worldly friends from the private school in Paris, and how their eyebrows always lifted in amusement when she told them where she was from. "San Francisco? Where on earth is that?" And for nearly six weeks now, first on board the steamer *Southern Star* out of New York, and then during that dreadful trek by trail and boat across the Isthmus of Panama, and now on this final voyage northward, she had indulged her hunger to make conversation at the expense of this patient old schoolmaster from Marseilles, Monsieur Ligon. The shipboard acquaintance had proven beneficial for both, of course; she had gained a grandfatherly escort and willing ear, he enjoyed the companionship of a stunning and well-educated young woman. And like so many shipboard friendships, each knew without saying that it would end when the *Panama* dropped anchor and they went their separate ways. Vanessa's eagerness to confide in him, a sympathetic stranger, assured as much. And she was, he recognized, a person of deep confusions.

"I hope that you can find yourself, mon cherie," he murmured now. "It is so difficult to be young. How sad that by the time we reach the maturity to accept life, our youth has fled."

"I do intend to find myself, Monsieur." She leaned beside him, searching the sea with violet eyes. A flock of seabirds swept past, breaking and diving into the *Panama*'s churning wake. Their quarrelsome screeches were high and thin against the beat of engines. The wind tugged at Vanessa's hair, causing it to billow in loose strands of reddish blond, the color of flame. "I cannot live merely as my mother dictates. I cannot play her games of make-believe."

The plan came back to her mind. It was audacious, yes; a wild, audacious thing to do. But for two years now, it had been forming and growing there. It had been spawned, she supposed, out of homesickness and teenaged despair in the first years at Madame Trude's. How lonely and isolated she had felt, living among all those European girls of wealthy families, who spoke always in French or stilted, drawing-room English, and who were wholly out of touch with the real world. Most excruciating was the knowledge that her own background and parentage was so different from theirs; that between her and them, there yawned a chasm that could never be bridged. She had been tempted to speak of her plan to the professor, but had not. Some things were best unsaid. And that included her own bastardy.

"Why do you wince, Vanessa?"

"Pardon?"

"Your expression just now, it looked as if you suffered pain."

"It is nothing, Monsieur." She thought, no, old man, it is nothing. I am merely the illegitimate offspring of a plainsman and a prostitute who got together on a buffalo robe. I never thought much about my bastardy until my mother sent me abroad, to learn French and table manners and how to balance a book on my head when I walked. And now I come home stuffed with knowledge about art and manners, and it's utterly useless because what I really want to do is to go off in search of my own heritage. I want to find out who my father really was.

"... can do it, whatever it is. And nothing should stand in your way. The old man was speaking again, his face flushed in the wind, white whiskers in disarray, eyes yellowing from age. He seemed to direct his thoughts in part to her unmet desires, and in part to his own. "You are only young once; and if you don't do it then, you never shall. Believe me, my child, you never shall "

The *Panama* chugged into the crowded harbor. The wharf was crowded with cargo, people, horses, wagons and carriages. As the anchor chain rattled noisily and lines were secured to stanchions ashore, Vanessa experienced an unexpected elation. Her eyes frantically scanned the crowd. She moved away from the railing and forward for a better view. Several males responded with the usual open-mouthed stares, but she ignored them.

At last she saw a splash of flaming hair in the jostling mass,

a flurry of iridescent taffeta and gathered skirts hurrying up
the gangplank. "Mother!" Vanessa shouted. The face of Maybelle
Stewart turned and her eyes anxiously swept the deck.
"Mother, over here!"

They ran toward each other, pushing through the human
crush. They embraced in the crowd, stepped back to hold
each other at arm's length, embraced again. Tears welled and
broke.

"How wonderful you look!"

"And you. Forever beautiful, forever young."

"Fiddlesticks. I'm an old frump and you know it. By my
word, you're a sight for these eyes. And how you've filled out
in all the right places!"

"Mother . . ."

"Well, you know what I mean." Suddenly Maybelle was a
dynamo of energy. "Hey there, young man! Let's get these
bags ashore. That's right, all of 'em. For God's sake, how
much luggage did you bring from Paris, Vanessa? Let's get a
move on, young man. We haven't got all day. Come, Vanessa,
our carriage is right there. Yes, yes. Right over there. You
won't recognize the house. I've had it completely redecorated,
and a new sunroom built with a lovely view of the bay.
They're all the rage nowadays, sunrooms. But your room is
the same. I didn't touch your room. We're having some lovely
people in for dinner tonight, your coming-home party and all
your friends—leastways, the ones that are still in San Francisco.
And tell me all about Paris. How was Paris? Oh, I'm so
excited."

As her mother rushed along, Vanessa looked back for the
professor, but he was nowhere to be seen. "Home sweet
home," she murmured.

"Here we are, then. Yes, young man, you can get them all
on board, I know you can. Right up there, plenty of room on
top. Lash 'em on there any old way. All right, then, just the
light bags and we'll send down for the trunks later. My God,
so much luggage."

"I shopped in Paris."

"So I see."

"I brought you a beautiful gown, a Paris original."

"Won't that be nice?"

"I know you'll love it."

"And the voyage? How was your voyage."

"Dreadful. Oh, I was seasick for days. I took the new

Cunard steamer to New York. And then there was another
steamship to Panama and that ghastly hot trip across the
Isthmus—there really should be a better way to go—and
then the final leg. Oh, be careful, Mother, you're going too
fast."

"It's this damned mare. Spirited beast. I should have had
one of the hired men drive. But damn it, Vanessa, I wanted
to do it myself. Does that make any sense?"

Vanessa laughed. Men's eyes followed the moving carriage.
Young blades smiled and tipped their hats, raising Maybelle's
protective instincts. "Mind your own business!" she muttered.
As they rattled through Portsmouth Square, Vanessa looked
back at the shining surface of the great bay sweeping outward
in its vast sparkling panorama. "The bay is so beautiful," she
said. "I had forgotten that our town had such a lovely
setting."

"Ain't a town any more. We've got a real city now and
there's no holding it back."

Vanessa patted Maybelle's arm. "Mother, it's good to see
you again."

It was true. How strange, she thought, after so many hard
feelings in the past to experience this unexpected warmth.
Maybelle had not changed all that much in four years. Oh, a
line here, a bit of loose flesh there; but obviously she still
worked hard at daily figure exercises. And the old vivaciousness
had not dimmed; the personality of Maybelle Stewart was
still overwhelming, especially when she smiled.

The frantic clanging of bells jarred Vanessa from her reverie. Around a corner, careening on two wheels, swept a
gleaming, red fire engine, gushing steam and drawn by four
white horses. As Maybelle fought her mare to the side of the
street, the terrible contraption rocketed past, raising a cloud
of smoke and dust. Dogs barked. Children screamed. Horses
shied and reared.

"Yaaa, horse!" Maybelle shouted, "Stop that dancin', you
carnsarned oatbag!" She flicked at the mare's rump with her
carriage whip, sawed the reins and managed to turn the
frightened animal. A crowd of louts laughed at her predica-
ment from the street corner. "You damned idlers," Maybelle
bawled, "why don't you go back to your saloon!"

The laughter increased. "Maybelle, you'd be better off
walkin'. It ain't safe, you drivin' on public streets."

"Ain't safe for who? For me?"

"Naw. For me!"

The joke brought fresh paroxysms of merriment. But by now the mare was under control and the carriage resumed its pace. "Damned fires," Maybelle grumbled. "They're the curse of San Francisco."

At last they were climbing Nob Hill, making small talk as Vanessa's eyes drank in the view. Her mother was prattling on about how nice it was to have one of her offspring at home again. "Your brother's doing real well in New York, I hear."

Abruptly, Vanessa's mood darkened. "How nice."

Maybelle glanced at her curiously. "He's getting rich in his own right. Always knew he could do it. Smart lad, Brack."

"Yes."

They rode the rest of the way in silence.

"Well, here we are." The mansion was fronted by a broad lawn and curving gravel driveway, its massive bulk festooned with ornate woodwork and tall columns. The roof was a thing of steep pitches and gables, bristling with lightning rods. A new wing had been added in Vanessa's absence and the whole painted a dull yellow.

"How do you like the paint job?"

"Hideous."

"Knew you'd be impressed. I wanted to paint the whole thing gold, but that didn't work out. This is the nearest color I could find."

"How interesting."

To Vanessa's dismay, homecoming inspired a round of parties and exuberant gaiety for Maybelle and her many friends. For a week, there were nightly soirees, dinners and dances in the mansion. A boisterous stratum of San Francisco society attended, with a free mix of political and entertainment luminaries, whites, blacks, Europeans, Asiatics, Australians, adventurers, tycoons, drifters, the rich and the broke. Vanessa found herself carrying on conversations in English, French and halting Spanish, or simply standing mute in the face of a barrage of happy Chinese.

The governor came, the mayor, a leading soprano appearing at the new opera house ("I hope she can complete her booking," mused Maybelle, "before the damn thing burns down."), members of the state legislature, the chief constable, a leading ornithologist, a British explorer, a pardoned Australian murderer, assorted gamblers, duelists and ladies of the night.

"Mother," Vanessa breathed, "this is a zoo!"

"Well, I kept the home atmosphere pretty sheltered while you were growing up. In the old days, these friends would have been entertained at the Nocturne. But with you away and all, the house was just a big empty woodpile. It was such a waste, having eighty rooms of dust and cobwebs. So I brought in some life."

In the process, of course, there were numerous advances from handsome young men. Vanessa was besieged with invitations for dancing and dinners, for carriage rides, horseback rides, croquet, boat outings, treks to the gold fields, marriage. She rejected them all. It was a mother-daughter discussion of this which kindled the first argument.

"It's none of my business, love, and I guess I ought to keep my mouth shut, but why in the devil do you turn all of those fellows down? You get offers that would make most young ladies drool with pleasure."

"I'm not interested, Mother."

"Not interested? Why not? It's rather natural, you know, for normal young women and young men to get together. That's been going on since Adam and Eve."

"Mother . . ."

"All right, all right." Seeing Vanessa's exasperation, Maybelle made a show of dropping the subject. But the subject would not drop. An hour later they were discussing it again.

"I really don't want to go into it, Mother. Suffice it to say that I find most of these men dull, self-centered and rather ignorant. Mostly, they're well-dressed American louts."

"Louts? The governor's nephew, Henry Beech, is no lout. And that good-looking young man from Virginia, Dabney Everling, has two university degrees and intends to go for his doctorate. Do you consider him a lout? He speaks better French than you do."

Vanessa could tolerate no more. Her eyes flashed, her temper exploded, and all the suppressed bitterness poured out in a torrent that, once started, she was powerless to stop.

"All right! If you must know, I'll tell you. Mother, I am not the normal young girl of your daydreams. I never have been and I never shall be. You sent me away to finishing school in Paris so that I could learn manners and language, so that I could discuss the arts and know which fork to use at a formal dinner. They saw to our good breeding and took us on outings to the Louvre. All my life this has been your goal, to see that

I had the education and polish that you lacked. You wanted to
make me into your own ideal of womanhood. Unfortunately,
Mother, I also had an opportunity to think, to compare myself
with others, to discover what makes for real quality in a
human being."

"Vanessa, please." Maybelle's face was suddenly drawn.
"Please don't say any more. Don't say things you'll be sorry
for later on."

"I'm not sorry for anything, Mother. You seem to want to
know what I think, and yet you don't want to know. Well, we
can't carry on our little charade forever, can we? And that's
what it is, you know. A charade. The rich bordello queen of
San Francisco wants her brat to be Miss Lah De Dah, to
mingle with the upper crust and marry well and have lots of
rich little brats who'll live on Nob Hill and warm Granny's
old age. You'd like a scion of Virginia aristocracy for a
son-in-law. You hunger for something that you never had,
respectability."

"There's nothing wrong with that!"

"No, there's nothing wrong with respectability. But respectability is something the individual earns for herself. It's
not a quality to be gained simply because one's offspring
marries well. The fact is, Mother, that I am me, Vanessa
Stewart. Putting a book in my hand and French in my mouth
and clothes on my back does not change that, does it? No
matter what you do to me, I am still Vanessa Stewart. And do
you know what that means?"

Maybelle's face was lifeless now, her eyes dull. "Yes," she
whispered, "I know what that means."

"It means that I don't have a father and don't have a
legitimate name of birth. It means that I was born out of
wedlock, the offspring of a whorehouse madam and a man she
met on a wagon train to California in the middle of nowhere;
a man she didn't even know! I am the daughter of a woman
whose primary function in life is to provide prostitutes to
satisfy the desires of men. And do you want to know the real
paradox of that, Mother? I'll tell you the real paradox. This is
no longer even necessary for our living. You got rich on a gold
mine, one that's still producing up in those hills, churning up
wealth for Maybelle Stewart. But you're not satisfied, are
you? Mother wants it all. Today you've got a string of
entertainment palaces all over California and Nevada and
God knows where else. There's not a mining town that

doesn't have a Nocturne. And every one is part dance hall, part restaurant, part bordello. Every time somebody gets fucked, Mother, we make another dollar!"

"Vanessa!"

"Do you have any idea what it's like to go to a private school—or any school, for that matter—knowing that you are probably the only bastard girl in the place? Do you know what it's like to hear other young people talk about their fathers and mothers, their wedding anniversaries, their respectable occupations, their friends and social lives, knowing that you have to keep silent or lie? No, I can see that you don't know. I doubt that it has ever entered your mind. For the truth is, Mother, you are concerned mainly for yourself."

"That's not true. I love you, Vanessa. I love you and Brack, and I've always loved you both. I've had to struggle alone to provide for us, to bring you up, see that you had a chance in life. This is a tough world, Vanessa. Things don't just happen because we will them to happen. I've employed hundreds of young girls just like yourself, and the only difference is that they have no one, no money, no friends, no parents who can see to their needs or even care. There are countless thousands of young people adrift in this country today, unable to read or write, working from the time they're eight years old in a mill or a mine. In Pittsburgh where I grew up, children went to work when they were old enough to pick up a shovel, and they worked that way until they died."

Vanessa smiled scornfully. "Mother, what do you know about that? The Stewarts were rich. Your father was a millionaire and your family is a dynasty."

"Yes. But that was them. It wasn't me. It was my father and my brothers. Everything was for the boys, schooling, opportunity, a place in the business. Nothing was for me. Father despised me. I had to leave, and so I did. I left there and never went back. Don't you see, Vanessa? We are ourselves. We've embarked on a whole new way of life in this big country, and made our way by our own rights. And it's all waiting for you, everything I've built up. It's waiting for you and Brack, equally, to take over and do with as you will."

"Mother, I don't want it. Can't you see that? I can't live in your mold any more than you could live in your own father's. I've got to be me. And the same for Brack. I can tell you some things about Brack, Mother, that aren't pretty at all. I understand him, you see. He is my half brother, after all."

"Brack is your brother."

"No, Mother. Brack is my half brother, because we had different fathers. But he is a bastard, too. His father was the man you worked for in New Orleans, the man called Maurice, who owned the first Nocturne."

Maybelle was silent. Her expression was that of a woman sick at heart. Vanessa wanted to stop, but could not. Her mind said, Stop! Her rage hurtled onward.

"You were employed by Maurice as a prostitute, Mother. He fell in love with you, and you lived together. He taught you the social graces, and how to play the piano. He was Brack's father. Maurice was murdered, and you took Brack and fled New Orleans to St. Louis. But his murderers followed you there, because you had taken money from them. Then you left St. Louis with two wagonloads of prostitutes and came overland to San Francisco. Right?"

"Yes, Vanessa." Her voice was very quiet. "That's right."

"Brack and I, you see, have been corresponding, and he filled in a lot of details. I also managed to find other sources."

"Yes. You have done well."

"Oh, that's merely the beginning, Mother. I intend to find out who I am, who I really am. I want to discover everything I can about my father, Van Harrison."

"How do you intend to do that?"

"By going to the places where he lived and made his fame. My father was quite well-known in certain circles as a plainsman and scout. He was a hunter and mountain man. There are many tales about Van Harrison, both legend and fact. I intend to seek them out, find people who knew him, and discover the other half of my heritage."

There it was: the plan. In fury, she had blurted it out. Well, no matter. She was committed now.

"Vanessa, those are mountains and deserts out there. It is a wild country, and no place for a young woman to be roaming about on her own. You don't know the first thing about such travel. You've never been out of civilization in your life."

"It doesn't matter. I can learn. I will learn. And I'll hire the best guides and companions I can find to take me where I want to go. I'll learn to speak other languages, too. If I can learn French, I can learn the dialect of a Sioux Indian."

"Please. Just because you're mad at me—"

"My mind is made up."

"I forbid it, Vanessa. I won't let you do this."

"No, Mother, you are not in a position to forbid anything. People will do what they must do."

"Think it over. Wait a while. There must be a better way."

"Oh, I have thought about it, Mother. As you can tell, I've thought about a lot of things. As I say, I'm not like everyone else. But then, neither is Brack. It may interest you to know that Brack is not the human being you'd like to imagine. Oh, he's a fox in business. Brack is utterly resourceful and will come out on top. He has already made his first million dollars. But I managed to make some discreet inquiries while I was in New York. It's amazing what kind of information money will buy in the right places. Did you know that my half brother takes his sexual pleasures from both women and men?"

"Vanessa!" Maybelle slapped her daughter's face, raising a red welt across the cheek. The two women suddenly confronted each other's wrath, eyes blazing.

Furious, Vanessa turned from her and stalked from the room.

They both knew that now there was no turning back.

News moves with amazing swiftness in the back country, especially as it applies to a unique event, an oddity of animal or human life, an event of magic, massacre or natural rampage. Word flies from mouth to mouth, over campfires and casual meetings. At times, so swiftly does it pass, the superstitious might deem that communication is borne upon the very breeze. And so it was that word spread from gold camps to Indian settlements of the white woman from the West who sought the cold trail of her father. She was a beauty, it was said, with hair the color of sunset and eyes that could dazzle a man, but cold eyes intent on far horizons. She was accompanied by two old Comanche Indian scouts whom she'd hired because they had traveled with her father, now dead. She sought out elderly people, Indians, isolated settlers, Mormons, anyone who had known of the man named Van Harrison. And as she went from place to place, riding a gelded, chestnut mustang and becoming proficient with rifle, tomahawk and skills of the trail, a protective mantle of superstitious awe settled about her. Sunset Woman and her Comanche could travel where no male stranger dared go without armed force at his back. To assure her safety, even renegade Sioux and Apache provided safe conduct through their hunting grounds and added escort from place to place. The Indians were amazed at the single-minded purposefulness of Sunset Woman, her special gift of tongues and the whispers of her magic. Her arrival at an Indian village invariably took a pattern as she sat down at council fires, where no female had ever sat before, to speak with warriors and chiefs.

"I am called Sunset Woman. I come from the west, beyond the great mountains, in search of my father's footsteps. He rode these lands before my birth, often at the head of the white man's wagon train. His name was Van Harrison. He was a plainsman, a mountain man and hunter."

"Yes, I have heard of him. It was a long time ago, in the days of my youth. He was tall, a tall white man of great courage. It is said that he killed a charging grizzly from one hundred paces with a single rifle shot in the eye of the beast. I do not believe it, for so many things are said. But those are the stories we heard."

"Did you ever see him? Did he come to your village?"

"I did see him, but only once. He came to my village to parley on behalf of white men who wished to cross our lands. He spoke our language, as you do, and once took an Indian woman as his wife."

The eyes of Sunset Woman were surprised. "I did not know that. Of what tribe was this Indian woman?"

"The Cheyenne, to the east. That is what I heard, that his woman was a Cheyenne. They are plains people and hunt the buffalo. Van Harrison's squaw died during childbirth."

"What tribe? How shall I find them?"

Silence. A scratching of heads and a pondering. "I do not know. You shall have to seek the answer from other tribes. Go to the east, find the Cheyenne and ask them."

"I will do as you say."

"Now let me ask a question of Sunset Woman."

"Yes?"

"It has been said that a visit by you is a good omen to a tribe. Is this true?"

"I cannot answer that question. Good omens exist in the hearts and minds of those who seek them. If you see my visit as such, as many others have done, then I am glad."

"Let us hope so. These are times of trouble for the Indian. The white man comes in ever increasing numbers. There is

constant talk of war and trouble. We need good omens,
Sunset Woman. I will consider your visit as such."

"Until we meet again, then."

"Sunset Woman, what a pity it is . . ."

"A pity?"

". . . that you were not born an Indian."

She moved by stages eastward, leaving the high mountains
at last for the plains. They wintered on good land at the base
of the mountains, in the shelter of massive foothills called the
Ramparts. Indians came from great distances to see Sunset
Woman, for the legend had spread widely that she brought
good luck. No one really knew how this had gotten its start.
Actually, Sunset Woman and the old Comanche knew, for
they were the ones who had contrived the fiction, and sent it
in advance of themselves by furtive talk as a clever means of
self-preservation. The eldest of the Comanche scouts, a grizzled ancient named Good Eagle, was especially convincing,
for he had an honest face and the manner of a shaman, a man
of strong medicine. Sometimes he was overly eloquent with
his own glowing enthusiasm, saying that Sunset Woman came
down from the sky on a cloud of gold. This would bring from
her an angry whisper in the Comanche tongue: "Old man,
don't get carried away!"

It was a hard winter with much suffering, and the blizzards
were heavier than anyone could remember. Sunset Woman
had never known such discomfort, as day after day she
huddled alone in a lodge of animal skins, feeding a smoky fire
with dwindling supplies of damp wood and bark. A month
passed, and two, and still the snow sifted down in heavy
drifts. The cold was so intense that even buffalo froze to
death on the plains. Food ran short. At last, however, the sun
broke through, the thaw came, the green grasses emerged in
melting patches of snow and they prepared to move on, into
the country of the Cheyenne.

They rode eastward onto the plains. Day followed day and
week followed week. Winter merged into spring and spring
into summer. At last they crested a bald hill and looked down
upon a green valley and the lodges of a Cheyenne village. For
maximum effect, Sunset Woman timed her arrivals for just
after dawn. In this way, they came out of the darkness upon a
village and gave the impression of having journeyed through
the night, while actually they had camped nearby. This also

gave her the tactical advantage of finding the elders and
warriors unprepared, for she would appear suddenly in their
midst without the warnings of a sentinel. She wore a beaded
chemise of soft white deerskin, which served to accentuate
the striking colors of her hair and eyes. Thus were the rumors
of magic reinforced, although no one had ever suggested
precisely what powers she possessed.

The village of the Cheyenne chief Shemkuk spread before
them in the first wash of morning light before the sunrise. A
few squaws picked about the camp and there were the usual
dogs rummaging for scraps of meat. Smoke from cookfires lay
a thin blue veil over the lodges, which were arrayed
symmetrically along the bank of a lovely creek. There were at
least a hundred lodges, and from the look of the camp, the
site was new. Things were unusually neat and well-ordered, a
sign of tribal discipline. Numerous buffalo hides, spread to
dry and cure, attested to recent successful hunts. Silently
Sunset Woman and the old Comanche scouts paced their
ponies into the village, riding past sleeping lodges into the
center of the settlement. Finally they came to the circle of
stones and dead ashes of the council fire. Here they stopped
their horses and sat quite still, waiting. Not even a dog
barked, so stealthily had they arrived. It was one of the
squaws who saw them first and yelped in surprise.

"Ayeee!"

Then the dogs came to life and there was a rushing and
bustling among the lodges. Warriors emerged, knuckling
sleep from their eyes and milling about in confusion. Several
men dashed to the largest of the lodges, a distinctive structure positioned near the creek. Commands came from some
source, because the young men swiftly organized themselves
and came trotting toward the center to form a ring around the
newcomers. A tall brave with angry eyes and a badly
pockmarked face demanded to know who they were and why
they had come. Sunset Woman looked at him coldly and did
not reply. The Comanche sat on their horses in silence. The
brave's bluster obviously was all for show, for the word
rippled through the crowd of onlookers and among the other
warriors. "It is the Sunset Woman."

"Sunset Woman, here?"

"That is Sunset Woman."

"How do you know?"

"I know from the sun in her hair and the paleness of her eyes."

A tall, broad-shouldered Indian emerged from the largest lodge. From his bearing and raiment, he was obviously a chief, but a young chief, not yet out of his twenties. As he walked toward them the crowd fell silent and parted to make way. He wore buckskins and a very light-colored shirt with colorful tassels and beads. his long hair was pulled straight back in a thick, neat braid. About his sturdy neck he wore a necklace of bear claws. Sunset Woman looked at him and caught her breath. He was the most handsome man she had ever seen. Calmly he strode through the crowd to her mustang and put his hand gently on the pony's nose. When he spoke, his voice was deep and resonant.

"You are Sunset Woman. Welcome to the village of Standing Bear."

She remained silent, looking down into his eyes. The old Comanche Good Eagle spoke for her.

"We have come to see the chief who is called Shemkuk."

The Indian kept his eyes fixed on the face of Sunset Woman. "And why do you wish to see my father Shemkuk?"

"To speak with him on a matter of the past."

"I see." The Indian smiled at Sunset Woman. His smile was even and self-assured. "I have heard of your quest, Sunset Woman. You seek your own father, and thereby your ancestral roots. Is it not so?"

Good Eagle started to reply, but Sunset Woman motioned for silence and answered the question herself. "It is so."

"Then please come down from your ponies and refresh yourselves. I am Standing Bear, the son of Shemkuk. I am chief of this tribe. You are welcome to our village." He glanced at an old squaw in the crowd and nodded. Then he turned and walked away. As Vanessa Stewart swung down from the mustang, she saw him go back into his lodge.

The Cheyenne treated them with warm hospitality. The old squaw who took charge of Sunset Woman was called Minnow, and her function was to prepare a guest lodge and see to her every need. The lodge to which Vanessa was taken was remarkably clean, with soft white buffalo robes in a roomy interior affording space for her things. Here she could also move about and have privacy. Accompanied by Minnow, she went to a secluded spot in the creek, removed her clothing and swam naked in cold, clear water The squaw busied herself cleaning Vanessa's garments When she had emerged from the water, Minnow dried her body with a large soft animal fur. Vanessa dressed in a fresh chemise The Indian woman brushed her hair lovingly, fascinated by its length and soft luster. "Sunset Woman should have wild flowers in her hair," the old squaw said. She went away briefly and returned with a spray of small white blooms taken from a nearby thicket. These she wound into Vanessa's hair in such a way that they seemed to be part of it, catching the sunlight like tiny beads of dew. Vanessa looked at her reflection in the creek and smiled. "Minnow is clever with her hands."

"Sunset Woman is clever in every way," the squaw replied. They exchanged knowing glances.

It was evening before Vanessa and the old Comanche sat down with Standing Bear and the tribal elders. The men silently smoked a great wooden pipe decorated with eagle feathers, passing it from hand to hand. Neither Sunset Woman nor Minnow, the only other female permitted to be present, shared in this. When the smoking was done, Standing Bear spoke.

"We have heard much of Sunset Woman and her travels. There is much information that I would like to share with her, for she has seen much in the year of her journey. But first, how can we of Shemkuk's Cheyenne be of help? It is said that Sunset Woman is filled with questions wherever she goes."

Vanessa nodded. The man not only was handsome, he was astute. Rarely did Indians suggest an exchange of information, and then it usually had to do with what game she had seen and where Indians could obtain guns and firewater.

"I seek knowledge about my father whose name was Van Harrison. I have been told that many years ago he took a squaw for a wife and that she was of Shemkuk's village. Where is Shemkuk, and how may I speak with him?"

"Shemkuk is no more. We have not chosen to have this widely known, for he was much respected by both our friends and our enemies. My father left us six moons ago for the land of eternal peace."

Vanessa's face betrayed her disappointment. "I am truly sorry," she said.

"It is the way of life."

"I was so in hopes..."

"But what you suggest is true. The white plainsman Van

Harrison did come to our village when I was a small child. He did take a wife who was called Eyes-of-the-Night. She was the daughter of a chief and there was bad blood in the tribe over this. Our people were divided into opposite camps, and some of that feeling exists to this day There are those who have anger in their hearts for all white men because of it."

"Did they stay in the village?"

"No. Feelings were so high that Van Harrison took his bride and left for the great mountains. We never saw either of them again. It is said that she died within a year, giving birth."

"And the baby?"

"The papoose died too, and Van Harrison buried them together. He did not return to us."

They talked on until the moon had risen. One by one, the tribal elders went to their lodges. Finally only Vanessa, Minnow and Standing Bear remained. Though he knew little more about Van Harrison, he seemed keenly interested in the things that she had learned. And so she told him of Van Harrison's great prowess as a hunter and scout, and how he had been among the mountain men who blazed the first trails to California. She stopped short of discussing her own mother and the romance between Maybelle and the plainsman on the hard westward trek. The searching eyes of Standing Bear seemed to bore into hers, however, and she had the uncanny feeling that he knew more about her than she told. At last they sat in silence, listening to the distant howl of a coyote. As night's chill settled upon them, Vanessa noticed with surprise that the fire had died down, leaving only a bed of embers.

"I will go to my lodge now," she said.

He did not respond, but stared into the embers lost in thought. She withdrew, followed by Minnow. Stooping to enter her lodge, she glanced back and saw that he was still sitting there, quite alone. She lay down on her buffalo robes and drifted into fitful sleep. But several times during the night she dreamed of the tall Indian with the searching eyes.

The days passed in an idyllic splendor. For the first time since leaving San Francisco, Vanessa felt at home and at peace. It was an illusion, she knew, rooted partly in the knowledge that her father had been with these people and had married one of their tribe a generation ago. She was free to move about as she pleased and did so, followed by the ever watchful Minnow and one of the old Comanche scouts. Her command of the Cheyenne dialect had been limited at first. Indeed, it astonished her that the first talk with Standing Bear had gone so smoothly, with the aid of sign language. But she improved rapidly. As was her custom in an Indian village, she sought out the tribal elders. A few had vivid memories of Van Harrison and his marriage to Eyes-of-the-Night. They seemed to feel a kinship with Sunset Woman, albeit as illusory as her own identity with Shemkuk's village. And for the first time in her travels, she noticed that no one made reference to her magic or to the legend that her visit was a good omen for the tribe.

Days went by without a sign of Standing Bear. At last she asked Minnow about him and learned that he was away, leading a scouting party.

"A scouting party?"

"There is a white settlement seven days ride from here, and soldiers. Some of our men have had trouble with them. Standing Bear is worried that this will bring open conflict. He has tried to keep the peace with the white man, as his father urged him to do, but there are those of the tribe who want war. This has been going on for a long time."

"But this is such a peaceful village, and fighting is so unnecessary. Why must there be trouble?"

Minnow's expression abruptly became a mask. The sparkle of life vanished from her eyes, leaving a stolid Indian inscrutability. "I do not know," she said. "I am a squaw. It is not my place to think of such things."

The scouting party was gone for nearly three weeks. When the warriors returned, there were fewer of them than had departed. Several men were wounded, and men and horses bore the signs of hard riding and exhaustion.

Standing Bear was among the wounded. He slid heavily off his pony. Several warriors hurried to him, but he waved them away and stood without assistance. The wound was in his side, a superficial shotgun wound. It was Minnow who led him to the creek, cut away his sweat-stained shirt and bathed him. The others, Vanessa noticed, hovered at some distance from their chief. Some of the women had begun a low keening wail, smearing ashes on their faces and tearing their garments.

"What is it, Minnow? What are they doing?"

"It is for their dead."

"Dead?"

"Three were killed and one was taken by the soldiers and is thought to be dead. He was badly wounded."

"But why did this happen?"

The mask dropped over Minnow's expression again. Vanessa went to Standing Bear and repeated the question. He sat staring into the still water of the creek, his naked side oozing blood. The bleeding appeared to have been started again deliberately, for the wound was open. Minnow was preparing a compress of herbs in an earthen dish.

"I went to parley with them." Standing Bear said. "Our purpose was peaceful, though we were armed for battle. There has been trouble with the whites of the settlement, but mainly involving other tribes. I thought that if we sat down and talked together we could heal our differences." He turned and looked up at Vanessa. His eyes were filled with confusion. "That is the way of the white man, is it not? To try to heal differences?"

"Sometimes," Vanessa said.

"But clearly the white men wanted war. Even as we were sitting down to speak, one of our men was attacked by a white who was crazy from drinking firewater. He had lost his family in a raid by the Sioux last year and was filled with hatred. He killed our man with a single blow of a tomahawk. We had to fight our way out. When the white soldiers arrived, we were badly outnumbered. There was nothing to do but retreat. I don't know what will happen now, Sunset Woman. My heart is heavy, for this is our first open fight with white men. I'm afraid that there will be many more."

Vanessa had not noticed the arrival of the pockmarked Indian. He stood slightly behind her, a towering figure of dark wrath. When he spoke, his words were filled with contempt.

"Standing Bear is an old woman," he said. "The blood of the warriors is on his hands and fills him with remorse. He sits here in the council of women with an old squaw there and this . . . this white squaw of the fire hair." The Indian spat in the dust at Standing Bear's side. "I say it is the fault of this woman. She is bad medicine and enraptures Standing Bear."

The eyes of the chief flashed. He came to his feet to confront his tormentor. "Black Feather speaks with venom in his heart," he said. "He did not choose to accompany his brothers to the white settlement, so blinded is he by hatred. Black Feather would rather send his men to certain death against the whites than to use his wit and attempt to parley."

"Parley is the way of the fearful. It is the weakling wolf who bares his throat to the strong."

The blood was streaming now from Standing Bear's wound. A pallor was on his face. Minnow rudely pushed Black Feather aside and muttered something that Vanessa did not understand. The pockmarked Indian withdrew, saying, "It is time for Sunset Woman to leave our camp."

The knees of Standing Bear buckled beneath him. Men came running. Minnow and Vanessa tried to grab his arms to break his fall but he tumbled in a heap on the ground. The warriors quickly lifted their chief and bore him to his lodge. Beckoning for Vanessa to accompany her, Minnow hurried into the lodge with her herbs and vessel. She quickly staunched the blood flow and closed the wound, actually sewing it shut with thread of sinew. The two women remained by his side all that night while he thrashed about in a fever, and the next day, and the next.

At last the fever broke. Vanessa was alone in the lodge, preparing a clean dressing for the wound. She sensed that Standing Bear had awakened. Startled, she turned to him and their eyes met and held. Something—some invisible power— passed between them, for suddenly she felt flushed and weak. "My lord is awake," she whispered.

"Yes." His voice was strong again. His smile was gradual and seemed to penetrate Vanessa's inner self. "And I find Sunset Woman in my lodge. It is a good omen."

"Does my lord have pain?" She bit her lip. Why did she use that expression? It had come out unconsciously, twice. Had he noticed? What was happening to her? "I shall call Minnow."

He lifted his hand. "I am healing. Minnow bled the wound well and used her medicines. The hot blood is gone. It is nothing now."

Minnow entered the lodge, bringing warm broth in a bowl. She placed it on the ground beside Standing Bear and said to Vanessa, "Give him this." She went out again. Standing Bear rose painfully on one elbow as Vanessa held the bowl to his lips. He drank the broth slowly, savoring its taste. The liveliness and color had returned to his face. When he had finished the broth, she made a cool damp compress and wiped his face. The facial bones were jutting and strong, the skin taut, the ridges precise as if each had been deliberately sculpted and put in place. Impulsively, she stroked his hair back with her hand. The touch of him caused a weakening in her stomach and her hand trembled.

"Sunset Woman has the gift of healing hands," he said. "Her touch is as soft as the brush of willow leaves, but brings strength pouring back into my body. Perhaps what they say is true, that Sunset Woman has magic." He lay back on the softness of his robes. The skins were of white fur, hundreds of tiny furs hand-stitched together. Vanessa had learned from Minnow that the young women of the tribe had done this, each vying with the others to serve their chief. He had never taken one for a wife, and this was curiously understood. For Standing Bear believed in the strong bonding of his people, and that their chief must be a part of them and yet detached.

"I have no magic," she murmured, "except the magic that is in my heart. And that is the magic of Standing Bear, who touches my life as the sunlight and the rain and the air I breathe."

He closed his eyes. "I will sleep now," he said.

The days passed as a curious blend of joy and sadness. Standing Bear was on his feet again, riding out with the hunters of the tribe to bring back meat. He also was the arbiter of disputes and the giver of laws; he sat for hours with his council to hear grievances of tribal members. The times that he could spend with Vanessa seemed all too brief. They would stroll together by the creek or ride side by side over the rolling bare hills. It was a sweeping land of rich grasses and scudding cloud shadows; a land of immense panorama, upon which a horse and rider would diminish to a distant speck and still be seen. Now, she habitually addressed him as "My lord" and the words fell comfortably and naturally upon her tongue. He asked her questions about her life in the world of white men and listened in rapt attention as she spoke of Paris and San Francisco and New York.

"Can it be true that men live in great cities such as you describe?" he said. "I find even the images of them elusive to my mind."

She drew sketches of the cities as best she could with charcoal on skins. She talked of the white man's culture, his art, his inventions of steamboats and trains, his ways of planting and harvesting, of making steel, of mining from the earth a black rock that burned even better than wood. He listened so intently that he seemed to absorb every word.

In return, Standing Bear spoke to her of his world, the trees and skies and open lands, the otter and the fox, the buffalo and the grizzly bear. His words imparted to her visions of a wild freedom now threatened with extinction. "Our ways of life cannot survive. My father knew this long ago, when the first white men arrived with their long rifles and possessive ways. The white man, Shemkuk would say, does not merely pass over and use the land as we do. He must possess it, build upon it, change it. More and more, I see how wisely my father spoke. In time, great cities such as those you have described will rise from these grassy plains. Men will lay claim to these lands and draw their holdings on pieces of paper and build fences to keep out intruders. These things I know. I see no way of stopping it. The white man is too powerful, too highly organized."

"Surely there must be a way that your tribe, your people, can survive," Vanessa said. "This land is so huge, so boundless. There is room for all."

Standing Bear frowned and shook his head. "I wish that it were so, Sunset Woman. But even now our days are dwindling. The white man's settlements and the pony soldiers keep coming in greater and greater numbers, and we are steadily pushed out of the path. It has been said that the white men even plan to bring the iron horse across our lands, to send it screaming through the valleys blowing smoke and showering fire. I know not of this, it is merely something I have heard. But my heart is heavy for my people, for we must decide whether to give ground slowly or dash ourselves to pieces in hopeless resistance."

"Your enemy, Black Feather . . ."

"He is not my enemy, Sunset Woman. Black Feather opposes me in many ways, but he is his own enemy, not mine. The wrath of Black Feather springs from his heart and will not be cooled. His voice is strong among our people for war against all white men. I listen to what he says, for in so doing I am better able to see the dangers of such thinking and thus avoid it."

In their moments together, each seemed to avoid repeating the intimacy of that day in his lodge. And yet the power of it was never out of her mind. In her dreams and while awake, she relived the memory. As the weeks slipped past, Vanessa lived for his eyes upon her, the sound of his voice, the casual brush of his hand, the scent of him—of sweat and leather and maleness—and even the joy of breathing the same air.

It was time to leave the Cheyenne. Clearly, there was no further reason to remain. Even the old Comanches hinted as much. Good Eagle kept his suggestions veiled. "The weather will soon be cold for traveling." And, "I have mended Sunset Woman's saddle blanket." His meaning was clear. But there was conflict in her mind. Never had she felt such a sense of belonging as here. The visit to this Indian village seemed almost too idyllic. She had grown to know its sounds and moods, to love the peace and beauty of life here. She was haunted by the curious mixture of sights around her: the village cloaked in the mists of morning and suddenly tipped with sunrise; the women bending over their cookfires, surrounded by children with dark, wistful eyes; the brilliant horsemanship of the braves as they galloped their ponies over the plain in Indian games, wheeling and dashing and flirting with danger, their excited yelps cutting through the sound of hoofbeats. ("Greatest cavalry in the world, the Cheyenne," a grizzled Army scout had once told her at a trading post. "I'd hate to have to fight them.") But more than any of this, there was Standing Bear. The irony of it caused her to smile. She was Vanessa Stewart, educated in Paris, taught to be at ease in the salon and the soiree, schooled in the nuances of art and pleasure and society, rich, pampered, sought-after. And where did she find joy? In the company of a savage unable to read or write, one who spoke a monosyllabic language augmented by signs, the leader of a people doomed to conquest and virtual destruction. He had fine Indian braves, but his weapons were a joke: knives and tomahawks and a few ancient smoothbore muskets against well-disciplined, well-mounted, well-armed United States cavalry.

"Sunset Woman is sad. There is trouble in her eyes."

"Yes, Minnow. The time has come for me to leave and I don't wish to leave."

"If you don't wish to do something, then why do it? Have you made promises that you must keep? Does the life of another depend on your decision? Minnow does not understand."

"It's just that . . . well, my world and my people are elsewhere. I am not a Cheyenne; this is not my world."

"Ah, then you weary of your visit among us. I understand.

You are sick in the heart for home and your people. Then certainly you should go."

"It isn't that either, Minnow. No, it isn't that way at all. I have no ties back there."

"No man waits for Sunset Woman?"

"No. No man waits. I came into the wilderness in search of something. The trail of my father, I thought. I wanted to learn all that I could about Van Harrison, because his blood flows in my veins and we are one. I thought that when I discovered everything I could about him and filled that vacuum in my life, I would be whole and complete. Do you understand? And yet, that wasn't my total purpose. Actually, I came to the wilderness in search of myself, to find something that would be uniquely mine. Does Minnow know what I mean?"

The face of the old squaw had that stolid, uncomprehending expression again. But then her glance strayed, she looked beyond Vanessa and a glint of cunning came to her eyes. "I think I do." Vanessa glanced behind her and saw Standing Bear approaching.

They walked together by the creek. He was troubled about the bad feelings with the whites of the settlement. "Our people wish to be at peace. The council thinks that we should pull up our lodge stakes and move. I must decide."

Vanessa did not speak of her own turmoil.

Then matters took an unexpected turn. Good Eagle was felled by a strange sickness. The old Comanche lay in his tepee, wracked by chills and nausea. Vanessa went to him, and he was filled with remorse. "I cannot travel with Sunset Woman. And the other scout, Crazy Otter, is not capable of guiding you alone. You must ask Chief Standing Bear for someone who can accompany you as far as the great river, to the place called St. Louis."

"There is no urgency, Good Eagle," she said. "Rest."

It was Standing Bear who resolved the dilemma, but not in the way she would have anticipated.

The late summer had come. The prairie grass was dry and the sound of singing insects strong upon the land. Hunting parties were out for weeks at a time, and squaws were busy drying meat and pounding pemmican for the winter. Standing Bear came to her lodge at daybreak. They mounted their ponies and rode toward the north, over gently undulating land that stretched as far as the eye could see. Life out-of-doors had streaked Vanessa's hair with white gold and turned her skin a tawny bronze. Her body had toughened remarkably in the sixteen months since she had left San Francisco. She rode Indian-style with only a blanket on the pony's back, and guiding with her knees. As had become her habit, she was silent, following Standing Bear with eyes upon his broad back. The sun passed its zenith and was tilting to the west when they arrived at last in a range of low hills with stands of willow and cottonwood flanking a bright, chuckling stream. Here they dismounted to rest in deep, soft grass. While the ponies grazed, the Indian lay on his back, face to the sky, and remained quiet for a long time. But at last he spoke.

"Is Sunset Woman leaving us?"

"I . . . I think I should. We had planned to go before now, but Good Eagle's illness complicated things. If I don't leave soon, the cold weather will come and we'll have to winter on the trail. We did that before, and it was very difficult. I had hoped to get to St. Louis."

"You will need a guide. Did you intend to ask Standing Bear for a guide?"

"It was suggested to me, yes. Good Eagle thought you might provide someone who could accompany me at least part of the way."

He was silent again. He picked a blade of grass and chewed it thoughtfully. She waited, intensely aware of the warmth of sunlight dappling upon them through the willows and the soft drowsiness of the afternoon. She looked intently at his face, as if to implant forever in her mind the strong lines of profile, the shining locks of black hair caught with a beaded headband, the thick, muscular neck and heavy torso bulging beneath his tunic of soft animal skin. The sheer power of the man filled her with a nameless force.

"Do you want to leave us?" he said. "Is it in your heart to go?"

There it was, a question that stripped away nonessentials and left her with none of the deceptions practiced by white men. Her answer came swiftly, not from the mind but from the heart, and whispered as lightly as the breeze.

"No. It is not in my heart to leave you, my lord."

His face turned to her. His eyes smoldered. "It is said that Sunset Woman has magic. I believe that. I am filled with her magic and it gives me no rest. The thought of her leaving turns my heart to stone."

Her tears came without warning. One instant she was dry-eyed and clear of mind, the next her emotions gave way as a dam would break. And as she wept, she spoke in a rush. "You can but glance at me, my lord, and I tremble like a leaf. You fill my mind and my dreams. Your touch sets my blood to racing, and my destiny is no longer my own."

He opened his arms and she went to him. And the sky and the earth were her transport on a sea of golden sunlight. Her senses swirled with the heat of him, with her bare opening to his urgent demand, with the quick stab of tearing pain that melded into a wild ecstasy. Her eyes were full of sunlight. Her throat cried her delight. And then she plunged headlong down, down the void of blue and green and gold into the mind-jarring explosion of blood and sinew and heart. At last the stillness returned. From somewhere, she heard a pheasant's call. The stream murmured in its eternal course. There was an odor of crushed grass.

"I will not leave Standing Bear," she murmured.

A fortnight later they struck the lodges, placed the old, the sick and newborn on horse-drawn drags of wood and skins and headed toward the southwest.

With them rode Sunset Woman.

XII

"Board! All aboard!"

Steam blasted from the underbelly of the Barrett Special locomotive. The whistle tooted. The conductor repeated his call through the echoes of Philadelphia's new central station.

"All aboard!"

Ruth clutched at Thaddeus's arm as if fearful of letting go. "Thaddeus, promise you'll write to me. You must, or I shall worry to death. You will write more often, won't you?"

"Yes. Yes, I'll write. Now, Ruth..."

"Good-bye, my boy." George Barrett stepped between

them and extended his powerful handshake. "You must hurry now. He must be off, Ruth. The train."

"Oh, dear," she said. "I do hate to see you go. We've had so little time to visit. Daddy, there's been so little time. Do make him come back. When are you coming back, Thaddeus?" Her auburn curls tossed and she gave him her Little Girl pout. Her eyes were large and luminous.

"All aboard!"

"Soon. I'll be back soon." With a final grip of George Barrett's hand, he detached himself from them. The train was jerking into motion as he sprang to the step and swung aboard, the conductor grabbing his valise. He waved back at Ruth and her father as the train to Washington gathered way. By the time the coach cleared the station canopy into bright morning sunlight, he was groping into his seat by the window. There was a sharp odor of wood smoke.

The train. It delighted him, fascinated him. He had ridden trains all the way from Illinois to Pittsburgh and then on to Philadelphia. It was a magic carpet on wheels of steel. Staring out the window, watching the city's sooty remnants hurtle past, he was conscious of the familiar metallic rhythm as it built momentum—*packetybum-packetybum-packetybum*—and the blurred vertical lines of the new telegraph poles. It was a remarkable time to be alive. Beyond the dreary, unpainted workers' shacks and tedious rows of red brick shops beneath belching chimney stacks, Thaddeus Stewart saw the bright tomorrow in a world of galloping technology. This train was flying along at thirty-five miles an hour. And those telegraph wires overhead carried the coded pulses of words that could flash in a single breath over half a continent.

The coach was crowded. A heavy, gray-thatched man in a cheap black suit and frayed linen sat beside him, breathing heavily and exuding odors of sweat and chewing tobacco. He was a boot salesman from Chester, Pennsylvania, on his way to Baltimore. "I tell you, young man, the railroad is a godsend to this country, a godsend. When I was your age a man couldn't move faster'n a horse could run, except by steamboat down a fast current. And now..." On and on he went, amid gasps for air and exortations to the Deity, his words spilling out in a compulsive rush. "They're talking in Congress about a railroad all the way to the Pacific Ocean. Oh, the wonders our Lord doth work! And it'll happen, too, if the Republicans get elected. That's my party, the Republican

party. A vote for Democrats is a vote for disunity, I say;
disunity, and the godless destruction of our hallowed Union.
We can't let that happen, boy. Can't let that happen. Can't let
slavery prevail. No. Slavery is a curse upon our very souls,"
—his eyes bulged and his face reddened, loosing streams of
sweat—"and an abomination in the sight of God."

There it was again, snapping and coiling like a serpent in
their midst. Had the entire country gone insane? Only in the
East had Thaddeus been conscious of such rising fixation, pro
and con, on the issue of slavery. But then, what did he know
of current events? For five years, since the Frémont expedition, he had been building the Illinois Central Railroad. The
closest he had come to politics was the frenzied activity of his
tall, gangling friend Abe Lincoln. The Illinois Central's sometime lawyer had made a name for himself two years before,
debating Stephen A. Douglas all over the state in an unsuc-
cessful attempt to wrest away the U.S. Senate seat. It amazed
Thaddeus the lengths to which men would go to grasp for
power. But even in failure Abe had accomplished something.
He'd become a national political figure, a strong contender
for the Republican nomination next month. Thaddeus recalled their last meeting, and saying to his tall friend, "Why
bother with politics, Abe? You make a good living prac-
ticing law. Hell, our railroad cases alone keep you solvent."
Lincoln had offered a sly chuckle and patted Thaddeus on
the shoulder. "Ambition, Thaddeus, is an itch you can't
scratch."

". . . surprise me none if the Democrats split between
North and South," the fat man went on. "And then, watch
out! It's Katie-bar-the-door, for sure. Uh, no offense intended
if you're a Democrat, friend. A feller never knows who he's
talking to nowadays." The train whistle punctuated his words
and they rocketed across a trestle spanning a gorge.

His mind drifted to Ruth—Ruth, with her glowing eyes
and feminine wiles. He had stopped off in Philadelphia at Ted
Judah's request. Judah's letter was still in his coat pocket.
"George Barrett is building a fine eight-wheel driver locomotive with a long-range tender that carries wood or coal and
water. Bring me the specs in Washington." And so in Cairo,
Illinois, Thaddeus had made his good-byes to the Illinois
Central and his friends there ("You can write your ticket with
this company, Thaddeus. You played such a big part building
this railroad, and now we need you to help run it.") and had

gone to see his old friend Barrett, the Philadelphia locomotive builder.

But it was Ruth who monopolized his time with her eternal closeness and perpetual parties. He'd wondered aloud why she was still unmarried—Ruth Barrett was by far the most beautiful and eligible woman in Philadelphia—and was surprised by the frankness of her reply: "Because, Thaddeus, you still haven't asked me." She had taken his arm in that possessive manner of hers, hugged it close to her breast and placed her head lightly on his shoulder. The excitement stirred him afresh, remembering. There had been several occasions when he could have made love to Ruth. They were frequently alone in the mansion, except for the servants. And one night in a hansom cab they had locked in fervid embraces, and he had wanted desperately to unclothe her in that lush darkness. The experience left him aching with lust. But the play of mutual flirtation was one thing, reality quite another. The reality was, he did not love Ruth. For all her beauty, her style, and his affection for her father, something prevented him from loving her. He tried to fathom this, and failed. Was it a quirk in his own nature? Was he simply incapable of loving? No, that was not the case. In his heart, he knew it was not. There was one whom he could love...

"Marguerite!"

She was there in the Washington depot, looking small and petite and ravishing as she stood between the two men who accompanied her. Thaddeus came off the train at a bound and hurried across the platform. She was shouting his name, and the light of a stray sunbeam turned her hair to spun gold. "Thaddeus! Oh, Thaddeus!" They embraced, and the sudden power of it made his senses reel. They were both talking at the same time, their arms interlocked, and he had the overwhelming need to keep her there, hold her there, never let her go. But then the presence of the two men came to his consciousness. The taller one in the uniform of an army colonel, was the tall, red-haired Southerner Peter Heflin, looking ill at ease. And beside him, a trifle older, a trifle grayer than when they'd last been together, stood the engineer Ted Judah. Marguerite withdrew from his arms, her lovely face strangely flushed, and he exchanged handshakes with Heflin and Judah while a porter came forward with his baggage and the crowd from the train spilled around them, jostling and shouting.

"My word, cousin, you're a sight to behold," Peter Heflin said. They were of equal height and the colonel, like Thaddeus himself, had filled out and matured. "Are all Stewart men such handsome brutes?"

It was Marguerite who replied, laughing and taking Thaddeus's arm. "This one is."

The day was balmy for the beginning of April. Bright afternoon sunlight poured down upon the city as they made their way from the depot in an open carriage. From her purse, Marguerite fished a perfumed handkerchief and placed it lightly to her nose. Thaddeus started to ask if she had a cold, but quickly found the question needless. The spring warmth had brought a stench to the air, a noxious mix of odors that lay over everything like an invisible pall.

"Phew!" she said.

"Welcome to the nation's capital," Ted Judah murmured.

"Where does it come from?"

"Everywhere. Open drainage ditches. They're filled with all sorts of refuse, dead dogs and cats, indescribable effluent. We've got sewage marshes south of the White House. Not to mention the fact that the horse population has become quite large, and the droppings tend to mix with the mud of the streets."

"Theodore!" said Marguerite.

"Sorry."

It was true, of course. Thaddeus recalled the general unsightliness of the city from before, but even then things had not seemed this bad. As the carriage, drawn by a superb pair of dappled grays, moved smartly down spacious Pennsylvania Avenue, he could see that the streets slanting off the main thoroughfare were still unpaved and muddy. Everywhere there were livery stables, saloons and dreary shacks nestled against gleaming new buildings of brick and granite. Pigs rooted here and there. Turning to look behind them, Thaddeus saw the uncompleted dome in its nest of scaffolding on the Capitol Building. Beyond, toward the Potomac, stood a spire, also in the process of construction.

"What is that?" he asked.

"The George Washington Monument, if they ever get it finished."

Finally they came to Thaddeus's hotel, the fortresslike Willard with its sign advertising running tap water in every room. Ted Judah had rented for him a two-bedroom suite with bay windows commanding a view. When the four friends were finally settled in the parlor, the engineer pulled aside a curtain and peered through the window toward the Capitol. "From now on," he chuckled, "that's where we'll do our most important work."

"I thought we were supposed to build railroads, Ted, not politick."

"These days, my boy, it's the same thing."

"I envy you two," Peter Heflin said.

"How do you mean, Peter?" asked Marguerite.

"With the country on the verge of tearing itself apart, they're thinking about building for the future."

A servant brought bourbon and cigars. Thaddeus puzzled over Heflin's remark. "I'm not sure I understand, Peter. I'm a bit dense about politics."

"Marguerite tells me you're a friend of Abraham Lincoln."

"In a way, yes. Abe has a multitude of friends, and I count myself as one of them."

"Well, Mr. Lincoln said it himself in the Douglas debates over slavery nearly two years ago: 'A house divided against itself cannot stand.' If memory serves me, he also warned that this country cannot endure permanently, half-slave and half-free."

"Do you mean to say there will be war?"

Heflin sighed. "I wouldn't be at all surprised."

Ted Judah shook his head. "I can't agree with you, Peter. This is eighteen and sixty, and I simply can't imagine America being plunged into the chaos of a civil war. I'm a railroad man, of course, and not a politician; but I'm often in the Capitol, and I sense that we will stop short of armed conflict between North and South."

"My word, Ted, can't you see that—"

"Gentlemen, gentlemen," Marguerite said gently. "If you don't stop, we'll have a battle right here in Thaddeus's parlor."

The two men chuckled, suddenly aware of their bickering. Thaddeus, deliberately changing the subject, picked up a newspaper he had brought with him from the depot and pointed to a lead article. "They've started a Pony Express from St. Joseph, Missouri, to Sacramento. That's over two thousand miles in ten days of hard riding, with relays around the clock. Ted, I thought you might be interested."

Judah snatched the newspaper from his hand, eyes widening.

"The Pony Express! By heaven, Thaddeus, what a stroke of luck. Listen, it says here the first run left St. Joseph before sunset on the third of April. The route"—Judah's excitement mounted—"goes straight out of Missouri and across Kansas Territory into, uh, the South Pass and Salt Lake. Then it's straight as an arrow to Fort Carson, Lake Tahoe and the American River Gorge into Placerville, California. The relays in the Sierra Nevada mountains bucked deep snowdrifts between Placerville and the Nevada line, but they made it. Ten days, Thaddeus. Ten days! And do you know the route they're following?"

"Sure. It's the old Mormon Trail. Most direct central route to California."

"The Mormon Trail." Ted Judah's eyes burned with an intensity Thaddeus had not seen since their days together plotting the final route of the railroad through the wild Niagara River Gorge. "The Mormon Trail!"

"And if the Pony Express can do it," said Thaddeus, "then why not the railroad?"

"Exactly," Ted Judah breathed. "Why not indeed?"

Washington seethed. Change crackled in the air as dramatically as the spring storms raking across the city. The storms were supercharged with lightning, and their thunder rolled down the Potomac like cannon volleys. Every political consciousness focused upon the major party conventions, where the issue of slavery would be joined as surely as fresh cloud masses boiled each day over the Capitol.

Thaddeus found himself caught up in the crazy spell of that tumultuous spring. His energies were whetted by Ted Judah's excitement over the coming-together of political forces that not only meant confrontation of the terrible issues between North and South, but also added stunning impetus to the long-fought question of the transcontinental railroad Filling in the backdrop of political intrigue and skirmish was the social scene, where powerful personalities from opposite polls came together over formal dinner tables, deftly cutting and parrying from behind disarming smiles. At the heart of it was Marguerite, who for the enhancement of her husband's career, and bolstered by her own magnetism and wealth had become the most popular hostess in Washington. At her soirees, teas, and formal dinners, Thaddeus found himself rubbing elbows with everybody who was anybody, from President Buchanan to the assorted legions of political savants, journalists, deputies, ministers, ambassadors, attorneys, bureau chiefs, career bureaucrats, opportunists and foreign dignitaries. Even the peppery grande dame of Capitol society, Marvella Clive, peered through a lorgnette from her six-foot height, bosom drenched in diamonds, and acknowledged that Marguerite was the social wonder of the age. "My dear," the aging hostess said dryly, "your beautiful cousin can wreak more havoc with the flutter of a fan than Colonel Lee with all his cannon."

"I know. She also has that effect on me."

"My dear Thaddeus, I'm beginning to get a clearer idea in my nasty little brain about why such a beautiful man as you has never married. And may I suggest in a friendly way that such hopeless fidelity is not only rare in this grubby world, in your case it is an absolute crime against the feminine gender. If I were thirty years younger, my pet . . . oh, never mind. I'll just cool my lusts with another glass of wine, if you will do the honors."

"Happy to do the honors, Marvella."

Talk swirled through the parlors of Washington. "Abraham Lincoln nominated by the Republicans! Of all people. That backwoods upstart rather reminds me of a grinning ape on whom someone has worked a colossal practical joke, dressing him in a black suit and stovepipe hat."

"Lincoln's the best they could get under the circumstances, I suppose. William H. Seward was everybody's favorite at the convention, but his antislavery position was just too radical for the party as a whole.

Stephen Douglas will settle Lincoln's hash this time mark words Marvelous orator, Douglas Absolutely spellbinding He makes that rube sound like he s gargling mouthwash

The verbal swipes at Lincoln galled Thaddeus He swallowed impulse to rush to the new   idate defense It was Marguerite who restrained him placing ɔ gentle hand   his

In Washington Thaddeus things aren t always what they seem People don t necessari   express their true ings. This is a city of whispers and deceptions Loyalties are changeable Just watch and listen m dear. In time you'll get the hang of it

In another arena, Congress it was Ted Judah who became his teacher and guide The engineer had developed into a shrewd lobbyist on behalf of the Pacific Railroad. This was partly from his passionate belief in the transcontinental link and partly as a direct representative of the state of California, which paid his salary. Judah was jubilant.

"The tide is running our way, Thaddeus. I feel it in my bones."

"Ted, I only wish I had your optimism," Thaddeus replied. And yet he knew that Judah's frustrations were multiple. As if Washington were not obstacle enough, California also had presented its share. Prior to coming east as a lobbyist for the railroad, Judah had roamed the Sierras for months with barometer—for measuring altitudes—and compass looking for a grade gentle enough for laying track. He had yet to find it. And then the engineer had been hired to build a small rail line from Sacramento to the gold fields of the Sierra Nevada, only to have his backers lose heart after twenty miles of track had been laid.

Asa Whitney and several other men joined them. Again, talk turned to presidential politics, and the prospect of war. "If war comes," Thaddeus was saying, "I would have to join on the side of the Union. I feel strongly—"

Someone had stepped to his side. A cultured voice intruded. "Gentlemen, sorry to barge in like this, but I haven't yet had the pleasure of meeting Mr. Stewart." He was a round-faced, bespectacled man wearing a party smile. His handclasp was soft and moist. Thaddeus recognized Poindexter Carp. His inner defenses stirred. He was uncomfortable and felt a prickly sensation at the back of his neck. Carp continued. "I merely wish to assure Mr. Stewart that I intend to bury this insane idea of a transcontinental railroad, this giveaway of federal lands owned by the taxpayers of this country. If need be, we'll filibuster it right out of the Congress."

An agitated Asa Whitney looked around them. Other party guests nearby had ceased speaking and were listening to the unexpected confrontation. From across the room, the hostess was threading her way through the crowd, wondering how she would control such a breach of Washington etiquette. "Poindexter," Whitney said, "I don't think this is the time."

"Of course it isn't," the senator said abruptly. The smile never left his face. "Forgive my rudeness." Again, the moist handshake. "Senator Poindexter Carp of New York, Mr. Stewart. Your humble servant, sir. And might I add that your cousin Francesca, my wife, sends her greetings. She has just arrived in Washington and is quite busy seeing to the new house. She could not join us this evening. I'm sure, however, that we will be bumping into one another now and again. Eh?"

"I'm sure of it," Thaddeus said coolly.

Poindexter Carp nodded and walked away.

Asa Whitney sighed. "Methinks, Thaddeus, I smell a family feud brewing."

Thaddeus did not reply.

Marguerite was a hunger in his soul.

He had tried at first to deny it, to convince himself that what had gone before was puppy love and no more. He told himself that surely Marguerite felt nothing for him beyond a cousin's warm regard. But none of this was true. The old intensity was back; indeed, it had never left. When they were together, which was often, the magnetism was too strong between them to be ignored by either. If Marguerite had struggled inwardly to resist the reality, she made no sign. Thaddeus himself gave up the pretense, and when they were apart accepted the fact that her memory would linger in the secret places of his mind and heart.

For all this, Colonel Peter Heflin's liking for this male cousin of Marguerite's was open and genuinely expressed. Marguerite's husband was a courtly, bright man with many Washington contacts. He displayed none of the resentments or jealousies one might expect and which Thaddeus suspected that he himself would be unable to contain had their roles been reversed. He almost wished that Heflin would show temper or hostility or wounded pride, for then it would be easier for Thaddeus to admit to himself: Yes, I am in love with your wife. Yes, I have always loved her and I always shall, even though she is my first cousin. He wondered at times where the dividing line really lay. How closely was he tiptoeing to the forbidden realm of kinship?

As summer advanced, Ted Judah and his wife Anna packed up and headed west on a packet steamer to Panama and then across the Isthmus and by boat again to California. Judah despised the jungle trek across Panama, despised it for the heat and mosquitoes and inconveniences of travel. From Panama City there came a card. "We're here, sweating, awaiting passage. What a beastly hot country! Can't wait to hit the Sierras again. Ted." The Sierras! They seemed to

shine in Judah's mind as strongly as the vision of Marguerite
did in Thaddeus's, and he wondered if there was any material
difference between one man's unreasoned passion and another's.

The summer gave way to fall. Washington tensed in expectation of the coming elections. Congress put the railroad act
onto its back burners of pending legislation, marking time
until the outcome of November's voting.

It was Peter Heflin, surprisingly, who became Thaddeus's
strong confidant and fellow enthusiast for the railroad act.
"There's tremendous support building, Thaddeus. Expansionism is the key. We've admitted three more free states,
Kansas, Oregon, and Minnesota, and created as many Free-
Soil territories in Colorado, Nebraska and Nevada. That's
going to provide you with a terrific boost for a nothern route."

"Peter, why do you feel strongly? You're a Southerner. Your
military career has had crucial backing from Senator Butler of
South Carolina and Jefferson Davis. This puts you in direct
conflict with them."

Heflin smiled. "Marguerite is partly to blame. She's so
enthusiastic that I could hardly afford to be otherwise. At the
same time, Thaddeus, I'm beginning to see this fixation of
yours and Judah's in a larger light. That link across country
not only will provide a fantastic direct route to California,
opening lands for western settlement and trade, it also will
bind together the Union, east and west. The distance will
always be two thousand miles from St. Louis to San Francisco.
But the railroad will shrink those miles, bring us more closely
together, force us to think and act and live as one people.
And though I was born and bred in the South, I can no
longer accept slavery as a natural order of man. It hurts me,
and I am torn within myself to reject my own people, but I
am given no choice. It behooves me to see that great western
territory solidified forever with our Union of free men."

Peter Heflin hesitated, suddenly embarrassed, and looked
away. "See what you've done, cousin? You've made me get on
a soapbox."

Thaddeus chuckled and reached into his coat pocket.

"Colonel," he said, "have a cigar."

Francesca Stewart Carp made her social debut in a manner
that plainly signaled a direct challenge to Marguerite's emi-
nence as a hostess. In their rented Tudor mansion, she and

her husband and mother-in-law Minerva Carp gave a party honoring President James Buchanan's last days in the White House. It was a brilliant opening stroke, for protocol demanded that everyone of Cabinet rank and all congressional leadership be present. Marguerite Heflin and her friends were included.

Marvella Clive was livid. "You must forgive my extreme bias, Marguerite, but I think your sister has the personality of a spider. Look at her over there, wrapping Jeff Davis around her little finger."

Another aspiring hostess tried to wither Francesca with a glance. "It's Buchanan, of course. He is such a pliable and bland President. Francesca simply moved in on him and refused to take no for an answer."

New York's Senator William Seward greeted Thaddeus with enthusiasm. "Some of my friends were involved with you in constructing the Illinois Central, Stewart. They tell me you made quite a name for yourself. How unfortunate that my colleague Senator Carp and Francesca are so hellbent on opposing your transcontinental railroad. I didn't know the Stewarts fought among themselves."

Thaddeus chuckled. "We're no different, Senator, from everybody else in this mixed-up country."

"Yes. Well, a friendly word of advice, young man." Seward moved closer and lowered his voice. "When you're walking in the jungle, keep an eye to your rear."

Three weeks went by before the cryptic comment began to make sense.

Gossip was the breath of Washington. It rippled and swirled with a life of its own, from cloakrooms to salons, parlors and assorted boudoirs where the mighty took their secret pleasures. In the steamy heat of that vicious summer, with sectionalism rising and malice honed to a cutting edge, the whispers took even uglier undertones. The most harmless liaison was suddenly suspect, the casual courtesy seen as an overture, the lightest whimsy proof of indiscretion.

No one could be certain where these things originated. They were borne like the swamp gas, out of sumps and bogs; they moved as subtly as the miasmas of the night, carrying their deadly bacilli. And one particular fresh morsel of gossip was more virulent than most, for it sapped at the marrow of the upper crust and picked as its target the very essence of Washington society.

"In love with her cousin, they say. Carrying on something scandalous, right under her husband's very nose."

"I thought they seemed awfully chummy."

"Anybody with a lick of perception can see it. Just look at her eyes, devouring him when he's near. They stare at each other across crowded rooms. My dear, I'm not a prude, but . . ."

"Do you really think they . . . they . . ."

"Of course, they are. Everybody knows it. Even the servants are talking. He goes to see her for afternoon tea, and then it's art galleries and social functions, this and that. They're constantly together."

"Lovers. No doubt about it. And first cousins, too."

"Lovers? You don't say?"

"Lovers."

"Handsome devil, isn't he? No wonder he doesn't take to any other woman."

"First cousins!"

"Lovers."

It was Marvella Clive who told them. The socialite was six feet of fury, standing in the middle of her own parlor in a flutter of ostrich plumes and dyed purple hair. When she had said her piece, speaking directly to Marguerite, Peter Heflin and Thaddeus, the silence settled upon the room like a brooding weight.

Heflin rose, white-faced with rage. "I would kill any man who suggested—"

"Please, Peter." Marguerite took his arm. "There's nothing you can do. You might as well fight the wind."

Thaddeus was bewildered and angry. He came to his feet, lit a cigar and strode brusquely back and forth through the smoke. "Why?" he said. "What's the purpose?"

"There is no purpose." Marguerite sighed. "It's just malicious talk. Washington is always full of it."

"Damn it, don't they have anything else to talk about? This whole country is about to split into a bloody shambles and they're talking nonsense about people's private lives!"

"A Stewart's life isn't private, I've discovered," said Peter Heflin. "And neither is mine."

"But to what earthly purpose?"

Marvella Clive smiled thinly. "Don't you know? Can't you even guess? I'd bet my last diamond that I know exactly where it came from, and why. It's Francesca Carp."

"Francesca? Nonsense. Francesca wouldn't."

"Francesca would, my dear. Between her and that mother-in-law, Minerva, I've never seen two more scheming women. Francesca will stop at nothing to discredit you, Peter and Thaddeus on this damned railroad bill. She has an absolutely insane fixation about it and intends to dash any hope of an act getting through Congress in the next session."

"But this is absolutely preposterous," Marguerite said. "Thaddeus and I . . . we are first cousins. We're like brother and sister."

"A handsome, dashing bachelor first cousin," Marvella said gently. "Please don't misunderstand. I love you all dearly, but I'm useless to you if I can't be honest. Thaddeus"—Marvella's heavily mascaraed eyes flicked toward Peter Heflin and her tongue darted nervously, licking her lips—"is probably the most sought-after young man in Washington right now. Female hearts from eight to eighty pine for him. We all know damn well that he's not one of those fruity men who don't like women. Thaddeus Stewart is all man. And that leaves the wagging tongues only one thing to wag about."

Thaddeus went to the window and turned off the rest of what Marvella had to say. It was true and frank and painful. No one else would have had the courage, or the love, to say these things. He felt flayed, drained, mortified. It was all there, the nuances and the implications, but suddenly public consumption had turned it sordid.

The calm maturity displayed by Peter Heflin amazed him, and the man's character again expanded in Thaddeus's mind. The pride of Peter Heflin turned outward and not against either Marguerite or Thaddeus or himself; the colonel's instinct was to throw up a common defense and to lash out at common enemies. He would undoubtedly challenge any man who spoke openly. But in a real sense, this was hopeless. Peter Heflin's frustration was complete. For how could a warrior duel with shadows? Of what use was the sword or the pistol against a will-o'-the-wisp?

Two days later, Thaddeus Stewart left Washington on the morning train for Philadelphia. There, he asked Ruth Barrett to marry him immediately. The wedding took place on the first of September in the presence of four hundred guests. Then the radiant couple departed for a honeymoon at Niagara Falls, New York.

It was noted that while many women shed the customary

tears during the service, the groom's stunning blond cousin
from Washington, D.C., Marguerite Stewart Heflin, sat beside her husband coolly composed and dry-eyed. Only later,
in the darkness of the night when she thought Peter was
asleep, did Marguerite weep. And then it was as if she would
never stop.

On the sixth of November, Abraham Lincoln of Springfield,
Illinois, was elected President of the United States.

The weather turned cold and damp. Weeks of low-hanging
clouds affected Washington's mood, matching the somber
news events of each passing day. Relentlessly, the South was
becoming more bellicose, as if determined to push the nation
toward conflict in the closing stages of James Buchanan's
lame-duck presidency. Thaddeus was appalled, a helpless
spectator to a tragedy in the making. His state of mind did
not improve with the strange turn of his personal life. Marriage to Ruth Barrett was turning out to be not at all what
he'd expected.

Some aspects were quite enjoyable. To his own surprise, he
took pleasure in suddenly sharing domestic life with a wife
after the years of bachelorhood. It was good to have a gentle
companion. And Ruth, beyond question, was a stunning
woman physically. In their early days together she demonstrated an insatiable appetite for love-making. Her cries and
writhings were such that he feared at times they would
disturb the neighbors around their townhouse apartment.
Thaddeus found himself enjoying their sexual awakening together, and it made his own prior experience seem limited in
the extreme. Ruth, on the other hand, displayed a remarkable skill and adroitness at lovemaking that seemed rather
excessive for a virgin. He did not speculate on this, however,
and accepted without question her admission that once she
had peeped into a racy novel filled with scenes of explicit sex.
"I was a naughty girl, Thaddeus. Reading it made me feel
all . . . all trembly and weak inside. Do you think a woman
should feel lust like a man does?" And so he looked forward
to their noisy romps in bed, finally admitting to himself that
the neighbors did not matter; they were probably doing the
same thing.

The difficulties between them, if one could call it that, took
a more subtle tack. One minor irritation had a touch of the
bizarre. This had to do with the doll collection. Even on their

honeymoon trip to Niagara Falls, Ruth had taken along two suitcases full of dolls. They were of varied sizes and types. She seemed to regard one of them, the big rag doll with sad button eyes, as a personal friend and confidante. She would cuddle the doll, stroke its cotton curls, talk to it. Thaddeus had regarded the dolls as having no consequence until they arrived in Washington. Over the back of their large double bed, Ruth had a broad shelf built on which she arrayed the dolls. Their constant presence became a distraction, giving him the feeling he was being watched. At last he said something about it. "Dear, do we have to have the dolls in our sleeping room?" Strangely, Ruth's temper flashed. She shouted that the dolls were her friends, her very best friends, and that they would remain. Then she pouted for two days. Thaddeus made no further mention of the dolls, but the incident—their first spat—smoldered unspoken between them.

Ruth Barrett Stewart had few interests beyond herself and an immediate circle of friends. She was bored by politics, national affairs and current events. To Thaddeus, who took zest from the hurly-burly of official Washington, such an attitude was beyond comprehension. When they made the rounds of teas, receptions, and dinners, Ruth could be charming enough—her beauty quickly stifled the ugly rumors concerning Thaddeus and Marguerite—but she did not enter into typical conversation and seemed detached from it all. Only among the men and women that she herself brought into their lives did she seem at ease. For the most part, they were wealthy young socialites with strong ties to Philadelphia's Main Line families, either by blood relation or social connection. They reflected indulgence and inbreeding, knew the same names and same code words, had gone to the same private schools and colleges. Among the males, concern about the turmoil in which the nation was engaged centered primarily on how it would affect the price of coal, iron and steel.

"My God, Humphrey, South Carolina is voting to secede. There's talk that they plan to seize the federal arsenal and try to take over the forts. People are dancing in the streets of Charleston. We're on the verge of an open break!"

"Tut, tut, Thaddeus, how you do take on. Nothing to worry about. The government will handle it. Shall we play whist?"

"Are we going to have a party on Christmas Eve?"

"But, Ruth..."

"Oh, pooh, Thaddeus. Don't be an old sour face."

Christmas brought the usual glow of candlelight and surface festivities to the Capitol. But larger realities continued
to undermine the holiday's mood. On the twenty-sixth,
Thaddeus and Ruth dined at the sumptuous home of Marvella
Clive. Among the guests were Marguerite and Peter Heflin.
But notable by their absence were numerous Southern
congressmen, senators and aides. Onrushing events dominated the talk.

"The harbor garrison at Charleston is being moved, I hear,
from Fort Moultrie to Fort Sumter. It's better situated, with
stronger works."

"Where are Senator Davis, Senator Butler and the others
tonight, Marvella? Are they snubbing you?"

"Haven't you heard, darling? People are packing. There's
going to be a mass exodus from Washington after the first of
the year. Congressmen, politicians, army and naval officers..."
Marvella Clive faltered, eyed Colonel Peter Heflin, cleared
her throat and took a quick drink of water. "It is such a
difficult time."

"What do you intend to do, Colonel Heflin?" The questioner
was a Southern lobbyist for the cotton industry, a pale,
black-haired man with a hawkish face and thin lips. There was
no warmth in his tone. "Do you stay, or go home to Carolina?"

Heflin's face flushed and he crumpled his napkin with a
meaty hand. "I find your question inappropriate, sir. This is
neither the time nor the place..."

"I understand Mr. Lincoln has invited Bill Seward to be
Secretary of State," Marguerite said smoothly. "What do you
think of that, Mr. Bates?"

"Shrewd move. It locks in Seward's considerable talents.
Very shrewd."

"Seward hasn't accepted yet."

"He will accept. Believe me, he will."

After dinner, Thaddeus finally was able to have a word with
Marguerite and Heflin. "What was that all about?"

"It's terribly difficult for Peter, Thaddeus. Jefferson Davis
keeps sending emissaries urging him to stand for the South.
They've offered him a general's command if it comes to war."

"Peter?"

"This is the hardest thing I've ever contemplated, Thaddeus.
I've got to turn against my own people. But this is something
I cannot escape."

"What do you think, Marguerite?"

"I've told him it is his decision to make. I... I will not leave Washington." Her eyes were troubled. Briefly they searched Thaddeus's face, then looked away. "I cannot support a cause which I find repugnant. Nor could I possibly leave here, leave my home."

Thaddeus felt strangely depressed on the carriage ride with Ruth back to Georgetown. A light snow sifted down. They made the trip in silence.

Two days later, Senator William Seward accepted the post of Secretary of State. In Atlanta, the Georgia legislature called on the states of Alabama, Florida, Mississippi and South Carolina to form a confederacy of the southern states. In early January, Senator Butler of South Carolina paid a personal call on Colonel Peter Heflin, urging him for one last time to resign his commission and return to his home state. Heflin refused. The feisty senator slammed the door angrily on his way out. That evening, Marguerite entertained with a small dinner party.

"Lincoln is standing firm. He insists the minority has no right to leave the Union. Jeff Davis argues that the Southern states have a right to self-determination."

"Thaddeus, someone would like to speak with you in the library."

"Speak with me? What about?"

"Just come along, please."

Marguerite led him from the parlor and through the hallway. The door to the library was closed. She opened it, ushered him inside, then withdrew. Secretary of State William Seward stood looking out the bay windows onto the snowy night, smoking a cigar. He turned, fixed Thaddeus with an appraising eye and came straight to the point.

"Stewart, we need your help."

"My help, sir? In what way?"

"This is strictly confidential, is that understood? Whether you agree to this assignment or not, you'll not speak of it to any unauthorized person, including your wife. I might say, especially your wife. Do you accept those terms?"

"Yes, sir."

"Good. Then here it is: I'd like for you to go to Springfield, Illinois, and prepare for the President-elect's train journey to Washington next month."

"Bring the President-elect to Washington?"

"That's right. You're to contact each and every railroad company that's involved and we'll map out a twelve-day itinerary that will take him on a speech-making tour of the North and the Middle West. I want to include stops at places like Chicago, Cleveland, Pittsburgh, New York, Philadelphia. Can you handle it?"

"Yes, sir, I'm certain that I can. But why me? Surely there are qualified railroad executives who'd be delighted to arrange it for you."

"There are several reasons. One is that you and Mr. Lincoln are acquainted. He knows you and trusts you. Also, you are not well-known outside Washington, and this might come in handy. Most important, however, is the matter of security. I know that you won't be tempted to boast about what you're doing or spread it all over hell's half-acre, as some politicians would do. I can't impress on you too strongly the need for discretion."

"May I ask why?"

William Seward frowned, his handsome face bathed in shadow from the lamplight. "Because," he said, "this city is crawling with hotheads who want to assassinate Abraham Lincoln."

An icy wind slashed off Lake Erie. Thaddeus leaned into it, clutching at his overcoat collar with one hand and his valise with the other, and hurried from the closed carriage into the railroad depot. Another depot, another train. In the past week, life had been an endless succession of depots, trains, hotel lobbies, and meetings with railroad executives, traffic supervisors, and stationmasters. Never had so complex a timetable been drawn up for the purpose of transporting one man and his retinue. But then, never had such public passion and outright hatred been generated over the election of a President of the United States. Each passing day, indeed each meeting, heightened the tension.

Double glass doors closed behind him, abruptly stilling the wind. Thaddeus unbuttoned the heavy coat as he walked across the depot, heels pounding the wooden floor. The structure was typical of the new style of railroad stations, a style which he found heavy, pretentious and tasteless: bare wooden floors with brass spittoons and dark woodwork, soaring carved beams of dark mahogany overhead, clerks peering from barred cages, a pervasive odor of smoke and oil and metal. On the platform outside, the train to Chicago panted and steamed in the cold.

"Mr. Stewart?" A man moved forward from behind a potted palm. He carried a black leather case and had the unmistakable austerity, in dress and manner, of the federal civil servant. Why do they never smile? Thaddeus wondered.

"I'm Thaddeus Stewart," he said.

The man's handshake was noncommittal. His eyes flicked about the depot. He stepped back to a secluded wooden bench and sat down, unsnapping the case. "I have a message for you from General Winfield Scott. Please sign here."

Thaddeus sighed. He wondered if all this hocus-pocus was really necessary, but then as quickly acknowledged to himself that it was. He scribbled his signature. A plain white envelope was thrust into his hand. He handed the messenger his own dispatch for Secretary Seward, and took a receipt. The man closed his case, rose quickly to his feet and walked away. He was disappearing through the double doors when Thaddeus heard his name called.

"Come on, slowpoke. I can't hold this train."

Major Herbert Willoughby, youthfully sporty in a civilian suit of the latest European cut, appeared from around a corner. He snatched up Thaddeus's valise and they rushed to the platform, boarding just as the conductor snapped shut a gold watch and tucked it with deliberate finality into his vest pocket. Thaddeus was slightly breathless as they settled into a private compartment. He opened the message from General Scott and scanned it, his expression darkening.

"Bad news?" Willoughby said.

"The usual. Baltimore is a hotbed of secessionists. In Washington, the plotters are lurking on every street corner. Scott has gotten word that the rebels want to seize the Capitol, block Lincoln's inauguration and shoot him dead. Secretary Seward is brooding over the President's chance of surviving the trip east, fearful that some lunatic will gun him down. The Baltimore plug-uglies want his head on a plate." He sighed. "Jesus Christ."

The train jerked into motion. Their conversation lapsed as it rumbled out of the station, gathering speed, and fled westward into the snow-clad Ohio countryside. Thaddeus thought of Ruth and the message he had received from her that morning. It was virtually the same at every major stop:

"I love you and miss you. I'm so lonely. Ruth." And occasionally there was condemnation for his failure to write frequently.

Willoughby seemed to read his thoughts. "Is she in a better frame of mind?"

"Ruth? Oh, I suppose so. It's our first separation, after all, and she took it hard. You can't blame her. Most men who've been married a little over four months don't go galavanting off on mysterious missions without a word of explanation. I finally told her it was government business, but her mood didn't improve much."

"Was the spat really that bad?"

"It was pretty bad."

This, he reflected, was an understatement. But there was no need to discuss his private life in detail. Ruth had reacted to the news of his assignment with a temper tantrum, screaming and rolling on the floor. She then withdrew into a shell, not speaking to him again until he was actually about to leave. At that point she burst into tears and hugged him fiercely, stammering apologies and declaring her love and adoration for him. Since then, the messages and appeals for forgiveness had followed him everywhere, but his own letters of reassurance seemed either unread or uncomprehended.

"True love ne'er did run smooth," Willoughby said gravely.

Thaddeus chuckled. "How wisely speaks the bachelor sage on matters of the heart."

On the last day of January, they pulled into Springfield, Illinois. Even as they rode in a carriage through the cold to the hotel, Thaddeus sensed the change in the town. There was a new sense of urgency and business. Uniformed troops were plentiful, streets busy. All this despite freezing weather and a threat of snow. At the hotel, the lobby was full and he waited for an hour to get a haircut. Everywhere the talk was of politics and Abraham Lincoln. At midafternoon the local marching band formed up outside and paraded in the cold in honor of a dignitary arriving at the depot. Springfield, a conservative town which Thaddeus remembered so well from his days on the Illinois Central, was supercharged by the magnetic power of the presidency.

"Mr. Stewart?" The messenger boy was wide-eyed, his face pinched with cold. "H-he would like to see you, if it's convenient. I mean, he asked if you could come over to where he is. 'Quietlike,' he said."

Thaddeus deposited his valise and followed the boy out of

the hotel and down the sidewalk, his face stinging in the wind. Several Springfield men called his name. He nodded in reply without breaking stride. At last they came to a nondescript building housing a general store on the ground floor. The boy pushed past a wooden door and led him up a narrow flight of creaking steps and down a dusty hallway. The boy knocked at another door and a voice said, "Come in."

Lincoln sat at an ancient rolltop desk on a straight-backed chair. It was chilly in the room and he wore a muffler around his throat and a heavy black suit. The room was used for storage, with assorted boxes and bales stacked to the ceiling on deep wooden shelves. A single dingy window looked out upon the cheerless afternoon. He pushed away from the desk; although he looked even thinner and more angular than before, his homely face creased in a smile. The face, always clean-shaven before, now sported a growth of black chinwhiskers. "Thaddeus, it was good of you to come."

"Mr. President!" Thaddeus took the big extended hand. He was almost as tall as Lincoln but had the odd impression that the man had grown taller. There was also a profound gravity about him that had not been evident before. The Abe Lincoln that Thaddeus had known, spinning stories around cracker barrels in country stores and riding in a buggy over his sprawling circuit as a lawyer, was no more.

Thaddeus looked about him in dismay. "But what are you doing up here?"

Lincoln chuckled, waved him into another straight-backed chair and sat down again. "I'm hiding out, Thaddeus. This is the only place I can get any work done. I've been working for days on my inaugural address. You know I can't make a speech unless it's all down on paper. But there are so many people wanting to see me, clamoring for federal jobs." He sighed. "They're like vultures. I've had a hundred and fifty here to see me already and more are coming into town every day."

"That explains all the hubbub outside. I've never seen Springfield like this."

"Neither have I. Tell me, Thaddeus, what's the mood in Washington? I get regular messages from Seward and the others, but I'm in a vacuum out here."

"You have your friends and your foes, Mr. President."

"That's politics. I'm told there are plots to assassinate me."

Thaddeus was startled at the candor of Lincoln's statement.

It was said without emotion, as though he were speaking of somebody else.

"Yes, sir. That's what I hear. We've drawn up a careful itinerary for your train trip to Washington. We're trying to avoid the southern and border states."

"I see." Lincoln grew thoughtful. "When do we leave Springfield?"

"On February eleventh, sir, if that meets with your approval. You'll be twelve days en route to Washington, with numerous speeches along the way."

Lincoln smiled. "Seward wants me to get wide exposure to the people and allay their fears. I'll try, but I can't promise much. Things are happening so fast. Mississippi, Alabama and Florida have already voted to secede from the Union. Georgia wants out. I look for Louisiana and Texas to follow any day now." Lincoln passed a hand over his eyes. Silence settled as he gathered his thoughts. The burdens upon the man seemed enormous, and he had not even assumed the presidency. "Do you know what I can't understand, Thaddeus? I can't understand why people would react so bitterly over my efforts to preserve the Union." The big hands reached for a drawer, pulled it open, drew out a sheaf of letters. Most of the letters were scrawled or block printed and bore drawings of Lincoln being stabbed, shot, garroted or hanged. There were many obscenities. One phrase caught Thaddeus's eye: Mad Man you wil Never Get to Washinton A Live. He handed the letters back to Lincoln without comment.

"I thought I was running for president of all the people." Lincoln's voice was heavy. "Why would so many want to kill me?"

"I don't know, sir. It does not make sense at all."

"Well so much for that Thaddeus, I want to ask a favor Before we leave here I d like to go down to Farmington and see my stepmother Sally I guess I ought to go on the train but with the least amount of fuss Do you think that can be arranged

sir It will be arranged

"Thank you Thaddeus I really do appreciate all done for me The big hand was extended again signaling the end of the conversation Thaddeus took it and then followed the messenger boy back down to the street

For no reason at all he felt an overwhelming sense of dread

There was no special locomotive and private coach immediately available—besides, such an arrangement would only draw needless attention—so they made the trip to Farmington in a caboose hitched to a freight. Lincoln was accompanied by Thaddeus and several lawyers and judges who were longtime friends. The President-elect relished the caboose. ("I've always wanted to ride in one of these things.") and his mood was jovial.

Farmington had no depot. Thaddeus drove one of the two ancient, open carriages which bore them toward the home of Sally Lincoln. The prairie was dusted with snow and an icy wind swept down. Lincoln sat beside him, eyes watery and nose reddened from cold. "My stepmother was the best friend I ever had, Thaddeus." The President-elect hunched in his heavy coat and stovepipe hat as the carriage bounced along over the frozen rutted road. "My family was in pretty sorry shape when she married my father She brought us a cheerful and positive change."

Again, Thaddeus wondered at the unabashed simplicity of this man who was about to assume the most powerful office in the land. Could such a humble spirit lead a nation at any time, much less now? He wanted to say something in warning, to say, Abe, Abe you re going into a lions' den! They'll tear a country bumpkin to pieces in Washington You've got to be devious and hard But then he remembered that Lincoln had been there before as a one-term congressman, he remembered that behind the homespun exterior this folksy man was as tough as any politician would need to be Already he had been unyielding in his leadership of the party, sending off daily exortations to Congress to resist any compromise on slavery The vulnerable exterior of Abraham Lincoln seemed an effective natural disguise disarming to his enemies and endearing to his loyalists Thaddeus stared out at the dreary expanse of Illinois prairie in winter, conscious of the profound paradox of this time and place and circumstance and thought That s me I'm a loyalist

Sally Lincoln the stepmother of the President-elect was not at all what Thaddeus pictured she would be The person who came out to greet her stepson who flung her arms about him and stood on tiptoe for a kiss was old and small and wrinkled Their embrace spanned a gulf of years since they had last seen one another, and both were in tears Lincoln's companions stood sheepishly in the cold hands plunged into

pockets, and tried to look away. They all then crowded into
her modest little house, which was overly warm from an extra
large fire in the grate, and sat sipping Sally's sassafras tea
while Lincoln held his stepmother's hand and reminisced
about the past and the hard life they had shared. Thaddeus
was spellbound, feeling as if he were eavesdropping on
treasured secrets. It had never occurred to him that Lincoln
came from such humble beginnings. His mood of unreality
continued into the midafternoon, when they went to the
small burial plot where Lincoln and Sally stood over the
unmarked grave of Lincoln's father. Tall and gangling, wiping
his eyes while the wind moaned about him, Lincoln muttered,
"I'll order a marker for you, Thomas. A man ought to have a
marker on his grave."

The hours had fled. At last they were ready to leave. The
horses stood in their traces, breath steaming. Lincoln held
Sally closely, stroking her face.

"Of all the family, I loved you best," he said.

"I worry about you, Abe," she said. "I worry about your
safety. I might not see you again."

They were silent. There was no more to say. The wind
whispered in the eaves of her little house. Lincoln released
her and climbed into the carriage. Thaddeus flicked the
reins. The carriage lurched into motion. Sally stood alone in
the road, waving, until she was but a speck in the distance
behind them.

A cold drizzle soaked Springfield on the day of departure.
Nevertheless, a thousand people gathered under a sea of
umbrellas at the Great Western Station. Inside, the waiting
room was overheated and smelled of unwashed bodies and
wet clothing. Lincoln shook hands all around and chatted
quietly with his wife Mary, a smallish, plump woman, and
their sons Robert, Tad and Willie. At a signal, they moved
out onto the platform and several voices shouted for a speech.
The President-elect waved the crowd to silence. His voice
was thin and high in the cold. Thaddeus had difficulty
hearing it all. "My friends, no one not in my situation, can
appreciate my feelings of sadness at this parting... I now
leave not knowing when, or whether ever, I may return." He
hesitated, groping for words. The crowd fidgeted. "I hope
and trust in God that all will be well." Then his tall, gangling
figure vanished into the presidential coach.

In years to come, Thaddeus would look back on those

twelve days of travel in fragments, rushing to this place and that, with crowds, crowds and more crowds. Lincoln's coach was furnished in rich carpeting, dark woods and tasseled fringe. The President-elect entertained a never-ending procession of visiting dignitaries at local stops. There was a uniformed military escort and official entourage.

The weather remained dreary as the train chuffed across country at thirty miles an hour, flags snapping and smoke billowing. Thaddeus's itinerary took them from Indianapolis across Ohio into western Pennsylvania and then back to Ohio again before moving into New York state. It gave them a seemingly endless succession of towns and villages. Crowds fluttered American flags. Lincoln obliged them with speeches but little reassurance. The words were there but the manner unconvincing. "There is nothing wrong between North and South . . . We entertain different views on political questions, but nobody is suffering yet." The cheers were ragged.

Lincoln became tired. They were all tired. Thaddeus heard him admit as much as the train chugged along to yet another rally in another bunting-draped town. "I'm worn out, unsure of myself." The President-elect passed a hand over his eyes. "I don't know what's going on in the South any more than they do."

In New York there was a brief stopover for rest and that night they attended an opera. Local opposition newspapers seethed with hostility. Lincoln was ridiculed for his western accent. Critics made much of his wearing black gloves to the opera and "hanging his big, ugly hands" over the edge of the presidential box. "How can this baboon be President?" one editorial asked caustically. Thaddeus, enraged, wished he could throttle the editor. Lincoln took it all with aplomb. "The unkindest cut," he chuckled, "would be for them not to write anything at all."

The train rolled southward through New Jersey's rolling hills and neat, picturebook towns. The engineer tooted his whistle to clear the tracks of children, dogs and chickens. Another packed reception awaited them at Trenton. Finally they pulled into the station at Philadelphia.

Thaddeus stepped off the train into the arms of Ruth.

"Oh, darling, I'm so happy to see you!" she cried. "I received Major Willoughby's telegraph message yesterday, and I couldn't sleep last night for excitement." She kissed him repeatedly while her father stood by looking embarrassed and

passersby smiled; Ruth's beauty caused the young men in the
military escort to stare in unabashed appreciation. "It has
been so lonely without you."

Thaddeus shook hands with George Barrett and took both
on board the train to introduce them to the President-elect.
Ruth gasped, fluttered her eyelids, curtsied. Lincoln remarked
upon her loveliness and exchanged a few words with George
Barrett about locomotives. Barrett was flattered that Lincoln
had heard of his engines and would have launched into a
lengthy technical discussion had not Thaddeus gently drawn
him away. As they left the train and rode to the Barrett home
in a hansom cab, Ruth was ecstatic. "Imagine, the President-
elect himself! My dear, no wonder you had to be so secretive.
Why I never dreamed..."

"A fine man," George Barrett said. "A rustic gentleman."

"Yes," Thaddeus agreed. "A fine man indeed."

That night, Ruth's physical passion was more than Thaddeus
could satisfy.

He was awakened before dawn. George Barrett stood by
the bedside in nightclothes. "I'm sorry to disturb you like
this, Thaddeus. There is a messenger downstairs. He says it
is urgent." Thaddeus drew on a robe and stumbled down the
stairs. Herbert Willoughby waited in the foyer, looking grim.

"What is it, Herbert? What's wrong?"

"I apologize, old man, but you're needed. I'll wait for you
to dress. Don't bother to shave."

Willoughby's urgency cut off further questions. Thaddeus
was ready in a few minutes. Their closed carriage moved
through dark, wet streets to Lincoln's hotel. They took the
steps two at a time and were admitted to the President's
sitting room by a short, bewhiskered man. He had red hair
and a Scottish accent. Lincoln, disheveled, sat in an armchair
wearing a robe.

"This is Allen Pinkerton, Thaddeus," Willoughby said.
"He's a detective for the Philadelphia, Wilmington and Baltimore Railroad."

Pinkerton frowned, fixing Thaddeus with piercing blue
eyes. "You're the railroad man, then."

"I am."

"There will be some changes in the itinerary, railroad
man."

"What do you mean?"

"Tell him, Mr. Pinkerton," Lincoln said.

The detective's eyes narrowed and he spoke with obvious reluctance. "Some of my men have uncovered a plot to murder the President-elect in Baltimore. The town is swarming w' Confederate sympathizers and plug-uglies..."

"Plug-uglies?"

"Street thugs. Bullyboys. Cut yer heart out quicker'n they'd say good mornin'. Yer plans has gotten out somehow, and they know you're supposed to change trains there. They want to kill him as he rides in the carriage from one train to another."

"There's no doubt of it?" Lincoln said.

"Not the slightest, sir."

Night closed over West Philadelphia. Rain sifted down upon the railroad depot. Abraham Lincoln, disguised in a change of clothing and a smallish brown hat, got out of a carriage and boarded the last sleeping car of the Baltimore train. He was accompanied by Thaddeus Stewart and Pinkerton. A sleeping berth waited. Lincoln, grumbling but cooperative, climbed into it fully clothed. The berth was too short, so that he was obliged to double up his long legs. The train lurched forward into the night. Thaddeus sat in a parlor-car seat, conscious of the eerie nature of this journey. Oil lanterns guttered at each end of the car, swinging to the motion of the train. It was shortly after three in the morning when they arrived at the outskirts of a city. Allen Pinkerton slipped into the seat beside him.

"This is it. Baltimore. You know what to do, Stewart."

"Yes. I know what to do."

The train groaned to a stop at Camden Station. Thaddeus listened to the sounds of trainmen talking outside and the noises of the sleeping car being unhooked.

"This'un goes to Washington, you say?"

"Them's the instructions I got, mate. You hook her up to the Washington train as soon as she's ready to go. And don't forget, or there'll be hell to pay."

The locomotive that had brought them moved away into the night. The trainmen departed. The sleeping car waited in its dark solitude. From where he sat, Thaddeus could see the berth, its curtain closed. No sound came from it. Shortly before dawn a drunk passed by outside the car, singing tunelessly, "I wish I was in Dixie, hooray, hooray. In Dixie land I'll take my stand, to live and (belch) die in Dixie..." At last the sleeping car moved again and, grinding and screeching, headed through a misty gray dawn toward Washington. As it gathered speed, the curtains of the berth parted and Abraham Lincoln emerged, stretching and running long fingers through his hair.

"Good morning, Mr. President," Thaddeus said. "We'll be in Washington directly. I trust you slept well."

Lincoln smiled. Obviously he had not slept at all. He asked about the regular presidential train, bearing Mary and the boys, and was told that it would follow on schedule today. Thaddeus brought him coffee from a small heater. Lincoln settled onto a seat by the window and his mood became pensive.

"Not a very auspicious beginning for a presidency," he said. "Not very auspicious at all."

XIII

Damn them! Damn all things Stewart! They were a hard-headed breed, hard-headed and acquisitive and mean. She was convinced of this and held to her conviction as absolute certainty. And who was to say otherwise? Who would dare challenge Maybelle Stewart's beliefs? A belief, after all, is one's most intimate possession, to be preserved, nurtured, defended. Even a belief rooted in misconception is the same. Sometimes even this thought crossed her mind, fleeting and disturbing as a shadow. She discarded it, cast it from her mind as vigorously as one would cast weeds from the garden. Damn them. Damn the Stewarts. Time would tell. She would have her vengeance, if only in the grim certainty of her isolation.

"This message, you say it came from Missouri?"

The Chinese man, Shingling, bowed. "From Missouri, yes. It came on the Pony Express and the clerk, he holler, 'Shingling! You takee to Mis Maybelle, chop-chop!'"

"No, no, Shingling. Don't say, 'You takee.' My dear, it's 'You take. Take this to Maybelle, quickly.'"

"Sure. You takee Maybelle quickly, chop-chop." The sturdy Shingling smiled, folded his hands, bowed. Behind him, the woman Lotus rolled her eyes in mock despair.

Maybelle gave an exasperated sigh. "But what if I don't wish to see him, Shingling? Did that ever occur to the lordly Stephen Stewart?" She paced the floor smoking a small cigar. "What if I don't choose to entertain him and Catherine here in San Francisco?"

"He your brother, Miss Maybelle."

"Oh, pooh! I promised myself years ago, more years ago than I'd care to admit, that these brothers of mine..."

She stopped at the great windows and looked down across the city and the bay. It was midmorning and San Francisco already was alive with pedestrians, horses and conveyances of every kind. Sunlight glistened upon ornate rooftops; balconies, bay windows, steep cobblestoned streets, and the masts and stacks of a vast array of ships in the harbor. The last of the fog was retreating in wispy shreds and rolling banks, but still obscured the distant hills beyond the bay. She thought, God, what a beautiful city! And with her wealth and powerful friends, Maybelle Stewart commanded it all. They called her the queen of San Francisco. But she would surrender, surrender everything, to have Vanessa back.

The lump came back to her throat. It was as big and unmovable as an orange stuck there, impossible to swallow down or spit up. If she let it happen—just stood there and did nothing—the tears would come back in a flood. She mustn't let the tears come again. She turned herself abruptly from the window and went to the desk, pretending a busy interest with papers there, while Shingling waited in respectful silence. Damn Stewarts, she thought. And damn astute Chinamen, too, who were too shrewd for their own good. "Well, why are you standing there like an oaf?"

"You want send message back to Missouri, Maybelle? I take."

"No, Shingling. Not 'I take.' It's 'I will take.' Oh, never mind."

"Never mind?"

"I mean, yes. I will send a message. Say, 'All right. If you wish to come, come on. I can't stop you.' Sign it 'Maybelle.'"

Shingling was gone then, followed by the ever faithful Lotus. How odd, Maybelle reflected, that a man could bring such change to Lotus's life. She had been a beauty, was still a beauty; in her day, Lotus had been the most beautiful whore in San Francisco, the prize of Maybelle's Nocturne. Then the sturdy Chinese farmer came into her life to be taught English by Lotus. Almost overnight, Lotus was no longer a whore. She gave up the profession, opened a cafe on the waterfront and seemed to exist for Shingling's periodic returns from the gold fields. In public she walked three paces behind him, awaiting his bidding, attending his needs. If the Chinaman noticed, it was not evident. He accepted Lotus's loyalty as one might accept the breeze off the bay. Only later, much later, did Lotus speak of it privately. And when she did, it was in an effort to make Maybelle understand, for she felt that she owed Maybelle this much. "I love Shingling. He is my man. I always loved him. But I have been unworthy of him, unworthy of his regard. Do you understand? I love him, and I would die for him. I thought that you should know this, Miss Maybelle." That was all. She never spoke of it again. But afterward, Maybelle remembered her own feelings for a man, the tall plainsman Van Harrison who had fathered Vanessa; and remembering, she understood.

Vanessa. Oh, dear God, where are you, Vanessa? She had haunted the places where the wagon trains arrived from their long treks, seeking word of Vanessa. From the wagoners there came hints and whispers. There was a white woman, a white woman with flaming hair and cool blue eyes whom they called Sunset Woman, and it was said that this woman lived with a Cheyenne tribe, and was the concubine of a chief. But it could not be proven. No one had seen such a woman with a tribe. It was talk that rippled around the campfires and the mining camps. And in that vastness, Maybelle knew, the tongues of men bore lies and legends as easily as truth.

So now, with this word that Stephen and Catherine were coming, she was almost glad. Again, how strange. The old hatreds were supposed to endure. Indeed, if this were her brother Nathan, or their father Isaiah, they would endure still. She remembered Nathan rejecting her plea for help so many years ago when she was desperate and adrift in New Orleans; she remembered and hated him still, even though he was dead. And the bitter gall of her father's rejection lingered as well, as wormwood in her soul. But there the hurt was compounded, mixed with thwarted pride and agony of frustration; for Isaiah Stewart had died too, and was beyond her vengeance—had died, they said, still refusing to speak her name.

"Damn you, I'm a human being!"

Her shout startled her. The words bounced back into her consciousness from the walls of the silent room. It was almost as if someone else had shouted, and not her. The others, the girls in their rooms and the servants below, had they heard? Maybelle stood still, listening for a footfall on the stairs, a rustle of cloth from the hallway. There was nothing. Only the measured ticking of the mantelpiece clock, and a whirring as it prepared to strike the hour.

Stephen, she thought. Brother Stephen is coming. Good Stephen. Stephen will help me.

The thought made her feel better.

It was a fantasy, of course. Her hatred was a fantasy, a striking back and nothing more. She had learned this much from her strange meeting with the mulatto Francis Drake Stewart. The handsome, swaggering ship captain was her blood, too, though distant. It gave her a perverse pleasure to acknowledge this, even in San Francisco society. Her liking for Captain Stewart had been instant. But she could not say the same for the Southern woman Elizabeth Chares who had accompanied him to Maybelle's soirees. For all her elegant clothes and lah-de-dah manners, that beauty had been plainly in heat, hungering for something that only Francis Drake could give. Maybelle chuckled. Elizabeth Chares' lust had been so palpable that one could smell it. They had gone off together, then, on his beautiful clipper ship, *Typhoon*, and occasional cards came back postmarked Hong Kong, Naples, London, Murmansk. Then the cards had stopped. From an old sea captain Maybelle heard that Francis Drake had sold his beloved *Typhoon* and bought a small steam-driven ocean cruiser instead. The woman had gone back to Charleston, South Carolina. It was said that Francis Drake vowed to follow her. But Charleston these days was no place for a free black man. Maybelle thought about him and worried.

There was a soft knock at the door. "Luncheon is served, Madam. And you have guests."

"All right, Susannah," she called, "I'll be right down."

Mercy, how the hour had flown. She barely had time to dress.

*   *   *

The ties of kinship are the most powerful known to man. For Maybelle, they also spanned time and distance and even those inner chasms once considered unbridgeable. She knew this, even as she saw them coming in an open carriage from the wharf: Stephen, Catherine, a tall Indian called Crippled Wolf and a stocky, good-looking man named Ted Judah. But then Maybelle's shock rooted her to the threshold of her front door. Her brother was half a man! His left hand was a claw, his left foot a peg leg studded with brass, and half of his face—that handsome Stewart face, almost too beautiful to be a man's—was hidden behind a flesh-tinted silken mask. It should not have been a shock; she should have been prepared. Francis Drake, after all, had told her. "Your brother is not the same as he once was, but he survives." Others had mentioned the steamboat explosion of so many years before, and the man in the silken mask. And yet she stood there, her mouth open, one hand at her breast.

"Maybelle?" He came stumping up the broad circular walkway and climbed the steps. "Sister Maybelle?"

The tears gushed then, they gushed and poured, streaking her face with eye makeup, reddening her nose and eyes. The arm that encircled her waist was powerful, the hand that caressed her face callused and hard from handling horses and work. The exposed half of his face was handsome still, though deeply seamed, and his hair was flecked with gray.

"Oh, Stephen, my God! It's been so long! And Catherine" —she turned into the embrace of the striking blond woman who was her sister-in-law—"after all these years."

They were inside, then, in the parlor with its high ceiling and great stone fireplace and massive windows and rich furnishings brought from Italy and Spain. The talk flowed while servants brought tea and little cakes, served on eggshell-colored desert plates with doily napkins. The Indian Crippled Wolf sat in somber majesty balancing a fragile trifle on his knee and sipping tea from a tiny cup. He seemed too large for the chair, and his big hands too ungainly for the cup. Maybelle could not suppress a giggle. "I've had some unusual guests for tea, but your friend—"

"Crippled Wolf," Stephen said gravely, "is a man of the world."

Ted Judah intrigued her. She had heard of the engineer

and his passion to build a railroad over the Sierras to connect the east and west, and once had even ridden the twenty-one miles of railroad he'd already constructed out of Sacramento. "Crazy Judah," they called him, forever poring over maps and prowling the rugged mountains that rose like an impenetrable barrier east of the coastal plain. "Mr. Judah," she said, "you must be the most persistent man in California."

Ted Judah offered a whimsical smile. "Persistence is not enough, I'm afraid. I can't seem to stir up the kind of enthusiasm that really gets things done."

"Oh?"

"He's talking about money, Maybelle. Ted can't get his backers to finance construction beyond what's already been built. The wagoners threaten a boycott, the steamship line between Sacramento and San Francisco is resisting, the legislature won't put up an appropriation and he's still not certain of his route through the Sierras. Right now, Ted's got a railroad to nowhere. That's why we're here. And Thaddeus is due to arrive next week."

"Thaddeus!"

The days swept past. Maybelle was caught up in a rush of parties and dinners. There were frequent daytime expeditions to show them the sights of San Francisco. They attended the opera and watched a prizefight and took a leisurely boat cruise on the bay. At last the steamship *Panama* arrived and Thaddeus Stewart stepped off the gangplank into a rush of hugs and handshakes. Again the eye makeup dribbled down Maybelle's cheeks. "I'm such a sentimental cuss," she sniffed. Catherine patted her arm. "You're beautiful."

Thaddeus had developed into a husky, handsome man. His appearance at dinner in the Nocturne caused a sensation among the hostesses. Maybelle drew several of the girls aside for a quick lecture. "Stop drooling and keep your hands off of him. He's my nephew. Besides, he's married." But that did not stop the covetous glances and wanton stares. Thaddeus seemed not to notice.

It was Ted Judah who wondered aloud why Ruth had not come with him to California. A shadow crossed Thaddeus's face. "She went home to be with her father in Philadelphia. Ruth does not enjoy traveling." The subject was not mentioned again. But Maybelle's instincts told her all was not well.

Finally, Maybelle was able to speak of Vanessa. It was a private family talk with Stephen, Catherine and Thaddeus.

She poured out her heart to these sympathetic listeners, and the act itself was an acknowledgment of their blood bond. "She's so rebellious, so headstrong. I'm going out of my mind with worry. Finally, just before Stephen arrived, I got a message. An old Indian brought it. They said he was a Comanche. Vanessa wrote, 'I'm well and happy.' That was all. The Indian disappeared before I could even ask him any questions. You know the West, Stephen. I thought maybe with your connections..."

Stephen pondered. "It's a big country out there, Maybelle. But then you know that as well as I do. I remember a time..." He hesitated. "Well, never mind. We'll do what we can. You have my word on that."

Maybelle seemed relieved. She wiped her eyes and blew her nose. She said, "You started to mention something else. You said you remembered a time. What was that?"

He smiled gently. "I remember a time when another headstrong young woman left home. We couldn't find her either, until she was ready to be found."

Maybelle's eyes welled up again, but she laughed. "Yes, I remember," she said. "I remember that time."

Ted Judah, Thaddeus, Stephen, and Crippled Wolf boarded the steamer to Sacramento the following morning. It was a journey of a hundred and fifty miles along the twisting waterway to the northwest and took them twelve hours. Judah, his mind filled with information gleaned from charts, looked out on the picturesque scenery and mused, "If we were birds, we could fly it in half the distance. And I figure a railroad from San Francisco would run nearly as straight." The engineer was a dynamo of enthusiasm about the region and the prospects for extending the railroad eastward into the mining country. As they disembarked from the steamer in the busy town of Sacramento, he was reciting the findings of his own private studies. "They mined two-hundred million dollars' worth of gold out of the Sierras since eighteen and forty-eight. Most of that was placer gold, and the miners carried it out themselves. Things are different now, the operations bigger and more expensive. There's a lot of rock mining and they wash down the ore banks with high-pressure hoses. They're doing hydraulic mining and quartz mining, and that takes heavy equipment. I found this out in my survey for the Sacramento Valley Line. There's plenty of business for an extended railroad. Plenty of business."

They boarded the train at Sacramento for its short run through the lush valley. The landscape flourished with grasses, wildflowers, grazing horses and cattle. The coaches were drawn by an eight-wheeled locomotive of twenty tons, laying a trail of blue woodsmoke. To the east, the Sierra Nevada range rose in mighty splendor, drawing them as if by some magnetic force. "Up there's where we've got to go," Judah said, squinting. "And that's where we'll do it."

Thaddeus was not sure that he understood what Judah meant. But he asked no questions now. All in due time, he thought. If Ted Judah said it, it was so.

The railroad from Sacramento did not end at a valid destination, but rather at a collection of huts and shacks and a dirt trail winding out to the main wagon road. Saddle horses and pack mules awaited them. In a short time they were mounted and moving eastward along an easy grade into the hills. At nightfall they camped by a clear meandering brook, and the following day they began the long winding climb up the western slope, giving way to heavy wagons that came rumbling and bumping down from above. A Pony Express rider clattered past them, bound for Sacramento, horse and rider running sweat. It was another day of travel before they arrived at the mining town of Dutch Flat, at the head of the Bear River. The settlement was a random scattering of tents, unpainted shacks, and lean-tos fifty-five miles northeast of Sacramento. But it was populous enough to have a dozen saloons, two bordellos, a horse doctor and a druggist.

"A druggist?" Stephen said.

"Dr. Daniel W. Strong, at your service, sir." He was a smallish, leathery man with a strong handshake and sharp features. He escorted him into his drugstore, a dark warren of cluttered shelves displaying medicines, potions and linament rubs. There was a glass case filled with combs, razors, barber shears, and several large jars of hard candy. "Appreciate your coming, Mr. Judah. Got something that might interest you."

"So your letter implied."

Daniel Strong brought out bourbon, glasses, and cigars. As they drank, he peered out through his dusty windows at the dirt street. There was constant traffic in wagons, horsemen, pedestrians. "Dutch Flat's an up-and-coming town, Mr. Judah. It don't look like much right now, but there's a big future here. Yep, a big future. My interest is business. The more traffic we can generate through Dutch Flat, the better it is for business. Now, I been hearing about your railroad plan, and that's all well and good. But I doubt if it would come through Dutch Flat. We sure could do with a good wide wagon road though."

"A wagon road?"

"A wagon road right through Dutch Flat and over the Sierras into the new mines of the Nevada country. Hell's bells, we could run wagons all the way to Salt Lake City."

"Well now, Mr. Strong—"

"Wait, before you say anything. Wait and see what I got to show you. Daniel W Strong eyed his saddle-weary guests and poured another round of drinks. "How would you gentlemen like to take a little ride?"

Undismayed by their pained expressions, he led them out to the horses, mounted his own chestnut mare and moved up the dirt street of Dutch Flat at a walk. Muscles aching and bones protesting, they followed. Thaddeus lost track of the time as they wound around the trail, moving toward a notch in the high spine of the range. Dr. Strong slowed his horse and pointed. "That's where we're going, Mr. Judah Recognize it?"

"No, sir. I haven't been up this trail before."

"That's Emigrant Pass, Mr. Judah. And beyond it is Donner Pass, and that leads right down to Donner Lake. A good wagon road over there ought to be passable the better part of the year." The druggist moved ahead again, up the slope.

At last, when it seemed that they would never arrive, the trail flattened, made another bend and they rode onto level ground. Abruptly the panorama made Thaddeus's heart lift in his chest. To the east as far as they could see rolled the mighty Sierra Nevada range. Behind them, sunlight broke through light cloud cover and set the mountains alight. The beauty of it, from blue hollows to jutting ridges and snow-capped peaks bathed in fiery glow, caused them to sit their horses in awed silence. Ted Judah finally dismounted in a flurry of excitement, removed his barometer and survey instruments from a pack mule and busied himself with measurements and sightings. The longer he worked the more animated he became. "Elevation six thousand, six hundred and ninety feet, Dr. Strong. That confirms the army's map readings. But the grade, the grade looks right! We could dig a tunnel here, blast a little there, bring it through. What do you say, Thaddeus?"

Thaddeus also had dismounted and had stood letting his eye trace the convolutions ahead. His excitement was rising to match Judah's. "Can't tell much yet without going over the ground. But I'd say yes, Ted. I'd say it's very possible."

"That's what I figured," the druggist beamed. "A good wagon road."

"Dr. Strong," Ted Judah announced, "we might do a whole lot better for Dutch Flat than a wagon road. You might just get yourself a railroad."

The druggist spat a stream of tobacco juice. "Well, if that don't beat all."

They returned to San Francisco ten days later in a mood of triumph. But as they rode in a carriage through the streets, Thaddeus sensed a strange undercurrent at work. People gathered in front of the newspaper office, reading from dispatches tacked to bulletin boards. Faces had the strained look of subdued excitement and pedestrians clustered on street corners, talking volubly.

When they finally arrived at Maybelle's mansion, it was Catherine who met them in the front foyer. Her face was taut.

"Oh, Stephen," she said, "they've fired on Fort Sumter. The President has called for troops to mobilize. The nation is at war!"

"War!"

They sat down in the parlor, stunned.

War.

Suddenly all thoughts of railroads swept from Thaddeus's mind. The monster was loose to stalk the land. It was too unreal, too devastating to accept at once. The thing they had so dreaded, the upheaval that must be prevented at all cost, had come to pass.

"Thaddeus, you're pale as a ghost."

"I . . . I must go back," he said. "I must go back east."

"Oh dear, what will become of us?" It was Maybelle, joining them from the other room. "What will become of us now?"

Thaddeus Stewart took the next steamer to Panama.

XIV

They came down the pike in hot, dust-blown columns, flushed with youth. July heat bore down, the sunshine baking green Virginia fields and fencerows. The columns made that restless, clanking sound of an army on the move, an army of haversacks and bedrolls, cartridge belts and canteens, sheathed bayonets and new muskets gleaming. Sweat saturated everything, the new boots and uniforms and bedrolls; dust sifted into eyes and noses and ears; dust rose in smoky puffs from marching feet and lay like brown smoke over the ranks. In the fields, the rich, rolling fields commanding panoramic views of distant blue hills and winding creeks, cattle watched them pass and robins sang from boughs of hickory, walnut and ash. Behind the infantry came the horse teams, in pairs, pulling guns and caissons. The guns lurched and bucked in the rutted road, dead weight on their heavy wheels; even in movement the guns made an ominous rumble. Artillerymen rode the big horses, whistling and harness-whipping them through the heat

The Brigadier was a florid restless man with the face of a red owl He rode straight backed and tense upon a nervous dappled gray, and was forever sending his aides clattering down the column on urgent matters of command The Brigadier had been a dry-goods merchant in Baltimore who gained his star by political pull, but bore a passion in his heart for the Union He vowed that his command would distinguish itself in battle

"We're going to whip their asses Captain Stewart The Brigadier squinted in the sunlight and mopped his face with a red bandana "War'll be over in two weeks mark my words Johnny Reb he'll get a taste of our musket fire and light out for Richmond." He cleared his throat noisily, leaned over in the saddle and spat.

"Yes, sir," Thaddeus said.

"Well, time to troop the line. Wouldn't you say so, Colonel Bibb? Time to troop the line, give the boys a show."

"The, uh, men need their break, sir. It's been almost an hour."

"Haw! Strong lads. We'll ride back a ways first, let 'em raise a shout, boost morale." The Brigadier wheeled the dappled gray and headed back along the columns at a canter, riding in the high grass at the fencerow. The staff, including Thaddeus and the colonel, followed.

The Brigadier was right. At sight of a real general, whether he bore one star or three, the trudging ranks straightened their backs, quickened their step and raised lusty cheers. "Let's hear it, boys, for the Brigadier. Hip hip, hoorah! Hip hip hoorah!"

Spirits soared, enthusiasm was at razor edge. Thaddeus himself felt it, a surging energy and anticipation unlike anything he had known before. After all the dismal weeks and months of training, encamped on the heights of Arlington overlooking Washington and drilling day after day in the fields, it finally came to this. The Army of the Potomac was marching to battle. General McDowell had led them out of the city in a holiday mood as crowds lined the dusty streets, cheering wildly, and young women rushed out to poke flowers into the barrels of their muskets. The army was accompanied by a strange assortment of spectators and hangers-on: congressmen, newspaper correspondents, socialites, women. By carriage, horseback, and on foot they followed along, some bearing picnic baskets and wine bottles, anxious to witness the army's triumph in the field. And now they were on the soil of Virginia, bound for a place called Manassas Junction where it was said that Beauregard himself—the villain who'd been in command at Charleston during the bombardment of Fort Sumter—blocked their march to Richmond with a ragtag force of rebels who trembled in their boots.

Voices shouted from the ranks. "Are we gonna whup 'em, General?"

"You bet we are!" the Brigadier declared.

"They're gonna feel Union steel, General!"

The Brigadier snatched off his hat and waved it, rearing the dappled gray. His hair was white and gleaming in the sunshine. The dusty columns loosed fresh volleys of cheers. Triumphant, the Brigadier cantered back toward the front of the columns, where it was not so dusty, the staff clanking along behind. Colonel Bibb muttered, "Good show."

They called a rest halt. The troops collapsed into the grass along both sides of the road, pulling out canteens and cutting fresh chaws of tobacco. Birds twittered in leafy green branches overhead. Sunlight filtered down in straight shafts. A warm breeze rippled the grass. There was a haunting beauty to it all.

"Lawd," Thaddeus heard a boyish voice say, "if it ain't a lovely day to go to war."

They went into bivouac at Centreville.

It took Thaddeus the better part of an hour to locate Colonel Willoughby's regiment. Willoughby shook hands eagerly. Trim, mustachioed and handsome, he was one of the army regulars on whom everything seemed to count these days. Thaddeus felt acutely his own lack of competence, and said so. "Herbert, without you regular officers and sergeants, this army would fall apart. I don't think we'd know enough to march down the pike."

Willoughby lit a cigar and grew thoughtful. "I'm glad you're with us, Thaddeus. I'm glad you took your commission. I'd hate to think of you out there as a private soldier."

"It's ridiculous for me to be an army captain. I feel so ill-prepared."

"We're all ill-prepared. Your brigadier was selling yard goods four months ago. I doubt if any greener army ever took the field for battle." Willoughby's tone was suddenly morose. "We need more time, more drill. Some of my commanders can't even deploy their battalions into a skirmish line yet, the troops are so raw. They've been drilling in platoons and companies. But tomorrow, or whenever it comes, we'll be trying to maneuver whole divisions and brigades. And not on a parade ground, either. In battle. We'll be moving them over hills and woods and fields, with hell breaking loose all around. Even the regulars are rusty. Good God, I've never been in battle myself."

"It probably won't matter, Herbert. Everybody says the war will be over in two weeks."

Willoughby frowned. "Don't count on it, Thaddeus."

Thaddeus was silent. His friend's tone intensified his own

somber mood. Events seemed to be pushing in around him, picking him up and bearing him along like a leaf in a whirlwind. Destiny was beyond his control. They were on the eve of something, a horror unlike anything he or Willoughby, or any of them, had experienced before. And for reasons he could not define, Thaddeus Stewart dreaded tomorrow.

"And your cousin Marguerite?" Willoughby said abruptly. "Is she well?"

"Marguerite is well," Thaddeus replied. Instinctively his hand moved to his breast pocket and felt the letter there, a letter haunting in its unexpected power and filled with the pangs of good-bye. Odd, that Willoughby would ask of Marguerite and not of Ruth. "Yes, Marguerite came to see us off."

"Colonel Heflin is doing well in Kentucky. He has a cavalry command. They've had some skirmishes already."

"So I've heard."

"And Ruth?"

"She remains in Georgetown. Her father has come down to stay with her."

It was desultory talk, now, almost as casual acquaintances and not as friends. There was a strain between them, and he sensed that Willoughby's mind had drifted to duty. An aide brought a message. Another arrived with a roll of maps. Thaddeus knew it was time to leave. He stood up.

"Forgive me, Thaddeus," Willoughby said. "There is so much to do."

"Of course."

They shook hands again, strongly. Willoughby's eyes searched his face. "Be careful, my friend."

"God be with you, Herbert."

He walked back to his own bivouac area deep in thought. The letter in his pocket was etched upon his mind, so many times had he read it. "Thaddeus, darling," she had written, "I am so worried. I had a terrible dream last night about you, almost a premonition. Oh, this dreadful war, how I wish it wasn't happening! Please, please watch out for yourself. You'll think me outrageous for writing this, and I know I shouldn't even think such things; but I could not imagine life without you, Thaddeus. I could not bear it. Wherever you go, my love goes with you." She had thrust it into his hand there in the shadow of the half-completed Washington Monument as the brigade formed up to march. And then, before the eyes of Ruth and Marvella Clive and assorted friends, she had flung her arms about him in a passionate embrace, bursting into tears. Even now, he could almost feel Marguerite's softness and warmth, smell the heady fragrance of her hair, feel it brushing against his face in waves of gold.

And Ruth. What was happening to Ruth? Upon his entering the army, she seemed to have withdrawn. There were bursts of recrimination and of passion, yes, but these were followed by long periods in which she seemed not to realize he was there, and periods in which the army was never mentioned. It was as if the army, the war, the Washington madness of shouted commands and marching troops and wheeling caissons, did not exist at all. She spent long hours, whole days even, in their bedroom, whispering to her dolls. But then she would come back, her eyes full of warmth and interest. And she would murmur, "Do you know how much I love you, Thaddeus? Do you have any idea?" The night before he was to leave, she had loved him deeply and warmly. For the first time, their lovemaking had not taken the form of wild, thrashing passion, but was slow, tender, rich with meaning. Briefly then, with a revelation that startled him, Thaddeus glimpsed a facet of Ruth that thrilled him deeply, a Ruth whom he could love. It was as if he were seeing for the first time a new person. Her climax to that lovemaking was the most intense he had ever known. But then the spell was broken, the mood passed. She turned away from him and was cold.

"Captain Stewart, sir?"

"Yes, Sergeant."

"The Brigadier has called a meeting of staff officers."

He tossed aside his cigar and hurried to the command tent.

He lay on his belly in the shadow, as still as death, watching the detail finishing its mess chores, watching them put away the last of the pans and vats, watching them douse the fire. Beside him, Fat Sam stirred restlessly in the weeds. He hissed for silence. But the soldier had lost his enthusiasm even for extra food and whispered back his complaint. "Damn, John Colby, how long we gonna lay here."

"Just a little more now. Shut up and be still."

It had taken longer than he had planned. Ordinarily, John Colby Stewart would have given up this lark an hour ago. But there was a matter of pride to be considered here. He prided himself as a scrounger, the best scrounger in the regiment, hell, best in the division. He had promised the boys extra rations, and extra rations it would be.

At last only the cook sergeant remained, a burly, tattooed old soldier fond of his liquor and his food. Tonight, as John Colby figured, the sergeant was in a mood for neither. He locked the wooden cupboards of the mess wagon, blew out the lantern and retired to his tent. The mess area was empty then, empty and still, and for miles around them the camp-fires were going out and quiet settled, leaving only the sentries to march their rounds.

John Colby rose from the tall grass, the bayonet clenched in his fist. He moved stealthily across the ground, keeping to the shadows, and made it to the back of the mess wagon. Easy, he thought. Piece of cake. He found the cupboard he sought, slipped the bayonet under the edge of the metal hinge and slowly worked it back and forth.

Creeaak.

Damn! He stopped, stood still, held his breath, looked to the cook's tent. There was no movement. Minutes went by. He resumed his task. Fools, he thought; they lock the cabinet front but forget that doors have hinges. At last the first hinge broke loose and tumbled softly into the grass. Soon the second was free. He opened the cupboard soundlessly, reached inside and began to fill his open blouse with meats and tins, loaves of bread and two bottles of rum. When he had all he could carry, he ducked down and away, slipping like a wisp of smoke into the woods behind the tent. Heavy footfalls sounded behind him, crunching dry twigs underfoot. He stopped, heart pounding, and prepared to make a dash for it.

"John Colby?"

His breath expelled in exasperation. "Damn it, Fat Sam, don't sneak up on a man like that. Here, carry some of this stuff."

They moved down the hill, stumbling in the darkness, splashed through a brook and climbed the wooded slope on the other side to where the others would be waiting. Light clouds scudded over the face of a half-moon which shed its feeble light onto the bivouac of an army wrapped in sleep. At last they came to five forms lying in blankets beside a dying fire.

"Here, we ain't going to have none of that," John Colby muttered. He nudged at a sleeping body with his foot, getting a grumble in response. Then he kicked. The form erupted from its blanket roll in a flurry of oaths. But when the youth recognized who had done the kicking, the oaths died on his lips. Soon all five were sitting up on their blankets, rubbing sleep from their eyes.

"You fellas said you was hungry, so me and Fat Sam went after food. Now you go to sleep on me. What kind of loyalty is that?"

"But you been gone two hours, John Colby. And we was tired."

John Colby laughed, drew forth one of the whiskey bottles and removed the cap with his bayonet. "Here, take a snort of red-eye and you won't be sleepy no more." To show how it was done, he took the first slug. The liquor burned down his throat like a pleasant fire. Finally, eyes teary, he handed it to the next man and belched. "You, Fat Sam, stir up that fire yonder."

"Yes, John Colby."

They pawed through the food he had brought and voiced their approval. There was tinned herring, fried pork, honey cakes, bully beef and bread. It was a feast, and the hungry troops made short work of everything. When the last morsel had disappeared, a weasel-faced private nicknamed Hucklebuck lay back on his blanket and gave forth a loud and satisfying fart. "Now that, John Colby, was what I call good eating."

"Compliments of Private Stewart and the Army of the Potomac," said another soldier. His speech was slurred from whiskey. With grave ceremony, he downed the last of a bottle, smacked his lips and chucked the empty into the weeds. "Fucking aye."

"We best be gettin' back to the company," said a private named Peterson. "They might miss us. You can get hung fer desertion, sneakin' away like this."

"Hell, they ain't going to miss us, Peterson. There's a war on, soldier. They got better things to do than worry about us."

"Sergeant Coker, he'll miss us. He's a mean 'un, Sergeant Coker. I wouldn't want to cross him."

"You're a volunteer, boy. Coker can't do a bloody thing to you. Besides, I happen to know he had a bottle of rye stashed in his kit."

"How do you know that, John Colby."

"'Cause I put it there."

Hucklebuck snickered drunkenly. "You are a caution, John Colby, and that's a fact. I guess you're about the biggest operator in this man's army. That's a fact. Ain't that a fact, Fat Sam?"

"That's a fact, Hucklebuck."

"Where'd ye get all this stuff, John Colby. Where'd ye get it?"

"He stole it, where do you think he got it?"

"Stole it? God a'mighty, I don't believe that."

"Foraged is the right word, Peterson. I foraged for it. In this man's army, foraging's an honorable pursuit. Man lives by his wits."

Conversation lapsed. They sat staring into the fire. A warm lassitude stole over John Colby. His body ached from the day's march, but the whiskey dulled the ache. The whiskey also went to his temper. He looked about him at the half-dozen who sat in their blankets, saying nothing. A fine lot. They were boys, nothing more; hayseeds and louts who attached themselves like leeches and followed his lead. Each of them he had picked deliberately, beaten in a fight, cowed and absorbed into his following.

It was Hucklebuck who spoke now. "John Colby, you ain't afeared, are you?"

"Afraid, you mean?" He glowered. "What's to be afraid of? A little shot and shell, a little smoke? That ain't nothing to be afraid of. Why do you want to know?"

"No reason special. I just wondered, that's all."

"You wondered. You wondered." His tone dripped with contempt. The bastard was afraid. They were all afraid. He could see it in their faces, Peterson, Hucklebuck, Fat Sam, Greaseball, all of them. "You ain't yellow, Hucklebuck. I won't have no yellowbelly around me."

"Yellow? Naw, I ain't yellow." Hucklebuck chuckled nervously.

"No need to hassle him, John Colby," said Peterson. "He don't mean nothing by it. We all wondered if you was afraid. None of us ever been in battle before. We don't know what it's like. And when you think about it . . . well, it's the not knowing."

"Don't think about it, Peterson. If it's going to get you all upset, make you want to puke, don't think about it. Bunch of lily-livered cowards . . ."

"We ain't cowards, John Colby. But everybody gets the jitters waiting. I'll bet everybody wonders, first time in, if he's going to stand up like a man or duck and run. Don't you ever wonder?"

John Colby laughed deliberately, mockingly. He repeated Peterson's words in girlish falsetto. "Don't you ever wonder? Don't you ever wonder?" He brandished his bayonet and stabbed it deep into the ground. "Let's see what kind of a man you are, Peterson. Let's see you go for this knife."

"John Colby, I don't . . ."

"Go for it, I said. Get outta that blanket and go for it."

"I didn't mean nothing, John Colby."

The others were silent, wide-eyed. Their fear of him was conditioned and palpable, and he gloried in it. He felt their fear, felt it warm his insides.

"Go for it, Peterson!"

Peterson paled, looked away, swallowed hard. His Adam's apple bobbed nervously. "No, John Colby. I don't want to." It was a whisper, a pleading. "I don't want to."

Elation filled him. He could be magnanimous. The strong prevailed. "All right, Peterson." He chuckled in his throat, drew out the bayonet, wiped it on his pants. The steel gleamed in the firelight.

"How come you joined up, John Colby?" Greaseball said. "I mean, you should have been an officer, or something. How come you be a private?"

"I joined to fight, Greaseball. I joined for one thing and one thing only, to kill me some Rebels. And I'm fixing to do that very thing tomorrow."

Tomorrow. He had pushed it from his mind, thrust it away like something evil. Tomorrow. John Colby spat into the fire. His spittle sizzled. He thought, What am I doing here? But he knew. Inside, he knew. At Pittsburgh, the chief constable had given him a choice, the army or jail. It was the penance for a series of petty thefts. The words of the constable still droned in his tormented consciousness. "John Colby, you're the blackguard of the Stewart family, and your grandfather would turn in his grave if he knew." The bastard. Well, so he was in the army. He was a Pennsylvania volunteer. And tomorrow or the next day, maybe, they'd meet the Rebs. Then he would show them, all of them. He would make the chief constable eat his words. No, more than that. He would make him eat dirt.

He smiled to himself, got to his feet and kicked earth over the fire.

"We'd best be getting back to the company," he said.

Morning. Gray light sifted off the tidal flats of eastern Virginia and Maryland, spreading westward across rolling green countryside, across hills and gullies and winding streams. The camp at Centreville was already broken and the army ramped southward by divisions and brigades along the Warrenton Turnpike, men stumbling in the early morning darkness. The mood was different now, without gaiety and songs. Gone the lighthearted banter of two days marching out of Washington. The cheers were silent. Men drew into themselves, into the quiet shelter of their own thoughts, watching the shadowy bootheels of the men ahead, shifting the weight of shouldered muskets for a comfort that could not be found. Stomachs cramped from the tension.

"All right, close ranks there," sergeants muttered. "You men, close it up and don't straggle." But the edge had gone from the commands, the sergeants adopted a more kindly tone. Strangely, it did not help, but only added to the unreality of what was happening, what was about to happen. They were civilians mostly—an army of thirty-five-thousand armed men, and mostly civilians. Scant months before, they had been shopkeepers, farm boys, factory hands, drifters, mill workers. Few had fired a gun in anger. And now they marched in route step down a strange twisting dirt road in a strange part of the country to an even stranger destination, to kill youths who were just like themselves. And nobody really knew precisely why.

Thaddeus Stewart felt the tension around him. There was new tension in the Brigadier. His round face was more flushed than usual, his voice pitched an octave higher, his movements so jerky they reminded one of a puppet on a string. All night, messengers had come and gone to the command tent, and the Brigadier had had little sleep. Few of them had slept, in fact, and Thaddeus was grubby and out of sorts because of it. They had pored over the maps by lantern light at three o'clock in the morning, the Brigadier poking at the map with the bitten-off stem of a stubby pipe. "Gentlemen, the scouts say they have positioned their lines along here, on a rise south of this little stream. It is called Bull Run. Good defensive posture. While the assault brigades maneuver for a flanking attack here, we are to take up reserve positions and await orders here. Are there any questions?"

Even as the brigades moved out of bivouac, the troops had seen the civilians. They lingered along the pike and dallied in the fields, traveling by carriages, wagons, saddle horses. Thaddeus saw several well-dressed women near a group of carriages and wondered if Marguerite could be among them. A lieutenant riding beside him muttered, "The Washington swells out to see the kill. Lah-de-dah."

"They don't want to miss the war," Thaddeus said. "They expect us to drive 'em clear to Richmond. Do you think that'll happen?"

"If you had asked me yesterday, Captain, I'd have said yes. This morning, after that army coffee and army food, I'm not guaranteeing anything. Except that my stomach's queasy."

The order of march had been altered since yesterday. Different units were in the head of the line now with their wagons and artillery. Horse droppings littered the road and ruts from heavy wagons made footing treacherous. Men grumbled. "I just stepped in it again. Horse shit."

The first booms were indistinct, but came from the south. Men lifted their heads to listen. The sounds had no pattern and were muffled. At times there was a single boom and at times a low rolling quality like thunder.

"What is it?"

"Cannon fire, what else?"

"Ours or theirs?"

"Both."

And then they were marching southward again, in a solid movement of twenty minutes at speed. More cavalry appeared in the fields and woods around them, but because of the trees and hilly terrain little could be seen. At last they broke through on a slight rise. The Brigadier led the command party off the road onto an open slope and drew binoculars. Thaddeus saw puffs of smoke on distant open ground, each burst opening like a deadly gray flower with a heart of flame. Horse-drawn artillery moved at a gallop over the slope immediately to their front; beyond, a ragged line of blue had shaken out on the edge of a wood.

"That'll be Hacker's brigade," the Brigadier said. "The Rebs are on the other side of that creek." He gestured to an aide, who quickly opened a map case and pointed. The

Brigadier made noises in his throat. "That's it, all right. That's Bull Run." From the valley there came a rolling popping sound like fireworks, and Thaddeus saw whitish smoke along the front of the blue line. The Brigadier put away his binoculars and led them back to the road.

"Now," he said, "it's time for us to be blooded."

They were the elegant and frivolous. War was something distant, a lark and a diversion. It was great fun to live in Washington at a time of crisis, and greater fun to view it all with detachment. Crisis broke the boredom of dinner parties and teas; crisis gave impetus to one's ambition, a finely dramatic edge to speeches. Anything and everything revolved about the rebellion, from appropriations bills to cloakroom intrigues. On the floor of the Congress and in committee rooms, one thing and one thing only determined the merit of a bill: How would it affect the war effort? Waves of patriotism swept over men and women to whom such emotions in the past were plebian at best, mundane in the extreme. Even those who before had vacillated on questions of slavery and states rights now championed the cause of the Union, once the lines had been drawn for them. Society matrons who never looked at a soldier with anything but disgust now rolled bandages and listened to patriotic speeches; congressmen who prior to the call to arms had swung somewhere between the opposite poles of debate now proclaimed their antisecessionist fervor. It was summer. It was glorious. And what nobler sacrifice of American youth than to give life for God and country.

Bull Run was an ecstacy. News of the impending battle coursed through the city with the force of hot blood. As the troops mustered on the open parade grounds sweeping down from the Capitol, boisterous civilian crowds cheered them on. Women rushed to hug blushing boys in blue, ripping off brass buttons and decorating the troops with flowers. No rose garden in Washington was safe from scavengers seeking blossoms. And at last, when commands echoed along the lines and the bands struck up martial airs—brasses shining splendidly in the sunlight—men and women wept openly, waving at the columns of departing heroes.

No one could say how the exodus of civilians started or who started it. The thing was spontaneous, a spontaneous rush to the field to see justice triumph and rebellion quashed. Barely had the last of the troops departed the city, leaving behind the dust cloud of an army on the march, when the first carriages rattled out of the city. It was a trickle at first, but soon became a stream. They were a great mixed lot, these followers of the army: congressmen and pages, newspaper artists and correspondents, society grande dames and ordinary citizens.

"Marvella, hurry! We'll miss the fun."

"What on earth are you talking about, Missy? What fun?"

"It's the army, Marvella. They're moving to meet the Rebs in battle, and we're following to see. Come, Marvella. We'll take my carriage. That young Congressman Hannah and his aide will go with us. We'll take a picnic basket."

"Missy, you must be out of your mind."

"Everybody's going, Marvella. Oh, please do."

"Well . . ."

"Please."

"Oh hell, how many times does one get to see a war? I'll come. And shall we ask Marguerite?"

"Marguerite refuses. She is quite upset. After all, you know who has gone to Bull Run."

"Yes, I know. I can't blame her."

And so they joined the exodus of civilians. It was twenty miles to Centreville and another five to a high vantage point overlooking the action. On the morning of the twenty-first of July, the crowd clustered to watch the show. Marvella and her friends raised parasols against the sunshine. There were several members of Congress scattered about. Spectators munched cold chicken and sipped wine. From the distance came early shell bursts that could be felt in the ground underfoot. Some fire from the Rebel batteries lofted far beyond the lines of blue, and burst noisily immediately below them. Conversation was disrupted.

"Congressman, do you think the fire would reach this far? I mean, we're not in any danger, are we?"

"Never you fear, ladies. We'll have 'em on the run soon enough. Behind the forces of our glorious Union, you're as safe as you'd be in your own front parlor."

"Oh, Congressman, you are such a comfort."

Marvella Clive sniffed. There was an odor of burnt gunpowder, and from somewhere came the distant scream of a horse that had had been hit. She sat down upon a fallen tree and scanned the far slopes with opera glasses. Prudently, she had kept the carriage parked nearby. The matched bays pawed nervously in harness.

"Marvella, isn't this just too exciting for words?"

"I'm not so sure I'd put it quite that way, Missy."

"Oh, pooh. Why not?"

Marvella frowned. "Because men are dying down there."

Noon. The heat was intense. No air stirred. Men sweated and baked. Gnats were a torment. John Colby squatted on his haunches near the stream. Sweat streaked his face and trickled down the back of his neck. A cloud of gnats swarmed about his head. He swatted and cursed. But the physical discomfort was secondary. A deeper unpleasantness nagged at his vitals, so intense that he would have gladly endured the one to be rid of the other. It balled in his stomach like a hard knot and made him want to vomit. It worked at his lower bowels and turned his joints to jelly. It filled his senses like a vast invisible miasma of the spirit. It gave him no peace.

John Colby Stewart was afraid.

"Get down, Stewart! Hit the dirt, man!" Sergeant Coker glared at him from behind a log. The troops were spread in sparse shelter near the creek. Beyond, a man-made storm raged. It exceeded anything that the human mind could accept. John Colby watched in a kind of mental paralysis. Men, swarms of them in blue, were running across the fields, bayonets flashing in the sunlight. Officers charged ahead on foot, sabers drawn. From the throats of the masses there arose a sound that was not human, a mingled roar of rage and bloodlust. It was a sound that penetrated to one's bones, mingled with the din of musket fire that rolled in volleys across the field. Artillery bursts fell in gross patterns, vomiting earth and steel.

"Ready!" It was Sergeant Coker, shouting from the middle of the line. "Ready, you men!" Coker was rising to his knees, peering ahead. The company tensed. White faces turned to the sergeant. The sergeant was everything. The sergeant was the one link to order and reality. Behind them, an officer rode up on a black horse. He rode in the face of the shot and shell, disdaining it. John Colby looked at the officer. He was a captain, their company commander. He saw the captain's mouth working, heard the scraps of command through the din.

"... now, you ... On your feet, Pennsylvania Volun ... them how Pennsylvanians fight ... geant Coker, bring your men ..."

No, John Colby thought. No, they were out of their minds. Nobody could stand up. Nobody could stand up and go forward in that. But around him, they were rising. They were coming to their feet. He clawed at the log, braced himself with the musket, pushed himself erect on shaky legs. His knees were water. He wanted to fall, to find a place to hide, burrow into the ground like a mole.

"Form ranks on right side company forward! Forward, you men. Forward, damn you! God damn you sons of bitches, forward!"

Someone dropped heavily beside him, almost knocking him down. He glanced down and saw Hucklebuck staring up at him. The eyes bugged crazily, seeming almost to pop out of their sockets. They looked stricken and surprised. The lower half of the face was gone.

A lieutenant was running ahead of him. The lieutenant faltered, caught in mid-stride. The lieutenant's arms flung upward, as if grappling for balance. The lieutenant's knees buckled and he went down slowly. The lieutenant lay still in a crumpled heap, a great gaping hole in his back.

No. The thought plucked at John Colby's brain. No. It ignited there, deep in his brain, and swept like a fire through his soul. No. And another thought followed it. The thought was I don't want to die. The thought linked with the no and made a brighter flame, all running together. No I don't want to die. No-I-don't-want-to-die. NoIdon'twanttodie!

Blast. Smoke. Acrid stench in nostrils. Screaming. A horse was hit. The horse screamed. The raging bellows of men drowned out the screams of the horse. He stumbled over something soft. A blue-clad body. Another. Another. He was running over blue-clad bodies through the smoke storm, and around him burst the thunderclaps of doom.

No.

He stopped running. He stopped and stood, eyes agape, staring. Someone ran into him from behind. The collision slammed him to the earth. A hot blast erupted nearby, and a body above him flew apart, disintegrating in a burst of scarlet.

At that instant, John Colby felt his bowels let go.

He turned away from it. He left the musket lying on the ground and simply turned away, crawling on all fours. No. He was dimly conscious of warm wetness oozing down inside the legs of his trousers. He crawled through thick green grass, breathing the scents of smoke and blood. He crawled around still bodies in grotesque positions. Behind him, the din was subsiding. He crawled for a very long time until he came to the creek. And at the creek he stood up, waded back through the red water that was littered with bodies and muskets and horses and equipment, and crawled up the bank on the other side.

More troops in blue were coming on. And then he started to run. Someone shouted, "Come back, Colby! You yellow-bellied coward, don't run away!" He ignored the voice. He ignored his own name. He ran, lurching clumsily over the rough ground. He ran away from the smoke and the stench and the dying, away from the screaming and the deadly bursts.

He ran and ran and ran, gasping for air until his throat constricted and he thought his chest would explode. He ran wild-eyed, while a desperate thought went tumbling through his mind: Oh Jesus. Oh Jesus, Joseph and Mary! Oh Mother! I've sh-shit my pants!

The Brigadier was ecstatic. "We've got them, by heaven. Look at that assault! A few more like that and we'll have 'em on the run!" He mopped his face with a red bandana and gloated. "Captain Stewart, I want you to take a message." An aide uncased another map. The Brigadier jabbed his finger toward the left side of the brigade's sector. "In this area you will find Colonel Bixbee's regiment. Please give Bixbee my compliments and tell him to attack immediately."

"Sir," a staff colonel interjected, "Bixbee has taken heavy losses already."

"No matter. We've got the Rebels reeling now," the Brigadier said. "One more good stiff punch in the belly..."

Thaddeus worked his way toward the left of the line, his horse under tight rein. The animal was young and skittish near shell bursts. As he moved forward, he became conscious of a lull in the sounds of battle. It was a welcome change to be away from brigade headquarters. All morning he had

remained at the Brigadier's side, more spectator than partici-
pant. Command, it seemed, was a process of receiving and
sending messages. Unfortunately, news of fresh developments
on the field of battle moved only at the speed of a courier on
horseback, who himself might lose his way in the turmoil, or
worse, become a casualty. At first, Thaddeus had considered
that the extreme confusion had been merely his own. Finally,
however, it became evident that nobody really knew what
was going on, and this included troop commanders themselves.

"Colonel Bixbee? You'll find him over there, sir." The
sergeant led a detachment of Zouaves dressed in fiery red
britches and blue tunics. The men rested in a patch of
stunted woods, their faces set in that glazed expression of
extreme fatigue and combat.

The colonel looked as battle-worn as his men. He heard
Thaddeus's message without blinking, then replied: "Thank
you, Captain. We have been in this position for exactly three
hours. In that time, we have repelled two Rebel assaults. If
you will kindly look out there to our front, you'll see the
condition of my troops."

Thaddeus looked. Along a slope below the command post
lay the remainder of a battered regiment. They occupied a
natural defile, but with scant protection from incoming musket fire. They appeared to be even worse off physically than
the Zouave unit to their rear, with more walking wounded
than fit men. Spread over the field to their front for a distance
of several hundred yards were the bodies of men killed in
earlier actions. Blue bodies were intermingled with gray.

"How much strength do you have left?" Thaddeus asked.

"We're down by a third. My remaining officers are a
captain and two lieutenants. The captain was my aide. He
commands a battalion now. The others are wounded, or—"

He was interrupted by a fierce cannonading to their front.
To Thaddeus's astonishment, a battery of Union artillery
came wheeling out from behind its own lines to the right,
horses galloping madly over the battle-torn terrain. The
movement awakened a Confederate battery opposite Bixbee's
regiment. Other guns from behind the lines set up a rolling
barrage of answering fire, and infantry units began pouring
fresh fusillades of musketry into the Rebel positions. The
Union battery quickly unlimbered in their exposed position
and began dueling fiercely with the Rebel guns. As they did

so, a second battery charged from cover to take up position beside the first.

A unit of Zouaves rushed forward to support the batteries. Shell bursts erupted all around the guns, but still the artillerymen went at their tasks. Finally, in order to get a better angle of fire, three of the guns were advanced to an even more forward position. The maneuver quickly turned out to be a dreadful mistake.

"My God, Look!"

From along the Manassas-Sudley Road, there swept a mass of Rebel cavalry. The charge, so swift and unexpected, scattered the Zouaves even before the guns could be swung and brought to bear. As the cavalry thundered into the Zuoaves, sabers flashing, a mass of gray infantry emerged from the shell-torn woods to the right of the line, advancing on the guns.

Bixbee whirled to Thaddeus. "Captain Stewart, I need officers. Will you take command of my second battalion and prepare to counterattack?"

"Yes, sir!"

Thaddeus swung into the saddle and galloped down the slope. A sergeant came running from the line of troops. A great wad of chewing tobacco made a lump in the man's jaw.

"Who is in charge here, Sergeant?"

"I am, sir."

"I'm Thaddeus Stewart, assuming command. We will prepare to counterattack."

The sergeant grinned broadly. He was a meaty, freckled man with a shock of red hair. "And it's pleased I am to welcome ye, sir! I'm Sergeant Clyde Bonner." He turned to a nearby soldier. "You there, Private. See to the captain's horse!"

There was no time, no time at all. Before them, the fire of the besieged guns was rising in desperate intensity. But thus far, the gunners had ignored the advancing Rebel infantry. With a shock, Thaddeus realized why. In the smoke and heat of action, the artillerymen thought they were Union troops! It was madness, madness. But madder still was the idea that he, who had never commanded troops before, now was to lead a decimated battalion of infantry into an attack!

"Sergeant Bonner," Thaddeus said quietly, "are the men ready to move?"

The sergeant glanced down the line. The worn, sweat-streaked faces stared back at him. Thaddeus thought, so young they are, so anonymous. "They're as ready as they'll ever be, sir," Bonner said.

Thaddeus nodded and drew his sword. "Might I trouble you, sergeant, for a chaw?"

Bonner drew a plug of dark brown chewing tobacco from an ammunition pouch. Sensing the eyes of the battalion upon him, Thaddeus calmly bit off a chunk, worked it into the side of his mouth and returned the plug to the sergeant. He strode to the front of the battalion, seemingly ignoring the whisper of miniballs flying overhead. It was an act, a ridiculous bit of stage business, but the best he could do at a moment's notice. How else was he to establish a quick identity? The sword in his hand now seemed so puny, his own mortality so insignificant.

The gray masses moved resolutely toward the guns. And at last, at last, someone awakened. Feverishly, the gunners tried to lever their pieces around, to bring them to bear on the new threat. But it was too late. Thaddeus caught this in glimpses, sickened by the reality. The gray infantry stopped its advance, the first ranks kneeling and bringing up their muskets. The ranks behind raised muskets, too, so that the lines of gray were in stair-step levels, bristling with weapons. The volley, when it came, was classic and rolling. Smoke belched from the line. A storm of mini-balls ripped across the afternoon. The gunners and horses were swept from their feet as if by a gigantic invisible scythe. In one instant men were furiously working the guns; in the next—as if in a blink of eternity—they were down, flung over the wheels and limbers and gun barrels, dead and dying.

The gray infantry broke its firing ranks and moved toward the guns. Thaddeus looked over his command, trying to inspect for a split second each frightened face. He had their attention. He turned, glared at the charging Rebel ranks, spat a deliberate stream of tobacco juice and swung his sword.

"Let's go, boys!"

From behind him, a drumbeat throbbed. He sensed the troops scrambling out of the defile in a ragged line, bayonets glistening. From the corner of his eye, he caught a glimpse of the flag bearer hoisting Old Glory, golden tassels snapping in the breeze. He moved forward at a brisk walking pace,

thrusting the sword before him. To the battalion's left and
right, other infantry also was advancing in a mass of blue,
flags and guidons streaming. The sight stirred in him a level
of emotion he had never felt before. This was a killing
ground. And yet there was a terrible majesty to it all, a
grandeur beyond the pale of normal thought.

The Union counterattack caught the Virginia infantry by
surprise. Rebel gunners sprang to the captured batteries, but
had no time to bring them into action. Blue-clad infantry
swarmed upon them and locked in a wild melee of hand-to-
hand combat. Men went down in an orgy of battle, bayonet-
ing, kicking, gouging. The ground was slippery with blood.
So spirited was the attack that the gray horde withdrew in
disarray, under covering fire from Confederate troops at their
rear.

The last furious individual encounters raged on. Thaddeus
parried a bayonet thrust with his saber. His opponent was
big, rawboned, strong as an ox. They locked in grim seesaw
struggle, grunting like animals and groping clumsily for advantage. Thaddeus lost his footing and went down in a heap,
losing his grasp on his adversary. The Virginian tore free with
an expression of insane triumph, swung his bayonet around,
aimed it at Thaddeus's belly, drove. Desperately, Thaddeus
rolled. The blade missed his stomach but plunged deep into
his hip and thigh, into the joint. The attacker jerked the
blade free, and hauled it back for another thrust. Thaddeus
felt his strength ebbing and tensed for the blade. But it did
not come. The man grunted, abruptly straightened, clawing
for his back, and dropped his musket. His hands waved
wildly as he doubled backward, and the point of a Union
bayonet emerged from his chest. He died falling and the last
thing Thaddeus saw before being engulfed in waves of pain
was the grinning face of Sergeant Clyde Bonner.

The tide turned after three o'clock. It turned on the pivot
of fate, as Confederate reinforcements poured onto the field
from a train arriving at Manassas Junction. McDowell's
exhausted Federal troops reeled backward in the face of fresh
assaults all along the line. Orders were to make a staged
withdrawal. But inexperienced troops quickly turned withdrawal into a rout.

For Marvella Clive and the civilian spectators, it came in a dreadful unexpected rush. They had waited all day for the certainty of victory, intent on joining the celebration of the troops. Marvella began to suspect early that things might not be going well, for there were far too many Union wounded and stragglers streaming back from the battle. Their spirits were not the spirits of a victorious army, but of troops used hard and tasting defeat. Congressman Hannah and his friends reassured her. "Nonsense, Marvella. These are the skulkers and the injured. That's to be expected among untested troops. Things are going well. We'll drive them to Richmond, you'll see." But in the fields and along the roads, the trickle gradually strengthened. At three o'clock in the dreadful heat, even the congressmen had lost their certainty. And by four, the tide of misery burst suddenly into full flood, and there was no longer any doubt.

"We'd better be getting back to Washington," a top-hatted lawyer said, nervously eyeing his pocket watch. The civilians climbed into carriages and mounted their horses. They moved into the stream of dispirited, unarmed soldiers, following along at a snail's pace.

Unexpectedly, in the heat and the dust, Marvella heard an odd sound passing overhead, a fluttering sigh. The shell burst somewhere ahead of them, followed by another and another. Women screamed. Horses panicked. "My God, they're shelling us!"

Pandemonium broke loose. Word flashed back that a bridge was blocked up ahead on Cub Run. Soldiers and civilians pushed, grappled and shouted. The rout poured into the fields. As retreating troops came up from behind, panic spread through the mass. It continued even after the shelling stopped.

Marvella saw a well-dressed civilian man stand up in a carriage waving two pistols at the horde of soldiers. "Go back!" he screamed. "Go back, you cowards, and fight!" They swept around him like a river at flood. With a sob, he lowered the pistols and sat down. The carriage moved slowly ahead in the crush.

A thought nagged at Marvella's mind. Restlessly, she eyed the faces of the human mass surrounding her carriage. At last, she could contain herself no longer. She turned to the young congressional aide who was driving the horses. "Stop the carriage!"

"Marvella," Missy cried, "are you out of your mind? The

Rebels are behind us. They'll start shelling us again. We'll all be killed!"

"Hush, Missy. I want this carriage pulled over and stopped."

The aide sighed and reined the horses. "Whatever you say, Marvella."

She stood up and watched intently the passing horde of beaten troops. Interspersed among the soldiers were the army wagons bearing their cargos of wounded. Each lurch of a wagon was punctuated by shrieks and groans. An hour went by, and the tide of misery and defeat flowed past without letup. Officers, on horseback and afoot, mingled with the dreary host. Marvella, in search of the familiar face, gazed at each officer. Few of the passing troops even bothered to look back at the tall woman who stood in the carriage wearing a frilly violet gown and clutching a matching parasol. And though she scanned with a special intensity the faces of the wounded, they did not respond either. The presence of such a woman in such a place was bizarre. But there had been too many jolts to the senses this day for the human mind to register another.

The sun settled upon the horizon, behind a bank of clouds that sent streaming fire into the heavens. The twilight came and still Marvella stood. The faces were masked in shadow, and the shuffling, clanking forms merged into blobs of darkness. At last, when it was impossible to see any longer, she sat down.

"All right," she whispered. "You can move on now." Her heart was filled with dread.

It was almost midnight, and raining, when the vanguard of the defeated Army of the Potomac slogged into Washington.

"Where can we find him, Marvella? Where can we begin to search?"

"I don't know, Marguerite. The army is still coming into the city. There are troops massed in the fields below the Capitol. Many of the wounded are there. But we're not certain. He could be anywhere. He could be wounded, or . . . or missing."

"We must go. We must look. Please. Go with me."

"Of course I will, Marguerite. You know I will."

They rode in Marguerite's buggy, drawn by a fast bay gelding. It was raining again, and the muddy streets were

softening into a quagmire. Traffic thickened as they neared
the Capitol area. Pennsylvania Avenue was a mass of carriages, wagons, buggies, army vehicles, troops, and civilians.
Marguerite veered off and took a route behind the Capitol to
a street opposite the main thoroughfare. Here it was easier,
restricted largely to army wagons. At last they came upon the
troops.

The Army of the Potomac huddled in the fields in the rain
without even adequate tents for shelter. Exhausted men lay
where they had fallen, sleeping on their arms and in mud-
caked uniforms still bearing the stench and sweat of battle.
The wounded were generally isolated in tight clumps of
misery. Army surgeons and orderlies moved along the rows of
men, some lying on the ground and some on cots. Work
details hastily erected tents in the rain, but it was a wet,
soggy business and quite slow. It mattered little, for most
of the men had lain in a downpour through the night and
were already wet to the skin.

The matrons of Washington were there, society women and
dowagers and politicians' wives, church women, housewives,
soldiers' wives. They moved among the huddled masses,
ladling soup from hot buckets, handing out bread and cheeses.
Many had brought bandages and utensils to care for the
wounded. The surgeons had set up operating tents, and there
was a stench of disinfectant. Morphine was plentiful, and
behind the surgeons' tents orderlies accumulated amputated
hands, arms, feet and legs to be hauled away for burial. The
saws and drills were busy in the tents.

For an hour, Marguerite and Marvella walked among the
wounded. They tried to shut their ears to the groans of the
sufferers and blind their eyes to the horrors of their wounds.
Hands reached out frantically to pluck at their gowns as they
passed, and they stopped to give water and comfort where
they could.

"My God," Marguerite murmured, "can you believe it?"

They almost passed him. He lay on his side beneath a tent
section which had been erected as a lean-to. He waited near
a surgeon's tent with a group of wounded officers. Beside him
sat a big, red-haired sergeant with a freckled face. It was
Marguerite who saw him after they had walked by. Only by
accident had she turned her head to look at the lean-to, and
peer more closely inside. The red-haired sergeant glanced up

but did not speak. She gasped, and stood stock-still in the rain.

"Marvella, it's him. He's under the canvas."

"Where?"

"There. He's there."

"Can't be, Marguerite. That's not him."

"It is. It's Thaddeus. I know."

Then she was running, running through the rain and the mud. "Thaddeus! Thaddeus!" She pounded past the sergeant, who half-rose to his feet, and fell on her knees at the lean-to. The rain poured down, soaking her hair and her face and mingling with her tears. "Thaddeus!"

He was pale, pale as death. His trousers were soaked with blood from a gaping gash in his thigh. At the sound of her voice, his eyelids fluttered. He opened his eyes, saw her face so near to his own. His dry lips formed the word, and it came out in a whisper. "Marguerite?"

"Well, I'll be damned." It was Marvella, standing over them, holding an umbrella against the rain. "If I didn't see it, I wouldn't believe it."

"Will you help me?" Marguerite said to the red-haired sergeant.

"Do you know him, ma'am?"

"He is my . . . my cousin."

"Of course, I'll help you."

"We will take him home now." She was kneeling still. Slowly, she bent over him. She put her face to his face. She kissed him on the mouth. She stroked his face and his hair. "We will take him home."

XV

It was a gray sky, lowering. Clouds raced down from the northeast in ragged ranks of flying scud. The sea heaved on black swells, white-frothed and crested. Francis Drake Stewart paced the narrow deck outside his wheelhouse, mentally gauging the wind and the roll of the vessel. The wind was rising, no doubt about it. They could expect a blow. Good! He rubbed his hands briskly against the chill. A blow would minimize Union gunboat activity. The Yankees were good sailors, right enough, but a fair-weather lot and reluctant to give chase in the teeth of a gale. There were too many discomforts already on board the gunboats, and most Yankee skippers lacked enthusiasm for battling two foes at one time— blockade-runners and weather. He tugged a heavy gold watch from his pocket and snapped it open. Fourteen hundred hours. Time and weather; for a change, both were on his side.

He returned to the wheelhouse, slamming the door behind him. Francis Drake was still not accustomed to running a vessel from inside. He spied the wheelman, a keen-eyed youth, studying the compass in its floating housing. Beyond the wheel stood the mate, Cochrane, glowering into the murky weather.

"Mr. Cochrane, do we have steam?"

"Aye, sir. Steam and in plenty. But I'd as soon take her in on sail."

Francis Drake smiled thinly. He knew what Cochrane was thinking. One had only to listen and look about him to know. They were canvas sailors at heart, and had spent too many years in the clean open world of the great clipper ship *Typhoon* to be at home on such a vessel as this, the steamer *Fury*. A man of sail pitted elemental instincts against the sea in all its moods, traveling by touch, by the feel of decks aslant beneath his feet, by the sound of wind, the creak of rigging and groan of timber. And the smells? Well, the smells were not of smoke and oil on a clipper; they were of salt spray and dank scuppers and bilge, of well-seasoned mahogany woods and wet canvas and rope. On board *Fury* it was all so new and strange. She was a stout enough craft, all right, and very fast—a converted brig fitted with a steam engine and small wheelhouse, oversize boilers and bins for fuel. She burned coal or wood. There were sails aloft still, to use in reserve; but most often it was the engine that drove her, a throbbing mechanical heart belching smoke from a single stack aft of amidships. At her stern, a whirling propeller powered them at good speed. When combined with adroit seamanship, this engine had outrun the best pursuit the Union picketboats could offer.

"We'll make the harbor right at dark, I'd say. What do you allow, Mr. Cochrane?"

"A fair estimate, sir. And we'll cut it close."

"Then bring her to four-oh degrees, helmsman, and steady as she goes."

"Four-oh degrees, sir. Steady."

They would make the run at a slightly southward arc, putting the wind to their backs so that if necessary they could also raise sail. He disliked the motion of the vessel on a following sea, but counted on her strength to withstand the buffeting. *Fury* had a strong hull and stout timbers; this he knew, for he had carefully gone over every inch of beam and warp and had set the engine mountings himself. Those side timbers were solid oak and could even withstand a hit from light cannon, if it came to that. He had toyed with the idea of shielding her with a thin armor plate, but reasoned that the weight would be excessive. He would not sacrifice speed for such questionable protection.

The run to harbor would be difficult, for he carried a heavy cargo. They had loaded from a British merchantman at sea, and the *Fury's* hold was stuffed with medical supplies, food, and, most important, a large supply of gunpowder and ammunition. The risk was considerable, for a lucky cannon shot could send them all to glory with a mighty blast. But such cargo also yielded maximum profits in gold. And for Francis Drake, that was the essence of it all. Gold. Gold in abundance. Already he had made a king's ransom, stashed safely away. And only he and Cochrane knew where.

Gold, he mused, could work wonders. Gold could almost change the color of a man's skin. He thought of Charleston and Elizabeth. The townspeople despised him, of course; despised him for being a mulatto and for keeping the company of a white mistress. It was Elizabeth who flaunted their love, and had from the beginning. There was a streak of bravado in Elizabeth Chares that he'd rarely found in any woman, a compulsion to risk anything for a lark. It amused her, he knew, to ride in his carriage through the streets of the city, her handsome mulatto lover decked out in a suit of dove gray and a black top hat that was the height of English

fashion. In a city of privation, they dined on English beef by
candlelight in the splendor of her father's Charleston mansion, and she wore new gowns of silk, expensively cut.

Elizabeth's father, a proud, brooding man, tolerated it all
in angry silence, having also made his compromises in the
name of patriotism and private profit. For what Southern
shipping magnate could refuse these days to have as his
partner the skipper of *Fury*, the fastest blockade-runner
afloat? Captain Francis Drake Stewart might be a black
man—and in other times and circumstances, likely as not
could have been one of Mason Chares' slave studs to put on
the auction block—but he also had the Midas touch. He ran
the blockade for gold, refused to accept Confederate currency, and had the connections abroad that could provide any
merchandise. Arms and ammunition alone shipped in by
Fury were a vital necessity as the Federal blockade tightened,
and the food supplies that stocked Mason Chares' warehouses
would keep Charleston fed when other cities starved. As for
Elizabeth . . .

"Uh oh, looks like trouble." Cochrane's words jarred him
out of his reverie. "Yankee picketboat yonder."

"Where away?"

"Three points off the port bow."

He squinted into the murk. Sure enough, there it was, a
shadow on the horizon, fading in and out of the misty spray.
By the set of her hull he recognized the lines of a cutter. Like
Fury, she combined engine and sail. And from the look of
things, she was laboring. Francis Drake reasoned that *Fury*
still had not been seen, but it was merely a matter of
minutes. Then he would be obliged to make a decision:
Continue his curving tack into Charleston harbor, or make a
straight dash for the shelter of the harbor batteries? He
decided on the straight dash.

"Bear two points to port, helmsman."

"Two points to port, sir."

"We're going in," Cochrane said.

"Is there a better way?"

The slight correction brought a change to the *Fury*'s motion. Now she had a kind of twisting yaw as heavy waves came
crashing at her hull from three-quarters aft. Timbers groaned
and the engine changed pitch as violent motion of the sea
frequently hoisted the propeller out of water. This would not

do! Francis Drake eyed the brig's sails, furled and lashed aloft. "We'll set the mainsail, Mr. Cochrane."

"Aye, sir." Cochrane sprang from the wheelhouse, speaking trumpet in hand. His bellow cut through the noise of wind and sea. "Hands aloft! Set mainsail!" Men leaped to the yards and scrambled upward. Within a minute, the mainsail was spreading in the wind, tugging at the lines. Immediately Francis Drake felt the change, a smoothing of the vessel as she gained headway against the sea. The engine bit full water and held.

An hour dragged by. The Union cutter had long since discovered *Fury*'s presence and turned to intercept the direct challenge. The maneuver turned the clumsy Yankee craft three-quarters to the wind and crashing seas, causing wild erratic motion and severe loss of speed. Nevertheless, *Fury* would cross her bows within easy range of the deck guns. Francis Drake eyed the cloud masses and felt the rising intensity of the gale. Seas were raging now. Towering combers poured in upon them, interspersed with short, choppy giants that threatened to rip the hull apart. Much more of this and she could broach, engine or no engine.

"Captain?" The mate, Cochrane, had taken the wheel. Now he eyed him questioningly. They had weathered so many storms together that both knew instinctively the thin line between acceptable risk and mortal danger.

"Steady as she goes, Mr. Cochrane."

"Steady as she goes, sir."

The Yankee cutter loomed up at a slight angle from their bow, pitching and yawing a scant three hundred yards away. On her decks, crewmen struggled to bring her single gun to bear and Francis Drake heard a thin cry in the storm. "Heave to! Ahoy the motor brig, I command you to heave to and prepare for boarding!"

"Order full speed, Mr. Cochrane."

The mate was already at the speaking tube. Barely had the words left Francis Drake's lips when Cochrane was relaying the commands to the engine men. "Full speed ahead. Let's pour the coals to her, boys!" Drake could only imagine the hell they were going through below, as stokers struggled to feed coal to the boiler fire while being flung about wildly with each lurch and toss of the ship.

The cutter's deck gun spoke. Francis Drake saw a dart of

flame in the gloom. The smoke was snatched away by the
wind. The report was a soft boom, muffled in the din of the
storm. But the pitch of the cutter lofted the shot high above
the *Fury* and sent it splashing harmlessly far beyond her
wallowing decks. Loading the gun for a second shot proved
all but impossible, so that by the time the gun again came to
bear the *Fury* had surged past the cutter and was drawing
away. Still, the shot hit hard by the brig's port side, showering
her decks with spray. Francis Drake saw the cutter turn in
pursuit, boldly trying to catch up.

"Stout fellow, that captain," Cochrane said. "A cut above
the others, I'd say."

But it was done now. They had the leading edge. A shift in
the wind was in *Fury's* favor, and she drove with the sea
straight for Charleston harbor like a terrier with a bone in her
teeth. Through a darkening afternoon Francis Drake saw the
jagged shape of Fort Sumter rising like a stone sentinel, its
guns now in the hands of Confederates and commanding the
approaches. He did not have to look back to see the cutter
giving up its pursuit; for a Union vessel to follow much closer
was to court disaster. Already he could make out the wharf
area with its menacing backdrop of heavy guns guarding the
old city from sea attack.

"Very good, Mr. Cochrane," he said. "Take her into an-
chorage if you please. I'll go below."

He left the wheelhouse, conscious of the eyes of the mate
and the helmsman upon his back.

When Francis Drake was out of earshot, the young helmsman said, "Talk about luck! I figured we was done for that
time, for sure."

"More than luck, lad," Cochrane growled, squinting for
channel markers in the dying light. "It takes a lot more than
luck."

Night fell over the city by the time they dropped anchor in
Charleston harbor. Francis Drake Stewart stripped naked and
plunged into the icy black water for a brisk swim. He then
climbed back aboard, descended into his cabin, shaved and
dressed carefully in a fresh uniform. He thrust a pair of heavy
cavalry pistols into his belt and a dagger in his boot before
donning a woolen cloak. The weapons had never been drawn
in Charleston, but he knew that their presence—and his
reputation for combativeness—undoubtedly had discouraged
countless would-be attackers. If many in Charleston depended

on the tall, mulatto blockade-runner for helping to supply merchandise for the Confederacy as well as for private profiteering, they also hated him for his hidden horde, and for his dalliance with the city's unrivaled fairest.

Cochrane rowed him to shore in a dinghy. A seaman stood in the shadows gripping the reins of the captain's favorite black stallion. "All quiet, seaman?" Cochrane growled.

"All quiet, sir." The seaman obviously was anxious to leave these hostile shadows and return to the vessel. "I ain't seen a living soul."

Francis Drake swung into the saddle, touched his cap in acknowledgment of Cochrane's salute and rode easily into the gloom of the Charleston waterfront. All was quiet, to be sure. But the night, even by the light of a few guttering torches, was filled with eyes. He felt them peering out from behind the shades of tall colonial windows as the stallion picked its way along the familiar cobblestoned route. In his mind's eye, he could visualize the pursed lips, the eyes slitted in disapproval, the hissing intakes of breath, the whispered epithet, "nigger." Uppity nigger, riding with the stiff-backed pride of a white man. Pride, they clucked, goeth before the fall.

At last the great white-pillared manor house loomed into view, its parlor windows dimly lit. The house of Mason Chares, dealer in cotton and slaves, occupied the better part of a city square in a setting of shrubs and magnolia. At Drake's approach, a shadow detached itself from the porch and hurried out to him. He recognized the squat form of the old black woman. Wordlessly, she took his horse as he dismounted and strode up the broad walkway. The front door swung open before his foot was on the step and Elizabeth came rushing to him. "Darling! Oh, darling!" She gathered him into a frantic scented embrace. "We heard the gunfire. Somebody said . . . oh, never mind. You're here!"

"Hey, what's this? Tears for old Drake?"

She grabbed his hand. "Quickly, into the house." Inside, she slammed and double-latched the door before throwing herself against him for a lingering, full-mouthed kiss that caused her breath to quicken. "There is treachery, so much treachery," she murmured against his mouth. "The Yankees knew when you were expected to come in, even knew the route you'd probably take. It's been all over the city. Oh, Drake!"

Elizabeth took his hand again and drew him into the parlor

with its velvet settees, rich European furnishings and heavy
draperies. He could scent her heat, and the lust filled him as
it always did, making his blood rush. She wore a white gown
with a plunging bodice, and the whiteness of her—mounded
and swelling and deeply cleaved—inflamed him. Her hair,
black as night, spilled wantonly over bare shoulders and full
bosom; the blue eyes, blue as ice and striking blue fire,
devoured him, gleaming with lascivious pleasure. In the
depths of his mind, in lucid moments, he sensed that she was
a witch and that the eyes could penetrate to the center of his
being, reading his thoughts, his needs, boring into his soul.
Once, only once—after they had spent a month in Paris—a
flicker of warning had come to him. It was the old black
woman who had said it, whispering through rotting teeth,
eyes veiled in malice. "She devours men, fool. She'll eat you
up and spit you out." The crone then had scuttled away in a
flurry of skirts, his laughter at her back.

They were on the red velvet settee in the darkened parlor
now, a candle flickering from a socket in the wall. Her mouth
clung to his, tongue darting, and her breath came in shuddering gasps. Abruptly she broke the kiss and the flimsy bodice
covering her breasts fell away. Gently, gently, she pushed him
back against the settee and undid him. He watched her face
and the ice-blue eyes locked into his, lynxlike. His senses
whirled. He panted for breath. The heat of her mouth was
upon him, but only for a moment. Lightly, lingeringly, until
he was on the verge of exploding.

And then she came up again, body writhing, ripping away
the gown. She lay back from him on the red velvet settee,
panting and murmuring, "Oh, God, there never was a stud
like you. It's too much, too much!" She was spreading before
him, spreading her billows of white.

He entered the cauldron of her.

Neither saw the shadowed figure watching from the stair-
case landing in the hall. Mason Chares, her father, did not
stir. But his eyes glittered with mortal fury.

Later, deep in the night after brandy and more lovemaking
and more brandy, Elizabeth led him to her upstairs boudoir
where he fell asleep in her arms on the great bed. Somewhere before dawn, he was dimly conscious of her nuzzling
his earlobe. A whisper sifted from the darkness, repeated
over and over. So subtle was it that later he would not be
certain if it was a whisper or a dream. The thought drifted

into the depths of his sleep. "My gold. Where is my gold? I must tell Elizabeth where my gold is. Tell Elizabeth. Tell Elizabeth..."

He rolled over, opened one eye, struggled to clear his brain. The room was silent but for the sound of rain upon her window. It was nothing, he told himself. Merely the rain. Merely the whisper of the rain.

XVI

Pain. It would not leave him. At first, in those first faltering steps with a cane, he had fought the pain and steeled himself to overcome it. The pain was exhausting in those early days and weeks; the pain left him drained, sweating and trembling in a chair. That's when he'd fought hardest, fought to overcome, forced himself to walk upright until he groaned aloud. In time the sharpest agony passed, the wound knitted, the body worked at repair. The pain settled into a dull ache. His physicians prescribed morphine. Thaddeus refused. Already he knew of wounded men who suffered the Soldier's Disease, a dependence on morphine, without which one suffered nausea, shaking, and sweats. He had had enough of that. He resolved to live with pain as he lived with anything else, as he lived with the dusting of gray in his hair or accepted the curious relationship with Ruth.

The wounding and its aftermath had caused, between them, a metamorphosis of spirits. First, there had been Ruth's insistence that Thaddeus be moved to their own home from Marguerite's. In the depths of his semiconsciousness, she had raised ugly scenes until finally, in an agony of jolting by ambulance, it was done. And then she had fussed over him, much as she fussed over her favorite doll Raggedy, trying to shield him from the doctor, the nurse, even Marguerite's daily visits. Then came the newspaper articles about Bull Run, and the emergence of Captain Thaddeus Stewart as the hero of the charge to save the guns. Ruth seemed to resent the attention this drew to their household and almost bodily threw out a newspaper writer who had come to find out about her husband's condition.

How slowly the body knit and the spirits revived! Ruth was unable to accept his pain, or the rage that sometimes burst from his lips as he struggled with himself. But at last the worst was past; he could move about again, accept callers, even go out. Ted Judah had been the catalyst for this. The railroad act was pending in Congress and faced a hard battle. "We need you," Judah told him, "to campaign for its passage." And so Thaddeus found himself dressing up in evening clothes to make a speech at Marvella Clive's Washington home. Clumsily he struggled with the velvet bow tie, muttering to his reflection in the mirror. "How stupid. Putting on evening clothes and going out. Doesn't Marvella know there's a goddamned war going on?"

Ruth looked dumbly at him. This, too, was an irritant. He wanted to shout at her, to shake her out of her lethargy. Even her rages of old would have been better than this. "Ruth, did you hear me?"

"I heard you. Please, Thaddeus, don't shout at me."

"Why do they insist that people put on these ridiculous clothes, this ridiculous monkey suit of mine and that ridiculous gown that you're wearing, when the whole country is being torn apart?"

"I'm sorry, Thaddeus."

He felt ashamed. Her tone was so helpless, so vulnerable, that he wanted to make amends, to fold her in his arms and shield her from whatever it was that she could not endure. He felt guilt, too, for the knowledge that in his heart he did not love Ruth, had never loved her, could never love her. Why had he done this to her, taken her into a marriage that he knew was wrong? He looked intently at his mirrored face and disliked it without really knowing why. He blinked his eyes, hard. Enough of that. They were going to Marvella Clive's, and he intended to make another strong pitch for the railroad. They had a fight on their hands, and by damn, he would jump into it with both feet. He stepped back, drew on his cloak, held Ruth's wrap for her, grasped his cane firmly and labored down the stairs against the rhythmic onslaught of pain.

"Let me help you, dear."

"No, thank you. I can manage." But even as he said it, he felt the cold sweat glazing his face.

They rode in the closed carriage without speaking. He retreated into the darkness, biting his lip. God, this street was rough! Didn't the carriage have any springs? By the time they arrived at Marvella Clive's mansion, where liveried footmen scurried out to open the carriage door and let down the folding step, he was ready to pass out. He concentrated instead on telling himself precisely what to do: slide out of the carriage, step down, brace against the cane, walk forward, do not show pain.

"Thaddeus! My dear!" Marvella Clive came charging from the front door, arms open, to fold him into a welcoming embrace. He and Ruth were ushered into the great house to a constant stream of Marvella's chitchat, morsels of gossip, and exclamations of affection. He had to smile at her effervescent spirit. Thaddeus felt his spirits lifting as the hostess steered him through countless greetings. The house was crowded with the cream of Washington politics and society. Many male guests wore military uniform. A string quartet performed from an alcove fringed with potted palms. Waiters passed through the throng bearing trays of liquors and cigars. Finally they all moved into dinner, served at long formal tables glittering in lamplight. Thaddeus looked about for Marguerite and finally spotted her on the far side of the room, in earnest conversation with a handsome young captain of cavalry. A flicker of jealousy went through him. He silently cursed himself for a fool, thinking, "She is not yours." But his resolve failed him and his ebullience evaporated.

War dominated the table talk. Another bloody battle had been fought at a place called Shiloh. Union gunboats skirmished with Rebel forces along the Mississippi. Thaddeus thought of his Aunt Catherine and her dwindling steamboat fleet, decimated by war seizures for government use. A letter from his Uncle Stephen at St. Louis had expressed it graphically: "Catherine is depressed by conditions on the river. She cannot keep a fleet running, and business is slow. There is no profit in the government's takeover of vessels for use in war shipments." Thaddeus listened to the drone of table conversation and lapsed into his own thoughts.

War engulfed them all. His painful hip was nothing compared to the agonies of the nation. From the field came daily dispatches bearing news of army movements, skirmishes and

fresh girdings for major battles. Bloodletting was fierce.
Songwriters produced a wave of doleful music to express the
domestic trial of suffering and death. He had heard another
song today, thinking that it was bound to become enormously
popular. "Just before the battle, Mother, I am thinking dear
of you . . ." Fresh levies of young men left their hometowns by
train to join the army, but festive crowds no longer tossed
flowers and brass bands no longer feted departing heroes with
martial airs. The mood was grim, the good-byes tearful, the
naive optimism was gone. A sense of tragedy sank in to the
bone and marrow of the nation. It was going to be a long and
costly war.

"Ladies and gentlemen." Marvella stood, tapping a glass
with a spoon. "Ladies and gentlemen. As all of you are aware,
a most important bill is to be introduced in the Congress this
month. It is the Railroad Act of Eighteen Sixty-Two. To tell us
about it tonight, we are most fortunate to have a man who
needs no introduction in this city. He is, of course, the
wounded hero from Bull Run, the officer who led the charge
to save the guns, our own—"

The applause began even before Marvella finished. Thaddeus
sat stunned as it rose to a volume that drowned out the rest of
her words. The crowd came to its feet, still applauding. He
rose from his chair, nodding gratefully. Only after he had
spread his arms for quiet did the ovation finally subside. As
the guests returned to their chairs, he struggled to bring his
voice under control. "I . . . I am overwhelmed."

He spoke hesitantly at first, giving them the background of
the railroad. It seemed odd to be speaking of railroads in the
midst of these terrible times. He said as much, but heard
himself adding, "We must think ahead as well. We must look
to the future of our great nation. My uncle, Nathan Stewart,
was privileged to participate in the building of the Erie
Canal"—another spatter of applause caught him by surprise—
"and the Erie opened our great northern tier of states, Ohio,
Michigan, Illinois and Indiana. The canal was a marvel of
engineering. And now we're talking about another marvel, a
railroad that will link the Atlantic and the Pacific oceans.
Travel that now takes weeks and months will be reduced to
mere days. The railroad will open the great western frontier
of America for settlement on a scale that boggles the mind. I
urge you, I implore you, to support the act in Congress to
make it a reality."

Thaddeus sat down to a wash of applause. When dinner had ended, and the men had retired to the main parlor for brandy and cigars, two California congressmen praised his efforts. "Good speech, Stewart. Caught the spirit of the thing nicely." Several other men, however, kept their distance. At last one large, black-bearded man detached from a group and sauntered over to Thaddeus.

"Pity to waste your considerable speaking talents on such a cause, Stewart. Pity."

"How do you mean, sir?"

"Beg pardon. My name is Calvert Bertram. I'm an associate, so to speak, of Senator Poindexter Carp. He is married to your cousin, I believe."

"Francesca, yes."

"This railroad act of yours is a bad thing for the country, Stewart. Terrible giveaway of federal lands. Do you have any idea of the financial plundering this would unleash? I tell you, it would be legalized larceny. Already the financial sharks are licking their chops. One of the most avaricious is another relative of yours, Brack Stewart. You know him, I presume?"

"I know of him . . ."

"Yes, I daresay. The man who plundered the Nolichuckey and Southern Railroad. Won himself a federal land grant, watered the stock, padded the contracts and drained it dry. It made him a millionaire. A disgraceful episode in high finance, absolutely without principle. But who is to point the finger, eh? Who among the mighty is without stain?" Bertram sucked on a cigar, blew smoke in a great blue cloud. His teeth were small and dulled from nicotine. "Brack Stewart is more praised than censured. And if your railroad act passes, the pillage will make the Nolichuckey and Southern episode child's play by comparison."

"I resent your implications, Mr. Bertram."

Bertram smiled thinly. "Your naiveté is refreshing." The comment seemed to be half to himself. "Well, no matter. I was quite impressed by your knack for speaking. I feel that it would be most, er, enlightening if you were to debate this issue with Senator Carp, face-to-face. Don't you?"

Thaddeus blinked, taken off guard. Congressman Burch frowned a warning and Marvella Clive, who had just joined them from the other room, spoke it aloud. "Careful, Thaddeus." The tall hostess twinkled her violet eyes at Bertram. "Calvert, here, is a resourceful and fascinating man. He goes for the jugular, as they say."

Something in the challenge nettled Thaddeus. It was Bertram's airy and supercilious tone perhaps. He looked into the amused face and heard himself saying, "I'd be delighted to debate Santaor Carp, or anyone else for that matter."

Bertram grinned broadly, raised his brandy glass in salute and waved his cigar. "Excellent!"

Congressman Burch drew in his breath. "I wish you hadn't done that, Thaddeus. Now we're in for it, I'm afraid."

The first debate against Poindexter Carp was arranged for a large public hall. As darkness fell, a noisy mob filled every seat and spilled out into the aisles. Thaddeus walked onstage to applause and catcalls. He fidgeted for ten minutes past the appointed starting time, eyeing his opponent's vacant chair. When the senator did arrive, he strode briskly to his place with a show of boundless confidence. From the beginning it was apparent that the crowd had been stacked, for Poindexter Carp's appearance brought cheers and prolonged applause.

A remarkable transformation had taken place in Carp since Thaddeus had last seen him nearly two years earlier. The moon face was still characteristic. But the thinning, mousy hair was now full and well-styled, evidently with a hairpiece. The fat was gone and his body honed to a muscular toughness from constant riding and exercise. His clothing was impeccable. The most dramatic change was in Carp's stage presence. The diffident mannerisms of old had given way to new vigor, strong gestures and a voice of astonishing timbre.

From their opening remarks, Thaddeus knew that he faced a forceful adversary. The feeling was heightened by the presence in the front row of tall, intense Francesca Stewart Carp, who sat with a plump, gray-haired woman who, someone said, was Carp's mother. Francesca did not return Thaddeus's nod of greeting. She looked at no one and nothing but Senator Poindexter Carp. Marguerite and Ruth sat several rows back, but Francesca ignored them as well.

"It is my pleasure to be sharing this platform with Captain Stewart." Carp acknowledged Thaddeus with a courtly nod. "All of us in the Senate are proud of the hero of the guns, as we are of all our fighting men. My only regret is to find Captain Stewart being used as tool of the special interests who would rob our beloved nation of its most priceless heritage, land."

The thrust caught Thaddeus unprepared. With cool detachment and a biting wit, Poindexter Carp then proceeded systematically to pick at every argument favoring the railroad. When he was done, he had managed to portray Thaddeus as a zealous technician, but blandly ignorant of the realities of life; a handsome boob, manipulated by devious forces scheming to plunder the public treasury.

Thaddeus left the platform knowing that he had been badly outclassed. Surprisingly, Poindexter Carp encountered him backstage afterward for a brief handshake. "Hated to do that to you, old man," Carp said. Thaddeus studied his adversary's face for a hint of guile, but found only genuine concern. "Things don't always turn out as we'd like for them to be." And then Carp was gone.

The debates continued, with varying results. Although others found him to be improving against the senator, Thaddeus could only retort: "Compared to what?" He could not shake a nagging feeling that out of his own stupid pride, the railroad act, and all that it meant to him and the nation, could go down in defeat again. A strange depressive lassitude settled over him. His state of mind was not improved by the persistent, odd behavior of Ruth. As social and speaking engagements became more frequent—they were now invited out four or five times a week—Ruth lost interest and drew into her shell. Even Marguerite, who had become swept up in the campaign and accompanied them regularly now, seemed unable to draw her out. Ruth's expression was vacant, her eyes without luster. She became careless of her appearance and would put on the same gown she had worn the night before. There was a hint of body odor, suggesting that she had neglected to bathe. Her face, especially around the mouth, began to draw. She paced the floor and avoided looking people in the eyes.

"What is it, Ruth? What's bothering you?"

"Bothering me? Should something be bothering me? Nothing is bothering me. I'm perfectly all right."

"Your disinterest, your appearance..."

"What's wrong with my appearance?"

"Nothing."

Thaddeus let it drop, sliding out of the conversation and deliberately changing the subject. He described a funny incident that had happened at a party. Her laughter had a shrill artificiality. She made no mention of the debates or of the people involved.

All things have a way of coming to resolution. In congressional politics, it happens in stages. And the first stage of the railroad fight took place in the House of Representatives. There, the issue had no powerful opposition. With Abraham Lincoln's floor managers twisting arms and the California congressmen Burch and Sargent leading the charge, the railroad bill passed. Thaddeus's elation was tempered by the fact that this was predictable.

"Now," muttered Ted Judah darkly, "for the Senate. Poindexter Carp has got the Senate in his pocket, Thaddeus. And frankly, I don't see a chance of passage there."

"It's my own damned fault. These debates . . ."

"It's not the debates. Carp was having his own way even before the debates."

"Do you think the President can help?"

"Maybe. But he's got so much on his mind."

"I'll try to talk with him."

Thaddeus's note to the White House brought a reply two days later in Lincoln's own hand, with an invitation. Even as Thaddeus's carriage drew up along the curved gravel driveway of the White House, he sensed the majestic isolation of the place. Lincoln received him in the presidential office. Thaddeus was shocked, for the President appeared to have aged ten years. After desultory small talk, he turned to the subject of his visit. Could Lincoln help push the railroad bill through the Senate?

The President offered a weary smile. "I'm afraid my influence isn't really worth very much, Thaddeus. Sometimes I wonder if I can get anything through Congress. They march to their own drummers on The Hill. From what I've heard of your problem, though, I strongly suspect that its resolution lies somewhere within your own family."

"My own family?"

Lincoln fixed Thaddeus with a shrewd eye. "Your cousin, Francesca, is a strong-minded woman. A strong-minded woman can move mountains. The man who underestimates her power is worse than a fool. No offense intended. It's been said that her hatred for railroads is extreme."

"Extreme? Mr. President, that's putting it mildly."

"I find myself in a political pickle here. Poindexter Carp has matured remarkably in the Senate, as you're probably aware. He continues to reflect Francesca's position on the railroad question. This has been consistent from the day he arrived in Washington. But the man also has taken strong positions on other worthwhile legislation, especially what I call 'people' bills. It might amaze you to think of Poindexter Carp as a populist senator, but that's what he has become. Quite an effective one, too."

Thaddeus left the White House moody and out of sorts, the image of Poindexter Carp looming even larger than before. That evening he brooded over a bourbon. Poindexter Carp. Poindexter Carp. My God, the man was a stumbling block. He thought about confronting Carp, trying to reason with the man. It made no sense to block such a stupendous project merely on the strength of the hatred of one's wife. But stranger things had happened in politics.

"What the hell are we going to do?"

It was Marguerite who decided to face things head-on. Her feminine logic left no other course. "I'll go to see him. Poindexter is my brother-in-law. If the whole damned railroad hinges on a family fuss, then I might as well throw in my two cents."

"Marguerite, you shouldn't," said Marvella Clive. "Francesca will hate you for it."

Marguerite sighed and looked at Thaddeus. "Francesca," she murmured, "hates me already."

It was a chore and a bother. His heart was not in railroad bills or financial bills. His heart was in things having to do with people. Poindexter Carp smiled to himself, thinking of Mr. Lincoln's phrase, "a populist senator." In times past, one would have thought such an idea preposterous. Poindexter Carp, the middling New York lawyer, a populist? To some, rich men who fancied themselves as kingmakers, it smacked of political eccentricity at best, virtual anarchy at worst. He remembered, however, the past; recalled life with his mother in good times and bad, and in the latter years—the years before Francesca—the gradual tightening of her purse strings and her prospects. They were descending into genteel poverty. A curious term, he thought. Genteel poverty was poverty with manners, poverty that one did not complain about but simply endured. It was poverty in a clean shirt. So he had come to the Senate aware of other facets of American life. And this, in turn, sharpened his sensitivity to the plight of struggling people: children in the sweatshops by the age of nine, Negroes in garbage-strewn shanties that ringed the city of Washington, workers toiling from dawn till dark in smitheries and mills seven days a week, Indians driven from their lands by the steady encroachment of the white man, sharecroppers and widows and the starving aged. From the vantage point of the Senate he managed to see them and their causes with a clarity denied most men. But he was aware, too, that one built a base of power not in human causes but in bills involving finance, taxation, industry, transportation, war.

On the question of the railroad act, Poindexter Carp felt that he owed something to Francesca. God knows they had little enough left together. Francesca had taken him like a piece of clay and molded him to the image of the statesman. Francesca had seen to it that he, a middle-aged man of more wit than ability to exercise it, was trained and conditioned for politics. Unhappily, politics was a demanding mistress; the gradual maturing of Poindexter Carp had caused ever-increasing strains on the marriage, and his wife had become more and more the female tyrant at home, prodding and demanding with no pretence at affection. In the process, she used Minerva Carp—pliable, grasping Minerva—as the means of exerting her dominance. The senator was torn between loyalties to his own identity and his mother's well-being. The debates with Thaddeus Stewart had occurred, quite spontaneously it seemed, against this troubled domestic backdrop. Poindexter Carp had easily bested the young man, cut him to pieces at times. And yet, oddly, he had a liking for the handsome idealist; a liking and, yes, a respect for his integrity. This side of the Stewart character was refreshing in a city crawling with larceny and deceit.

Marguerite caught him unawares. He was riding his favorite hunter at midday over the broad fields near the Capitol. She came up from behind on a five-gaited mare, flushed and breathless from a run. Her golden hair streamed in the wind and her face had a pinkish glow that accentuated her beauty.

"Hello, Poindexter. I didn't realize you were such a superb rider." She laughed, reining the mare into place beside him. "What a marvelous day for it, too."

He stammered, both delighted and startled. Marguerite had rarely spoken with him directly before. The avoidance was not deliberate, but rather a matter of chance. So strained were relations between the sisters that neither made overtures to the other, and Poindexter rarely found himself even in a position to converse with his sister-in-law. The meeting gave him a quick surge of pleasure which quickly expanded into friendly exchange. They walked their mounts, chatting amiably about their relative good qualities. Marguerite's mare, he saw at a glance, had the deep chest and strong long flanks of a thoroughbred. Instinctively he speculated on her racing ability. Marguerite seemed to read his thoughts. "She's a good sprinter," she said gaily, "but her best distance is the half-mile. Excellent wind for it."

"So I see." Carp heard his name called, turned and nodded to several midday strollers—members of the Capitol staff, out for midday constitutionals. He saw their eyes shift to Marguerite with open admiration. This gave him an extra measure of self-esteem. "Wonderful, wonderful."

"My mare?"

"No"—he turned back to her and smiled—"my absolutely stunning sister-in-law."

"Why, Poindexter Carp, I think you're teasing."

"You honor me."

They chatted on, randomly, pleasantly. Carp was enjoying himself hugely. A slight annoyance crossed his mind. What if Francesca heard about this? He quickly discarded it. That was Francesca's problem.

Marguerite suggested they dismount and walk the horses. He complied. They strolled over the spring grass. Carp found himself conscious of jonquils and green buds and the fresh odors of new grass. Spring lay over the city like a magic carpet, filling one's senses. He even whistled a catchy tune.

Carp was only mildly aware of the shift in conversation from green buds to railroads. It was done smoothly, almost as an afterthought. But then, moments afterward, they were seated together on the rim of a new fountain, and Marguerite was speaking earnestly about cousin Thaddeus, the Railroad Act and the enormous impact it could have upon the nation.

"You know my commitment, Marguerite." He kept his tone cordial, but inwardly felt his defenses rising. "All this is terribly detailed and the issues are clearly drawn."

"Fiddlesticks, Poindexter." Her blue eyes flashed and a wisp of golden hair fell over her forehead. She swept it back with a gloved hand. "That's rhetoric and you know it. Poindexter Carp has emerged in the United States Senate as a decent and honorable man. Frankly, I was surprised to see you developing in the way that you have, surprised and...pleased."

"Now you're playing games with me, sister-in-law."

"No games, Poindexter. If we can't speak as equals without games and guile then we should not speak at all. But I insist on speaking. I believe that you've been locked into a course of action that would not be your real intent, had the decision been yours alone to make."

"You're treading on thin ice."

"So, I'll tread. Francesca is my sister. I'm the closest blood relative she has, and that gives me certain rights in this matter. If I thought this were a contest of wills between you and cousin Thaddeus alone, I would not stick my nose into it, no matter how strongly I felt. But when it comes to the railroad and your opposition to it in the Senate, you do not speak your own mind. It is not a contest between you and Thaddeus but between Francesca and Thaddeus."

"Marguerite, really. You presume too much."

"On the contrary, Poindexter, I presume too accurately. Francesca's interest in this is not purely philosophical; there are other, selfish considerations. And if you are going to weigh an issue fairly, if you are going to lay your political prestige on the line for a point of view, then it's only reasonable that you recognize it all."

Carp remained silent. Unexpectedly, he did not feel well. His stomach fluttered and the atmosphere seemed inexplicably heavy. The charm had gone out of the day.

"To begin with, Francesca's hatred of railroads is emotional. You know this, Poindexter; you've always known it. Her feelings stem directly from the death of our father. In that single event, the seeds of her twisted reasoning took root. Everything else—the argument against the giveaway of federal lands, the argument about the cost and the threat of financial plunder, and even the argument about the inherent evil of a speeding locomotive—has been built up in her mind to reinforce and perpetuate that original hatred. And you, Poindexter, you are the instrument of her vengeance, the tool of Francesca's design. It is for this reason, and this alone, that she married you in the first place."

Poindexter started to rise. His mouth worked, but nothing came out. His mind tried to blot out what she was saying, tried to will his tongue to lash back. Marguerite put her hand gently on his arm, restraining him. He sat down again.

"I know this is painful for you. But many things are painful in life. You have a commitment to Francesca, yes. You also have a responsibility, Poindexter, a responsibility to yourself and to your country. Some of the things Francesca warns of happening might happen. Yes, there are vested interests waiting to profit on the railroads. Profit is the middle name of any enterprise taken on such a scale. I know this, Thaddeus knows it, Ted Judah knows it. But fear can't be permitted to stop progress. Our nation today is a house divided politically, as Mr. Lincoln has said, and a house divided against itself cannot stand. It is also divided geographically east and west by those vast reaches of empty land. If Francesca speaks of the federal grant as a giveaway, then I say, a giveaway of what? Of what value is twenty million acres when nobody lives there?"

Marguerite stopped speaking. She gazed intently into the round face and felt pity. The man looked stricken. Impulsively, she took his hand. "I . . . I'm sorry, Poindexter."

He stared at the Capitol building, still nested in scaffolding as workmen continued the seemingly endless task of constructing the great dome. "Things are complicated," he said. "We're only human beings and none of us is perfect. I have a commitment. You might say that I have a debt to pay."

Marguerite sighed, stood up and walked to the mare, which was grazing nearby. She mounted and rode away, booting the horse into a gallop.

She did not see Senator Poindexter Carp burst into tears.

The following evening, at dinner, Fransesca was in a fury. "You were seen having your little midday rendezvous with my sister. I suppose you think that such behavior would be overlooked because you happen to be a United States senator. Having yourselves a nice little horseback ride, sitting by the fountain in heart-to-heart conversation, touching hands. I've never been so mortified in my life."

"My dear, Marguerite was—"

"Oh, don't tell me about Marguerite! Spare me the sordid details. I know my little sister, Poindexter. I'm no fool. What astonishes me is that you sneak around to be with your blond hussy, and that you are fool enough to succumb to her wiles. Of course, Marguerite doesn't let blood kinship stand in the way, so why should she be deterred from making sport with someone as remote as a brother-in-law, eh? When I think of all that I've done for you! How much I've sacrificed for your public career! Well, I've spared this from Mother Carp. It would break her heart. It would absolutely devastate her."

She pursed her lips. Her eyes glittered in the light reflected from silver dinnerware and cut crystal. "The very idea..."

It went on this way, interminably, subsiding only when the servants were present to attend them for dinner. Afterward, she withdrew to her study to go over the daily business reports from New York, leaving him in the solitude of the parlor with his newspaper and his stomach cramps. At bedtime she took the unusual step of visiting him in his rooms for a further tirade before finally whisking away in an angry flurry of taffeta, trailing a scent of cold cream and rubbing alcohol. Only then did it occur to him, with a sense of profound relief, that his mother had not once made an appearance but had chosen to spend the evening in her own apartment.

He thought of his mother and of what Francesca's lashing tongue could do to her. Such unpleasantness could bring on another of Minerva Carp's sick headaches, which invariably unnerved him. Senator Poindexter Carp did not sleep well that night. His mind was in a turmoil.

There is an aura of sanctity to the United States Senate. It mingles with the air one breathes in those chambers. To Thaddeus, by now an experienced maneuverer in the Capitol, the Senate represented the ultimate in political prestige, short of the presidency. Its contrast with the hurly-burly of the House was marked by subdued manner of debate, more splendiferous trappings, a conscious courtliness of proceedings even amid volatile issues.

But on the day of decision, Thaddeus arrived at the Senate's spectator gallery in a mood of defeat. He was accompanied by Ted Judah, Marguerite, Marvella Clive and the California congressmen, Burch and Sargent. Barely had they taken their seats when Francesca Carp, trailed by a retinue of antirailroad people, swept into a tier of nearby seats. Francesca caught Thaddeus's eye and offered a thin smile of triumph. His spirits sank even more, for her eyes told him that the vote was a foregone conclusion.

Marguerite, seated beside him, reached over and gently squeezed his hand.

Below, the double doors swung open and the members of the Senate poured into the room, taking their places. Poindexter Carp marched resolutely to his desk, not even glancing up toward the gallery, and sat down stiffly. He ruffled through a sheaf of papers from a leather folder, but more out of distraction than purpose. From his high desk, the president of the Senate—the nation's Vice-President—pounded a gavel and called the body to order. Several preliminary matters were dispensed with before the presiding officer intoned gravely, "The chair recognizes the distinguished senator from the great state of Connecticut."

The senator from Connecticut rose to stand beside his desk. A spare, white-haired man, he had become within the past year one of Poindexter Carp's closest associates. Already the word had leaked out that it was he, rather than Carp, who would lead the debate against the railroad. As the New Englander began to speak in a thin, nasal tone, Thaddeus leaned forward and cupped his ear to hear. ". . . come to regard this as one of the most wasteful proposals ever presented to the Senate. Gentlemen . . . impractical and expensive, not to mention its questionable technical merit . . . this giveaway of federal land, our most priceless . . ."

There was a rustle in the chamber. Poindexter Carp had risen to his feet and stood waiting to be recognized. His round face was curiously set and his expression—Thaddeus tried to define it from this distance—was one of physical pain. Carp leaned on the desk as if for support and peered across the chamber toward the presiding officer. The senator from Connecticut looked at Carp in surprise and his words trailed off into silence.

Carp's strong voice filled the chamber. "Mr. President, will the Senator yield?"

The Connecticut senator swallowed, eyed the presiding officer, blinked.

"Will the Senator yield?" the chairman asked.

"I yield to the distinguished Senator from New York."

"The Senator from New York has the floor."

Poindexter Carp nodded, ruffled the papers at his desk, dabbed at his face with a handkerchief, cleared his throat. In the gallery, Thaddeus glanced at Francesca. Her face was oddly pinched, with an expression that was part perplexity and part impatience. She appeared to be thinking, "What is the fool up to now?" His attention reverted to the floor as Carp began to speak.

"Mr. President, distinguished colleagues of the Senate. It was not my original intent to speak on this matter today. My position has been well-known and I saw no purpose in amplifying it further. Circumstances, however, do change in life and so do the minds of men. In recent days, I have had occasion to take a new look at the question of building a transcontinental railroad and my own part in these proceedings. As you all know, I feel a deep sense of commitment to the United States Senate and to the burden of trust which the people of the great state of New York, and indeed our sacred Union, have placed upon me. In pursuing my duties in this august assembly, it is incumbent upon me to seek those programs which will be in the best interests of the nation as a whole, and to avoid—" Carp hesitated, licked his lips nervously and let his eyes flick for an instant toward the gallery. "—to avoid narrow personal considerations, no matter how painful this may be."

Thaddeus's heart seemed to swell in his chest. What was this man saying? He did not dare let his mind speculate further. But in the intensity of the moment, his own pulse quickened and his hands gripped the gallery railing so fiercely that his knuckles were white. His eye strayed again to Francesca. She had turned even paler than usual and sat riveted in place, hardly seeming to breathe. Behind her, in the press section, newspaper reporters scribbled savagely in their notebooks, trying to get down every precious word and syllable.

"And therefore, Mr. President, in what I now choose to believe is the best interest of the nation and its future—when hopefully this accursed war is done—I hereby withdraw my opposition to the transcontinental railroad and to this Railroad Act which will bring it about."

A stirring and murmuring began in the Senate chambers. Thaddeus heard a door opening in the press gallery and the sound of running feet. The murmur on the Senate floor rose to audible exclamations, and finally, a rippling of applause.

"Stout fellow!"

"Hurrah for Carp!"

"Hear, hear!"

". . . And Mr. President, I hereby announce it my intention to cast the first vote in favor of the Railroad Act!"

A female voice shrieked from the gallery: "You can't! You can't do that! I won't let you!" Heads turned. The sergeant-at-arms started to move, recognized the standing, swaying form of Francesca Carp and stopped in his tracks, confused. "Damn you, Poindexter Carp, you've betrayed me!"

Senator Carp did not look to the gallery nor speak again. He sat down at his desk and stared toward the rostrum in silence.

Friends escorted Francesca from the gallery.

Thaddeus felt Marguerite's grasp upon his arm. "He did it! Oh, Thaddeus, he did it!"

The president of the senate hammered his gavel for order and threatened to clear the gallery if there were further disturbances. As calm was restored, voices on the floor clamored for a vote. The roll was called. Senator after senator responded, "Aye!" It was clear that the tide had turned dramatically. When the voting was done, there were thirty-five ayes and only five nays.

In the jubilation that followed, nobody noticed that Senator Poindexter Carp had slipped out a side door and left the senate.

Carp walked for miles through the city, a round-faced but distinguished-looking man for whom even vagrants and foot-pads respectfully gave way. At nightfall, he returned to the center of the city and took a suite at the Willard Hotel. The quarters consisted of two bedrooms and a sitting room. Before going to bed, he wrote a brief note and gave it to a bellman with instructions to deliver it that evening, in person.

He did not sleep well, and arose for breakfast the next morning still weary and out of sorts. The newspapers featured the story of his abrupt reversal resulting in passage of the railroad bill. For that day's editions, the news even equaled that of the end of General McClellan's seven-day battle for Richmond which had caused heavy casualties on both sides. He remained in his suite all day. At noon, a knock on the door caused him to bolt from his chair; but it was merely a message from the President thanking him for his "courageous and selfless action." There was not another knock until evening. This time he found his mother standing in the hallway, along with a porter bearing her single trunk. Minerva Carp embraced him and kissed him on the cheek.

"I'm sorry," he said. "I couldn't keep up the pretence any longer."

"And I am so proud of you," she said. "I am proud of my strong bright son."

Mother and son sat by the fireplace, as they talked and lingered over hot chocolate. For the first time in his life, Poindexter Carp was his own man. He accepted with relief

the news that Francesca was returning to New York and
intended to arrange quietly for a divorce, under the terms of
their marital agreement.

He sighed. "We owe her a great deal, I suppose. After all,
Francesca made this possible. Without her, I never would
have amounted to anything. In a way, I feel badly."

Minerva sipped chocolate and shook her head. "The raw
material was already there, Poindexter. You don't have to feel
beholden to Francesca Stewart for anything. She had only
one objective, and that was to use you for her own purposes.
We both did, in a way; I was as much a part of it as she. What
we didn't bargain for was that as a senator, you would find
your own way, discover your own strengths and responsibilities.
I'm thrilled that finally they proved to be greater than
Francesca's. Ultimately, you had to be yourself. Anything less
would have been tragic."

He poured brandy and lit a cigar. The light from the
fireplace gave the liquor a fine amber glow. Tomorrow he had
an important committee meeting at the Capitol, and in the
evening, he would attend a formal reception. Already there
were plans for the formal signing of the Railroad Act by
President Lincoln the first of the month. And today's action
had won him powerful allies in the senate, allies who could
elevate him to a committee chairmanship with the start of his
next six-year term. And beyond that . . .

Poindexter Carp smiled into his brandy glass. Suddenly the
future looked promising indeed.

XVII

The voices were insistent. *"Ruth is a bad girl. Bad girl,
Ruth."*

"Stop that," she said. "Stop saying that about me."

"We don't like Ruth. We think Ruth is ugly."

"I said stop it."

"*Raggedy thinks so too. Hee-hee-hee. Raggedy thinks Ruth is a witch. Witch! Witch! Witch!*"

"I'm not a witch. You've got to stop saying that."

"*Make us stop. Make us stop. Ruth is ugly. Ugly, ugly Ruth. Ruth is a witch. Ugly witch Ruth.*"

"Very well, if you persist, I just won't listen to you any more. You can say what you please, and I won't listen."

"*Stop us. Make us stop.*"

"I'll tell Thaddeus."

"*Hee-hee-hee. Thaddeus doesn't care. Thaddeus loves Marguerite. Thaddeus doesn't care. Hee-hee-hee. Poor Ruth.*"

"No! No! No! I'm beautiful. See how beautiful I am? Look in the mirror. See my long hair? See my body? Men stare at me, you know. They've always stared at me. They want me. But I don't want them, because they're dirty. Dirty men. Thaddeus is all I want. Thaddeus isn't dirty."

Sometimes Ruth pacified the voices. She discovered, quite by accident, that the voices would be still if she danced for them. And so she danced. She put on a long white negligee and danced in the gathering twilight of her room. But mostly, she danced with nothing on at all, nude, in front of the full-length mirror. Sometimes she danced in the dark, imagining the turns and leaps and pirouettes. That's when the voices approved. That's when the voices said nice things.

But sometimes they made her cry.

"*Nobody loves Ruth. Thaddeus doesn't love Ruth. Raggedy doesn't love Ruth. Mommy and Daddy don't love Ruth. Ruth is all alone because nobody loves her.*"

This made her cry. She would curl up in a ball, a tight, tight little ball, and cry. She would curl up and pull the blanket over her head and put her thumb in her mouth and cry. And after a while the voices would get tired and go away.

And sometimes they confused her. Sometimes they deliberately confused her. This happened when they pretended to come from people standing near her. They were watching her and hating her and saying bad things about her, these people. Except their lips didn't move. The Lady on the Second Floor did this. And so did the Man Who Delivered the Ice. Frequently she saw the Lady on the Second Floor talking with the Man Who Delivered the Ice, and she knew they were talking about her. She saw the eyes shifting in their sockets and staring angrily at her, heard the voices even if the lips did not move.

"*There's Ruth,*" said the voice from the Lady on the
Second Floor. "*She's a bad neighbor. Bad, bad, bad. I hate
her.*"

"*Yes,*" said the voice from the Man Who Delivered the Ice.
"*I hate her, hate her, hate her.*"

The lips did not move. For the space of a heartbeat, the
faces seemed cut in stone. She would blink her eyes and look
away. When she looked back the stone faces were smiling.
And she wondered if it was a trick, if the voices were playing
tricks.

And sometimes they terrified her. They did this when they
taunted her about Thaddeus. "*Thaddeus doesn't love Ruth.
Thaddeus hates Ruth. Thaddeus loves Marguerite. Thaddeus
will leave Ruth. He'll go away and leave Ruth all alone. Alllll
alone.*"

She whimpered when that happened, whimpered and grew
angry all at the same time. And she talked back, in her Little
Girl voice, that it wasn't true. No, no, no, it wasn't true.
"*Thaddeus loves me! Thaddeus loves me! Thaddeus loves
me!*"

But Ruth kept these experiences to herself. They were her
secret, secret life. She didn't tell anybody. Not even Thaddeus.

The strange behavior of Ruth Stewart had taken unexpected turns. Friends thought that she would be better off
remaining in Washington than to go with Thaddeus on this
latest jaunt to the West. While the airs of the Potomac
certainly were not the most healthful at any time of year, at
least there were people to look after her while he was away,
people who cared. It was not to be, however, for the thought
of Thaddeus leaving seemed to terrify her. Ruth had several
unmanageable fits of temper which ended in weeping and
bitter recriminations. And so when the steamship *Caribbean*
pushed off from the Norfolk docks, Mr. and Mrs. Thaddeus
Stewart occupied a large stateroom in first class.

The sea voyage was pleasant and seemed to have a calming
effect. Ruth's spirits improved by the second day out and she
actually made the acquaintance of other passengers. Thaddeus
noticed that she also paid more attention to her appearance.
The long, straggly hair was combed, the body bathed and
powdered, the nails done. Even at her worst, Ruth's physical
beauty was evident; with improvement, she drew the appre-

ciative stares that had always been her due, and reacted in kind. By the time they disembarked in Panama for the sweltering, mosquito-ridden journey across the isthmus, she was the most talked-about woman in the traveling group. Not all of it, of course, was friendly. One middle-aged matron was heard to murmur peevishly, "With a handsome brute like her husband around, I don't see why Mrs. Stewart must flirt with mine."

At San Francisco they stopped briefly for a visit with Maybelle. Ruth was enthused further by a large formal dinner party in the Nob Hill mansion. In the midst of it, as a string quartet played in the main parlor and couples swirled to the latest dance steps, she stood at the great windows overlooking the lights of the city and the shipping in the bay. "Oh, this is the way to live," she breathed. "Yes, yes. Oh, my!" It seemed rather odd to the servants who heard, for at the time Mrs. Stewart was standing quite alone. After two days of visiting, Maybelle was alert to little oddities of her nephew's wife. It was nothing one could put a finger on, but . . .

"Has she seen a doctor, Thaddeus?" Maybelle asked. "Perhaps it's a case of nerves."

They moved on to the high Sierras the following day, first by steamer to Sacramento, then by rail on board the Sacramento Valley Railroad and, and finally, by stagecoach, lurching and bucking up the steep slope toward Donner Summit. Beyond the summit on the down slopes, travel was by horseback and pack animals. Ruth rode well—indeed, she had grown up around horses—and seemed to accept with stolid indifference their trek into the wilds. Her enthusiasm, however, was flagging badly. By the end of the week she rode silently behind Thaddeus, expressing no interest in the mountain splendors that soared at every hand.

"Look, Ruth, a bald eagle!" Thaddeus thrust his hand toward the great shape that wheeled high overhead in an evening sky the color of copper. She murmured something that sounded like I don't care. But he could not be sure. They made camp in a dry wash, near the steep eastern face of the Sierras, and as darkness fell the heavens were ablaze with stars. The sight reminded him of the nights on the Frémont expedition years before, and he talked at length about his adventures to the silent figure seated rock-still by the fire.

That night she was up repeatedly, pacing back and forth in front of the tent like a wild animal unable to find rest.

The purpose of the trek was to complete Ted Judah's survey of the Truckee Valley. Day after day, in scenes of splendid vastness, Thaddeus took his sights and barometric readings for precise measure of angles and altitudes. On his topographical charts, he sketched likely places for tunnel gradients and cuts in the mountainsides, painstakingly following the preliminary instructions from Ted Judah's records. The work gave him fresh appreciation of Judah's exhaustive detail work, and he recalled vividly his friend's expression of the surveyor's role: "Nothing can happen, Thaddeus, until a man with a dream stands and peers through a glass."

During the hot days, Ruth remained in her tent. When he returned in the evening, nothing had been done; their bunks remained unmade and no meal had been prepared. One evening, after an especially trying afternoon in which he had narrowly escaped an attack by a puma, shooting the beast in a split second of self-preservation, he voiced his discontent. "You could help a bit, Ruth." In reply, she flashed him a look of undisguised hatred and shrank away. He noticed that her hair was again becoming long and unkempt and she made no effort to bathe, even when they happened upon a mountain lake or stream.

"I hate it out here," she murmured. "The voices say we ought to leave, that you ought to take me back somewhere. Why did you bring me out here, Thaddeus?"

"The voices?" He lowered the match with which he had been lighting a cigar. "What voices?"

"My voices, of course. They talk to me and tell me things. Now they tell me they don't like it out here. It's too wild and weird. The silences. Thaddeus, when you're away I can't stand the silences." Her eyes glittered in the firelight and her mouth was drawn downward in a grimace.

He made his voice gentle. "Then why don't you come with me, Ruth? The hiking will do you good."

"I don't want to go." It was her Little Girl voice, sounding high and disembodied. "I want to stay here with Raggedy."

"Raggedy?" It was then that he noticed the doll. She was soiled and torn, sitting by the tent in the firelight. One of the doll's button eyes was missing, as if plucked out. "I didn't know that you had brought Raggedy."

"Raggedy is my friend." She stared straight ahead, her eyes

oddly fixed. He waved his hand but got no response. It was as if she had lost contact with him and was gazing at some fascinating object in her mind.

The next day, they started their trek back to civilization.

The physician in Sacramento was vague and evasive. He made noises in his throat, checked her heart and lungs, examined her throat and the pupils of her eyes. He said it might be a touch of altitude sickness and that Ruth ought to go to bed with a toddy of hot, sweetened lemon juice and a warm water bottle on her chest. "Nothing serious," he assured Thaddeus. "Your wife is a fine, healthy girl." He went away, humming to himself.

Ruth refused to accompany Thaddeus to the ground-breaking ceremony for the Sacramento railroad bridge. "I have terribly important things to do," she told him. "Terribly, terribly important things to do." And she smiled a strange, impish smile which haunted his mind as he left her and gently closed the hotel room door.

"All right, boys. Whup it on down!"

Sunlight blazed from a cloudless morning sky. On the outskirts of Sacramento, the marshes spread toward the American River where the bridge would be flung across at six feet above flood crest. On a near slope, the pile driver machine stood poised above a group of spectators. At Charlie Crocker's shout, steam gushed and the dead weight of a one-ton hammer plummeted downward, striking the top of a great redwood piling standing thirty feet high.

Whack!

Despite his troubled mind, Thaddeus was thrilled by the sound. The steam engine gushed and huffed, raising its hammer for another stroke, struck again, raised its hammer, struck again, a living mechanical creature setting up the rhythm of work. *Chuff-chuff-chuff-whack! Chuff-chuff-chuff-whack!*

"Music to your ears, ain't it?" Charlie Crocker shouted. The superintendent of the Central Pacific Railroad spat into the dirt at their feet. The man was two hundred and forty-four pounds of restless dynamo and had sold out his dry-goods business to take on this job. Thaddeus liked him immensely, for Crocker shared enthusiasm for building. "By God, Stewart, we're on our way!"

A ragged cheer lifted around them. Slow-talking Leland
Stanford, the tall, bearded ex-grocer who'd gotten himself
elected governor of California and was also president of the
railroad, made a brief speech that was drowned out by the
piledriver's racket. Champagne flowed. Thaddeus found himself in conversation with a group of merchants and bankers
and, as usual, went at the task of trying to sell the obvious to
people lacking the vision to see.

"Now you're going to be watching a railroad under construction." He raised his voice above the din. "This bridge
will have nearly three thousand feet of approach trestle alone
over the swamp. The two main spans, they'll be a hundred
and ninety-two feet."

A merchant was asking a question, and from the noise he
heard two words ". . . iron track?"

"Well, you can't get steel in this country. Only the British
are making steel tracks. So Ted Judah ordered the heaviest
iron rail we could buy." Thaddeus hesitated and swallowed
hard. The mention of Ted Judah's name still affected him. It
was inconceivable that Judah was dead, cut down by yellow
fever at the age of thirty-seven. He forced the thought from
his mind and continued. "Right now we've got commitments
for five thousand tons. You'll see 'em piling up on the Front
Street dock . . ."

Deftly, Thaddeus shifted the subject to the route across the
Sierras. From where they stood, the formidable mountain
wall was a blue mound on the horizon. "It's a long, inclined
slope between the two deep river valleys. That route,
gentlemen, leads you from the Sacramento Plain up to Donner
Summit at seven thousand feet. You can stand up there and
look down on Donner Lake." He paused, took another swallow of champagne and lit a cigar. The men listened gravely
but without comment. The old familiar frustration knotted his
stomach. He wanted to grab the nearest man by the shoulders and shake him, shouting at the damn fool to wake up,
grab hold, help push this thing through! He curbed the
impulse. His nerves were on edge. He snuffed out the match
and blew a thin stream of cigar smoke. "And once over the
hump, most of that track will ease down the other side along
a shelf we'll notch in the mountainside. It's a hundred and
twenty-three miles from Sacramento to the Truckee Valley.
We'll just follow the valley in easy stages clear to Nevada."

He smiled and winked at his listeners. "Slick as grease." But they weren't charmed.

A banker brought up the subject of money. It was always the bankers. "They ain't buying Central Pacific bonds," the banker said to his companions. "Collis Huntington is having a hell of a time in Boston and New York. He's shrewd and crusty, Collis is, but if you ask me, Jesus Christ couldn't put this one across."

"Oh, they'll buy," Thaddeus heard himself saying. "The message hasn't gotten across to them yet, that's all. They aren't aware of the stakes."

The banker smiled thinly. "You've got to build forty miles of Central Pacific before you collect a dime. And with your costs going up all the time . . ."

Costs. The man was right, of course. When the pile-driving ceremony had ended and they took to their carriages for the return trip into town, Thaddeus found himself brooding upon the passing landscape, his thoughts in a turmoil. Sharing the carriage were Charlie Crocker and morose Mark Hopkins, the hardware dealer who had helped to organize the railroad company. The two men made small talk, respecting Thaddeus's silence.

Any way one looked at it, they were in a bind. By Ted Judah's estimate, the first fifty miles of railroad alone would cost more than three million dollars to build. The resourceful Collis Huntington, vice-president of the Central Pacific, had wired back that two hundred and fifty thousand dollars in bond sales was the best he could do. And Stanford himself, a mediocre but plodding man, had described their dilemma rather succinctly: "The plain truth of it, Thaddeus, is that nobody wants to invest huge sums in a transcontinental railroad when there's fortunes to be made in war materials."

Insurance costs were up. There was the rising expense of transporting multiple tons of iron track, locomotives, switches and other heavy equipment by ship from the east coast around the Horn to Sacramento. Even the damned terrain refused to cooperate. Grading contractors easily scraped off two feet of topsoil only to encounter the concretelike subsurface, a cemented mass of sand, rocks and pebbles. They paid four dollars a day in wages and couldn't find enough men to fill the jobs; those who did respond to newspaper advertisements were merely seeking enough cash to return to the gold

fields at the first opportunity. Fresh mounds of earthen fill
dribbled across the floor of the valley reaching for the Sierra
foothills. In the meantime, Sacramento's Front Street docks
accumulated stacks of redwood piling brought by schooners
from Santa Cruz, trestle timbers from the forests around
Puget Sound in Washington Territory and enough precut
track ties to kindle the world's biggest bonfire.

How short-lived had been the exuberance of victory! Already the great Railroad Act for which he and Ted Judah had
labored was turning to ashes. And then, tragedy of tragedies,
Judah had died from the ravages of yellow fever contracted on
yet another journey through the region he'd so despised, the
Isthmus of Panama. It thus became Thaddeus's task to try to
pick up where Judah had left off, breathing life into the
flagging dream. This meant constantly prodding these men
who'd responded to Judah's plea to form the Central Pacific
in the first place.

"We're not the only ones having trouble." The voice of
Charlie Crocker jarred him out of his contemplation. "It's not
the season for transcontinental railroads, I guess."

"What do you mean, Charlie?"

"The Union Pacific's dying on the vine. I hear Tom Durant
is worse off than we are. He put his stock on the market for
ninety days, nationwide, and guess how many subscribers
came forward. Seven! The Union Pacific broke ground there
at Omaha with nothing between them and the West but high
grass and prairie dogs. But they couldn't get men to work
either. All the workers are back east, or in the army. They ran
out of money, ran out of men, ran out of supplies."

"And they haven't driven a spike in six months," Thaddeus
concluded lamely.

They dropped him off in front of his hotel. As the carriage
rattled away and the noises of this bawdy capital town assailed
him, Thaddeus suddenly remembered what awaited him in
the suite of rooms overlooking the river. Ruth. A vague
displeasure overtook him. He did not wish to go up there
right now. To postpone the inevitable, he strolled the muddy
streets while around him flowed the teeming masses of
California humanity: miners and gamblers, Chinese, waterfront toughs, adventurers, gamesmen, teamsters. A constant
stream of heavy wagon traffic rumbled past, splashing mud.
Drivers cursed and whipped their teams. Thaddeus's hip
pained him again—he had been on his feet too long—and he

limped heavily as he walked along the boardwalk, leaning against his cane. Everywhere there were the sounds of hammering and sawing. Construction was as never-ending in Sacramento as it was in San Francisco. There were mingled odors of mud, horses, sweat, hot tar, and raw wood.

Thaddeus found a saloon on Front Street, went in and ordered whiskey and water. He needed time to be by himself and think. He drank, lit a cigar and thought about Ruth. An hour went by.

She was an alien presence. This was the sum of it. Ruth pondered the thought. An alien presence. The sum of it. Out there beyond the window lay the town, a town of raw wood and raw people and dusty streets where drunken men fought with their fists. In the room, even with the windows and doors closed, she heard the angry sounds from the street, the constant bawling and bickering. Somewhere a piano tinkled. In the saloon directly beneath her on the ground floor of the hotel, a chair crashed and splintered followed by a heavy bumping and thumping. The terror welled from deep inside her, welled up until it filled her chest and filled her throat. She sat on the bed and shrank back into herself. And so the hours passed.

"Ruth must hide."

The light of afternoon filtered through drawn blinds. Shafts of sunlight stabbed through the cracks, making splotches on the floor. The splotches moved across the rug and up the wall. She watched them dispassionately, listening to the whispers in the room.

"Ruth must go away and hide where nobody can find her."

Finally, when the last splotch of sunlight had disappeared and the afternoon was turning to gray, a distracted smile played upon her face. Slowly, slowly, she removed her clothing and dropped it in a heap by the bed. Slowly, slowly she got up and took the first subtle steps through the shadows. The air was cool upon her body and she was light as a zephyr, moving, moving. The mirror at the dresser caught her image and sent it back. She danced through the gathering shadows.

"Ruth will never be afraid again."

After a long while she settled onto the bare floor in the foyer, the bare floor of cold tile. Cold, cold, cold. She sat rigidly, feeling the cold. It was not unpleasant. Something filled her lower abdomen, a tingling sensation; something liquid that wished to flow. She let it flow. Ruth let it flow. And warmth suffused her naked hips and private parts where it flowed. Where the warm golden liquid flowed. She placed her hands in the liquid and bathed her face with it, her face and then her hair. And it was dusk around her, but she no longer heard the sounds from outside. She heard nothing but the sighs and whispers, felt nothing but the warm golden liquid.

"Ruth will never be afraid again."

And that's how Thaddeus Stewart found his wife. She sat naked on the tile floor in the foyer of their hotel suite, eyes glazed and a fixed smile upon her face. She had smeared her face and hair with urine.

Six weeks later on the outskirts of Philadelphia, accompanied by her father George Barrett, Thaddeus committed Ruth to Thornwood Asylum for the Insane.

"Yeeeeeee hawwwww!"

They thundered out of the draw at full gallop. Men shouted, slapping leather in the sweat and the dust, harness and weapons clattering. As columns cleared the trees they broke to left and right, fanning into a ragged blue line. Brigadier General Peter Heflin stood up in his stirrups, saber flashing, and bellowed, "God damn you, come on!" The exhilaration surged through him and his blood ran hot. "At 'em, you blue-bellied sonsabitches!" He kicked his spurs into the black stallion's flanks, felt the beast drive headlong into the fray, swung his saber in a mighty arc. His long red hair streamed in the wind; his bearded face, caked with sweaty dirt, twisted with rage. Amid the thunder of hoofbeats, men howled in a wild chorus and the first ragged volleys from Spencer rifles made the popping sounds across the blazing afternoon.

Ahead, up the green slope and along the tree line, he could see tiny figures running now, figures in butternut gray swarming in confusion among the tents and log huts. Puffballs of smoke burst among them spasmodically at first and then with a rising intensity of fire. The running figures merged. Steel gleamed in the sunlight. A line of gray spat sheets of flame. From behind him, Heflin heard the sharp bark like drumbeats of his own light artillery pieces. Deadly black blossoms with fiery hearts burst in the Rebel positions.

"Yeeeeeeeeeeeee!"

Men dropped from their saddles. Horses reared and plunged, shrieking. But the charge carried. At last they were upon them. Heflin saw startled white faces upturned, eyes wide with shock, mouths open and screaming, throwing spittle. The impressions burned into his brain as he crouched over the stallion's neck, swung the saber downward, chopped away at faces and necks and arms. Blood gushed. Bullets picked at his hat, his sleeves. The saber blade was red, redder than his wild flying hair, as he stroked it down again. Again. Again. And then he was through, bursting into the clear and still in the saddle, turning the stallion and charging back into the melee. Many horses were down, writhing. Men, blue and gray, were locked together hand-to-hand or had fallen, trampled by feet and hooves. There was a stench of gunsmoke and fresh blood. Abruptly, the charge broke. Riders with lighted torches went for the big tents and log huts. There was a crackling of flame, a sudden billowing of smoke. More men were down at the railroad line, ripping up track, burning crossties and throwing rails into the flames to warp and bend.

At last it was done. The guns stilled. Fires crackled across the afternoon. Smoke columns stood high in a sky the color of slate. They gathered their wounded onto the wagons and buried the Union dead. Heflin rode among the work parties, calling a man's name here, uttering praise there. Captain Morton, his aide-de-camp, moved along beside him.

Heflin said, "Odd, the elation of battle. Eh, Morton?"

The captain looked curiously at him. "The men are exhausted, sir." It was a gentle suggestion to let the troops relax a bit, make camp, put out picket patrols.

Heflin recognized the tone but made no acknowledgment.

They came upon a cluster of Rebel prisoners under guard. It was a ragged lot. Many were barefoot. Eyes followed Heflin from lean, sunburned faces. He envied such men. They could march all day on a handful of cracked corn. By a turn of fate, he would have commanded them.

"What shall we do with 'em, General?" A grizzled major of cavalry laconically touched his brim and spat tobacco juice. "Got several officers here, too."

Heflin glanced over the prisoners' faces. The shock of battle was still upon them. Eyes peered dully from expressionless masks. Only one face, that of a tall, ragged Confederate colonel, showed any interest. The colonel was staring at him curiously.

"Hell, give 'em some rations, if we've got any to spare," Heflin replied wearily. "Break up their muskets and turn 'em loose. They can tend to their own wounded and dead. We can't take prisoners."

The Confederate colonel spoke hoarsely. "Peter Heflin. You're him, aren't you?"

"That's right." He searched the man's face without recognition. "I'm Heflin."

The colonel spat into the dust. "Devil Heflin. Traitor to your kind."

Heflin slapped the officer across the face and grabbed his tunic. "Shut your filthy mouth, Reb, and show some respect." Heflin leaned over the neck of his horse and looked into the angry eyes. "Where are you from, Colonel?"

"Don't you know, General? Didn't you see our standard? We're South Carolina men, same as you. We're your blood and kin"—the eyes were reduced to twin slits—"and my people used to know your people." He looked up the slope to where the worst carnage had taken place. "I 'spect you got cousins lying up there, Heflins that you took down with your saber stroke. Does that make you happy, Heflin?"

"Don't pay no attention to the Reb, General Heflin," said the major. "He don't know what he's saying."

"Oh, I know all right," the Confederate colonel said. "And Devil Heflin knows that I know. There ain't a more despised man in the whole state of South Carolina. No Heflin will claim his kinship. His own father is ashamed. And the general knows that, too. The traitor—"

Peter Heflin slapped a glove against the side of his boot. "One more word out of you, Colonel, and I'll kill you where you stand."

The colonel offered a mocking smile. "May your soul rot in hell."

Heflin grabbed for his saber hilt. The stallion shied and tossed his mane.

"General, no!" It was Captain Morton, putting a restraining hand on his arm. Instinctively the stallion backed away from the prisoners. Heflin released the saber to bring his mount under control. He glared into the defiant eyes.

"There is some question, Colonel, about who is the real traitor here." He turned the horse and trotted away.

Peter Heflin's cavalry withdrew at nightfall from the wrecked Rebel supply depot and rode all night in a drizzling rain. Exhausted men, many of them wounded, silently cursed their commander and dozed off in the saddle. At daybreak they made a bivouac in a wood near several war-ravaged farms. Foraging parties were dispatched to take food and livestock.

The general withdrew to his tent and drank whiskey.

His mind was tormented by visions of pale, upturned faces beneath his saber stroke, the fresh bodies heaped on bloody ground, the hatred in the eyes and words of the Rebel colonel. "Traitor. May your soul rot in hell. Traitor." It galled him and yet oddly stimulated him, too. His thoughts played over the bugle calls, the charges, the galloping ranks, the saber strokes, the bodies, the guidons snapping in the wind.

He drank his whiskey straight. The liquid fire went down his gullet. "Traitor. May your soul rot in hell." Well, they could all rot in hell, all their souls. He would be in good company. But they knew Heflin, knew and feared his cavalry from Front Royal to Seven Pines, Cold Harbor and Antietam, from Richmond to deep into Georgia and Mississippi. They whispered in awe of the red-haired devil brigadier who led his cavalry charges brandishing a blood-soaked saber, while his men howled like banshees. Devil Heflin ranged over thousands of square miles to strike deeply and unexpectedly in the very heart of the Confederacy.

But never before had he encountered South Carolina troops. Not straight out like this, not beneath the hooves of his own war horse. The white upturned faces, the twisted mouths, the slit eyes of the colonel...

He shook his head, poured another whiskey, tossed it down. This was war, goddamn it. He did what he expected his own troops to do, for war was killing. They were fantastic troops, these cavalrymen. He had molded them, driven them, put fire in their guts and steel in their spine. He had made them killers, goddamn it. Killing was the essence of war, the thrust and purpose of war. When all the politicians in their black suits with their clean hands and sharp words were done plotting and scheming, it took other men to go out and perform the killing they had ordained. And it took men like Devil Heflin to command them, lead them, and deliver the first saber stroke. And why not?

A fly buzzed past his head and settled on the dirty white

canvas of his tent. He watched the fly. The fly rubbed its
forefeet and twitched its wings, unaware of anything beyond
its own miniscule existence. Heflin chuckled aloud. He could
swat the fly or let it live, and had the power to choose. It was
a power almost unspeakably sublime, a power of life and
death and fate. It was so with flies and it was so with men.

War engulfed him. For nearly two years now, he had led
men in the field. Before, there had been others in his life.
Marguerite. His mind drifted to her, to the perfect face in a
halo of golden hair, to the limpid eyes and voluptuous mouth.
Marguerite? Her letters still found him, letters filled with
warmth and pride and loyalty. His own replies were less and
less frequent, although his need of her brought agonies of
desire. Marguerite. But he no longer thought of her as a
companion, a sharer of his life; rather, she was an object for
his need, a fantasy to dwell upon when the agony drove him
to quick, unsatisfying masturbation on his cot.

For a new and unrelenting mistress controlled him now.
Her name was War. Killing was her essence. And upon Peter
Heflin, she had conferred the powers of life and death. She
made him a god. He loved war. He loved war with a sure and
fatal passion.

He drifted off into a drunken sleep. Even the shattering of
the glass as it fell from his hand did not wake him.

The marvel of creation was a constant reality, swelling and
moving in her abdomen. Through winter snows and ice
storms they had flourished, her own life and the life within
her. The phenomenon was as timeless as eternity and yet
always fresh and filled with wonder. Even when the bitter
winds of January lashed the high plains so that a warrior and
his mount returning from the meager hunt appeared as
moving white figures of ice, the miniscule inner life warmed
Sunset Woman. Never had she been so preoccupied with her
self, never so inwardly content. Beyond this, the miracle
transformed her identity as well. No longer was she remote
from the Cheyenne, but one with them; for within her she
carried the seed of Standing Bear, and the fetus that quickened
beneath her heart was Cheyenne life, of the Shemkuk tribe.
And so in this mood the spring had come, thawing the
deep, crusted snow and ice-choked rivers. Sunlight flooded

the cold air, the white expanses and the cloudy breaths of women as they gathered sticks and newly exposed buffalo chips for the cookfires. She went out in her chemise and furs, laboring clumsily through the melting snow, to do the woman's work of Standing Bear's lodge. And always she was accompanied by the ever-vigilant squaw Minnow.

"Will I bear him a man-child, Minnow?" They sat on a buffalo hide at the rippling brook, the snow lying in splotches and the grass spreading its cloak of deep green, sprinkled with wild flowers. "Tell me, old woman, what do you think?"

"It will be a man-child." Minnow braided Sunset Woman's shining hair, after it had been washed. "You have strong haunches for bearing. It will be a man-child."

"And if it isn't?"

"If it isn't, then she will be as lovely as the sunrise and the delight of her father's heart."

Vanessa laughed. "You always know the right thing to say, Minnow."

"I have lived long and seen many springs." The old woman grew wistful, her dark eyes measuring the horizon. "Yes. And I had my own springs, too, and life stirring within me. It is the lot of woman to bring life to the earth, to replenish the tribe, to create strong warriors that they may protect and perpetuate the race." But then something passed over her eyes like an invisible cloud, and she sank into silence.

"What is it, Minnow? Why do you brood?"

"Our troubles multiply. I fear that the days of our race are numbered."

Seldom was it spoken so directly, and in times past, Minnow would not have said such things aloud to an outsider. Sunset Woman had become such a part of the life of Standing Bear's people, however, that one forgot she was not of the Cheyenne. Even her expectant motherhood enhanced this sense of permanency. And so she became acutely aware of the ominous portents as spring advanced. For even as wildlife rustled and warm winds blew across the lands of the Cheyenne, there came fresh tidings of distant tall riders and wagon trains. There were occasional brushes between Indians and whites; and rumors came to the campfires telling of pitched battles farther west, especially between settlers and the Sioux.

"They are a very warlike people, the Sioux," Standing Bear

himself muttered. "They arouse the wrath of the whites against all Indian people, for whites recognize no difference between one tribe and another."

"My lord, will there be fighting again?" She lay beside him in the lodge, which was her permanent sleeping place now. His hand was on her bare swollen abdomen, feeling for the kicks and movements. "Will there be trouble?"

"A strong baby," he murmured. "He kicks like a mustang."

"My lord?"

Standing Bear sighed in the darkness. The burden lay heavy upon him. "Yes. And some of it originates within our people. There is much blood already on their hands. I must confront my enemies both from within and from without. It is enough to try to live in peace against the onslaught of the white men. Their wagon trains and stagecoaches travel constantly through our ancient hunting grounds. Their guns take down the mightiest buffalo, and kill them as easily as one kills flies. Their wires-that-talk now reach across the distant mountains. They insist that we live in peace, and yet wreak violence upon us. They smile with false faces, utter lies while looking you full in the eyes and sign treaties that are worthless. In a way, one cannot blame Black Feather and his impatient young followers. They are angry and offended. And yet they go too far. I know that on their expeditions, they seek out white men and slay them for scalps. They have too long flaunted my authority, and these acts are becoming a danger to our people. I must confront Black Feather."

Vanessa lay silent, swallowing her fear.

The confrontation came sooner than anyone expected. Black Feather mustered his force of renegade Cheyenne and prepared to set forth. Word came to Standing Bear that they intended to raid a settlement for whiskey, horses, and guns. He strode to the fire circle and spoke to Black Feather as the warriors mounted. "If you do this, you break tribal law and must be punished." Those who listened recognized a tone of authority in which Standing Bear rarely spoke. He addressed the warriors as one who will tolerate no further defiance.

Black Feather snorted, reining his restless pony. "And who will punish us, O chief of the squaw's tent? We have turned our backs upon the white man too long already. We are expected by our chief to act as old women without teeth. Well, I have teeth." Black Feather brandished a new Sharp's rifle he had brought back from an expedition the previous year. "I intend to use them!" Rearing and turning his mount, he galloped away, leading his companions in a cloud of dust.

The party was gone for eighteen days. They returned leading four horses without riders. Of the fourteen braves Black Feather had led out, four had been killed and as many more wounded. One of the wounded, hit by a rifle bullet in the thigh, was dying as he slid off the pony into the arms of his squaw. Even as the females began to wail for their dead, Black Feather stalked to the lodge pole in the center of the village and hung fresh scalps. "I count my coups," he announced, turning to face the gathering tribe. "Our people no longer will cower in terror of the white man, but will stand as Cheyenne, unafraid."

Standing Bear walked from his lodge. He had donned the full dress of a Cheyenne chief, with fresh buckskin trousers and tunic, full beads at his throat and the formal headdress of solemn ceremony. He had received already a full account of Black Feather's deed from others. Without warning they had attacked the white trading post at Antelope Bend, killing a white woman and two men before the settlers could mount a defense. It had been wild hand-to-hand fighting and firing at close range. But Black Feather's desire to plunder and rape had not been fulfilled. Unexpected white reinforcements had arrived in the form of a telegraph surveying party. The attacking Cheyenne had been driven off, but not before Black Feather had taken the scalps of his victims.

"You have committed murder upon helpless people who did you no wrong." Standing Bear spoke facing his nemesis, hands by his sides and a tomahawk at his belt. "I have suspected you of similar crimes in the past, but lacked proof. Now there is proof and there are witnesses. Equally grave, Black Feather, are your deliberate attempts to split the loyalties of our people. You have tried to weaken their unity and create confusion. This must be resolved in trial by combat."

The entire tribe had gathered to listen. Standing Bear's words stirred a babble of voices. He raised his hand, and the babble stilled. Vanessa hovered at the back of the crowd, numbed by what she heard.

The eyes of Black Feather burned in naked hatred. "I welcome the chance to drive my tomahawk into the brain of this chief of the squaw's tent." The pockmarked face mottled with fury. "I will hang his scalp on my lodge pole and drive

the birthing Sunset Woman and her whelp from our midst."
He spat, and the spittle barely missed Standing Bear's foot.
"The squaw chief knows no pride and is beneath contempt."

"Tomorrow morning, then"—Standing Bear pointed to the
east—"when the rim of the sun appears on the horizon."

Black Feather nodded once, turned his back and strode
away.

The afternoon waned in an atmosphere of silent tension. In
the village, all life hung suspended. Even the ever present
dogs ceased to bark. As night drew over the plains, Vanessa
felt stifled by the mood. The moon rose, casting the village in
its lurid silvery glow and lighting the mist of the creek. Night
creatures chorused from dark thickets. An owl hooted. A fox
barked. She went to his lodge, enveloped in an inexplicable
sadness. As she lay down on the buffalo robe beside him, the
life within her kicked and fluttered in a strangely frantic way.

Standing Bear was silent, lying on his back in the darkness,
breathing evenly. She knew that his eyes were open.

"My lord," she whispered, "is there no other way?"

He did not reply.

"I beg you not to do this, my lord. You can simply handle
him as any of the tribe's lawbreakers would be handled. If his
offense is a capital offense, then he can be banished from the
tribe." She was speaking boldly, and beyond her place. But it
had to be done, for how else was she to communicate her
thought? "The tribe will follow you without question, and will
abide by your wishes. This . . . this is so great a risk to
everyone."

"There is no choice," he said. "Now be silent."

"But my lord . . ."

"Be silent."

She did not speak again, but lay wide awake beside him
until just before the dawn. He arose at last in the cold
darkness, lit a tallow lamp, and prepared himself for the task
ahead. As Vanessa watched from the buffalo robe, Standing
Bear painted his face with war paint, put on arm bracelets of
carved bone and secured his hair with a leather thong. He
donned clean trousers of doeskin and beaded moccasins
tightly laced. He smeared bear grease upon his shoulders,
neck, and upper torso, so that his long muscles rippled in the
tallow light. Finally he cleansed his hands thoroughly, dusted
them with a finely ground powder, and selected a handsome
battle tomahawk from a rack. This he stuck into a leather

thong at his waist. He also strapped on a large hunting knife. Each weapon was sharp enough to slice hair. Without a glance at Vanessa, he pushed open the flap of the lodge and stepped into the gray wash of dawn.

Quickly she got up, wrapped her swollen body against the chill and followed him. The dread stuck in her throat like a stone. And even as she waddled clumsily across the dusty ground to where the crowd had already gathered in dark silence, she sensed an increasing pressure in her body and knew that the birth would be very soon.

The combatants were equally matched in stature and strength, but it was evident to all that Black Feather would enjoy a slight advantage of reach. Six feet apart and facing the east, they crouched at the center of the hard-packed council fire circle. Each man's breath could be seen in the cold gray air. The crowd stood hushed, all eyes on the eastern horizon as it slowly gathered light. In years to come, Vanessa Stewart would remember this moment as one of suspended agony, separated from place and time, her eyes shifting frantically from that terrible line of earth and sky to the handsome, immobile face of her beloved, and back again. The light brightened with a dreadful intensity until it was the color of blood, shooting rays aloft in violent hues. And then, with heart-stopping suddenness that brought a murmur to the crowd, the first silver-thin slash of sun, angry as molten fire, cut the edge of the earth. The war cry of Black Feather came to her like the shriek of doom.

"Ayeeeeeeeeeeeeeeeeeeeee . . !"

They smashed together, knife-to-knife and tomahawk-to-tomahawk. Feet and knees flailed, bodies twisted. In hushed silence the tribe watched this struggle. The movements of the combatants seemed a ritualistic dance. Stamping moccasins raised puffs of dust. Grunts punctuated blows and knife thrusts. Black Feather spat into the eyes of his hated adversary, sprang free of the deadly weapons-lock, swiped the air with his tomahawk, loosed a cry of vengeance. Standing Bear's moccasined foot lashed out, struck a knee joint. There was a crack of breaking bone as Black Feather dropped. But even in falling, his sudden knife thrust brought first blood, an arc slashing deep into the tendons of Standing Bear's knife hand, rendering it useless. The chief's knife fell into the dirt and he hacked with his tomahawk, blade smashing blade, backing away.

Vanessa stifled a cry. Pain struck her deep in the body, forcing her to kneel. No, she thought. Not now! It can't start now! But it did, and in her heavy stress the labor set in much more rapidly than she had expected.

The battle wore on, each man panting from exertion, weakened or hobbled by his injury. Again they crashed together and locked in deadly embrace, struggling to free their weapons for the mortal blow. They toppled and rolled in the dirt, Black Feather grunting from the pain of his shattered knee. Time went by. The sun blazed down and sweat streamed down the grease-smeared bodies of the men, to mingle with blood and dirt.

It was Minnow who turned and saw Vanessa down. Wordlessly, the old squaw helped her to the shade of a cottonwood tree. The pains were swift and fierce, and in the lulls between them Vanessa looked desperately toward the unheeding crowd. But she saw only glimpses of the shifting feet of the fighting men. And still the time dragged on. The sun rose to its zenith and tilted into the afternoon. She lost track of reality, her consciousness overwhelmed by the pains and her own task. As the moment drew near, Minnow hissed an order and several old women turned from the struggle to circle around Sunset Woman, shielding her birth throes with their bodies. To Vanessa, there were only the shadows of the women, and the warm, coaxing voice of Minnow in the Cheyenne tongue. "Push, my child. Work hard." And at last the final labor came, and the birth was forced free of her body. A strange elation flooded her being. There was the sound of a whack, and a lusty cry.

At that instant, a shudder went through the tribe. A woman cried out. There was a confusion of vocal sounds, and then silence. The crowd shifted and parted, to make way.

Standing Bear, exhausted, battered, and bleeding from many cuts, stepped across the body of the slain Black Feather and walked painfully past the crowd to claim his firstborn son.

Vanessa Stewart whispered, "My lord."

At home, he preferred the velvet smoking jacket. It was wine red and enhanced his coloring. Brack Stewart appraised his image in the full-length mirror. Yes, the smoking jacket would do. It looked well with the dark gray trousers and dove gray cravat. Besides, this was only a cousin coming to call, and a supplicant at that. No need to be formal for Thaddeus Stewart. Brack smiled at his image, smoothed his jet-black hair once more with the matching silver brushes—he kept his hair dyed, against an increasing onslaught of gray—and dashed his face with cologne. Then he went downstairs to discuss luncheon.

"Will you have the squab, Mr. Stewart?" Howard, the manservant, spoke with a lofty precision denoting order and excellence. "It is quite fresh. May I suggest peas and small onions, a shell of potato with cheese sauce. Quite good. Very appropriate for this time of year."

"Very well, Howard." He enjoyed these discussions of the meals. Howard was a jewel at seeing to things. He was also quite discreet. Brack had brought him from London. "The squab will do nicely."

He had a small glass of sherry, more to occupy his hand than to drink, and strode lightly through the lower rooms of the house. He loved it here, loved his things. Brack had been as careful with his architect and designer as he had been in selecting a manservant. They had to be people who reflected his own tastes. And his own tastes, of course, were artistic and traditional. The house was a greystone tucked in behind its black wrought-iron fencing on Fifth Avenue. Exquisite leaded windows, accented with stained glass, offered intimate glimpses of the rose garden, the immaculate lawn, the avenue. Here he lived with his carpets, his paintings, his vases, his superb collection of jade. It was a house of quiet wealth, understated and in impeccable taste.

Thaddeus was on time. At the stroke of the hour, Howard announced his arrival. Brack regarded such punctuality, under the circumstances, a bit gauche. It inflated his own sense of superiority as he stood up from his chair. But the illusion quickly evaporated. The man who entered his parlor was quite tall and strikingly handsome. He walked with a decided limp, using a black cane with a heavy worked handle. He was dressed impeccably in black, and gave his hat to Howard with an offhand gesture that brought from the manservant an instinctive bow. The voice, when it spoke, was deep and of rich timbre.

"Cousin Brack. How good it is to see you."

"Thaddeus, my word. A pleasure!"

Thaddeus settled onto the divan, accepted a small sherry

and lit a cigar. The smoke was especially mild, and he explained that the tobacco was grown in Cuba. "Finest cigars in the world come from Cuba." They exchanged small talk, family talk. Brack was impressed by Thaddeus; recognition of his favorite Ming vase and appreciation for the jade figures displayed about the room. "You have excellent taste, cousin," Thaddeus said. "But then, I'm not surprised."

"Oh?"

"I've met your mother, my Aunt Maybelle. A striking woman. And she's quite proud of your accomplishments in finance." Something in Thaddeus's tone implied that he did not necessarily concur. Brack was immediately on guard.

"I take that as a high compliment, Thaddeus, considering the source. You have managed to create quite a stir of your own in railroad circles."

"Yes, well"—Thaddeus rolled the cigar in his fingers, studying its shape—"I wish I could say the same. The fact is, cousin, we're still sitting on dead center. I can't seem to get the finances moving. Except for a few of us enthusiasts, nobody's willing to invest. The Union Pacific's bonds are gathering dust, the Central Pacific is working hand-to-mouth to build a few miles out of Sacramento. So I decided to come and see you; I thought you might have some ideas."

"Ideas? My word, Thaddeus, what could I possibly suggest?"

Thaddeus eyed him shrewdly, the amusement in his gray eyes stifling the words in Brack's throat. Brack realized that this cousin was not a man to be deflected.

"Brack, you're one of the sharpest operators on Wall Street. The Nolichuckey and Southern deal was as cold-blooded a bit of financial piracy as ever crossed a broker's table. You've got your fingers in a half-dozen other ventures, including Cornelius Vanderbilt's idea to grab control of both the New York Central and the Erie lines. And your personal profits in war materiel—on both sides of the Mason-Dixon Line—are reckoned in millions."

"You flatter me unduly, Thaddeus. But where did you hear all this claptrap?" Brack plucked a handkerchief from his breast pocket and dabbed at his face.

"Common knowledge, Brack. Common knowledge. So I figured if there was a way to attract investors to the transcontinental railroad, short of dragging 'em in by the heels, then you would be the man to see it." Thaddeus flicked cigar ashes into a brass ashtray, his smiling eyes artfully buffering the bluntness of his speech. "But with one provision." The gray eyes locked onto Brack's. "We deal honestly."

Brack felt strangely uncomfortable under the scrutiny, and yet he was intrigued. There was enormous possibility here for gain. His mind did a quick analysis.

"Part of your problem, Thaddeus, is the war. It does compete for the investor's dollar. But I don't have to tell you that. Another problem is the meagerness of the federal subsidy."

"But Brack, we've got a promise of millions of acres of land. It's a potential bonanza!"

"Potential, yes. But all that land isn't worth a penny until a train runs through it. And this makes the risk very high. Your precious railroad will easily cost over one hundred million dollars to construct. My advice to you, Thaddeus, is to go back to Congress and get them to sweeten the pot."

"Sweeten the pot?"

"Sweeten the pot. And while it's commendable to be upright and proper in your dealings with Congress, I'm afraid that in politics, virtue must be its own reward."

"I don't get your meaning," Thaddeus said.

"Virtue does not move reluctant politicians. Politics, cousin, is a greedy business and politicians are venal men. There's hardly a foot of railroad in this country that doesn't owe its existence to the self-enrichment of public officials. You certainly ought to know this."

Thaddeus eyed him levelly, a frown creasing his forehead. Brack felt an inner excitement. It took not just miracles to move mountains, he had learned long ago; it took profit as well. And before all this was over, Brack intended to take a sizable chunk for himself.

"If I were in your shoes, Thaddeus, I'd work toward doubling the size of your federal land grants and speeding those subsidy payments to get a worthwhile cash flow. That would be a very good beginning. Then something could be worked out."

Thaddeus sighed. His cigar was dead in his hand. He dropped it into the ashtray. "I guess my work's cut out for me in Washington."

Brack nodded. "And cousin..."

"Yes?"

"Take along lots of cash."

* * *

Thaddeus despised this activity. It made him feel unclean. "Politicians," Brack had said, "are venal men." The phrase dogged his mind as he smiled into the porcine face of Congressman Hench, controller of a dozen votes in the House, and heard himself saying: "Congressman, it is the desire of my colleagues to make a substantial contribution to your reelection campaign."

"Well, well, well." Hench flushed happily. His wattles quivered. His eyes made bright beads as they saw the five thousand-dollar bills. A moist hand folded swiftly over the cash and tucked it out of sight. "A pleasure, Mr. Stewart, to serve such a worthy cause as your transcontinental railroad."

There were three of them involved in the effort: Thaddeus, Collis Huntington and Dr. Durant. The latter, whose own attempts to move the Union Pacific westward out of Omaha had faltered also for lack of financing, took a practical view. "Don't be too dismayed, Stewart. It's the system. Spoils are the name of the game."

Even Marguerite agreed. "If this is the way it must be done, dear, then go ahead and do it. Otherwise, forget about your railroad. Even Poindexter Carp agrees that you have very little choice."

And so the time dragged by. July brought broiling heat. Anxiety was stirred by fresh rumors of a Confederate thrust northward. But Thaddeus's spirits surged as the amended Pacific Railroad Act soared through Congress and was signed by President Lincoln. The new act doubled the size of land grants and made federal loans immediate with each twenty miles of track laid. Twenty-one million acres now lay potentially in control of the Central Pacific and Union Pacific Railroads. Thomas Durant celebrated over whiskey and cigars, convinced that his Union Pacific would now march boldly westward from Omaha. "Damn it, Stewart, nothing can stop us now!"

Thaddeus disliked the man without knowing why. Durant, a former physician turned railroader, flaunted wealth. His suits cost a fortune, his surroundings were invariably posh, he entertained lavishly. "It pays to make an impression," he declared. "If you want to attract railroad investors, you've got to look successful. And that means rich." Thaddeus's feelings turned to apprehension one evening at a dinner party, when Durant commented, "I've met your cousin Brack in New

York. Bright young man. His ideas look promising. Yes, very promising." The railroader's lean face glimmered with avarice.

Thaddeus left Washington and went back to California.

Contractor Charlie Crocker and his meager crews of laborers were building roadbed east of Newcastle. In command of the field forces now was a hulking new foreman, James H. Strobridge. A Vermont-born Irishman, Strobridge tongue-lashed and cursed his crews even when the task involved no more than make-work grading. Thaddeus had known the man slightly many years before in Illinois and approved of Crocker's choice.

Already, Strobridge's mettle had been tested. Not long before, they had blasted out the Bloomer Cut, a defile slashing at sixty-three-foot depths for eight hundred feet through the granitelike conglomerate rock east of Newcastle. Strobridge, eager to see that the black powder charges were properly placed, had been caught in an explosion and lost an eye. Within weeks he was back on the job and had the empty socket filled with a glass eye. "Dig, you goddamned Irish loafers!" he bawled to his grading crews. "We ain't payin' ye four dollars a day to sit on yer butts!"

Charlie Crocker sighed. "I told him he shouldn't talk so abusively to the men, Thaddeus. 'They're human creatures,' I says; 'Don't be so rough on them.' Jim Strobridge just grunts at me. He says, 'You can't talk to them like they was gentlemen. They're about as near brutes as you can find.' After a bit, I just figured he knew what he was doing and let it go at that. The trouble is, even if we get the financing to go full steam ahead, I don't see where we'll get the labor."

Thaddeus wagged his head. "First things first, Charlie. First things first."

He returned to the East in time for Christmas. A quick trip to Philadelphia and Thornwood Asylum had left him dispirited. The director of the asylum, a bewhiskered, intense man named Dr. Phineas Delacorte, escorted him to Ruth's room. It was a padded cell, lacking furniture or sharp objects of any kind. She lay in a corner in the fetal position, staring into oblivion. Beside her lay the battered doll, Raggedy. He knelt, touched her face and called her name. "Ruth? Ruth, it's Thaddeus." There was no response. As they walked through

the brooding brick building, the director offered little hope
for change.

"She suffers from a disorder we call dementia praecox, Mr.
Stewart. I've also heard it termed schizophrenia. Very little is
known, either of its cause or cure. She is in a state of
catatonia, withdrawn from the real world. I'm afraid the best
we can do is to keep her as you see her now, warm and fed
and reasonably clean. She is subject to periodic angers beyond
our control. Therefore, we thought it best that she occupy
one of our padded rooms. It's to minimize risk of injury to
herself."

Thaddeus arrived in Washington expecting to find Marguerite waiting at the station. She was not there. It was Marvella
Clive who led him through bitter cold and blowing snow to
her closed carriage. As they rattled off toward the Willard
Hotel, Marvella seemed to evade his questions about Marguerite. "What's wrong, Marvella?" he persisted. "Is she ill?"
At last, with two brandies under her corset in the comfort of
his suite, Marvella blurted it out.

"Peter Heflin came home on leave. He drank heavily and
there was a terrible row. The . . . the man has changed,
Thaddeus. This beastly war! A few drinks and he became a
savage. Treated his wife like a common prostitute. Oh, I hate
even to utter these things. The servants were shocked. I hear
that Heflin assaulted her dreadfully. He threatened to kill her
when she resisted. Anyhow, she is still bruised about the face
and simply could not have you see her in that condition. She
swore me to secrecy about this. But, my dear, I thought you
of all people should know." Her violet eyes rolled in chagrin.
"I hate myself for being a blabbermouth."

A rage filled him. He stood up, fists clenched. "Heflin.
Where is he now?"

"He's gone, Thaddeus. He left Washington and returned to
his troops. He said war is the only reality he can tolerate any
longer. What does that mean?"

"I must see her."

"Please, dear. Don't. Not until she . . ."

"I must see her!" He stalked out, leaving Marvella gathering up her things from the settee.

A hansom cab rushed him through icy streets to the
white-pillared manor house. A servant attempted to block his
way, but he pushed past the man and took the stairs two at a

time. The door of her boudoir was open, and he walked in. She looked up, startled, from her dressing table.

"Thaddeus!"

The fury was like bile in his throat. Feet planted apart, fists on his hips, he glared at the dark splotches beneath her eyes and the swelling that distended her mouth. "That bastard," he breathed. "How dare he touch you. How dare he!"

She turned away, hands covering her face. "Please, darling. Don't look at me, please."

And then he was beside her, dropping to his knees and gathering her face in his hands. He searched her eyes and was overwhelmed by the hurt and shame there. "My dear," he murmured, kissing her cheek. "My dear . . ."

He held her then, as she wept and talked. "I . . . I couldn't l-let him . . . touch me, Thaddeus. I couldn't b-be a w-wife to him. Oh, Thaddeus, I'm so miserable. It wasn't Peter's fault. He c-couldn't help himself. The war has changed him, Thaddeus. I barely knew him."

At last she was composed. They sat in opposite chairs, holding hands. She wiped the tears from her eyes and tried to smile. "He looked the same," she said. "And yet I could hardly recognize Peter as the man I'd married. He is so . . . so brutal. I know you'll think I'm crazy, Thaddeus, and maybe I am a little bit, but it was very obvious to me—Peter enjoys war. He loves war, Thaddeus. His whole life is killing. And he loves it. Do you understand what I'm saying? My husband loves war!"

Thaddeus remained in Washington through the winter, in order to be near Marguerite. Spring of 1865 came early, with pale green buds freshening the Potomac willows and jonquils thrusting up in yellow splotches around the Capitol. The newspapers bore daily recitals of somber war news as Grant battered Richmond and Sherman marched ruthlessly through Georgia to the sea. Lists of dead and wounded grew longer. But at last, in April, church bells rang over Washington. People poured into the streets, shouting and singing. A bellman in the lobby of the Willard shouted to Thaddeus the electrifying words: "Richmond has fallen, Mr. Stewart. The Rebs are on the run!" A week later, on April 9, Robert E. Lee surrendered to General Grant at Appomattox Courthouse in Virginia. Washington was in a frenzy. And Thaddeus and Marguerite joined a jubilant crowd outside the White House to hear brief remarks by the President. "We hope for the southern states to return to the Union as soon as possible," Lincoln said. The crowd cheered lustily.

Someone plucked at Thaddeus's arm. "Mr. Stewart?" It was one of the presidential assistants. "Mr. Lincoln asks if he could have a word with you in his office." The man turned an admiring smile to Marguerite. "And he'd like for you to bring the lady, too."

Lincoln was in a buoyant mood. He charmed Marguerite with compliments, exchanged wry humor with several other visitors, and finally was able to have a few words with Thaddeus.

"It's a great day, Mr. President."

"Indeed it is, Thaddeus. A glorious day. I was beginning to wonder, frankly, if Providence would ever smile upon us again. How puny is our faith at times."

"You've suffered much. Victory must be sweet."

"We've all suffered, Thaddeus. Your own wound is evidence of that. We've spilt more blood than we can ever hope to justify. And now we must find a way to bind the wounds and put it all back together again. It is men such as yourself who'll have the means for that."

Thaddeus's heart sank. "I only wish that you were right, Mr. President. But it isn't happening and sometimes I think it isn't going to happen. Sometimes I think we've bitten off more than we can possibly chew."

"Nonsense. That railroad will go through, I'm certain of it. Your associates are men of vision and daring. You have the opportunity to forge this nation into a colossus. And it will be done."

"Right now," Thaddeus said bleakly, "the Central Pacific is still hauling passengers over thirty-one miles of track at ten cents a head, and the Union Pacific hasn't gone beyond the city limits of Omaha. That's not much of a colossus."

Lincoln chuckled. "You're an engineer and a political lobbyist, Thaddeus, and you're damned good at both. Finance, on the other hand, is a skill you haven't yet mastered. Sometimes for a thing to succeed it takes combined talents of all kinds." Lincoln turned in his chair and pulled a bell cord. "There's someone waiting outside who might be able to help."

An aide arrived, accompanied by a smiling, thickset man with gray hair, a massive head and big shoulders. Thaddeus recognized the congressman from Massachusetts, Oakes Ames. At age sixty, the wealthy industrialist was a newcomer to the House but had served on the Select Committee for the Pacific Railroad. His enthusiasm was keen and his integrity absolute. Lincoln saw the smile lighting Thaddeus's face and grinned. "I see that you two know each other already."

"We do, Mr. President. A pleasure to see you again, Congressman."

"The pleasure is mine, Mr. Stewart."

"I've asked Oakes to take hold of this with you, Thaddeus. I think he's the man to get things moving. What he doesn't know about high finance isn't worth knowing. Eh, Oakes?"

"Don't give me too much credit, Mr. President. I'll fall on my nose for sure." The industrialist smiled. "But I'll be glad to do what I can."

"Excellent, excellent." Lincoln was pressed for time. As always, there were many who wished to see him and the schedule was tight. He seemed to want to talk further of commonplace things, but it was not to be. As Thaddeus rose to leave, Lincoln said cryptically, "If I'm not around to ride hard on this project, I expect you men to do the job."

Thaddeus started to speak, but Lincoln's whimsical smile confused him. He left the office with the feel of the rail-splitter's powerful grip warm upon his hand. Standing with Marguerite in the East Room, he asked Oakes Ames, "What did he mean by, 'If I'm not around'? He's got more than three years to go in this second term."

The congressman lifted an eyebrow. "That's Old Abe. You never know when he's pulling your leg."

Thaddeus left the White House troubled in mind.

April 14, 1865, Good Friday. The day dawned hazy and cool. Thaddeus awoke early and stood at the window of his Willard Hotel suite. Holiday quiet lay over the city. Few people stirred in the streets. Most government workers would have the day off. He was in a happy state of mind. Peace, at last! For a week, Washington had hardly drawn a sober breath. Bars and clubs did a land office business. The previous evening, the city had swirled with celebration as crowds ranged through the streets, singing war songs. Thaddeus himself had attended a gala victory party and danced with numerous giggly young women beneath cut-glass chandeliers. Later he had accompanied a group of Senate friends and their wives to St. Aloysius Catholic Church, where many parishioners came to pray through the night. The stations of the cross were decorated in purple. Although he was not of religious mind, the experience had stirred him deeply. Even now, memories of guttering candles and priestly chants plucked at his memory.

Restless, he found the newspaper at his door and settled down to scan it. There was little of real interest to catch his eye. The usual list of war dead began on the front page, left-hand column, then continued inside. Lee's surrender still dominated the news. A congressional subcommittee expressed concern over the horde of convalescing wounded sleeping in the basement of the Capitol. Sherman's troops had laid waste to Charleston, South Carolina. President and Mrs. Lincoln planned to attend a play at Ford's Theater this evening. People were upset about outrageous prices in the markets, with butter at 30 cents a pound, coffee at 21 cents a pound and ham at 28 cents a pound. A physician advertised his latest cure for cancer at $2 a visit. There was criticism of Lincoln's order to lift the blockade immediately and his magnanimous terms for reconstruction of the South. Thaddeus tossed the paper aside.

At nine o'clock there was a knock at the door and the maid announced the arrival of Brigadier General Herbert Willoughby. Thaddeus rushed to greet his old friend with handshakes and backslapping. "Willoughby, you war-horse. By God, you survived!"

"Some of us, Thaddeus, are too worthless to kill." Willoughby appeared to be lean and physically fit, but his face was stamped with the fatigue of long campaigning. A single star of new rank glittered in gold braid on each shoulder epaulet. "I never thought I'd see this day."

"We'll celebrate with the damnedest breakfast you ever ate."

"Good. I'm famished!"

In the Willard Hotel dining room, they polished off eggs, bacon, biscuits, oysters, black coffee and a pint of whiskey. Slightly tipsy, they then donned their cloaks and ventured out for a morning stroll. Willoughby observed that Thaddeus was moving about quite well despite his war wound, and the cane gave him distinction. They turned onto Pennsylvania Avenue.

"Well, they finally finished the Capitol dome and the Washington Monument, General. Wouldn't you say they add a bit of class to the town?"

Willoughby smiled. "Now, if we could just shoo the goats and tent squatters off the White House lawn..."

A thin mist still lay over the city, casting a surreal light. The air, a heady mix of odors, hinted of rain. As they walked along the single sidewalk bordering the avenue, a horsecar trundled past carrying a few passengers. The White House rose like a gleaming square pile facing the avenue, paths crisscrossing the grounds. Nearby there sprawled a teeming slum of Negro shanties.

"Where did they all come from?" Willoughby asked.

"The South. They're freed slaves, mostly, come to be near the man in the White House who is their deliverer. They've got no jobs, no prospects, no hope. Freedom is a mixed blessing."

Willoughby sighed. "I don't know how we're going to put it all back together, Thaddeus. Things will never be the same again. And the country is still torn apart by sectional hatreds."

Thaddeus clapped him on the back. "We'll build us a railroad, Willoughby."

They strolled past the open-air market, where men were at work gutting shad and butchers tended great brine vats of beef. There was a stench of fish and rotting produce. A train beginning its forty-mile trip to Baltimore whistled as it left the B&O's ornate wooden station. Thaddeus drew out his heavy gold watch and unsnapped the case. "Right on time. She'll be in New York City in nine hours."

"Nine hours," Herbert Willoughby mused. "Unbelievable."

They returned to the Willard at noon and talked, over glasses of sherry. Other friends joined them in the early afternoon, including Collis Huntington, Oakes Ames and several members of his committee. War still dominated conversations and the air filled with cigar smoke.

"It's left us with six-hundred-thousand dead, North and South, and God knows how many wounded. The national debt is two and a half billion dollars. And what in the world's to be done with four million Negroes who used to be slaves and now are free?"

Conversation turned to the Central Pacific. Huntington was in a dour mood. At long last, bonds were being sold to finance the work. But now a new headache had developed.

"It's manpower we need, Thaddeus. Strobridge advertised for five-thousand laborers. He thought he'd be swamped with applicants. God knows, there are enough cutthroats and loafers around Sacramento and San Francisco. But there were only eight hundred takers, and we lost two hundred of them payday. They get drunk or take off for the mines in Nevada."

"And what about the Union Pacific? What do you hear from Tom Durant?"

"Still no real progress, I'm afraid." It was Oakes Ames who spoke. The big-shouldered millionaire sighed. "Durant has got his survey parties out, all the way to the mountains. But Indians are on the warpath all through that country. Unless we can put them down, there'll be hell to pay laying track."

Herbert Willoughby looked intently at Ames. "Then that explains it," he said.

"Explains what, General?"

"Peter Heflin is taking a division of cavalry west. He will have field command of troops from Nebraska clear to Utah. He intends to clear a hundred-mile swath along the route of the Union Pacific. Knowing Heflin, he won't rest until there are no Indians left in his jurisdiction."

Thaddeus digested this news with mixed feelings. Attempting to keep the edge from his voice, he asked: "And is Heflin coming to Washington at all?"

"No." Willoughby looked at him curiously. "No, he's going straight to Fort Kearny. At least, those are the orders I saw. And they were issued by the Secretary of War at Heflin's specific request."

Oakes Ames fingered his steel-gray growth of chin whiskers. "Thaddeus, Tom Durant and some of his friends have come up with a way of breaking their financial logjam, at least as far as the Union Pacific Railroad is concerned."

"How's that, Congressman?"

"They've created a separate corporation to handle the Union Pacific's contracting and financing. It's called the Credit Mobilier."

"The Credit Mobilier?"

"I'm still hazy on details, but I understand your cousin Brack Stewart is involved. They're predicting enormous success. He is quite the bright star in financial circles these days."

"Yes," Thaddeus mused, "quite the bright star . . ."

Later in the day, Thaddeus declined an invitation to attend

the play *Our American Cousin* at Ford's Theater, preferring instead to reintroduce Herbert Willoughby to old Washington friends at a dinner party at Marguerite's. As the evening progressed amid gaiety that typified Washington these days, he was glad to have made the choice. Laughter and bubbling conversation restored his spirits. Dinner was just ending, and the men had gone to the parlor for brandy and cigars, when a cavalry lieutenant pushed past the butler demanding to see General Willoughby immediately. The man was in a high state of excitement and his shouts brought them to their feet as the butler led him into the room

"What is it, lieutenant? I'm Willoughby. What's wrong?"

"The President, sir. President Lincoln's been shot! There are assassins loose all over the city. Secretary Seward was attacked in his home."

Willoughby sprang for his hat and cloak. "Thaddeus! Let's go!" Together they pounded down the steps behind the lieutenant, jumped into a carriage and whipped the horses into a gallop.

People were weeping in the streets. A woman stood at the corner of Tenth Street shouting, "Murder! Murder!"

The carriage careened around the corner and rocked toward Ford's Theater, slowing in the face of thickening crowds. Finally they were inching along. Thaddeus said, "We'll make better time on foot." They walked then, at last elbowing through the crush toward the lights of Ford's Theater, haloed in mist.

Troops with fixed bayonets blocked the way, facing a jostling mob. Men and women were sobbing and shouting the President's name. Willoughby collared a captain of the detachment. "I'm General Willoughby, presidential staff. Where is Mr. Lincoln?"

"Over there, General. In that house across the street."

"Come along, Thaddeus."

They passed through the lines and mounted the steps of a narrow, nondescript house at 453 Tenth Street, directly opposite the theater. Thaddeus's mind registered fleeting impressions: a gloomy interior lit by guttering gaslight, a narrow hallway, a parlor with a coal grate and black horsehair furniture. Several women sat weeping on a couch. He recognized young Clara Harris, a senator's daughter, and the bulky figure of Mary Todd Lincoln. A young man in shirt-sleeves met Willoughby in the hallway. "I'm Dr. Leale."

"What's his condition, Doctor?"

Leale, who had been in the theater crowd and attended the President since shortly after the assassin had fired the shot and fled, shook his head grimly. "The wound is mortal, General. It is not possible for him to recover."

"May we see him?"

Leale led them into a small bedroom beneath the stairway. As Thaddeus ducked through the doorway, the walls closed in. The wallpaper was of a color resembling oatmeal, the furniture a mixed set of cheap maple. On the bed, in a state of terrible immobility, lay the giant body of Abraham Lincoln. He was covered by a blanket, his bare feet protruding grotesquely beyond both bed and blanket. They had placed him diagonally across the bed or he would not have fit on it at all. Extra pillows were wedged beneath the great head with its black locks and whiskers. Gaslight glowed from a wall fixture, accentuating the pallor and deep hollows of the face. There were sounds of stertorous breathing and an occasional sigh.

"The bullet," Dr. Leale said, "entered the back of his head on the left side. We think it is lodged behind the right eye."

Thaddeus knelt beside the bed and held the big, lifeless hand. His mind was a turmoil; grief lodged in his throat. The others stood quietly behind him. His thoughts picked over the past, the talks they'd had, the train journey from Springfield to assume the presidency, the long, hard years of war and how they had ravaged Lincoln's spirit, the death of the son Willie in the White House, his dreams of the railroad to the Pacific. "It isn't fair, Mr. President," he said quietly. "It isn't fair." At last he stood up and walked out, followed by Willoughby, into the grieving city.

Crowds stood all night in front of the house on Tenth Street. At dawn, rain began falling. It was a chill, cheerless rain that seeped into everyone's bones. And at half past seven on the morning of April 15, Abraham Lincoln was dead.

Again, Thaddeus Stewart was called upon to take charge of the presidential train. Only this time, the train was draped in black crepe and bore the hulking body back to Springfield and eternal rest. With Willoughby in command of the military escort, Thaddeus rode part of the way in the cab of the locomotive. Rain sifted down periodically, as the slow-moving train chugged past towns and villages. Somber clusters of

people stood under black umbrellas, mopping their eyes and
waving sodden handkerchiefs. At one point, as they passed
through a busy switching yard, Thaddeus remembered the
words that Lincoln had spoken in their final meeting at the
White House. "You have the opportunity to forge this nation
into a colossus!" Well, he thought, it will be done, Mr.
President. It will be done.

The engineer turned and looked at him curiously. "What
did you say, sir?"

Thaddeus, unaware that he had spoken out loud, shook his
head. "Nothing. Nothing at all."

XVIII

"Make a run to Natchez?" Catherine was incredulous. She
walked across the office of the St. Louis compound and stared
from a window down the slope to the Mississippi. Two battered
steamboats lay at the wharf, only one of which was capable of
taking on a head of steam. Her eye took in the once majestic
Isaiah Stewart, flagship of the fleet. The great triple decks
were rusted and sagging, the superstructure a dingy gray.
Even the vessel's twin stacks, thrusting thirty feet into the
balmy air of late spring and topped by battered metal crowns
once resplendent in gold leaf, resembled something out of a
junkyard. "Make a run with what? The Stewart fleet is a
shambles."

"With the *Isaiah Stewart*, Miss Catherine," the visitor said
quietly. "She'll make steam. And my people, we'll act as
crew. We can stoke wood to the fires and handle the cargo."

"I don't even have a captain, Mr. Probish. No captain, no
crew. My steamers are scattered the length of the Mississippi. Those that weren't commandeered for military use, or
sunk, lie rotting in a dozen sloughs and bayous."

"We're desperate, Miss Catherine. People around Natchez

are going hungry. There ain't no cattle left, no hogs, no chickens. There weren't no able-bodied men to make a corn crop."

"I know that." She could not look at him. She remained at the window, her back turned, and hated herself. A dozen of them waited outside, Natchez people who had come upriver on a miserable clutch of rafts and canoes seeking help. They needed everything: food, grain, tools, animals. The war, she thought, the war was bad, and now peace was even worse. "The war has extracted its price from us all," she said aloud. "My husband and I will have to start over building this fleet. The only thing we've got left is hulks. *Pittsburgh, River Queen, Vicksburg Pride, New Orleans, King Creole, Belle of the South*—they were grand in their day, Mr. Probish. No grander vessels afloat. And now? Now there's not a one of 'em worth a hundred-dollar gold piece."

"Yes, ma'am." He waited, hat in hand, eyes too big for his bony face, eyes full of hunger.

"Not a one of 'em could be launched for commercial use without a heavy overhaul. And that's what I've told every person who has come to my door."

"Yes, ma'am."

"You're not the first, you know."

"Yes, ma'am."

She whirled around, eyes blazing. Catherine had aged gracefully, and her lithe, tall frame and long, gray-blond hair still drew appreciative glances from men half her age. "Hell, Mr. Probish, even if we try it with *Isaiah Stewart* I can't guarantee we'll make ten miles downriver. Those channels have had four years of neglect. They're full of sandbars and snags that nobody even knows about now. Rip the guts right out of a steamboat." She hesitated, thinking one thing and saying another. "And like I say, I haven't even got a captain."

"I heard you, ma'am."

She fell silent, looking into his eyes. The quiet was intense. From outside where the others waited, she heard a woman's rattling cough. She thought of Stephen. How would Stephen handle this? But Stephen was not here to ask; he was in St. Joseph with the twins, Bradley and Colette, tending to the stage line and the wagon business. It was up to her to decide. Catherine Colby Stewart felt a great weight upon her mind.

"All right," she said quietly. "I'm not promising anything, but I'll try."

He smiled. He sank down to his knees and bowed low to her. He said, "Thank you, Miss Catherine. Thank you very much."

"Oh, get up off the floor, Probish. For God's sake..."

Only an old clerk, Cavendish, remained in the office. He sat behind an ancient desk brought from Pittsburgh years before, presiding over an enterprise of virtually nothing. She had kept Cavendish on the meager payroll during the war and watched the rest of the staff disintegrate. Now she needed a captain, and there was one man who might—just might—do the job. Cavendish would know where to find him, if anybody did. "Cavendish," she said, "where is Ezekiel Potter?"

"Who?"

"Potter. Captain Ezekiel Potter. Where do I find him?"

"Well, Miss Catherine..." Cavendish hesitated, dabbed at his brow with a blue bandana. "Captain Potter, he's been in St. Louis, but he ain't been well. No ma'am, he ain't been well at all."

"He's not sober, you mean. Probably hasn't drawn a sober breath in four years." She sighed, glowering. "All right, then. Where do I find the body."

"Oh, you wouldn't want to go there, Miss Catherine. Ezekiel, his accomodations ain't the best, and you wouldn't—"

"Come on, Cavendish. I'm running out of patience!"

"Well, then..."

An hour later, with a dagger in her boot and a Colt revolver holstered under her coat, Catherine Stewart strode down the meanest street in St. Louis. Dark corners emitted odors of vomit and urine. Whistles and catcalls came from drunken idlers lounging in front of saloons.

"My, my, my, what've got here?"

"Hey, missy, wait a while. Give us a toss, eh?"

"It might be old, but it sure sets me afire."

"I got what you're lookin' fer, lady, right cheer."

She ignored them. One drunken giant staggered into her path, blocking the sidewalk. Catherine stopped, flicked back the coat to show the Colt and waited. He saw the fury in her eyes, belched softly and stepped clear. "'Scuse me."

She found it at last, a rundown hotel with a grimy facade and a sign, Rooms to Let. At the desk a slovenly woman looked up with hostile eyes. "Yes?" The eyes widened, absorbing the presence of the tall, handsome visitor. "Yes, madame?" The slattern straightened and smoothed her soiled dress. Catherine spoke Ezekiel Potter's name. The woman pretended ignorance. A gold piece provided inspiration. She led the way up a grimy stairway, pushed open a sagging door and entered a room drenched in odors of decay. A gnarled finger pointed to a huddled figure on the bed. "There he is."

"Bring me a basin of cold water and a washcloth."

"Yes, madame."

"And coffee, if you've got any. Strong."

"Coffee. Yes."

Catherine knelt to her task. It was twenty minutes before she managed to bring him around. He came awake resentfully, as one who'd long sought the release of oblivion and surrendered to it with profound relief. She persisted, splashing cold water into his face and calling his name. "Captain Potter? Captain Potter, do you hear me? Captain Potter, I want you to wake up. I need you."

"Huh? Huh? Huh?" The eyes opened, tried to focus, rolled in their sockets.

"Captain Potter, I want you out of this bed immediately. We've got work to do!"

"Whork... Got whhork..."

Finally he was on his feet, a thin, bewhiskered apparition, wheezing and pale as death, swaying in her grasp. "Got whhork to do," he mumbled.

And then they were down the stairs and out into the dying afternoon, the tall, straight-backed woman leading the shambling drunk by the arm and speaking earnestly into his ear. "Ezekiel Potter, there's nobody else who can do it but you. No other captain knows this river so well. You've got to take the *Isaiah Stewart* down to Natchez with a cargo of relief supplies. The people are starving and desperate. Do you hear me, Captain Potter?"

"God damn, Miz Catherine, I ain't even sober. Ain't drawed a sober breath in a month of Sundays. Besides, there's a war on. Didn't you know there's a war on, Miz Catherine? We could get our (belch) asses killed!"

"The war's over, Captain. The war's over and we're going downriver on the *Isaiah Stewart*. And you're going to take us to Natchez, the whole damn works."

At last he stood on the wharf focusing his eyes at the *Isaiah Stewart*. His face wrinkled in disgust. "That ain't your steamboat, Miz Catherine. That's a scow. Your steamboat's the

flagship of the fleet, pride o' the Mississippi—all gleamin'
white and touched with gold, three decks fore 'n aft. This
here's a pile o' kindling wood."

"Maybe so, Captain Potter, but her heart's still strong.
And you're going to take her to Natchez, come hell or high
water."

"If you say so, Miz Catherine. If you say so . . ."

Ezekiel Potter's knees buckled and he tumbled onto the
dock, fast asleep.

In town, the merchants were more than dubious. Bankers
and business interests had watched the decline of the Stewart
line and clucked their tongues. When it came time for
rebuilding—as inevitably it would—there wouldn't be much
collateral left on which to base loans. Not that the Stewarts
had ever required loans before, but there was always a first
time. And now, as word circulated in St. Louis that Catherine
Stewart was accumulating livestock, grains and stores to help
the South, the critics' clucking grew louder. "Do you think
it's wise, Miss Catherine," a banker friend muttered, "to
treat with a fallen enemy so soon?"

"They're people, Clyde. People like you and me. They
need help."

"Well, yesssss." He said it with a hiss. "But Natchez has no
money except Confederate money. And I doubt, frankly, that
a Johnny Reb's credit is worth much."

"I take it you mean that if I need financial help, don't come
to you for it. Right?"

"Now, Catherine, I didn't say that. Stewart business has
always been valued in this town."

It troubled her, of course. Her cash reserves were low.
Only in an emergency would she ask Stephen to help. They
kept the enterprises separate—by mutual agreement—and
had done so ever since he'd lost their entire Ohio River trade
on a damnfool bet many years ago.

The thought of Stephen warmed her. What would he
advise her to do? She knew, of course, what he would advise.
"If you've got to do it, do it. The details can be worked out
later." And so as days passed, the last cash was poured out for
cattle, pigs and chickens; for corn, wheat and barley grains;
for sacks of flour and drums of salt. Then she made a visit to
the St. Louis Bank & Trust Company.

Afterward, the clerk Cavendish was aghast. "You mortgaged the river compound?"

"Yep. Mortgaged the whole damned thing, including that desk you're sittin' at, Cavendish."

"But Miss Catherine, there never has been a mortgage on Stewart property."

"There is now."

"Those people"—Cavendish, a staunch Union man who had lost two grandsons in the war, looked out the window to where Probish and his people were busy loading the *Isaiah Stewart* in the middle of the afternoon— "they won't even appreciate what you done."

"We won't worry about that right now, Cavendish. We'll just do it. And I'll thank you to keep the accounts."

The clerk muttered into his white mustache and returned to his ledger sheets. "Yes, ma'am."

Ezekiel Potter quarreled and snapped at the volunteer labor, his quavering voice keening over the noise of mooing cattle, crowing cocks and bleating sheep. "Carnsarn it, ye damn fools, ye can't put all them barrels on one side of the boat. She'll be unstable 'fer sure. And tie up them cattle, don't leave 'em to wander around. This ain't no pasture, it's a foredeck!"

"How's it going, Captain Potter?"

"Miss Catherine, I don't know. It's a darnfool thing to be doin', if you ask me. These folks don't know how to load a steamboat. I shudder to think what's likely to happen when we get underway." He eyed the thin curl of steam issuing from the single usable boiler, manned by an uncertain Mr. Probish. "If we get underway."

But at last the morning of departure dawned. A light mist rose from the muddy waters. The sun came up over the woodlands, burning off the mist and sprinkling the mighty Mississippi with reflective jewels. Jumping fish broke quiet waters, making widening ripples.

"Cast off yer bow lines!"

"What'd you say, Cap'n?"

"Cast off yer bow lines! Stand ready aft!"

"Whut's a bow line, Cap'n?"

"Oh, hell. Untie that goddamned rope."

To a rising accompaniment of mooing, bleating, crowing and clucking, the battered *Isaiah Stewart* shuddered to the reluctant turning of her great stern wheel and limped into midstream. In the wheelhouse, Ezekiel Potter—a skeletal apparition suffering the torments of the newly sober—spun the great wheel and shouted his commands fruitlessly down a voice pipe to uncomprehending ears below.

It was Catherine who now stoked wood to the fire under the watchful gaze of Mr. Probish and two ancient and arthritic helpers. "Now this is the way you do it, Mr. Probish. You got to cut these wood lengths to size, see? Get a good solid fire but don't overload. Bang the door shut like this, and be sure it catches; don't need to lose more draft control than's necessary. Here are your dampers and ventilators. And if she gets too hot"—she eyed the two crippled ancients who stood by to relieve Probish at his labors— "Well, never mind. She's not goin' to get too hot."

Catherine made a tour of the craft, toweling sweat from her soot-streaked face. The great main salon, once a glittering scene of gaming tables where a string orchestra entertained well-dressed crowds in a blaze of lamplight, now was piled high with crates, bins, sacks, and boxes. The promenade decks, where fancy ladies and gentlemen once had taken the air, now were alive with animals and fowl. And to tend all this in place of the burly, profane riverboat crews, was a handful of undernourished women, old men, and children.

Catherine climbed to the wheelhouse, breathing in the clear air of late spring and letting her gaze drift across the wide, muddy expanse of river. Willows in full leaf crowded the banks. Distant fields and woodlands spread away in a panorama of emerald green. A hawk cruised overhead. And in the midst of all this beauty, the *Isaiah Stewart* moved along like a living relic, paint peeling and superstructure sagging, stern wheel biting at the muddy flow with broken teeth which tended to propel the hulk at an odd angle.

"Well, Captain Potter, how's it going now?"

"Now?" Ezekiel Potter muttered in his throat. "Now I know how Noah felt."

It was a slow business for more reasons than weak fires in the boiler. The river, even to the canny eye of Ezekiel Potter, was a thing of new mysteries and lurking traps. Sandbars appeared where none had existed before, stobs and snags lurked just beneath the murky surface. There were hidden logs, sneaky currents, treacherous turns. Catherine placed every available eye on the foredeck to watch for perils and shout the alarm. Ezekiel Potter spun his wheel, shouted into his voice pipe, cursed, and longed for a drink. They tied up at night, roping securely to trees along the shore, and waited each morning for the mists to clear before proceeding. It was a slow, arduous voyage; a voyage, Catherine thought whimsically, of the lame and the halt, as aptly demonstrated by the wheezing bleat of the steamboat's once mighty whistle.

Other river traffic was sparse: a military gunboat here, plodding upcurrent while uniformed men stared, stolid and unsmiling; a raft there. Now and then they even passed a keelboat, floating along downstream in the timeless way of bygone travel. From the shore there came occasional waves and shouts from lone men or small groups signaling them to make landfall. It was Captain Potter who offered the advice to ignore them. "These are perilous times, Miss Catherine. You don't know what kind of riffraff is waiting behind them trees." And so they made no unplanned stops.

Catherine was beginning to think they would never get to Natchez. As she'd been accustomed to speed and power on this river, and the great lighted boats sweeping along day and night, the fitful voyage seemed eternal. At night, bedded down amid the odors of cattle and fowl, she dreamed of sailing forever on a derelict steamboat down a muddy torrent of no return, while a cantankerous, drunken skeleton continually shouted down a voicepipe with no one to hear.

But, finally, the Mississippi took one last turn, a line of familiar bluffs loomed to their left, and Mr. Probish shouted from below, "There she is! There's home!" Catherine herself was at the wheel, having spelled Captain Potter for lunch. She reached for the whistle rope, tugged, and for the first time got a full, rich blast that sent echoes racing through the valley. On the decks below, the makeshift crew raised a ragged cheer and waved their hats in the sunshine. Catherine loosed another whistle blast as the town itself came into view, cresting the bluff and spilling down to the water's edge. Even from this distance, she could see the people begin to emerge from the houses and buildings. Doors banged and windows flew up. More and more of them appeared, waving and jumping up and down and hugging each other. As Catherine spun the great wheel, swinging toward the shore, the human trickle became a tide, bursting from the houses and pouring down the slope. Many were bone-thin and dressed in rags.

Wild cheering erupted, a rippling, disjointed sound punctuated by the high-pitched Rebel yells. The sound grew into a thunderous roar engulfing her senses as Catherine worked the *Isaiah Stewart* into the dock. Eager hands grabbed coiling bow lines. The gangplank thrust shoreward. The vanguard of the mass surged onto the deck of the steamboat, enveloping Probish and his friends in welcoming hugs. Catherine descended from the wheelhouse into a joyous pandemonium. The people of Natchez rushed to grasp her hand and embrace her, tears running down their faces. Abruptly, she felt herself hoisted aloft. Chanting and laughing, they bore her on their shoulders around the deck and then to shore, while as if by magic a small fife and drum band appeared and struck up a lusty, tuneless air. As they deposited her before an elderly, bewhiskered man wearing a vastly oversized suit and the sash of official office, Catherine could no longer hold back her own tears.

The mayor grasped her hand and uttered the thanks of a grateful city.

Catherine mopped her eyes, stammering, "I feel like a damn fool."

"You will never know what this means to us," the mayor said.

"We've got a new beginning," Catherine said. "Isn't that something? We've got a new beginning!"

Around her, the crowd roared.

Heat baked the ruins of Charleston. It was a town of rubble, shattered pillars, shattered walls and shattered hopes. Black children squatted in the dust, skin and bones, their faces covered with unheeded flies, eyes staring. Men and women in tattered clothing poked in rubbish heaps and garbage cans. The warehouses of the dock area lay in ruins. The wharf was a broken shell, collapsed into the harbor. Once elegant homes faced the sea as blackened shells. There was a pervasive odor of despair.

Francis Drake Stewart no longer rode his black stallion from the Chares mansion to the docks. The stallion had long since been slaughtered for meat. The mansion was a wreck of broken pillars and shattered glass. Only his vessel, the *Fury*, survived at anchor in the harbor. For he had been at sea when Sherman's troops came to bombard the city, to pillage and burn and ravish. Otherwise, *Fury* undoubtedly would have gone the way of the rest of it.

Francis Drake swatted a mosquito at his ear, mopped perspiration from his face and walked through the dust in the

Chares house. Behind him, Elizabeth Chares, her father and several former hired hands began the tedious business of putting the house back in order. But it was a make-work process without real enthusiasm; for like everyone else in Charleston, the Chares were hungry and there was little food to sustain them.

"What will you do, Drake?" she had asked him. "How will you help us?"

"I'll do what I can. It's going to take time."

"But we're hungry. Blessed be, Drake, can't you see that? We don't have time, honeychile. I'm hungry and Daddy's hungry, and we got to have help."

"I'll do what I can."

Yes, they were hungry. But it was worse in the town. The whites suffered, having less than they had ever had before. Even the Chares, however, had managed to lay a little aside, cached in hiding places and in the fields; a sack of beans, a box of flour, a little fatback. The whites suffered, but the blacks—Drake's own people—were in agony. Francis Drake walked the dusty streets with Cochrane at his side into the slum-ridden Negro section of Charleston. It wasn't a section, really, but an infestation of dire need; paper shacks and wooden lean-tos and packing boxes housed whole families. The children sat in the dust with distended bellies and huge eyes staring from heads that were too big for their scrawny necks and emaciated bodies. He felt the eyes burning at him from the children and from the adults, sinking in their shadows; felt the eyes flicking over his tailored clothes, his well-fleshed body and near-white complexion.

"Good Lord," said the mate Cochrane. "What're these people going to do?"

"I don't know," Francis Drake muttered. "I don't think anybody knows. They're freed people now. That means nobody's responsible for their upkeep, except maybe the federal government. But the federal government's in Washington, not Charleston. It'll take a long time for the bureaucracy to gear up and take charge. And while that happens, people will simply starve to death.

They found the railroad depot, or what had been the railroad depot. Now it was a burned-out ruin. Even the tracks were gone, ripped up and burn-warped into useless junk. They followed the right of way for a distance, and it was the same. The railroad would have to be rebuilt through here, for miles into the countryside. "And that means we can't get anything shipped in by land, not for a good long while. It's got to be by water. And since *Fury* is the only serviceable vessel left, that means us."

"Sherman's men really did a job on Charleston. Why, Captain?"

"They blamed South Carolina for starting the war. Out there"—he peered across the sunlit harbor toward the ruins of Fort Sumter—"is where it all began. The city was a symbol, and the symbol was a prime target for destruction." Drake sighed. "If you ask me, it was all a damned senseless waste. Except"—his eye fell on a clutch of Negro children who smiled shyly from the shadows of a burned-out building— "except that it achieved the purpose of eradicating slavery. That was an evil this country could no longer tolerate."

"Let's get the hell out of here, Captain," Cochrane said. "There ain't no sense in hanging around this place. We can get into legitimate shipping. Jesus Christ, you've made a pile. Buy another merchant ship, get on the China run. Hell, start a fleet. There's riches to be made, now that the war's over."

Francis Drake did not reply. They returned to the *Fury* and he retired alone to his cabin with a bottle of whiskey. His lamp burned all night and the deck watch could hear the sound of his boots pacing. At first light he emerged, haggard and needing a shave, and went ashore alone in the dinghy. In the early afternoon, Francis Drake stood in the wrecked parlor of the Chares house facing several of the leading merchants. The former slaver Mason Chares eyed him stonily. Elizabeth sat nearby, avoiding her father's glance.

"We've got to put it back together," Francis Drake was saying. "The city is starving, and black people are suffering even more than the whites. My first mate suggests that we take the *Fury* and go"—the words stirred a muttering of protest, and several eyes glanced at Elizabeth Chares as if beseeching her help—"but I have decided not to." He looked into the white faces, the faces of men who had despised him in the past and who were still unyielding in their enmity. A part of his mind wondered why he was doing this, but his eye fell upon Elizabeth, and he knew the answer. Elizabeth, with her tumbling black hair and pale blue eyes, her luscious mouth opening slightly as she caught his gaze. "Instead, we will use *Fury* to make a run to Norfolk for supplies. The blockade is no more, so it will be an easy matter. In the meantime, I would like for you gentlemen to draw up a list of priorities for restoring the dock area and the warehouses. I think I can get us some help to rebuild the railroad, at least so that food and supplies can be brought in by train."

"But what about money?" one of the merchants said. "We haven't got any money. Confederate currency is worthless. And as for gold..." The words hung suspended, the mood suddenly ugly. Gold. They knew who had the gold. The eyes narrowed, searching his face.

"First things first," Drake heard himself saying. "And gold, for a while anyway, is not a problem."

Afterward, as the sun went down over the jagged silhouettes of the town, Elizabeth Chares clutched at him in her boudoir, whispering. "Oh, darling. Oh, my darling. What would I do without you?"

"Elizabeth..."

"Here. Put your hand here. Feel my heart hammering? I want you so. Oh, Drake, I need you so." She was moaning as he lowered her to the bed, undid his trousers and bared his jutting shaft.

The plaque was small, discreet, done in polished brass studded to the marbled wall. "Stewart & Associates, Consultants." Francis Drake dropped his cigar into a potted palm and pushed through the mahogany door. The reception area was a model of tasteful elegance: brass fixtures and lamps, Oriental rugs, high ceilings and windows, velvet drapes with gold tassels. The female receptionist was blonde, young, nubile. Drake had an impression of firm breasts straining against rich cloth, a pouty mouth, jaunty gold spectacles.

"May I help you?"

"Brack Stewart, please."

"You are Mr.... Mr...?"

"Francis Drake Stewart." He smiled gently. "His cousin."

The eyebrows lifted. "One moment." She disappeared through another mahogany doorway, returned, offered a winsome smile that took in his eyes, his mouth, his shoulders. "This way, please."

Brack was up and striding toward him across the office. He looked tan and fit, his black hair brushed straight back, his suit a dark gray, perfectly fitted, his linen immaculate. "Drake! Good to see you, Cousin." He waved him to a leather armchair, offered brandy, chatted about the weather and the rising price of gold, sat on the edge of his massive desk idly swinging a foot booted in soft black leather.

Drake chuckled. "You've got style, Brack."

"And you"—Brack snipped the end of a small cigar with a gold cutter, lit it, blew smoke—"have got another favor to ask."

"I'd call it another business proposition to present. The risk is not without opportunity."

"Well, your last one paid off handsomely. I must say that running the blockade into Charleston proved damned profitable to both of us. And our gold holdings increased handsomely, wouldn't you agree?"

"Handsomely is hardly the word."

"How does it feel to be a millionaire and not yet forty?" Drake chuckled. "Wonderful."

Brack's eyes narrowed and the smile faded. "Now then, what's on your mind?"

"I want to rebuild Charleston. At least part of it."

"Rebuild Charleston? Tall order, I'd say."

"Just the commercial part. They're starving down there. Sherman's army hardly left a house undamaged. The docks are a ruin, the warehouses wrecked, the railroad torn up."

Brack's thin lips curled. "Good enough for them."

"Maybe. But it's not just the white gentry that suffers. The poor people are a hell of a lot worse off. Sherman's punishment, if that's what he intended, was meted out to those least able to absorb it."

"But where does Brack Stewart fit in?"

"The railroad. I thought you might like to extend loans to rebuild that railroad. I can put you in touch with the company. I suspect that you could name your terms."

"And?"

"And I'll work on the docks and the warehouses. It's not a bad investment, all things considered."

Brack pondered. Drake could visualize the nimble mind at work, figuring percentages, potential for control, potential for graft. Cousin or no cousin, it was like inviting the devil himself into partnership. But he had no choice. Wealth begets wealth.

"I'll think about it," Brack Stewart said.

"Fine. Think hard."

"I always do."

Drake declined an invitation to dinner. This cousin's social company made him oddly uncomfortable. As he took his hat and was going out the door, Brack's parting words stayed his step.

"By the way, Cousin. Since when did Charleston white gentry start welcoming a black business partner?"

Francis Drake smiled. "Since they got hongry, Cousin. Since they done got hongry."

But the question nagged at him for many days after that.

The months fled in a frenzy of activity. After securing loans in New York against his personal bank accounts, Drake placed orders for a vast quantity of building supplies, from sawmill parts to nails and hardware. The first shipment was carried back to Charleston in the holds of the *Fury*, but more arrived on board commercial schooners. Hiring gangs of black workmen and returning white soldiers, Drake and Cochrane supervised the work of dismantling wrecked structures and constructing new ones. Laboring crews attacked wharfs and docks, pulling out charred and broken timbers. As the sweltering summer passed, the infusion of capital and construction triggered a burst of restoration zeal. By autumn, the first shipments of lumber, pine tar and turpentine had gone out from the new warehouses. Brack Stewart's loans, in the meantime, fueled reconstruction of the railroad. Schooners began arriving to unload track, construction equipment, even an entire dismantled locomotive. As the new local Reconstruction regime arrived to take charge of city affairs, sharp carpetbagger administrators quietly approved the works. Francis Drake shrewdly kept his distance from these hard-eyed men, who handpicked ignorant blacks for key political positions. Graft and corruption flourished. Federal troops acted more as occupation forces than public servants come to restore order. Hatreds seethed between local residents and the newcomers.

But finally, the day arrived when Francis Drake could look from the deck of *Fury* upon a rebuilt waterfront, with two great warehouses and another under construction, new docks and piers and a bustling activity of loading and unloading ships. Beyond, the city itself was rapidly face-lifting, and the majestic white columns of the Chares mansion rose in freshly painted splendor.

"You've invested your whole fortune in this town," Cochrane grumbled at his side. "I hope you ain't disappointed."

"Disappointed? Why should I be?"

Cochrane seemed to have something on his mind. When Drake mentioned that he planned to visit Elizabeth and her father that evening, the mate frowned. "It ain't none of my business, Cap'n, but how sure are you about Miss Chares?"

"As sure as I could be, I suppose. I never gave it much thought. Why do you ask?"

Cochrane turned away from the railing and wiped a hand across his meaty face. "Nothing, I guess. Nothing at all."

Along the way to the Chares house, Drake reflected upon the strange mood of his mate. He drove a light gig now, flicking his whip at the flanks of a fine trotter. The gig took its usual route from the dock, past the warehouses and the newly refurbished business buildings, past the old church with its fresh coat of paint. He wore a suit of fine cut, a soft hat with a low crown, a gold watch chain across his vest. But there were few greetings from those he passed, and no smiles. White merchants turned away, busy with their sweeping or their conversations. Women glanced at him furtively from beneath the brims of sunbonnets, but gave no outward sign of recognition. Even the blacks did not acknowledge him, as if to say that while he was lightly of their blood he was not of their kind, being a man of wealth and substance. As the gig passed the new livery stable of Mason Chares, Drake touched his hat in greeting. The stable owner seemed not to notice.

For weeks now, he suspected that Cochrane had been trying to tell him something but was unable to find the words. The mate's behavior was nettlesome, for they had served together too long and too closely for secrets. He had noticed at times, especially at night in Charleston, that one or two men seemed to be following him. At Cochrane's suggestion he had taken to carrying a small pocket pistol. There were idlers and rogues about, and their numbers increased as prosperity returned to the city. There was also the sullen mood of many Confederate veterans, still without employment or means of a livelihood in the aftermath of war. They could be hard and bitter men and there was a special enmity between them and the occupying Union troops. His own position was uncomfortable; for while he was in the center of Charleston's rebirth—indeed, one of the catalysts for it—those who had depended on his enterprise now kept a distance.

And so he was a part of the community and yet not a part of it; a friend of Charleston who was without friends. Even Elizabeth . . .

The ache returned to the pit of his stomach. He could not fathom the strain developing with Elizabeth. He disliked her sullen moods and growing petulance. Most of all, he disliked the weakness in himself and the pain of rejection she caused him. "Are you saying I'm unfaithful, Drake? What do you think I am, one of your waterfront strumpets?" Lately she had found various reasons for postponing his visits to Chares house—she suffered a headache, or had some pressing social matter to attend to, or her father was unwell. He had extended a loan, unsecured, to Mason Chares in the amount of ten thousand dollars in gold the previous year. A handshake implied that the debt would be repaid. But there had been no mention of it for months, and Chares was rarely available to discuss the matter. Elizabeth became angry when it was mentioned, and once had burst into tears and rushed to her boudoir, slamming the door in Drake's face.

"Watch your step in town," Cochrane had warned him a week ago.

The trotter turned onto the street of Elizabeth's house and he drew up the gig at the ornate new hitching post in front. Late afternoon sunlight pitched steeply from the west, bathing the church steeple and buildings in gold. Beyond, in the harbor where *Fury* rode at anchor, the water was a sweep of dazzling blue. Seabirds wheeled in and out of the sunlight in brilliant feathered bursts.

He knocked at the front door and waited. There was no response. He turned the doorbell several times, loudly, before someone finally came. It was the old black woman, eyeing him through a crack in the doorway. "Miss Chares, she ain't home."

"Where is she, then?"

"I don't know. She gone out. She didn't say when she'd be back."

Angered, he pushed at the door, demanding admittance. He would simply wait until she returned. The old woman tried feebly to stop him. He pushed harder and the door opened. Six paces brought him to the front parlor. Elizabeth rose hurriedly from the settee, straightening her dress. A handsome blond Army officer remained seated, eyeing him with amusement.

"What are you doing here?" Her eyes blazed and her cheeks flushed scarlet. "The very idea, barging in like this!"

He felt cold. The cold began in his stomach and flooded his being. He glared at the officer and then at Elizabeth. He felt his fists clenching and unclenching.

"You told me the darky wasn't coming around anymore, Elizabeth." The officer stood up slowly, adjusting his belt and buttoning his tunic. He was broad at the chest and as tall as Drake. The insignia of a captain's rank rode on his square shoulders. Blue eyes turned insolently upon Drake. "Get on outta here now, boy. You're not welcome."

Something burst within him. Later, Francis Drake would not be able to comprehend the fury that exploded in that instant of time and space. The words struck him like a lash. With a growl of animal rage, he was across the parlor and upon the man, pummeling the mocking face with his fists, smashing the groin with his knees, grabbing for the throat. Locked in struggle together, they somersaulted over the settee, overturning furniture and smashing glass. He was dimly aware of Elizabeth's screams and something beating at his head and shoulders. Fingernails clawed at his face, and his fingers locked about the throat of his adversary. But the man was strong, the body rock-hard. Even as the face turned purple and the eyes bulged grotesquely, a fist smashed the side of Drake's head, bringing a blaze of stars and breaking his death grip. Catlike, the captain rolled to his feet. Drake rolled instinctively as booted feet came smashing down at his head. And then he was up, circling as his enemy circled. He lunged again with the strength of rage, and broke through the battering fists with his own attack. Their feet entangled. The officer groped for balance, dropping his hands. Drake's fists smacked full into the white face. Bone crunched. Teeth cracked. Blood gushed from the nose and mouth. The blue eyes glazed and the man went down, crumbling like a laden sack in a shambles of shattered furniture.

Francis Drake backed to the middle of the room and stood, chest heaving, fists still clenched. His eyes blazed at the unconscious form. His clothing was in tatters. His mouth dripped blood. Blinking, wiping his face with one hand, he turned and saw her kneeling in the corner, staring at him with eyes of hatred. Strangely, the passion had gone out of him. His heart was a dead and unfeeling thing. He felt nothing for her. Nothing. He spat blood on the floor.

"Bitch," he said. He walked out.

The mobs formed at nightfall. A warrant had been issued by the Charleston military command for the arrest of Francis Drake Stewart, a Negro male, on multiple charges of trespassing, breaking and entering a private dwelling, and assault and battery upon an Army officer. The mobs moved onto the waterfront and, as darkness fell, put torches to the warehouses built with Stewart money. "Good enough fer the nigger!" voices bawled as fire licked at the night. "Burn 'em! Burn 'em!" So rapidly did it all take place that Drake was cut off from the slip where the dinghy was tied.

On board *Fury*, First Mate Cochrane broke out weapons and distributed them to all hands. Then, debating whether to go ashore or stay with the ship, he remained on deck. As the fires cast the waterfront in their lurid glow, Cochrane scanned the dark waters for sign of movement. Finally, he heard a splash and saw the water surface break. "Give me three men aft," he shouted, "to take aboard swimmer!" As feet pounded across the deck, he went over the side on a rope in time to grasp the arm of the exhausted Francis Drake Stewart.

Cochrane chuckled. "Welcome aboard, Captain. We've got steam and we're ready to hoist anchor."

In the firelight he could make out the shapes of men at the docks climbing into rowboats and pushing off toward *Fury*.

"And I'd say the sooner the better."

Commands barked across the ship. The anchor lifted from the waters of Charleston harbor. Steam valves hissed, pistons surged and *Fury* put her stern to the swift-rowing boatmen silhouetted by fiery destruction. A few shots came from the boats, but thudded harmlessly into the stout wooden hull of the steamer.

At last they were clear. Francis Drake Stewart leaned on the aft rail, watching the diminishing light of his crumbling warehouses.

"Orders, sir?" Cochrane asked quietly.

"Make for the Bahamas, Mr. Cochrane. We'll take on stores at Nassau and try to load a cargo for England."

"Bahamas it is, sir."

"And how are we for fuel wood?"

"I took the liberty of stocking in, captain. We're in good supply."

"Very well."

Drake lit a cigar. The smoke whipped in the breeze. He

sensed the first surge of open water beneath his feet, heard the chug of engine and the slap of rigging. It was good to be at sea again.

"Mr. Cochrane . . ."

"Sir."

"We wouldn't have been happy on dry land anyhow."

"No, sir." The mate spat over the side and grinned. "That we wouldn't."

XIX

"Son of a bitch." Big Jim Strobridge said it thoughtfully, spat tobacco juice and squinted with his one eye at the ruggedly majestic heights. "There's where we're going, Thaddeus. Way up high where the birdies fly. Before this is over, by God, we'll ride a train right up them cliffs that you and Ted Judah picked out for us to climb."

Thaddeus grinned, mopping sweat. It was June, 1865. Behind them, in the rising foothills of the Sierra Nevada, eight hundred laborers hacked, blasted, and scraped at the stubborn rock conglomerate subsurface. In broiling heat, there was a constant clanging, shouting, and raising of dust. "Nothing to it, Strobridge." He liked the hulking, profane field boss for Charlie Crocker's construction company. "Just like climbing a dinosaur's back."

"Hunnh! Some dinosaur. We got ten tunnels to blast through solid granite by the time we hit the summit. Ten tunnels in seventy miles! Our competition"—he spat again, demonstrating what he thought of the rival Union Pacific, whose oncoming tracks would follow gently rising plain from Nebraska, eighteen hundred miles away—"won't dig their first tunnel till they're seven hundred miles west of Omaha. And in between each one of your dinosaur's vertebra, we've got to bridge a ravine with a mountain of dirt or a trestle. Some dinosaur." Strobridge turned back to watch the work gangs. From here, looking downslope toward the coastal plain, they resembled a small army of ants. A pitifully small army. Thaddeus saw the worry knit his friend's broad face. "But goddamn it, how are we supposed to build a railroad when the most I can find to hire is eight hundred workmen, and two hundred of them laid off drunk after every payday?" He made a noise in his throat. "Irishmen."

Even as he spoke, a squat figure came riding upslope astride a stocky sorrel mare. Thaddeus recognized Harmon, a straw boss designated by the men. The man had a stubborn, mulish face and disposition to match. Harmon reined in the sorrel and glowered at Strobridge. A sudden quiet settled over the works below. Thaddeus saw that the men were leaning on their picks and shovels, watching.

"What is it Harmon?"

"The men are tired, Mr. Strobridge."

"Tired? Hell, they ain't hit the rough stuff yet."

Harmon's eyes flicked up at the brooding massif. "That's the point, Mr. Strobridge. Seein' as how we're there now, and you got a shortage of labor, the men figure they're worth more than thirty-five dollars a month plus board. So this here is a way of sayin' they don't intend to move no more dirt right now. Not till the wages goes up."

Strobridge turned to Thaddeus. "Mr. Stewart here is overseer for the railroad. What do you think about that, Mr. Stewart?"

Thaddeus stared without blinking into the mulish eyes of the straw boss. They were bringing the railhead to Clipper Gap, just forty-three miles east of Sacramento. Now came the brutal work of blasting and filling roadbed up the clifflike faces of Bear River Gorge. The financial realities of the Central Pacific Railroad nagged at his mind. Collis Huntington had described it bleakly in their last talk before Thaddeus had left New York. "Damn it, Thaddeus, we're on a shoestring. Our hardest, most expensive work is right at the beginning of the project. We need cash in advance for tunneling, trestles and mountain grading. But the government bonds can't be issued except in twenty-mile sections that're ready for use and approved by the government commissioners. Right now we've got two million dollars to work with. The rest is on faith."

"Mr. Stewart?" Strobridge repeated his question.

"Tell 'em to go to hell," Thaddeus said.

It was a gamble. Harmon wheeled the sorrel angrily and clattered downslope. The work gangs dropped their shovels and crowded around the straw boss. Thaddeus saw the intense discussion and eyes glancing his way.

Strobridge chuckled. "Think you'll get away with it?"

Thaddeus drew a cigar from his shirt pocket and struck a match. "Do we have any choice?"

"No, I reckon not."

Three hundred men walked off the job. Those who remained merely picked at the soil, moving with studied slowness. Burly Charlie Crocker came up from Sacramento, raging and cursing. Strobridge, his one good eye shining angrily, moved among the men verbally kicking asses. It did no good.

Two days later Thaddeus was in San Francisco for a promised visit with Maybelle. He brooded into a glass of straight bourbon. "We're going to need two thousand men, three thousand men. Hell, before this is over we might need ten thousand. And where are we supposed to find them? The only available manpower is idlers from the city, and most of them light out for the gold fields as soon as they get a stake. Their minds are on mining in Nevada, not struggling with a railroad in the Sierras at a little over a dollar a day."

That afternoon he accompanied Maybelle down into the city. As always, San Francisco impressed him as a dumping ground of the world's humanity. Streets along the waterfront teemed with Indians, Irishmen, Australians, Europeans, Orientals, Yankees and Southerners, Mexicans, South Americans. "all these people," he was saying, "and not enough to—"

A disturbance broke out in the street. A large open wagon drawn by a two-horse team had come out of the dock area laden with Chinese men. They sat upright on plank seats shoulder-to-shoulder, quiet little men with almond-shaped eyes peering out beneath the brims of big, conical hats. They wore blue cotton tunics with flowing sleeves, floppy trousers and canvas sneakers. Each man's hair hung down his back in a braided pigtail.

From the sidewalk, a group of drunken idlers jeered.. "Hey, look what we got here? What is it, pray tell me?"

"Chinee boys, from the looks of 'em. Shit, from the smell."

"Haw, haw. Chinkee likee ridee wagon? Haw, haw."

From the wagon, eyes darted fearfully, inspiring their tormentors to fresh vigor. Several men moved alongside the wagon, shouting obscenities. Someone threw a clod of dirt. More clods flew, pelting wagon and riders. The Chinese raised their arms against the missiles and chattered noisily. The next missile was a chunk of brick, which smacked one of the unfortunates in the side causing him to double over in pain.

"What the hell?" Thaddeus said.

"Bullyboys," Maybelle sniffed. "It's their favorite sport, goading the new arrivals."

"But the constables, where are they?"

"Looking the other way, more'n likely. They don't like Celestials either. Nobody likes 'em. They've tried to get a bill through the Legislature to prevent the brokers from bringing in more. The commercial importers haul boatloads from China to work the placer mines and do menial labor. They make damn fine houseboys and cooks."

One of the street thugs raced up behind the wagon, grabbed a pigtail and yanked. The luckless owner of the hair somersaulted off the back of the wagon onto the hard brick street. As he scrambled to his feet, head bleeding from a deep cut, the attacker—a muscular Irishman—cocked his fist for a blow at the face. "Take this, you fucking—"

"Stop it!" Thaddeus shouted. Swinging along on his heavy walnut cane, he covered the distance in four strides. "Leave that man alone!"

The bully's eyes widened in surprise, fist still poised. Seeing the cane and the tall, well-dressed man, he whirled with a snarl and lowered his head in a fighter's crouch.

"Thaddeus! Careful!"

Thaddeus did not wait for the attack nor lift the cane for a swing. With a short, savage thrust, he drove its point into the man's beefy midsection. The air went out of him with the force of a spent balloon. Thaddeus shifted his grip on the cane and brought the handle down smartly with one savage chop behind the right ear. The body collapsed heavily onto the street. Ahead, the wagon had come to a stop. "Here, my man." Thaddeus helped the Chinaman back into the wagon, then turned to the crowd on the sidewalk. "Anyone else?" There was no response.

From the wagon, the singsong babble rose in volume and he looked up to see a dozen faces smiling and nodding to him from beneath the ridiculous conical hats. Thaddeus waved the driver on and walked back to Maybelle.

She eyed him admiringly and took his arm. "Nice work, nephew."

Smoke billowed from the cookfires behind Big Sing's warehouse. The newcomers clustered over their rice bowls, shoving gobs of steaming rice into their mouths to the click of chopsticks. Rarely had Shingling seen newcomers' spirits so high and heard talk so animated. He stood listening, welcoming the diversion as he waited to see Big Sing. The conversation was all about the tall, lame American who had beaten off the attack on the wagon. Each speaker tried to outdo the other with his description of the swinging cane, the thundering voice, the hooligan dropping in the street. Shingling's curiosity sharpened when a pigtailed farmer exclaimed, "Ahyeeee, and the woman of the fire hair! She was with him. Did you see how she clapped her hands?"

"What does that mean? I have never seen a female react so. No Chinese woman would make such public display."

"You are not in China now, ignorant one. You are in Gum San. All things are different here. Women do not walk with their eyes cast upon the ground."

The woman of the fire hair? Only one female in San Francisco matched that description, of course. Maybelle Stewart. And the tall man with the cane must be her nephew, Thaddeus. The thought brought Shingling back to his mission today, and what he intended to do if things did not go well with Big Sing. These Chinese crowded into the yard of Big Sing's warehouse—these newcomers, none of them yet a week off the boat—were both a problem and a challenge that must be faced. And what irony that he, an ignorant farmer from the valley of Sheh and Shah, must be the one to face it.

An elderly cook with whom Shingling had once worked in the gold fields joined him beside the warehouse.

"You come to see the merchant?" the cook asked.

"Yes. I come to talk with him about this." He nodded at the crowd of eating men. "So many new arrivals, week after week."

"Do you think he will listen?"

"I doubt it. But I must try all the same."

"The merchant is a shrewd man. He thinks of his own rice bowl. It has made him rich. The wise petitioner will appeal to that." The cook was an old man from one of the northern provinces. He had seen much of life and many of its wrongs, and no longer believed that the wrongs would be righted. Nor did he regard the human species as either enlightened or practical. "An idea is like a bolt of cloth, something best exchanged by barter."

Shingling did not offer a direct response. "This is a good lot, good workers. They recover quickly from the voyage. I remember my own trip over and how uncomfortable it was. We were packed like cattle in the steerage and there was much rough weather."

"That is the rule rather than the exception," the cook said. "I can understand these young fellows. A man comes to Gum San filled with fear and questions, a stranger in a strange land. One is bound to his own kind by ignorance of the language, by custom, by the hostilities of the whites." He spat upon the ground. "You are learning English rapidly, I hear. Already this has elevated you to a position of prestige. The men speak well of you."

"I do not feel like a leader. As for English, I can only stumble through. It is a dreadful language, all grunts and hisses, absolutely impossible to master."

"But your teacher, she makes the labor a pleasure, eh?"

Shingling searched the cook's face to see what the words implied, but the face was inscrutable. "Is this what the others say?" he asked.

"I mean nothing by it, my friend. Please do not read into my words what is not there."

"You are a wise one, old man."

"I am an old man whose heart has cooled and whose brain is addled. All I do is cook rice and shrimp."

The old man drifted away. Shingling watched his countrymen finish their meal. They must seem a curious lot indeed to westerners, with their conical hats and floppy trousers. What was it the old cook had said? "A man comes to Gum San filled with fear..." Yes. And by his own ignorance—especially of language—he was bound inexorably to his own kind and wholly dependent upon shrewd entrepreneurs who controlled his destiny. Entrepeneurs such as the merchant Big Sing...

A voice at his side said, "Mr. Sing will see you now." It was the merchant's assistant, Hong, a mincing, smirking functionary who affected blue silk pantaloons and a haughty manner. He glided away and Shingling followed around the corner and through a small garden to a side door of the warehouse. He pushed through a bamboo curtain that fell quietly about his shoulders. There was an odor of incense and warm tea from a charcoal brazier. The merchant sat cross-legged on a pile of silken cushions in the manner of some benign Buddha, a massive figure of fat and silken robes in mandarin red. He wore a silken skullcap and his fingernails were curved talons painted the color of fresh blood.

Shingling bowed. "I am honored to be admitted to the presence of Big Sing. You are most gracious to give of your time to one who is unworthy." He waited in silence while the seated giant sipped tea from a cup made of porcelain. At last the painted fingernails waved him to a cushion and he sat down, feeling inferior in his western work clothes.

When he spoke at last, Big Sing's voice barely rose above a whisper. "So. Now that you learn the language of the Americans, the men designate you as their speaker."

"I am an ignorant farmer from Canton, as you well know. I do not choose to be anyone's speaker. But they feel it is necessary for someone to express their needs, and I am selected to make the attempt."

"And what is it you are to tell me, Shingling Chou?"

"We are too many working at the mines, Big Sing. There is not enough gold dust being dug out to pay us all. As you know, the white men will not allow Chinese to stake their own gold claims, and so we have only the tailings to work. The yield of such diggings continues to decline. And yet you keep on sending the newly arrived workers from China into the mines. Lately there has been trouble between them and the older men, and there are many complaints."

Big Sing stared from the shadows, the light of the brazier casting a lurid glow upon his face. The eyes were small and intense, buried in folds of flesh. Shingling knew that the merchant had grown enormously wealthy importing Chinese workers and handling their financial affairs, including sending portions of their earnings back to families in China. For these services he took a cut of each man's wages. Individual indebtedness to him was so great that some men were ignorant of their sums. Big Sing thus held in virtual bondage thousands of fellow Chinese whom he had arranged to bring to Gum San in the holds of rotting ships. And yet it was a bondage of convenience. The more presentable of his clients got jobs with wealthy California families as cooks, houseboys and gardeners. Some even went into business for themselves.

Such people managed to clear their debts to him and be free. Shingling himself had achieved this simply by the good fortune of having been one of the early arrivals to Gum San when gold mining paid well. He still chose to work the mines in preference to being a servant, if only for the freedom such labor provided. Now he confronted the scrutiny of Big Sing and felt his earlier nervousness diminishing.

"I have no responsibility for what happens at the mines," Big Sing murmured. "Those are the men's affairs. I cannot help it if they have grown soft and do not wish to earn their fortunes in Gum San. Ignorant farmers come here believing in the myth of the Golden Mountain, and lament loudly to learn that life here is not guaranteed. To take their ease, they would steal rice from the mouths of honest businessmen."

"But we face a very serious problem, Big Sing. It is not that the men lack desire to work, they welcome the opportunity. The newcomers, however, are simply flooding the gold fields so that there are too many Chinese for too few jobs. Many of these men go hungry and cannot provide for their families back home. They are deeply in debt to you and to the moneylenders. The interest that you charge can put a man in servitude for life."

Big Sing frowned. "I am a businessman. It is my business to provide a service."

"But if only you would slow down your import of additional labor . . ."

"There are many who wish to come to Gun San, and they wait for the opportunity in China. They will come just as you did, Shingling Chou. Would you selfishly deny them that right?"

It could not continue. The conversation was resolving nothing, and further effort was futile. The merchant would not yield. Shingling rose abruptly, leaving his cup of tea unfinished. "Perhaps," he said, "it is just as well. Now I will seek another remedy."

"Another remedy?"

Shingling bowed to the merchant and withdrew, leaving Big Sing's question hanging in the air.

He left the warehouse and the workers' yard and walked briskly into the heart of San Francisco. Shingling had long since cut his pigtail and abandoned his Chinese clothing for western wear. Thus, he was not as quickly recognizable as an Oriental by the street toughs who lounged in front of the saloons looking for easy prey. He walked for nearly an hour, so that the sun was settling into the Pacific, laying a path of fire upon the great bay, by the time he entered the bustling heart of town. High up the slope of Nob Hill, he could see the great yellow bulk of Maybelle Stewart's mansion, commanding its panoramic view. And then he was walking along the wharf in the sunset, the air pungent with the odors of fish and the sea.

It seemed so long, now, that he had been here; so long ago that he had left Canton province on borrowed passage in the steerage of a brigantine. All those days and nights of seasickness, packed into that stinking hold with all the others, lingered with him as but a fading memory. And yet how many times had Shingling cursed himself for a fool to have left the valley of Sheh and Shah in pursuit of his father's dream. Well, that was done. Now he still toiled in the mines in search of the yellow dust, laboring with the dusty gang with pick and shovel. His hands were thick and hard, his muscles bunched and shoulders stooped. But he had paid off his indebtedness to Big Sing long ago and earned enough to send back money to his mother and two brothers. Someday he might go back to China to find a wife, he supposed. But all in due time. He could not afford to keep a wife just yet. Besides, there was this strange relationship to his teacher Lotus. When he was in the hills her memory plucked at the edges of his mind. He thought of her as instructing, instructing, forever instructing. Whenever he came back to San Francisco, she was always there for another lesson in the impossible language of English. And she was coldly efficient in his presence, very proper in her manner. It was fitting, the attitude of a higher intellect toward one who plodded and was so terribly slow to learn.

"Now then, Mr. Chou. You say it after me: The quick brown fox jumped over the lazy dog's back."

"Qlik blown fox he jump ovel back of lazy dog."

"No, no, no. The quick brown fox jumped over the lazy dog's back. Now, again."

"Sure, sure. Qlik blown fox he..."

Exasperated, she despaired of him and rose to stomp angrily about the room, and his embarrassment was complete. But then, strangely, he would catch her watching him at other times, the luminous eyes soft and warm and the picture-book mouth open slightly, full-lipped and ripe. It was a look that caused him an odd and perplexing pain, for it implied something that could not be. This Lotus was too intelligent for a lowly Cantonese farmer. And, besides, she was a woman of pleasure and not of the hearth; no man of dignity could possibly think of taking such a one as wife, or even as concubine. Too many men had shared her secrets. Too many men could gaze knowingly into her eyes.

But then, abruptly, she had given up being a whore. Lotus had left the employment of Maybelle Stewart, taken her savings and opened a cafe on the wharf. The Lotus Cafe. And there he could find her when he came down from the hills for more lessons in English. And she always seemed to be waiting. And even now, as he pushed open the door of the Lotus Cafe, a young waitress saw him and hurried toward the back room, her slippers making rapid scuffing sounds, and called out in Chinese: "Miss Lotus! Miss Lotus, he is here!" And the face, the lovely face beneath its mass of soft black hair appeared framed in the doorway, smiling at him in that strange way that seemed to cause a tightness in his chest.

She whispered, "Mr. Chou..."

He followed her into the small back office and they sat down to tea, rice, pigeon wings and rice wine. As always, he was vaguely unsure of himself in her presence and yet filled with a subtle pleasure as well. She wore a plain green frock for working in her cafe. Strange, but she no longer displayed a taste for silken gowns and jewelry. Except for her rare and natural beauty, the woman who sat opposite him was a simple, tasteful woman wholly unaware of the other, earlier life. She questioned him gently about his visit to Big Sing. His replies were candid and self-deprecating. "I did not do well," he concluded. "Mr. Sing was not impressed. Perhaps someone else of greater stature..."

A flicker of annoyance crossed her face. "And what will you do now, Mr. Chou?"

"I will do as you suggest. There is no choice."

"Good. And you will accompany me now to Maybelle's house?"

He swallowed nervously. "Yes."

She smiled, snapped her fingers for one of the servant girls and ordered her buggy brought around. "Then let's be on our way."

Dusk fell over the city. As they walked to the buggy, he was acutely aware of her nearness and the faint, sweet scent

that followed her. She was almost as tall as he, and this
renewed his feelings of uncertainty. He thought, I have no
gift with women. I am a farmer and nothing more. I am out of
place. But then he gave her his hand to step into the buggy,
and her eyes glowed from the rocklike grip that steadied her.
Lotus seemed momentarily to lose her breath, and this left
him in confusion. She drove the black mare expertly, in
silence. Shingling watched the lamplights of San Francisco
passing by and could think of nothing to say.

When they arrived at Maybelle Stewart's mansion, it was
the butler who answered their knock. Frowning slightly, he
led them into the library. "Miss Stewart is entertaining her
cousin this evening," the butler said gravely, speaking to
Lotus, "I shall tell her that you wish to see her." He backed
out through the double doors and closed them softly behind
him. Moments later, Maybelle herself burst into the room
accompanied by a tall, handsome American who walked with
a cane.

"Lotus, my dear! And Shingling! How nice of you both to
drop by."

Shingling was puzzled by the enthusiastic welcome. But
then an exchange of knowing glances between the two wom-
en told him that all this had been prearranged. He took the
proffered handshake of Thaddeus Stewart and smiled happily,
speaking in English. "Please-a met you, Misser Stewart. I
hear what you do today in-a street. It all over Chinatown,
everybody talking. Yesss. We very grateful."

"Shingling?" Thaddeus Stewart said.

Maybelle spoke. "Shingling was a farmer from Canton
province. He came here to work the tailings of the gold
mines. One day he saved me from a runaway horse. We've
been friends ever since. A lot of Chinese are out there.
They're the best workers you could possibly find, diligent and
loyal . . ." She hesitated as if measuring her words. "And so
many of them. Incidentally, Shingling has an idea that I think
you might find interesting."

"An idea?"

"Tell him, Shingling."

Shingling was nervous. He licked his lips and glanced at
Lotus, who suddenly seemed preoccupied with a potted
plant. He held his heavy hands together to keep them from
trembling. If he failed now, he would have nothing to take
back to his men. He would have failed them. He tried to

make his voice sound firm and self-assured. The English troubled him, and he spoke more slowly than usual. "Sure, Miss Maybelle. I speak my idea. Ah, I hear tell you need men workee railroad, Misser Stewart. Right?"

Thaddeus nodded. "Yes, we do need men."

"Ah, good. See, we got lotsa Chinese men, needee job. Good workers, like Miss Maybelle say. Very strong. Why not you workee Chinese on the railroad?"

Shingling stopped speaking and peered up into the face of the tall American. His own stocky body was so short that his eye level came to Thaddeus's shoulder. He could see that the railroad man was studying and doubting that a Canton farmer would have the strength to labor all day with pick and shovel on a railroad job.

Thaddeus shook his head. "Chinese on the railroad? Not a chance."

Maybelle smiled, patted Thaddeus on the arm and winked at Shingling. "Remember, they built the Great Wall."

Thaddeus shook his head again, smiling. "Chinese on the railroad..."

Later, as they rode back down Nob Hill in the buggy, Shingling was so disappointed that he thought his heart would break. "I am so ignorant, so unworthy," he said. "Now they will all laugh at me and call me a fool."

And suddenly, Lotus's hand was upon his arm. She stopped the buggy and her eyes were shining in the lamplight. "You are no fool," she whispered. "You are Mr. Chou. My Mr. Chou. You are a great man. It is..." The eyes looked away quickly. "It is I who am unworthy..."

"You're out of your mind, Stewart!" Charlie Crocker's face flushed. "Hell, they ain't got the strength God gave a duck. Great houseboys, sure. But they wouldn't last a week out on the line. Haw, haw, haw. You've got to be kidding."

Strobridge was not even amused. His big face was set in an expression akin to outrage. "Not on your life," he growled. "I'll not boss Chinese or work 'em alongside white men. They couldn't begin to build a railroad. And just trying to feed 'em the weird things they eat would be out of the question."

"Let them provide their own cooks, their own food."

Leland Stanford was equally adamant. In his campaign for governor in 1862, the president of the Central Pacific had termed the hated Chinese "the dregs of Asia" and pledged his support for legislative ban on their further immigration.

"The Chinese are despised," Stanford said. "They've flooded California. The Irish laborers look upon them as usurpers."

"There are no better laborers anywhere," Thaddeus persisted. "And they'll work for less than whites do." He was out on a limb and knew it. The enmity against the Orientals was spread throughout California. "Try 'em, Charlie."

"It's up to Jim," Crocker said.

"You might change a few minds," said Stanford. "But you won't change a whole state's mind."

"Hire fifty of 'em, Strobridge. What the hell have you got to lose?"

The big field boss stroked his jaw thoughtfully. Thaddeus knew that his only consideration was their mutual regard. But it was stake enough. The others watched silently. Finally, Strobridge offered a slight nod. "All right, Fifty. Fifty Chinks, and we'll try 'em on handcarts, grading."

Two days later, Shingling brought fifty Chinese in wagons up to the line. Irish laborers leaned on their picks and shovels laughing. "Thaddeus Stewart's army! Haw, Haw."

"Looks like they let the little boys outta school."

"Whatja say they eat? Fishheads and worms?"

The newcomers walked silently through the white camp in their strange hats, blue cotton trousers flopping.

The next day, with Shingling in command, the fifty went to work as a group on a separate stretch of grading. The work involved breaking loose the hard conglomerate subsurface with picks, loading the debris onto handcarts, dumping it into a ravine, and smoothing and tamping out a graded roadbed twenty-six feet wide. Observers from the Irish work gangs noticed immediately that the picks of the Chinese drove with less power; the rhythm, which a strong man made to sound like *chunk . . . chunk*, came out as *peck-peck-peck*. Men snickered. "Like a buncha pullets peckin' out corn." The newcomers worked without letup, however, and were refreshed from time to time by swigs of tea served by a Chinese who went around bearing two jugs slung from a shoulder pole. Two days went by.

It was Charlie Crocker who first spoke of the results. "Strobridge, the Chinese right-of-way is smoother and longer than the other."

Strobridge grunted. "Thaddeus, tell your boy to bring me fifty more Chinese."

White laborers were incensed. As the work became more difficult, and as they moved higher up the wild, rugged slopes east of Newcastle, Harmon came to Strobridge with the word. "We ain't gonna work near them Chinks. Not within a hundred rods of 'em, Strobridge."

"Suit yourself, Harmon."

The white crews stepped up the pace of their work and cut back the lunch breaks. Still, by the end of the week the methodical Chinese were well ahead.

"Bring me more Chinese, Thaddeus."

The track crept beyond Clipper Gap, forty-three miles east of Sacramento. They were 1,750 feet above sea level and climbing. Powder blasts boomed and rock and shale came spilling down the slopes beneath frowning embankments. Behind them, the work trains chuffed incessantly now, bringing up supplies. The Chinese continued to increase in numbers, as day after day fresh infusions of manpower arrived.

"They're too frail to swing sledgehammers, Strobridge. That's where we've got to depend on the Irish."

"We'll see, Sam."

Two more days went by.

"Thaddeus, tell Shingling to bring more."

"You've got a thousand Chinese now, Strobridge."

"We need two thousand."

The showdown came at a night meeting of the white gangs. Harmon stood before the bonfire, thumbs in his belt, facing Strobridge, Thaddeus and Charlie Crocker. The crowd behind him was sullen. "Strobridge, we've come to a decision. We want the Chinese off the job for good, and we won't settle for less. It's either them or us. Now which will it be?"

It was Thaddeus who stepped forward. The issue, he felt, was between the workers and the Central Pacific Railroad, not contractor Crocker and his field boss. He let his voice carry past Harmon to the workers massed on a slope beyond. "You men have done nothing but grouse and complain. I've had a bellyful of it. We can't get enough white labor to build this railroad. But by damn, we're going to build the Central Pacific anyhow. If it takes Chinamen to do it, then that's how it's going to be done. Either you men get along with them, or we'll let all of you go and hire nothing but Chinese labor." He

paused, hearing the angry murmurs of response. "The choice
is yours." He turned and walked away.

The next morning, Harmon was nowhere to be seen. But
six hundred Irish laboring men were on the job as usual. And
two dozen of them, the strongest sledgehammer drivers on
the line, had teamed with Chinese drill-holders to drive steel
into the merging granite rock of the dinosaur's back.

Settlement of the laborers' standoff came at a critical time.
As the work gangs climbed higher on the ascending ridgeline
in brutal July heat, the first yawning gorges waited to be
conquered. Now came the building of high trestle bridges,
matching the manual labor of the Chinese with the skill of
white carpenters. Out of the great forests of Puget Sound in
the far northwest, by schooner, riverboat and railroad flatcar,
came immense timbers to be set vertically in masonry and
then bolted into horizontal beams. While men swarmed over
the vast structures, the trestles inched forward across yawning chasms like gigantic centipedes, each leg pair planted at
sixteen-foot intervals. They gobbled up timbers, struts and
beams by the tens of thousands. So voracious was the demand that it consumed wood as fast as it could be hauled up
the snaking track by the work trains: wood for ties, for
bridges, for trestles, for freight sheds and stations.

Between engineering chores, it was Thaddeus's lot to
shepherd visiting dignitaries and potential investors in Central Pacific bonds, providing a running explanation of what
was going on. "This forested ridge we're climbing is like a
vast backbone of fossilized rock. You curl the track around
each one of the vertebra and bring it across the gaps.
Originally, we planned earthen fill. But it wouldn't work. Soil
on this ridge is rarely over a foot deep. That's a mighty thin
supply of dirt to scrape up when you need fill fifty feet deep
and hundreds of feet long. So we're building trestle instead,
for now. Later on, when we've got trains, we can haul in dirt
from elsewhere, dump it in and replace the trestles."

"Looks . . . damned spindly to me Mr. Stewart. And them
ravines . . . it makes me sick to my stomach to look down into
them ravines."

As the white-faced visitor spoke, they stood on the brink of
Deep Gulch Trestle, a span one hundred feet high and five
hundred feet long.

"Them Chinks is good, Mr. Stewart. I got to hand it to 'em,

even if they ain't white men. They can do most anything. But I know one thing they won't be equal to."

"What's that, Mr. Slade?"

"Rock work. No Chink's going to match an Irishman for rock work. Especially where it's high climbing and settin' charges by hand."

"We'll see, Mr. Slade. We'll see."

By July, the work force had grown to four thousand men—mostly Chinese—and five hundred teams of mules and horses. By October, when the tracklayers had spiked down their lead rails at the new town of Colfax, fifty-five miles from Sacramento, they had five thousand men and six hundred teams.

"They'll never do rock work. Not like the Irish."

And now, Strobridge and Thaddeus stood looking up at the seemingly impossible. The route to Dutch Flat wound up the face of a gigantic cliff jutting out in a solid wall fourteen hundred feet above the American River Gorge. In awe, men had already named it Cape Horn.

"Not even a goat path," Strobridge grumbled.

An Irish foreman shook his head. "My men ain't about to dangle like human flies on that monster trying to chip out blasting holes. I get the willies just thinkin' about it."

Shingling heard the talk and squinted up at the mighty formation, a thought germinating in his mind. He resolved to see Cape Horn from a closer vantage point. And so the following morning after breakfast he left the work camp and climbed the steep twisting trail. His leg muscles cramped against the strain and sweat saturated his shirt. At noon he paused for a handful of cold cooked rice and a swig of tea. Not until midafternoon did he finally come out on a ridge adjoining the massif. Below, the gorge was a yawning blue abyss cut by the silver river. Wind moaned among the rocks and tugged at his clothing. The whole was an immensity of silence and isolation. He felt himself an intruder in a domain of eagles. Squatting on the brink of a rock ledge, Shingling stared at the face of Cape Horn, impressing each hump and wrinkle upon his mind. The thing was indeed gigantic, a whole mountainside in one colossal hump. Suddenly the audacity of his idea threatened to overwhelm him. But he could not give in to fear. The mountain must become his personal adversary and not a thing of paralyzing fright. He studied the granite face and thought, I am not afraid. I will conquer you. In this immensity of space, distance and spirit, I am but a grain of dust. But then, is not the mountain itself but grains of dust?

The sun settled and the blueness of the gorge rose up to engulf him. He sat, watching and sensing, while the night came on bringing the moon and the stars. The cold spread across the mountain and seeped into his bones. He set his mind against it and remained motionless. The night passed. At last the morning came with a shrieking of mountain birds. Sunlight exploded over the peaks of the Sierra Nevada. He came to his feet, still facing Cape Horn. He bowed slightly to his adversary and said aloud in Chinese, "I shall return." And then he went back down the trail toward the camp. Several of the Chinese workmen came out to meet him and peppered him with questions. He shook his head, offering no reply. He went to his tent and fell down upon the pallet into a deep sleep.

It was dark when he awoke and the work gangs were finishing the evening meal around their fires. He summoned a dozen of the headmen and spoke at length of his plan. They heard him out in silence and when he was done erupted in furious debate.

One said, "It is too dangerous. You are asking us to risk men's lives on the high rock."

Another said: "Ahyee! You speak as an old woman. But then, what can one expect from a lowlander? Let upland men decide. Our ancestors built strong forts in the Yangtze gorges. High work is no problem."

"You are a braggart, Chung. Your courage is in your tongue. We'll see what happens when you hang like a spider over the great chasm!"

"You have seen it? It is that bad?"

"Did you not hear the words of Shingling?"

"Shingling, how high is the cliff?"

"As high as the sky. The view from down here is impressive, but nothing to what you see up there. It is a sight that you feel in your belly."

"What do the Irish say, Shingling?"

"The Irish boast that they are better stoneworkers than we, but they do not like the mountain. They fear Cape Horn. The foremen don't wish to send their men onto the face."

"Then why should we send ours?"

Shingling looked intently at the speaker, a hulking gang

boss for whom he had no liking. "The railroad must be built. Our job is to build it. That's what we are being paid to do. And that's what we will do. Any man who does not agree with this need not remain, but can return to the service of Big Sing."

The gang boss glowered. "I say we should take a vote."

"A vote? That is ridiculous."

"There are evil spirits on the mountain. I feel it every time I look up there."

"Is this true, Shingling? Are there evil spirits?"

Shingling thought about this question. The group was silent again, watching him. The point was delicate. He thought back, remembering his night in the moaning wind facing the great jutting hump of granite. Unwittingly perhaps, the questioner had given him a means of stilling this dispute and rallying the men. A spirit was something a Chinese laborer could understand and guard against. His life was filled with spirits—spirits of the sun and the wind, of luck and tragedy, of light and darkness. Evil spirits were always more significant by their presence than their absence. He looked into the faces gravely and said, "I think there are evil spirits upon the mountain."

"Ahyeee!"

"And so we must take every precaution."

"Yes."

"We carefully weave the baskets by which our men are lowered over the cliff face. And in the eyelets for each rope tie, we shall paint symbols against the spirits—north, south, east and west."

"Our best weavers must be put to work on it."

"And who shall be the first to confront Cape Horn, the first man down in a basket?" a headman asked.

The question hung in the air. The faces turned to Shingling. His reply was quick and firm. "I shall be the first. The mountain is my nemesis."

There was a murmuring among the others, but no one challenged him. Several of them now avoided his eyes. The gang boss did not speak again. But later, after the meeting was ended, he came to Shingling's tent and stood at the front flap until his presence was acknowledged. "It is a brave thing you propose to do, Shingling. We have had our differences, but I respect this act."

"I have not spoken to the white bosses yet. I'm not certain that they will agree."

"I think they will agree," the gang boss said. "But when they do, you will need advice. You are from a valley village, I understand, the valley of Sheh and Shah."

"Yes."

"That is lowland country." The gang boss spoke carefully, keeping his voice neutral of regional differences. "My people are mountain people, and I have done high work. I will be glad to make suggestions. If you think they might be of help."

Shingling smiled. He reached out and grasped the hand of the gang boss. "Thank you," he said.

The following morning, accompanied by the headmen, Shingling spoke to Thaddeus Stewart and Jim Strobridge about his plan. The big Americans were dubious. "We're thinking of hiring steeplejacks," they said. "Cape Horn will be a brutal job. It means high work, with blasting powder. The dangers . . ."

"Beg pardon, Misser Stewart," Shingling said, "but Chinese men have no difficulty. We used to this work. Ancestors built strong forts in-a river gorges. High work no problem. But we must send to San Francisco Chinatown for reed."

"Reed?"

"To weave wicker baskets, Misser Stewart."

Thaddeus glanced at Strobridge. "What do you think, Jim?"

The big field boss shrugged. "Charlie Crocker's going to think I've lost my mind. But what the hell, give it a try."

Shingling was astonished that word of the Cape Horn project got back to Lotus in San Francisco. He had not seen her for three weeks since her last visit; but lately, she had been much on his mind. There was growing between them a bond that seemed to transcend distances and time. It was something that he could neither comprehend nor control. And then Lotus herself arrived one evening on the work train at the railhead. She walked to his tent heedless of the stares of the workmen. Shingling had been seeing to the completion of the basket weaving by a hundred upland Chinese, selected by the gang boss for their knowledge and dexterity. These same workmen ultimately would entrust their lives to the baskets they weaved. Each basket was

decorated with painted symbols against the evil spirits of the
mountain. Their chatter ceased as the woman appeared.

Lotus wore the plain clothing of a country person and a
conical hat against the sunlight. Her face was without makeup, her figure hidden in the folds of floppy work trousers of
the kind that a man might wear. She faced Shingling and
spoke in English. "It is said that you are risking your life
tomorrow against the mountain."

He was flustered. "Why have you come here? This is not a
place for you."

"It is true? You are going up there?" She pointed to the
looming bulk, its granite face glistening in the late afternoon.

"I am going up there, yes. We must begin blasting it away,
to make a shelf for the tracks. This is something that must be
done. It is of no special consequence."

"You are a lowlander. You have never worked the high rock.
This is what they are saying. They are saying that Shingling is
taking a terrible chance against the mountain. They say that
Cape Horn is evil. Many are wagering that you will not
survive."

"Chinese will wager on anything. They will wager that the
sun will not rise tomorrow."

"Listen to me." She grasped his arm and held it. "There
are men who can do this better than you. Maybelle Stewart
sent me to ask you not to try it. It is too dangerous. You have
never even worked with blasting powder, much less tried to
drive a blasting hole with a hand drill while slung in a flimsy
basket over the edge of a precipice."

"So it is Maybelle who sends you?"

"I would have come anyway." The face was set in determi-
nation and the eyes flashed.

He turned from her. The basket weavers watched them
without expression, not understanding the language but sensing
what their conversation was about. "Please go back to San
Francisco."

"I will stay," she said quietly.

He was angry and embarrassed. He tried to put this
unexpected confrontation out of his mind and to concentrate
on the matters at hand. She sat down on the ground in front
of his tent and remained there. Shingling went to the gang
boss, to see to final preparation of the ropes. The gang boss
did not mention the presence of Lotus. They discussed the
ropes, their length and strength, the organization of the

gangs that would manipulate them in the morning. Lotus remained at his tent. She was still there as the evening came on and the high peaks were bathed in the last sunlight. The dusk drew a blue mantle about the mountains until finally even the sunlight was gone and a hush lay upon the land.

He brought her food, a steaming rice bowl with chunks of shrimp and pork on a tray. They sat together and ate in silence, while the work gangs clustered at their cookfires. No man approached them or looked their way. By unspoken accord, the privacy of the man and woman was observed.

His belly was full. He lay on his back and looked up at the stars, aware of her silent presence and knowing that she was gazing at him. At last he asked, "Why did you come here?"

"To be with you," she said.

"I do not understand."

"Neither do I."

"That is not an explanation."

"It is enough."

"What do you intend to do tomorrow?"

"I intend to be there, where you are, as you go over the cliff and as you drill the blasting holes in Cape Horn. I intend to watch every move you make. And if you die—if a rope breaks and sends you plunging into the gorge, or the men do not pull you up fast enough to escape the blast—then I shall throw myself off the mountain."

He swallowed hard. What was this? This made no sense at all. He peered into her face, searching for something—some glint of the eyes that would tell him she was mad. "I do not understand," he said.

"No, you do not understand. You do not understand what you are and who you are. You do not understand how the men have come to look for your leadership and your counsel. You do not know what they say about Shingling Chou, who liberated them from Big Sing."

"I am a farmer, a working man, and nothing more. I don't know what you are saying."

"It does not matter. I am saying that I must be where you are, that I am unworthy of you and your attention but it is no matter; I wish to be with you. Is that so difficult to understand? I am a woman. You are a man. I have never in my life loved a man in my heart. It is a strange new experience that I thought would never come to me. I don't understand it myself. But there it is."

His mind digested this, and the impact of it struck him like a blow. The words repeated themselves in his mind, "I have never in my life loved a man in my heart..." His conscious mind tried to reject it all. She was Lotus, one of Maybelle's girls. She was a prostitute. He, Shingling, would be the laughingstock of the railroad camps, to consort in this way with a prostitute. He thought of the valley of Sheh and Shah, and of the grave on the hillside, and how he had stood there in the agony of loss. Not since then had he shared the company of a woman, any woman, until this one came into his life, teaching him English.

"I cannot change the past," she said. "I cannot change what I am or what I was. It is a part of me, and is the shame I shall carry to my grave. All I can say is that I would never, never think of returning to that life; that I would prostrate myself upon the ground for you to walk upon me, if it would attract your notice. My life, of whatever value it may be, is yours, Shingling Chou; and that's all I have to offer."

She was silent then. The hours passed. The fires died. The night deepened. The mountain cold came. She got up from the ground and brought blankets from his tent to spread over them, and then lay close beside him without touching. At last he fell asleep and dreamed of Lotus and of the brooding mass of Cape Horn rising above them both.

In the first brush of morning light, he awoke, stood up, stretched and went down to the main camp, whistling up the work gangs. By sunup, a mass of men were moving up the winding trail of the mountain bearing ropes and man-size wicker baskets, heading for the great granite face that soared into the fiery morning sky. At the head of the mass trudged Shingling, and beside him the woman called Lotus.

The wind. The wind had a power and caprice all its own. It freshened early this day, swooping up from the gorge and whipping along the mighty face of gray granite. The wind was more powerful than it had been on his previous visit to this place, and its deep moaning power seemed to cut into his vitals. The basket was ready, lashed into a fork of ropes, but tossing like a child's plaything in the wind. Atop this steep sloping, rounded hulk of mountainside, the basket appeared from a distance as a yellow speck and the massed men on the rough ground above it as a horde of ants.

"Here is your hammer and drill-spike, with a drill to spare. Stick them into your belt, just so." The gang boss worried and fussed about Shingling, tugging at his safety rope, double-checking and triple-checking the main rope lashed to the basket. That main rope, hundreds of feet of it, extended up the slope and through a block and tackle attached to a platform jutting out from the crest of the granite face. Farther up, behind them all, a gang of haulers waited—the rope in their hands—for signals to spring to action.

"And the blasting powder?"

"Here, in these paper cylinders. You have the powder, the wadding and the fuse. This is slow-burning fuse. You set the charge, put in the wadding, light the fuse, and at your signal we haul away bringing you up out of range of the blast. Do you understand?"

"I understand."

"Now take your time. There is no rush. Once you're down there, get the feel of the basket and the granite face. You should try to find faults in the granite, for drilling. That will help you to take out more rock with the blast..."

He had difficulty understanding it all. The wind whipped words from the gang boss's mouth. Shingling's own mind was a confusion. Tension knotted his stomach, and the power of the abyss beneath them was awesome. He looked up at the rope gangs and saw, with astonishment, that a great mounded shelf of the mountain was covered with spectators, Chinese and Irish workmen all drawn together in a vast silent throng. At a nearer vantage point stood the tall American construction chiefs Thaddeus Stewart and Jim Strobridge along with the portly contractor Charlie Crocker. On the exposed brim of the abyss, not ten feet from the basket, sat Lotus. Her hands were folded in her lap. Her eyes never left Shingling's face. He felt her powerful presence as, at last, he stepped away from the gang boss, grasped the rope above the tossing basket and swung his body into it. At his signal the rope gang began paying out line and the basket swung out over the gorge and down.

A blast of wind caught him with fresh fury. Sickeningly, his flimsy woven vehicle lurched and swayed in a gulf of emptiness. Suddenly it was as if there were nothing between him and certain destruction but the thinnest of reeds, offering no more sturdy support than so much paper. Beneath his feet he could feel the give and sway of the thin matting. Around him,

chest high, its fragile weave creaked and popped alarmingly
with the strain. Above, the lengthening rope grew thinner
and thinner, curving in the wind, until its strand was the
relative thickness of a spider's web. The descent was slow,
and because of the slope the basket clung to the granite face,
bumping and scraping. He looked over the edge. The awesome vastness of the gorge struck like a blow in the stomach,
almost causing him to vomit. He shut his eyes against rising
nausea and did not look down again. At last he reached a
prearranged depth for this initial descent to a creviced overhang offering good possibilities for a large rockfall. The descent stopped and Shingling faced the granite wall in his
bucking basket, fumbling for the steel drill-spike and hammer
at his belt. The crevice was within easy reach, although a
couple of inches high; but several times the wind tossed the
basket so violently that he almost dropped the drill-spike. At
last he was able to place the steel point and give it two solid
hammer blows before another gust swung him away, the
basket tossing and twisting. The drill-spike remained in its
crack, and by the fourth blow was secure enough for him to
hold in a solid grip, anchoring the basket against the face
while he worked.

Plink! went the hammer. *Plink! Plink!*

Quickly, the strenuousness of his labor began to assert
itself. Muscles knotted with the strain and small bolts of pain
coursed through the muscles of his arms and back. He was
surprised to find his breath coming in great, shuddering
gasps, so that he was forced to rest briefly while hanging onto
the drill-spike. Time stood still. The abyss at his back seemed
to want to swallow him as it would a flyspeck on the face of
eternity. Each blow of the hammer sank the shaft a mere
fraction, and his toil was measured in taps of steel upon steel
and tiny puffs of loosened granite dust. An hour went by.
Two. Three. Sweat poured from his body and saturated his
clothing. The sun blazed down upon his back. Heat radiated
off the granite face in merciless waves.

Plink! Plink! Plink! Plink!

He lost all track of time, place, substance. This was life and
toil, and he but a fragment of time. The mountain was his
nemesis, and he the diligent ant determined to chip it down
blow by blow by blow. *Plink! Plink!* He thought of his father
and the water buffalo, trudging endlessly, timelessly, through
the muck of the rice field, year in and year out. He thought

of the great flocks of field birds, specks of life in dazzling vistas of green, bursting out of clouds and sweeping over-head. He saw in the eyes of his mind the graves on the hillside, and heard the voice of his father through the corri-dors of time: "There is a land called Gum San, which is the Golden Mountain. The roads are paved with gold and a man can grow rich from his labors..."

And at last, it was done. A final blow, and the spike was buried into the hole. He withdrew it from the granite and dropped it to the bottom of the basket. He mopped the sweat from his face and leaned against the edge of the basket catching his breath. He brought out the heavy paper cylinder of black powder, slid it into the hole and tamped it carefully. He inserted the wadding and tapped it in upon the charge, along with a length of fuse that whipped in the wind. He secured the fuse into a loose coil. He looked up for the first time at the tiny figures high above, and waved one arm to the gang boss in the signal that he was about to light the fuse. To the right of the gang boss he saw the figure of Lotus, seated on a knob of rock. She was looking down at him and not moving at all. Now he put his back to the wind, cupped the flint striker in his heavy hands and lit the fuse. Sparks sizzled and smoked. He dropped the flint striker and waved both arms, shouting into the wind, "Haul away! Haul awayyyyy!"

The basket jerked upward. The violence of the jerk hurled him sideways, so that he lost his footing and clutched franti-cally at the ropes. The basket was rocketing upward. Abruptly, it began to pitch forward into the granite face. A sharp chunk of granite outcropping snagged the wicker and dug into it. With a mighty jolt, the upward momentum stopped. As Shingling fought to keep from being pitched out of the wildly swinging basket, he was aware of frantic pulling and shouting above. Each tug by the rope gangs only drove the rock snag deeper into the side of the basket, locking it to the cliff face. Ten feet below sparks showered from the sputtering fuse. In desperation Shingling tried to signal the gang boss to slacken the main rope, so that he could push the basket free of the granite. It was Lotus who understood his dilemma, being able to look down from her slightly different position on top of the cliff. Lotus shouted something to the gang boss and Shingling felt the ropes loosen. As the combined weight of the basket and his own body sagged upon the granite snag, he flattened his hands against the rock wall and pushed.

Still the mountain refused to set him free. Sweat poured down his face. Again he was conscious of the terrible gorge at his back, the wind smashing down with renewed force, the cold shock of fear in his belly. His pushing achieved nothing, for the flimsy side of the bucket gave his back no support for leverage and the glistening gray mass of Cape Horn mocked his puny struggles. He glanced upward and saw Lotus rising from her ledge on the rock. She walked to the very lip of the gorge. She stood there with the wind tugging at her body, an inch from eternity. What was she doing? What in the name of the gods was she doing? And then her words came flashing back to him; those words that had seemed so senseless when she had spoken them before, words that had seemed so much woman-prattle. "I intend to watch every move you make. And if you die... then I shall throw myself off the mountain."

No! Again he pushed with futile strength at the rock, and again the basket simply flexed in response. Down there at his knee he could see the ugly spur of rock jutting through the jagged hole in the weave; the hook of granite with which the mountain intended to destroy its human tormentor. His foot moved, and the hammer clinked against the spare drill-spike.

The hammer!

His heart leaped. He bent down, seized the heavy hammer and began smashing at the rock. So confined was the space that he could not swing a full blow, and the steel glanced off the ugly spur. But a piece of the spur's top abruptly sheered off. He struck. And struck again. Another chunk gave way. Now he used the drill-spike to enlarge the hole in the basket. And suddenly...

"Haul awayyyyy!"

Above, Lotus seemed to hear his shout into the wind. Even as he stood upright again and began waving his arms, she was signaling wildly to the rope gangs and screaming instructions in Chinese. The rope jerked. It jerked again. The basket tilted perilously. And with a mighty ripping of reed, it broke free. In one second Shingling was still bound to the rock; in another, the basket was loose, swooping upward and away, its torn side open to the yawning emptiness of space. Within the time of a dozen heartbeats, he was within hearing range of the screaming pulley wheel, as the rope poured through it with a speed that raised smoke. Before Shingling's astonished eyes, the cliff face swept down and down, the great hump itself seeming to fall away. He saw Lotus, still standing on the brink, nearing; and the gang boss, shouting and jumping up and down; and the rope gangs, gripping the lifeline and running uphill, men slipping and falling in their frantic haste...

Boooooooommmmmmm!

The explosion came like a thunderclap. Its power struck him with a wave of energy that rocked the fleeing basket in midair. Shingling looked down to see a great belch of black smoke, hurling a blast of granite chunks outward and down. The cascade of debris plummeted down, down, down in a slow-motion display, turning upon itself in a massive death plunge toward the silvery ribbon of river cutting the blue void far below. In the stillness that followed, smoke curled upward around his airy vehicle, a mute submission of the mountain to man's enterprise.

And then, as the basket swung toward the crest again and Lotus stepped back from the abyss, eyes shining, a new sound came to Shingling's ears; a thin roaring sound, as if from some mighty mountain cascade. Puzzled, he looked up toward its source and saw the army of workmen massed around the mountain's crest, so many that they seemed to be literally poured over the peak. Then he recognized the sound.

They were shouting, "Shingling! Shingling! Shingling!"

"Hell on wheels. That's what we call it."

It was an army sprawled on the plain: graders, teamsters, herdsmen and cooks, tracklayers and gandy dancers, mule-skinners, bridge builders, pick-and-shovel men. As the Union Pacific train chuffed westward, Brack Stewart tried to absorb the sheer enormity of it all, and failed. "We got a mixed force of laborers," the general was saying. "Irish, mostly. Former Union and Rebel soldiers, mule skinners, ex-miners, adventurers, runaway boys from families back east, disgruntled farmers, gamblers, drinkers. We got Swedes, Irish, Finns, Negroes. It's a hard lot." He blew his nose on an old bandana. "They wear pieces of cast-off uniforms, subsist on beef, potatoes, bread, coffee and raw whiskey, fight and—when the opportunity presents itself—fornicate. But we're building, Mr. Stewart. By God, we're building."

Brack Stewart took a pinch of snuff, sniffed, sneezed deli-

cately against the back of his hand, sighed. "I daresay." He
disliked the man. Grenville Dodge, chief engineer of the
Union Pacific and ex-major general of the Union Army, was
short, stocky, sloppy in appearance. His face was a weathered wedge, pain-pinched from old war wounds and framed
in black whiskers streaked with gray. Dodge had a driving
spirit, however, and that meant profits. The Union Pacific
might be suffering its financial shortages still—indeed, Jack
Casement, the squat, short-tempered tracklaying contractor
was forever carping about delayed payrolls for the thousands
of men—but profits poured into the coffers of the Credit
Mobilier in a stream of pure gold. Credit Mobilier had been a
brainstorm, partly Brack's and partly that of Thomas Durant
and a few associates. By serving as prime contractor and
supplier of everything, from rails and fishplates to rolling
stock, locomotives, even herds of cattle on the hoof which
ambled along with the work gangs to provide a steady supply
of beef, the company had complete control of every Union
Pacific dollar. "Like a fox in the hen house," shrewd old
McRoberts Hagen, Brack's mentor, had said ecstatically. "And
you, my dear boy, are the fox."

It was all well and good for Hagen to speak. But the fox was
not without vexations. A major irritant now was proving to be
his cousin, Thaddeus. It was in the interests of the Union
Pacific for the California railroad builders to remain stalled in
those dreadful Sierra Nevada mountains as long as possible.
Every mile of track laid brought each company control of
virgin federal lands along the right-of-way. By a quirk of
geography, the Union Pacific thus stood to gain a vast domain
by racing across the flat plains while Thaddeus and his
Central Pacific toiled yard by yard in the mountains. Brack's
spies told him of the headaches his rival was having hiring
labor.

But at the same time, Thaddeus was asking troublesome
questions. From California there had come notes in his firm
hand, asking, "What is Credit Mobilier?" Brack had not
replied. Another note said, "Our railroads must not be tainted
by sharp practices." This had caused Brack's temper to flare.
The cheek of the man! He wasn't even a major stockholder in
the Union Pacific.

But Thomas Durant had advised caution. "Thaddeus has
powerful friends. It's best not to antagonize him."

And so Brack had finally written, assuring Thaddeus that

nothing was amiss with Credit Mobilier; that as prime contractor for the Union Pacific, the company was committed to
success.

"... But what about Indians, General?" It was Oakes Ames
who spoke. The aging millionaire rode in the seat behind
Brack, dozing intermittently as the plush excursion car rocked
westward over an endless plain. "They're a real nuisance, I
hear."

Brack smiled inwardly. Ames might be a shrewd industrialist, but he was easy prey in this league. The Massachusetts
congressman and his brother Oliver had pumped two million
dollars of their own cash into Union Pacific the previous year
in a desperate effort to get construction going. Ames's
involvement with Credit Mobilier, however, had glossed it
with his own image of unshakable honesty and drawn major
investors who otherwise would have remained on the side-
lines, despite—or perhaps because of—the heavy involvement
of Brack Stewart.

"More than a nuisance, Congressman. The redskins have
given us a fit. The Cheyenne and the Sioux are the worst.
War parties are out all the time. They hit the Missouri
settlements first, burned people out and slaughtered 'em.
They've ambushed our troops, hit the surveying teams out
front. We put military escorts on the survey parties and even
on the track gangs." Dodge glanced out at the rolling prairie.
"Our men are equal to it, though. They've been soldiers,
most of 'em, and every man has got a rifle handy."

"General Grant wants to make peace with the Indians. His
commissioners are parleying—"

"They parley with the old chiefs, Congressman. The young
braves want none of it." Dodge settled back in his chair. He
spoke as one who understood the Indians' plight, and yet
would brook no interference. "It's them or us. They hate the
locomotive worse than anything. The locomotive frightens off
the herds of bison, antelope and elk, rushes along making
terrible noises and showers sparks that ignite prairie fires.
They've tried to lasso locomotives, tried to derail 'em by
stretching leather thongs across the track—they gave that up
when the braves holding the thongs were yanked under the
wheels—and ripped up tracks."

"Heavens to Betsy!" It was the pretty Mrs. Delaney who
spoke from her seat opposite the general. Again, Brack
leaned forward and glanced across the aisle at the bosomy,

brown-haired woman whose husband, Sharpe Delaney, bossed
one of the survey crews. She had come along on the excursion tour intending to join Delaney at Fort Kearny, and was
accompanied by an aging and disapproving aunt. Brack caught
her eye, smiled, and deliberately let his glance stray down
the front of her dress. Her face flushed and she fanned
herself with a newspaper. "Goodness!"

"No cause to worry, ma'am," General Dodge said amiably.
"We are well protected."

The excursion train rocked and swayed through the valley
of the upper North Platte and finally ground to a stop at a raw
new station of unpainted wood in a muddy town of tents,
shacks and false-fronted buildings. As they crowded into the
aisle, Brack managed to press against Mrs. Delaney, who
responded with a breathy giggle. General Dodge chirruped,
"Welcome to Helltown! Uh, begging yer pardon, ladies."

They filed off the train into a sun-drenched afternoon
teeming with horses, men, mules and mud. Along the main
street, saloons flourished and signs advertised games of monte, faro and chuck-a-luck. From inside came sounds of piano
playing and loud talk. The visitors climbed into stagecoaches
and rocked westward for a mile, until finally they came to the
railhead. Gigantic sleeping and dining cars of the work train
were drawn up on makeshift rail sidings, while ahead labored
swarms of men, laying track, spiking, grading, scooping,
filling, blasting. Sledgehammers rang across the afternoon.
There was a constant clatter of picks and wheels and hooves.
From the distance came the muffled boom of powder blasts.

Brack Stewart watched in amazement. For the first time,
the vast dimensions of it all began to focus in his mind. Under
the driving influence of Grenville Dodge, the Union Pacific
had come two hundred and fifty miles from Omaha in a year's
time. Omaha, the jumping-off town, the capital of Nebraska,
was flourishing. Even Brack had been impressed by the new
buildings rising everywhere, the masses of humanity streaming through, the new white statehouse commanding its mile-
long slope down to the muddy Missouri River. But Omaha,
he could see now, was only the beginning; for on their train
journey, they had passed through raw new villages like this
one, spawned as mobile hell-towns. Ultimately each tempo-
rary settlement moved on, leaving a settled population behind. The arithmetic of his intellect picked at the potential
profits. With twenty million square miles of federal land

alone up for grabs between Omaha and Sacramento, they were dealing with ...

"Stupendous!" Oakes Ames said, standing beside him on the dustblown right-of-way. "Absolutely stupendous!"

A small group of Army cavalry came trotting toward them from the direction of Fort Kearny, a few miles to the west. The party was led by a tall, red-haired brigadier general whose seamed face was dusted with freckles. He rode with the rocking half-slouch of one long conditioned to the saddle. The general dismounted and handed the reins to an aide. Grenville Dodge shook his hand.

"Congressman Ames, Mr. Stewart, ladies, may I introduce General Peter Heflin, commander of troops west of Omaha."

Heflin's blue eyes nested in his face like bits of steel. They bored into Brack's with a special intensity. "Stewart?" How interesting."

"Yes," Brack said carefully. "I am related distantly to your wife, I believe. A cousin, on my mother's side.

"I see." Heflin turned abruptly to Mrs. Delaney, tipped his hat and bowed. But Brack noticed that he reached first for the hand of the chaperoning aunt. "Charmed." The aunt curtsied, simpering. The Delaney woman looked up into the sunburned face with eyes full of luster. He bent over her hand and brushed it with his lips. Brack felt a stab of envy.

Hours later, in the dining tent, Heflin held forth with Southern charm and gallantry. As Mrs. Delaney listened, enthralled, he engaged in disucssion of the Indian problem. Congressman Ames expressed sympathy for the dilemma of the tribes forced from their lands despite long-standing treaties. "The gold seekers have swarmed into Montana country, which is the home of the Sioux under treaty."

"That may be true, Congressman, but my command will defend settlers, travelers and railroad construction crews against attack. This is our duty. I also believe it is in the interests of the nation to clear these savages from the route of the Pacific Railroad, by whatever means."

Brack could not surpress a smile. Ah, General, he thought, what music to my ears. Indians also stood in the way of profits by hindering the Union Pacific's cross-country race. He wondered what Heflin would think if he knew of the private fortunes riding on his high-flown sense of Duty. "Admirable," he said aloud. Heflin acknowledged his response with a somber nod.

Mrs. Delaney spoke. "But, General, under treaty the tribes have the right to open hunting grounds, even in the right-of-way. They can wander where they please."

Heflin's face reddened. Brack noticed that the man had partaken freely of red wine. "Does Congress intend to back down and surrender the future of this nation to a few bands of roving Indians?" Heflin snapped.

"Well, no . . ."

"You are not dealing with a civilized people out here. These are savages with no more feeling for life and death than a cougar or a grizzly bear. On the upper North Platte, a detachment of eighty-one troops under Captain W. J. Fetterman rode into an ambush of more than two thousand Sioux, Cheyenne, and Arapaho." Heflin lifted his wine glass, drank, banged the glass onto the table. Red wine splashed like blood over the white tablecloth. "They were slaughtered to a man."

A strange quiet settled over the gathering. It persisted through the remainder of dinner despite Grenville Dodge's attempts to clear the air. Afterward, General Heflin and his aides left early, to the disappointment of Mrs. Delaney. "I intend to be in the saddle early with the troops," Heflin announced. "We are patrolling in strength."

When the officers had departed, Brack turned to Jack Casement. The contractor, ironically, also had served as a brigadier general during the war.

"Dedicated man," Brack said.

Casement frowned. "Perhaps too dedicated."

Mrs. Delaney's displeasure quickly passed. As conversation grew desultory, Brack found her eyes upon him. Hazel eyes, they were, bold and appraising now. His excitement stirred. As the gathering began to break up, he managed to step closely enough to whisper lightly into her ear. Again, the flush of cheeks and quick intake of breath. But she nodded.

Shortly after midnight, Brack Stewart left his stateroom in the excursion coach and stepped off the platform. He wore his cloak against the chill. A half-moon cast its silvery light over the gently rolling landscape. From the main street of the new Helltown, half a mile away, there came sounds of piano music and boisterous male conviviality. The lights glowed in two large tents which, he had been told, served as bordellos. He strolled a dozen yards from the train, stepped behind a tool shed and lit a cigar. The cigar was not yet half-consumed

when he heard light footsteps crunching through dry grass.
She rounded the corner of the shed and stopped.

Brack smiled. "Ah, Mrs. Delaney."

"Evelyn."

"Evelyn, then. Come here, Evelyn."

She approached him hesitantly. She wore a dark coat,
drawn over her nightdress. He opened his arms and she came
to him. She was shivering. He kissed her, open-mouthed,
and drew her body close.

"Oh," she said. "Oh . . ."

They walked away from the train, through the dry grass,
until he found a dark place in a small copse of cottonwood.
He spread his cloak upon the ground and drew her down,
shaking and panting with heat. Her thighs opened.

"Be gentle with me," she whispered. "P-Please be gentle."

Summer passed into autumn, and storms lashed the valley
of the Platte with their special fury. Awesome things they
were, violent in thunder, lightning and wind. Black clouds
disgorged rain and hail and, sometimes, multiple tornadoes
that advanced in fours and fives as if from the mouth of Hell.
Peter Heflin commanded five regiments of troops, one of
them consisting entirely of Pawnees. The Pawnees were
mortal enemies of the Sioux and Cheyenne, and often took
extra delight in orgiastic scalping of fallen foes. Heflin deafened
his ears to the screams. A good Indian was a dead Indian, and
there was no horror more certain than that which redskins
meted out to their own kind. It justified him, and salved any
personal remorse for engaging in a campaign of eradication.

"Remember the Fetterman massacre," he told his troops,
and led them in kind. They were a hard-riding, hard-bitten
lot, survivors of both armies during the war. He thought of
this now, hunched in the saddle beneath soggy hat and cloak
against the lashing rain. They were a good forty miles north
of Laramie—the newest Helltown near the railroad—riding
in regimental strength. The Union Pacific crews had easily
surpassed their original goals of a mile of track a day, and thus
extended the area for cavalry patrol. Indian raiders had
mauled stagecoaches in Wyoming and stripped Colorado
ranches of their horses. Telegraph lines, which the Indians
called "talking wires," were ripped down by the mile and

crews were attacked as they arrived to repair the damage. The emissaries from Washington still parleyed—ye gods, did they know nothing else?—while good people died in ways that were appalling even to an old war horse. Heflin thought of the locomotive fireman, trapped in an engine wrecked by Indians and literally roasted to death while he screamed for someone to shoot him. He thought of the blond-haired surveyor, badly wounded and scalped, who'd managed to crawl away from his attackers in the darkness and escape, carrying the bloody remains of his hair.

Was there no justice for these victims? Was there no retribution? A bolt of lightning slammed to earth on a mighty surge of power, causing his horse to shy. He reined back, speaking soothingly to the animal. As the horse settled back into stride, Heflin pondered his resolve. He would not yield until accounts had been squared. He would not surrender to the savage horde. He intended to bring down upon them the wrath of a vengeful god.

They camped in a wash beneath a line of hills. The night was pitch black and stormy. But even without foul weather, there was no possibility of lighting fires; the weather covered them, giving Heflin's troops maximum opportunity to gain complete surprise. He issued orders requiring that every man see to his arms, and extra ammunition was distributed at midnight. Sleep came fitfully. Wrapped in his cloak on the wet ground, he dreamed of cannon fire and awoke to find the lightning flicking anew and more rain threatening. The dawn broke gray and chill, in a drizzle. They ate a cold breakfast of hardtack and bully beef. The hills were misty as they mounted, the bugles silent and commands whispered from man to man. Peter Heflin turned out ahead of his force. They rode up the slope, and near the crest, shook out the ranks into a skirmish line. The troops reined in along the hilltops, silhouetted in the morning light. Beneath them sprawled a war camp of the Sioux, distinctive by its lodge poles displaying a mass of scalps. The camp lay along a winding creek, clear and shallow. Smoke curled upward from the vent holes of several lodges. In one of the lodges, a puppy whined at its unaccustomed rawhide leash.

Brigadier General Peter Heflin stood up in his stirrups and drew his saber. Along the line, there was a metallic clatter of Spencer repeating rifles being cocked. Each rifle was balanced on the rider's hip, aslant toward the angry, ragged sky.

He looked at his troops. For some strange reason, he thought at that instant of his wife's foppish cousin, and how out of place the man had seemed two months previously in that rugged setting of the West—the New York financier with his elegant suits and superior airs. How would Brack Stewart react now, doing what they had to do in the next few minutes? He would probably vomit in his soup.

Peter Heflin's war cry ripped across the morning.

"Chaaaaaarge!"

Such a sight had never been seen before in these mountains by man or beast. Especially beast. In the half-light of an autumn drizzle, the partially dismantled black steam boiler and piston assembly of the locomotive *Sacramento* inched up the twisting road toward the summit of the Sierra Nevada. To passing horses and mules, pulling wagons and stagecoaches, it was a nightmarish spectacle. Grinding and groaning, the iron monstrosity was slung to a huge platform of heavy timbers on massive rollers. The whole was drawn by a twenty-mule team augmented by swarms of rope-hauling Chinese, jabbering excitedly.

"Good God Almighty!" The stagecoach from Virginia City came lurching down the slope, rounding a curve. On the high seat, a wide-eyed driver opened his mouth and dropped his cigar. The lead horse took one look at *Sacramento* and shied, whinnying.

"Whoa, hoss! Whoa, you goddamned... What is it? What in God's name..."

"Get them hosses in hand! Look out, they're boltin'!"

"Mr. Stewart, watch fer the team!"

"I see 'em. Driver, rein those horses!"

But the lead animal was already slamming against his harness, trying to prance sideways and gallop at the same time. Its partner in the traces, an old bay, a veteran of mountains and plains, rolled fearful eyes at the great iron hulk and side-wallowed wildly. The stagecoach, out of control, bucked and lunged downslope and away, leaning heavily on the turns while irate passengers shook their fists from open, side windows.

And so it went during the tumultuous first day and the next and the next. Mules shied, horses reared, teamsters bellowed, mule skinners turned the air blue with curses. On the third evening, as the great bulk was stilled for the night before resuming its noisy uphill odyssey, Charlie Crocker eyed Thaddeus over a flickering campfire and pulled at a pint of bourbon.

"You and your bright ideas."

"How was I supposed to know?" Thaddeus said defensively.

"Well, that's a fair enough question. You can't read the mind of a horse."

"Or a mule. Or a teamster. And I don't know which is more spooky."

"You got to figure out something, Thaddeus. We're scaring them animals out of their wits."

"I'll think of something, Charlie."

Charlie Crocker spat tobacco juice into the fire. As the spittle sizzled, he eyed the black bulk squatting in evil majesty a hundred yards away. The Chinese massed around it on their haunches, chattering and shoving boiled rice into their mouths with chopsticks from wooden bowls. Shingling and his army had taken the latest task as a lark, treating the mighty hulk of *Sacramento* with the deference of a pet dragon. "Sometimes," Thaddeus said aloud, "I think it is a dragon."

"I still say it's a damn fool idea," Charlie Crocker muttered. "Hauling the steam boiler of a hundred-ton locomotive up a mountain seven thousand feet high. What if we get it there and it don't work?"

"It'll work."

"It's never been done before."

"None of this has been done before."

"There must be a better way to dig a tunnel."

"Tell me."

Crocker sighed, grinned, scratched himself. Thaddeus knew the contractor was chiding him, knew he was pleased. Summit Tunnel was a monstrous piece of work, more than sixteen hundred feet of hole through solid granite. Upon completion, it would be wide enough for double track. Work gangs of Chinese toiled in twelve-hour shifts at the granite face with rock drill, hammer and blasting powder. The tunnel men were part of a force of ten thousand now swarming on the cruel ridges.

Work was in progress on a dozen tunnels between the raw new town of Cisco, ninety-two miles from Sacramento, and the Nevada line. Supply trains made a constant shrieking procession up the western slope on grades pitched as steep as one-hundred-and-sixteen feet to the mile. The Chinese had dug out Grizzly Hill Tunnel and Emigrant Gap. Working by lamplight, the gangs advanced against their granite faces at a rate of one foot every twenty-four hours. But there was nothing like Summit Tunnel. Nothing.

"We'll never get it done," Charlie Crocker sighed.

"That's what you said before."

"I remember your first brainstorm, Stewart. You and John Gillis. You said, 'Hell, why attack the granite just from two ends of the tunnel? We'll sink a shaft down the middle too. Drop two more gangs in there.' That's what you said."

"Your memory's very good, Charlie."

"So it took 'em four months to cut the shaft, seventy-three feet down. Then it turned out you wasn't so damned smart after all." Charlie Crocker chuckled. "Couldn't get the debris up fast enough, right? Not with a hand-operated derrick."

"Nope."

"So here we are, hauling up this monster to give you a steam lift on the mountaintop." He wagged his head and sighed. "Know what I think sometimes, Stewart?"

Thaddeus lay back and rolled into his blanket against the mountain chill. He took a final slug of bourbon from the pint, tossed his spent cigar into the fire and closed his eyes. "What do you think, Crocker?"

"I think I should've taken my mother's advice and been a preacher."

The following day, an oncoming four-horse team harnessed to a heavy freight wagon became hysterical. The brutes kicked the traces and went galloping away while the wagon overturned. That's when Thaddeus came up with his solution to the problem.

"Blindfolds!" he announced.

"What's that you say, Stewart?"

"Tell every teamster and mule skinner coming downslope to blindfold his animals before they get to us."

And they did. And it worked. And at last, the *Sacramento's* mighty boiler made its final turn, its last lumbering lurch and rolled into place atop the yawning black hole above Summit Tunnel. Braced and bolted onto solid foundation, the firebox was ignited, steam pressure expanded in the vast works, the wheel piston surged and Summit Tunnel's power winch took

strain. Her creators slapped each other's shoulders triumphantly
and lit fresh cigars.

"By God, there's nothin' a man can't do," said Charlie
Crocker ecstatically, "with a little ingenuity and five hundred
Chinamen to help him out."

Autumn advanced with mixed blessings. It broke the broiling
heat of late summer, which had forced grading crews into
night work by lanternlight. Daily progress on the roadbed
improved. But then came rain. Scattered showers grew into
daylong downpours. Formerly dry gulches turned to torrents.
The red dirt of the lower slopes became quagmires of oozing
mud. On the Dutch Flat wagon road, wagons sank into the
muck, and horses and mules struggled up to their knees in
sludge. The Virginia City stagecoach mired down and had to
be abandoned, its passengers completing their journey by
horseback. A Chinese worker was buried alive in a mud slide.
The body was boxed and shipped back to Hong Kong.

Thaddeus was tired. They all were tired. He sat in a
construction shack reading the latest letter from Marguerite.
The flowing handwriting on an envelope bearing his name
never failed to lift his spirits. But the news was not good.
"Ruth is declining. Marvella Clive and I visit her twice a
month. She does not recognize either of us. You asked in
your letter if a visit from you might help. Honestly, darling, I
don't think so. The doctor shares this view. I'm afraid you
would only be depressed, and such a long, hard trip seems
hardly worth it." A note from the director of Thornwood
Asylum confirmed Marguerite's opinion.

Thaddeus put down the letter and stared at the waterstreaked
window of the shack, listening to the rain drumming on the
corrugated iron roof. Trouble compounded itself. As if Ruth's
condition were not enough to hound him, there was the
added vexation of Brack Stewart and his shady dealings with
the Union Pacific. Brack's Credit Mobilier clearly was siphoning
off the potential profits of that luckless railroad. Thaddeus did
not have the details, but fraud was becoming evident. Despite
the rapid pace at which Union Pacific work gangs were
advancing now, each mile bringing in huge sums of federal
loan guarantees and great tracts of new land grants, the
railroad was badly in the red. Informants in the eastern
financial establishment warned Thaddeus of flagrant abuses.
"Your cousin and his friends are bleeding that railroad for
every nickel, Stewart. Can you do nothing to stop it?"

Equally as bad, Brack and Durant had embarked upon a wild race for spoils, trying to gobble up every possible acre of land grant property and, thus, profit hugely at the expense of the Central Pacific whose progress was stalled in these infernal mountains. Clearly, the Central Pacific must push through as rapidly as possible, for every day of delay gave Brack Stewart and Credit Mobilier an added advantage.

A knock at the door broke his train of thought. It was Shingling, smiling and soaked. "You wanted me, Misser Stewart?"

Thaddeus's spirits lifted. This stocky Chinese farmer's magnetism affected them all: Strobridge, Crocker, Thaddeus, the men. He wondered if the man was even remotely aware of what a gigantic presence he had become in the scheme of things for the Central Pacific.

"I need your opinion, Shingling. It's about the tunnel work."

The Oriental face flashed dismay. "The tunnel work? We ain't doing good job?"

"You're doing a great job. But winter's coming on. The first blizzard will sock in this mountaintop. If these rains are any indication, we're in for a rough time of it. But our progress is very slow." He picked his words, decided for complete candor. "Frankly, we're in a race against the Union Pacific. It could cost us a fortune; hell, it could cost us everything. So I propose that the tunnel work go on right through the winter. Otherwise we'd lose three months, maybe four. It's a gamble, though. The dangers will be high. The choice is yours. It's up to you and the men."

Shingling nodded. "I ask the men, see what they say." He bowed, put on his soggy hat and went back out into the rain.

The following morning, Shingling returned. "The men, they make decision, Misser Stewart. They decide to tunnel through winter."

Thaddeus nodded gratefully. If he had known what hell awaited them, he might have acted differently.

The rain persisted. Moisture-laden storms swept across the California coast from the Pacific, ascended into the Sierras and turned to snow. By the first of November a foot of snow clung to the new settlement of Cisco, where tracklayers were spiking down the last rails. Thaddeus's winter tunneling inspired Charlie Crocker to take other work gangs down the eastern slopes, to work below the snow level, backward toward Donner pass. This meant hauling supplies from the Cisco railhead down the eastern slopes over the wagon road. As the weather grew progressively more foul, mule skinners and teamsters went at the task with a will. Fortified by whiskey, tobacco and loud oaths, they whiplashed their teams through the blizzards, moving in a steady stream of wagons in weather that cloaked man and beast in layers of white.

At the tunnels, drifts accumulated. Storm after storm raked the high passes. Chinese work gangs dug paths through the snow to the job and, twelve hours later, dug back to their shacks in the work camp.

Shingling and the men labored on in the tunnels, hammering and blasting, raising clouds of dust by the murky light of lanterns and candles, penetrating each day deeper into the mountain. December passed, laying five feet of snow. January brought eight feet, February another ten...

"Where is the warehouse, Stewart?"

"Buried over there in the drift."

"Good Lord, that building's thirty feet high!"

No longer was it possible to clear snow between the tunnel mouth and the living quarters of the men. And so they tunneled under the snow, shaping white corridors high enough and wide enough for two horse-drawn sleds to pass. Other corridors swung off to the side, for carting away and dumping debris from the dig.

A new word was coined among the Irish teamsters who still fought their teams along the supply route by sheer numbers somehow keeping the wagon road open. They called it White Hell.

By late April, the heaviest drifts were fifty feet deep. Great brows of snow jutted above the sheer western slopes, to break and plunge downward for a mile sweeping everything from their paths. The mountains cracked and boomed with fresh avalanches. And in the murky depths, the work went on around the clock in a smoky world of dim lights, ear-shattering blasts and choking dust.

Word came to the Summit Tunnel camp that twenty Chinese had perished in a snow slide, lower down to the east. Routinely, individuals disappeared in avalanches or by stepping into concealed air holes in the drifts. A man might go to relieve himself and never return. They found the bodies later, as the weather warmed and the spring meltdown sent torrents rushing toward the valleys. Some of the men were still clinging to their picks and shovels in the positions in which they died.

At last, it was the middle of June with new grasses blowing in the wind and wild flowers nodding on the coastal plains far below. There remained ten feet of snow in patches between Cisco and the Nevada border. But Thaddeus Stewart stood on a point and watched, amazed, as an army of fourteen thousand Chinese attacked the earth more than a hundred miles east of Sacramento. The Central Pacific was spending eight million dollars a mile.

"Thaddeus, we got no choice. We're going to have to build a roof over that entire length of track in the snow belt. I'd say thirty miles of it, maybe more."

"The cost, Collis. It's going to be enormous."

"Appalling is a better word."

"It'll be like railroading in a barn."

Collis Huntington, vice-president, uttered a weary sigh. "Sometimes I think I'd change jobs with just about anybody."

In October, 1867, converging crews broke through to each other in the Summit Tunnel. Within a month, the tracks were spiked through. Jubilation swept the high camps, and laborers swarmed to the site from elsewhere along the line. Charlie Crocker broke a champagne bottle against the tunnel's mouth and they rode through on a flatcar in triumph.

"By God, Stewart, this is a glorious day!"

"That it is, Crocker. That it is."

Charlie Crocker squinted toward the east, where the long winding slope already was being cut to take the Central Pacific down into the valley of the Truckee River and the gentle meadows far below. Beyond, in stages of diminishing difficulty, would lie the towns and whistle stops of a blessedly flatter terrain.

"From now on," Crocker said, "it's duck soup."

Thaddeus wished that he could be half as sure.

He spun the barrel of the big .44, squinted down the gunsight at the startled face of Mose Hacker and squeezed the trigger. *Snick!* The face winced. John Colby Stewart laughed out loud, a raspy, guffawing laughter. Then he removed the barrel mechanism from the revolver and began the absorbing ritual of cleaning it with rag and oil.

"God damned, John Colby," Mose Hacker bawled. "You

near scared the piss outta me. Whut if there was a round in that chamber?"

"Then you wouldn't have no face, and I'd have done the world a favor." He laughed again.

Hard living was upon him now. The years had done their work, and John Colby knew it. Whiskey had red-veined his cheeks and nose. The eyes, once dark and clear, had turned cloudy. But he could still give a whore a good romp, and that's what mattered. As for the rest . . . well, he had not seen the family for years. The only living thing on earth that wanted him was the army, for desertion under fire. And he still bore in his heart the old hatred; the older he got, the deeper it ate into his soul, like a cancer.

"John Colby, are you cleanin' that pistol again? Damn, man, if that ain't the cleanest gun west of the Mississippi."

He looked up from the cleaning. The speaker was Montcliff, a cold-eyed bear of a man whom he instinctively feared. His eyes drifted down the icy draw to the others as they finished the meal. There were eight, including himself, and they were all big men with cold eyes and meanness in their hearts. Montcliff was a caricature of the human race, dirty, corpulent and foul-smelling. But the others were no better. They were banded together in the strange brotherhood of outlaws and drifters, living by a cruel code, and had accompanied him west of the Mississippi for reasons of their own. It was vast country, the West; the law was loose and men asked no questions.

"Go to hell, Montcliff," he said. But he smiled.

The .44 was special. The gun had character. John Colby tended it lovingly, as an extension of himself. Guns fascinated him. He loved to stroke them, love them. A gun was power, the ultimate arbiter. He had lived a torment of the damned after Bull Run, sick from the terrible knowledge of his cowardice. And then he had found the gun and its uses, had shot down strong men from ambush and felt the thrill of it, had reasoned that Bull Run wasn't really his doing, but Fate's doing; it wasn't him that ran away, but some demented boy who hadn't grown up yet and didn't know about power. That soothed him. He put Bull Run out of his mind. He killed for the hell of it now, and lived for the gun. Like this one, this .44, its black steel gleaming in the snowlight. He had killed the Indian with it, the half-breed Creek who had ridden with him and would steal pennies from a dead man's eyes. He had killed the fat merchant with it, back in Ohio, blubbering and whining for his life. Bang! The bark of the .44 was a terrible thing, and would tear out a man's lungs and guts and leave him to gulp out his last breath on bubbles of scarlet spit. He had pressed it to the temple of the fat woman in Cairo, the one they'd accosted in the riverfront bar; had held it to her temple while she pleaded for mercy and Montcliff rode her like a crazy stallion. The memory of her fear, fear sounds and fear smells, still gave him pleasure. And then he had shot her.

But all that was nothing. Over the years, there had grown in his mind the certainty that there was one man he intended to kill. The others were whims of time and circumstance, meaning nothing. One man was his nemesis; one man bore the responsibility for all that had happened to John Colby Stewart. He had resolved to do this during a drinking bout, and it had remained with him when he'd sobered up. Yes. He would use the .44 and would kill that son of a bitch Thaddeus Stewart. But first, he'd have him on his knees, begging for mercy.

" . . . begging for mercy."

"What'd you say, John Colby? What was it you said?"

"Huh? Nothing, Montcliff. I didn't say nothing."

It was cold, bitterly cold. The cold knifed down on a north wind out of Canada, sweeping the plains, driving ice and snow. It was a miserable cold that cut a man clear through, even through his sheepskin and a mountain of underclothes. Stiffly, now, they climbed back into the saddles and, leading the pack mules, continued the trek cross-country. Up ahead, Hacker kept a weather eye for Indians. He was a sharp man at cross-country and could smell redskins a mile away. Hacker despised redskins more than rattlesnakes. Nobody asked him why; it was nobody's business but Hacker's. John Colby didn't want to know. The less you knew about a man, the better.

They rode southwest, heading for the railroad. It would be easier going along the Union Pacific tracks: not as many deep snowdrifts to plague a man and his animals. John Colby rode, feeling the tug of the pack mule's reins at his saddle horn. Thaddeus Stewart, he thought. Thaddeus Stewart . . .

"Thaddeus Stewart? Sure. He's workin' on the Central Pacific Railroad. Some kind of big shot, engineer. I got it from his uncle, Stephen." It was a bartender who had spo-

ken, in the booming town of St. Joseph, Missouri. This was
three weeks before, when John Colby and Hacker had gone
into town to see what they could see. Supplies and manpower
for the Union Pacific poured through St. Joseph in enormous
quantities. Day and night, the town was a lusty center of
groaning freight trains and hooting steamboats. Stewart steamboats were making a fortune hauling heavy equipment up the
muddy Missouri to St. Joe, and Stewart freight yards handled
nearly everything that passed through, from mountains
of cottonwood ties to vast stores of spikes, cable, tools, foodstuffs. In nosing around, John Colby had learned that the
contractor for the Union Pacific, something called Credit
Mobilier, had figured it was cheaper to arrange for Stephen
Stewart to handle the goods at St. Joseph than to build a
freight operation of its own. John Colby had made no effort to
see his father or mother in St. Joseph. And in a sudden desire
to get away from all that, he had vetoed a plan by the others
to push on westward to a place called Laramie in Wyoming
country. It was said that there was plenty of action in Laramie.

"John Colby, Hacker's makin' a signal."

They rode up a slope to where Hacker sat his horse,
looking down into a valley dominated by a single knoll. A
campfire burned brightly and several Indians—he counted
five—were busy butchering meat from a buffalo kill.

Hacker's eyes glittered. "Red devils." He motioned for
them to draw back down the slope. They dismounted and
gathered in a circle. "I want them savages," Hacker said.
"And we could use the meat."

"The redskins ain't bothering nobody, Hacker," someone
said.

"It don't matter. Listen, we're going to get 'em. Here's
whut we're gonna do. We'll wait here till after dark, and
then . . ."

They withdrew into a line of trees half a mile back and
settled down in the cold. It was miserable. John Colby
wished for a fire, a warm meal, whiskey. He thought of the
coming night and what Hacker wanted to do.

Nausea rose in his throat.

The wind blew down from the northwest, driving stinging
crystals of ice and snow. The sky was a dark mass of swirling
gray clouds, flying across a desolate land of stark white. Stand-

ing Bear leaned into the wind, bringing his pony around to face it. So intense was the cold that his breath stuck in his throat; cold burned the lining of his mouth and nose, and stabbed at his eyes. Behind him, the scouting party moved in black silhouette across the frozen plain, each brave hunched in the saddle. Standing Bear thought of Sunset Woman and the child, whom he had left in their lodge on the Creek-of-Many-Branches. They had picked a strategic pocket in the terrain for the camp, but that had been in the fall when the creek was in flow between steep banks. Now the creek was frozen, the banks drifted over with hard-packed, icy snow, and the camp of the Shemkuk Cheyenne less well-protected against attack. The force remaining in the camp was mixed, Cheyenne warriors augmented by some of the Sioux. He hoped they would suffice to protect the weak and old, but uncertainty nagged at him.

"Hyeeee, Standing Bear!" It was the voice of Broken Knife, from behind him. He reined in and waited for the Sioux chief. Broken Knife's great nose protruded like a beak from the fur robe in which he had wrapped himself. "I see them down there, beyond the knoll." He pointed into the distance below them. "To the right of the knoll. Look."

Standing Bear followed the directions of the Sioux chief and could make out several dark shapes scattered in the snow. Yes, it could be the bodies. Leaving two men on the high ground as lookouts, he led Broken Knife and the eleven others into the draw. The snow was loose here, the going hard, but at last they came to the bodies. There were five of them, Shemkuk Cheyenne who had left the Creek-of-Many Branches camp two weeks earlier in a hunting party. The bodies lay in the same stillness as the rocks and the snow. Around them the snow had been wildly trampled by many horses, and there were splotches of blood. Three of the bodies were scalped. One man's private parts had been cut off and stuck into his mouth, from which they protruded obscenely. "That is Little Wolf," one of the warriors muttered. "He has a new son in his lodge." The comment was unnecessary, for they all recognized the bodies: Little Wolf, Running Elk, Big Hand, and the others. Running Elk's body hung by the heels from a cottonwood tree over the black remains of a small fire. His brains had been cooked until he died.

"White men," grunted Broken Knife. "See the tracks?"

They were indeed the tracks of white men, for the hooves

of the horses had been shoed. Nearby they found a discarded
Army canteen, but Standing Bear did not believe this to be
Army work. Army troops did not torture and mutilate. "Ren-
egades," he said.

Broken Knife looked into his face expectantly. The Sioux
had lost none of his own men here, but it was of little matter.
The tribes were joined now in a common war.

"We will follow the tracks," Standing Bear said.

The trail led toward the southwest into rough country of
rising foothills, angling toward the tracks of the Iron Horse.
This was troublesome, awakening afresh the conflict within
him between desire for peace and the will to survive. It was
impossible, of course, to stop the iron horse as it catapulted
westward; one might as well try to stop the whirlwind.
Besides, the great black engine had no life of its own, but ran
on the same steam that rose from a squaw's cookpot. But
what else was to be done? He had parleyed with the emissaries of the Great White Father Grant, heard their meaningless
promises and deceits. The Indian could roam as he pleased,
hunt as he pleased, in the old ways over the old grounds. But
words and realities were separate things. The white man was
as numerous as the grasses of the plain. And so, as Cheyenne,
Sioux, and Arapaho had risen to battle the iron horse, Standing Bear had seen no choice but to join. He had sent his
braves to rip down the high wires that blipped with talk and
to tear up rails behind the masses of men who put them
down. Others, young hawks of the allied tribes, bushwhacked
isolated surveyors, bridge builders and tie cutters. His own
Cheyenne army had escaped a pony soldier dragnet led by
the red-haired general they called Heflin, he of the bloody
sword. But then, angry Shemkuk Cheyenne had ambushed a
repair train at Plum Creek and killed six trainmen. And the
more the Indians fought back, the more troops in blue
poured into the region. It was said that Heflin now commanded
five thousand men, well mounted and armed with the terrible Spencer repeating rifles.

Through it all, he had seen the worry in the eyes of Sunset
Woman. She had suckled his man-child Spotted Deer at her
breast, guided the boy's toddling steps as he grew to walk,
taught him the thoughts and tongue of the whites. Now,
riding in the gathering darkness in deepening cold, Standing
Bear warmed his mind with thoughts of her body pressed to
him in the darkness, her scent of musk and crushed blos-

soms, her voice in melodic whispers at his ear. "My lord, my life is empty when you are gone. I dread the day you are taken from me. I feel... a sorrowful sense of tomorrow." It was always so with women, but none had ever given it such words before; no Indian woman would dare to speak so frankly. And yet her very openness enriched his life and filled his heart, for she was friend as well as woman, a wise counselor. He could not conceive of meaningful life without her.

The ponies followed the trail of the iron-shod hooves. There were eight of them, by Broken Knife's reckoning, and they were mostly heavy men, slowed by pack mules, utensils, weapons. Night came, but the trek went on. The stars appeared, pinpoints of frozen light in the black mass of sky, casting enough glow in the icy wastes for them to see. The wind moaned and slashed. Coyotes chorused from dark hills. They traveled through the night and the following day, passing a campsite at which the ashes of a small fire were still warm to the hand. There they rested. On the afternoon of the third day they saw blue smoke spiraling into a stand of cottonwood trees.

"Do you want them alive?" Broken Knife said.

"Alive or dead," Standing Bear replied, "it does not matter."

His warriors went in at the rush, plowing through heavy snow. But even as the attack launched, Standing Bear knew it could not succeed. Abruptly they had thrown away the element of surprise. The white men were quick to take cover on the ground and squeezed off their rifle shots with terrible accuracy. Spencers! The weapons gave the eight defenders firepower of a hundred men using Indian single-shot rifles. Horses screamed and tumbled into the snow. In a single charge, half of his force was shot down. Two braves managed to break through, and each took a white life before dying under the guns. Standing Bear and his survivors withdrew.

"I am sorry, Standing Bear," said Broken Knife. "We threw away our advantage. I did not expect..."

"The fault is mine. What's done is done."

They remained through the night and into the next day, watching to see what the white men would do. But the whites merely waited, six surviving men who were expert shots with plentiful ammunition. From this distance, Standing Bear could have shot the pack animals and riding mounts, but his heart was not in it. Finally, retrieving their dead

under cover of darkness, the Shemkuk Cheyenne abandoned
the attack and turned their ponies for the long trek back to
the camp at the Creek-of-Many-Branches.

Sunset Woman came running when the word of their
arrival passed among the lodges. She ran clumsily, holding
her heavy skirts in the snow. "My lord! My lord, you're
returned!" And then she was beside him, running in the
snow with a strong grip at his stirrup, joy suffusing her
upturned face. She wore her flaming hair in tight Indian
braids caught in a beaded headband. Her features flushed
with cold. He thought he had never seen so beautiful a sight.
He reached down, caught her under the arm in a powerful
grip and swung her up astride the pony at his back. Her
arms encircled him tightly and her head lay against his
shoulder. "My lord, welcome home."

That night, in the silent warmth of their lodge, he loved
her with slow and infinite delight.

They rested by the Creek-of-Many-Branches and gathered
strength. More Sioux and Cheyenne came to join them,
pitching their lodges in the snow. A month went by. There
were earnest discussions around the council fires while pipes
passed hand to hand. Scouts had wandered into the helltowns,
Julesburg and Dry Gulch and Laramie, and returned with
wonders to tell of the white man's ways. None had been
caught by the ever present Pawnee who served the white
man as warriors against the Indian and were despised.

"They drink the firewater and argue loudly, sickened in the
brain. There are many shootings in the place called Laramie."

"White man and Indian?"

"No, white man and white man."

"How many are there now, working the iron tracks?"

"As many as there are warriors of the Sioux and Cheyenne
everywhere. It is said ten thousand workers and a thousand
horses and mules. I don't know what that means."

"Ten thousand is a way of numbering. It is one hundred of
the number of lodges in this camp."

"Standing Bear knows much of the white man's ways."

"It is good to have knowledge. To be ignorant is to be blind."

"There are rivals among these men. White men despise
one another. They rob and steal from their own kind. And
many men will line up to use the same white squaw, and pay
her money for serving them."

"Strange practices."

"Unclean."

"We have not only one group of iron horses to worry about. It is said that another has come over the great mountains from the west, and its tracks now rush toward the east as wildly as this one rushes to the west."

Derisive laughter greeted this revelation.

"You speak in riddles. It is not possible to bring an iron horse over the great mountains. Not unless it can fly like the eagle. And I have never seen an iron horse fly."

"Nevertheless, it has come over the mountains and even now is said to be within six days' ride from here. The western iron horse is attended by strange yellow men who have slits for eyes and wear hats like the mushroom."

"Now I know you are fooling us."

"It is true!"

"Let us ask Standing Bear what he thinks. What do you say, Standing Bear? Is this true?"

Standing Bear stared thoughtfully into the fire. The white men not only were as numerous as the blades of prairie grass, they possessed magic far beyond anything he had imagined before. They possessed the skill of putting thoughts on pieces of paper and making wires that talk and creating fire-belching black monsters that could outrun the strongest pony. They created these rifles with which the Cheyenne and the Sioux could kill a running antelope beyond reach of the strongest bowman. Was it true that the iron horse also could leap mountains, borne along by strange yellow men?

"I do not know if it is true," he said at last. He looked about the council fire at the faces of these tribal leaders and felt, inside, a sudden sense of doom. "I do not know."

Sunset Woman could not sleep. She lay awake with the man-child at her side in the buffalo robes, waiting for Standing Bear to return from the council fire. At last the flap of the lodge opened and he came in, bringing the icy air and odor of wood smoke. He stripped naked, slipped into the furs and gathered her to him.

"My lord has much on his mind."

"We have argued long at the council fire and could not find agreement. There are those who wish to widen the war and those who favor a withdrawal to the north."

"And what does Standing Bear think?"

He sighed. "I am almost ready to heed the advice of the government agents and take our people to a reservation. I see no advantage of further fighting; and it is pointless to withdraw to the north, for we will merely have new conflicts there. The buffalo herds are being driven off and destroyed. They shoot at the buffalo and elk from the iron horse, and leave the carcasses to rot. Why do they do this?"

She buried her face into his shoulder, breathing his man-smell. The sinews and muscles of his body were as familiar now as her own, and yet always wonderful and new. Each touch of him was a fresh excitement, as if for the first time. But this talk of white men and their strange ways troubled her always, and she wished they could avoid it. Vanessa felt shame for her people, but could not seem to convince him that all white men were not deceitful, greedy and wantonly cruel. "Why does the Indian torture his captives in war?" she said.

"It is the custom of certain tribes. It is often a way of letting a beaten foe display his courage before dying."

"White men call it savagery of the cruelest sort. Neither can they understand the taking of scalps."

"A scalp is a symbol. It is a symbol of a warrior's deed in battle."

She was silent. Enough of this, she thought. They must not bicker. They could not change the world. Life was too brief to waste. And suddenly, for no reason at all, this thought sent a cold ripple down her back.

"My lord"—she pressed closely to him— "you are the light of my life."

"And you," he murmured, "of mine."

The camp by the Creek-of-Many-Branches settled into sleep. From the hot ashes of the council fire a remnant of smoke curled into the night. A half-moon rose late, casting the icy landscape in bright silver. The cold deepened, so that the ponies' breaths formed ice crystals on their muzzles. The animals shifted restlessly at their hobbles. The form of a wolf glided noiselessly through the camp and vanished into a dark copse by the creek. The Sioux chief, Broken Knife, had posted two lookouts, but the cold drove them into the warmth of their blankets where they fell asleep. From the creek came an occasional sound of cracking ice. The moon arced slowly across the sky. Night held the earth in a frozen embrace.

In the dark lodge, Vanessa's eyes flew open. Her heart pounded strangely. She turned and felt the small body of

Spotted Deer. The three-year-old stirred in his sleep. She heard the rhythmic breathing of Standing Bear. Familiar shadows hovered in the lodge, silhouetted against moonlight filtering through the animal skin. Why was she alarmed? She listened intently. There was no sound beyond the breathing, the settling of ice, her own heartbeat.

"Chaaaaaaaaaarge!"

The cry had the sound of a sword blade ripping across her mind. With it came a distant rumble in the snow, the clatter of hoofbeats on ice, the whinny of horses. Men's voices bawled across her consciousness, punctuated by keening yelps that pricked at her surging fear like knifepoints. She was fighting the cumbersome buffalo robe, groping for Spotted Deer, scooping the child to her body, rolling to her feet. Standing Bear was already up, grabbing for rifle and knife. She cried, "What is it?", but he was diving headlong through the lodge opening, his naked form glistening in moonlight, a snarl of rage at his lips.

They came across the frozen creek at the gallop, shouting war whoops. Spencer rifles, fired with one hand and rhythmically recocked, poured fusillades into the lodges. Sabers flashed in the moonlight, scything down upon the first running forms that burst from the tepees. Vanessa dashed from the lodge carrying Spotted Deer, clutching a robe. Her eyes widened as she watched them come, horses and men coated in frost, broad-brimmed hats low, blue capes flying, brass buttons rippling in moonlight. Cavalry! In front, standing in the saddle of a huge black stallion, saber swinging, mouth open in full cry, charged a figure of terrible wrath. His bellow came as if from the mouth of hell: "Die, you redskinned sons of bitches! Die, you whelps of the devil! Chaaaaaaaaarge!"

More bodies burst from the lodges, tumbling and scrambling, falling in the snow. She saw the old squaw Minnow, rushing toward her through the snow and screaming something. Minnow faltered as bullets thudded into her chest; her forward motion stopped as if striking an invisible wall, her body jerking erect and vaulted backward into an explosion of snow. Screaming children dashed under the thundering hooves and went down. Warriors were cut in half by saber strokes. A pregnant squaw was shot dead by a massive trooper encased in frost. He spun his charger over her, whooped wildly, spurred the horse's bloody flanks and went barreling through a tepee roaring like a madman. From nowhere came the

flaming torches, arcing across the night sky from the hands of
galloping troopers, thumping into lodges. Tongues of fire
roared up, licking the night.

"My lord!"

He was ahead of her, shouting to a group of milling
warriors, kneeling naked in the snow and firing his single-
shot rifle into the face of a charging cavalryman. The rider
lurched backward, dead in the saddle, wrenching his galloping horse off-stride. Horse and rider somersaulted into a
blazing tepee. Standing Bear darted and dodged, knife slashing, shrieking the Cheyenne war cry. In the firelight his neck
muscles stood out like whipcords. He whirled, looking for
her. As he did so, Spotted Deer shouted, wrenched free of
Vanessa's grasp and darted across the open space toward his
father.

"Spotted Deer! Come back!" She was running, running
clumsily, still clutching the robe, floundering through the snow
on icy feet. "Spotted Deer!" A streak of silver caught the
corner of her eye. She saw him coming low on the neck of his
stallion, eyes blazing, hat brim plastered back against his
forehead in the wind. The saber rose, arced as if in slow
motion. Her legs churned with dreadful slowness through the
snow. The stallion was upon them, mouth foaming at the bit,
eyes rolling white. She had an impression of an open-mouthed
face, flushed red, splashed with freckles, and streaming red
hair beneath the hat.

A heavy form appeared, leaving its feet in a broad leap.
The body crashed into Spotted Deer, sending him flying,
rolled in the snow, came up again under the forefeet of the
stallion. The saber stroked down. A fountain of blood burst
from the half-severed torso of Standing Bear. He turned, war
cry still pouring from his mouth. His eyes found hers, locked.
He fell heavily, and the snow was flooded with scarlet. The
horseman thundered past, neither wheeling nor stopping,
intent on another target. She grabbed up Spotted Deer,
lurched back to the side of Standing Bear and sank into the
bloody snow at his side as the first sobs wracked her.

She lay there, numbed, while the slaughter advanced
onward through the camp. Finally the last shots went off
sporadically in the distance, the last screams and wails abruptly
cut off. The roaring fires died down. Still she lay with the
child at her breast, seeing nothing, clutching at him, feeling
his breathing, sensing the open watchfulness of his eyes.

Beside her, the big naked body was losing its warmth. And then there was only the sound of white men talking, and horses moving back and forth in the charred wreckage of the camp. Several times men walked past her, and one nudged at her with his boot, only to pass on. But at last, after the daylight had come, a cavalryman grabbed her by the shoulder and rolled her over. She looked up into his grizzled face, eyes glaring.

"Goddamned Cheyenne bitch..." He lifted a tomahawk to strike. A beam of sunlight flicked from a cloudbank and burst upon her hair. The tomahawk hesitated. The tobacco-stained mouth opened. "Well, I'll be blowed." The tomahawk lowered. "Hey, get General Heflin! You, soldier, go tell the general we got a white woman. We got a white woman here!"

They met in Tom Durant's private car at the railhead of the Union Pacific. Between their rival groups, Thaddeus Stewart sensed the heavy air of animosity. Opposite him across the highly polished table, Dr. Thomas Durant avoided his direct scrutiny. Grenville Dodge brooded over a lighted cigar. Brack Stewart stared past Thaddeus out the window, his face set. The black eyes had an odd, flat cast, Thaddeus thought, almost reptilian in shape. He shook his head. A trick of the light. Beside him, big Jim Strobridge returned to the subject of discussion. "Durant, we're both in real trouble unless you slow down your work gangs. Somebody's got to decide where our railheads finally join. If we can't agree like civilized men, then it's going to have to come from Washington."

Durant smirked. "We can't help it if your Chinamen lack the spunk—"

"Now hold on there!" Strobridge surged from his chair, almost knocking it over behind him.

Thaddeus placed a restraining hand on the arm of the field boss. "Cool down, Jim. That's not the way." He looked into the face of Brack Stewart, caught the black eyes and held them. "It's between you and me, isn't it?"

Brack did not reply. The eyes shifted away again, the handsome face offering a sardonic half-smile. The others grew silent, waiting for the simmering feud between the cousins either to explode or resolve itself. It did neither.

"I know what you're doing," Thaddeus said quietly. "And I promise you, cousin, I don't intend to let it go. The time will come..." But his words sounded hollow and boastful. They were not making an impression. Across the table, the Union Pacific men exchanged glances. Beside him, Charlie Crocker stirred restlessly. Thaddeus fell silent.

"We'll see," Brack Stewart said.

No one was certain, afterward, who suggested the final race for a tracklaying record. In the intensity of the moment, it literally fell onto the table, not a resolution of the conflict, but a new element of confrontation. If nothing else, it would salve the pride of both sides. The Union Pacific held the advantage. Jack Casement, Durant's tracklaying contractor, already had pushed his crews to the limit and laid eight miles of track in twenty-four hours. No track gang in railroading had ever performed at such a pace.

Durant's manner was confident. "All right, Crocker, I'll make you a deal. If your Chinamen can beat Casement's record, then we'll agree to a meeting point for the railheads. We'll send a wire to Washington"—he turned to a map spread over the conference table, and studied it for a moment—"and designate this place, here." Durant's long, bony finger tapped the map. "Promontory Point, Utah."

Crocker nodded. "Fair enough. And if we don't beat you?"

"Then you back off for a distance of one hundred miles from your present point of advance."

"A hundred miles!"

"Take it or leave it."

It was Thaddeus who spoke now, staring into the flat, black eyes and feeling the malice that radiated from them. "We'll take it." The eyes did not blink.

"Thaddeus," Crocker protested, "you can't—"

"Listen, Thaddeus," Jim Strobridge said, "a hundred miles is a fortune. You're talking about a quarter of a million dollars in cash federal loans and nearly a million acres of land grants. Hell, we'll resolve this thing in Washington and it can't make over twenty-five miles difference either way."

But Thaddeus only half-heard. Opposite him, the black eyes were filled with mockery. He heard Brack Stewart murmur, "You don't have the nerve..."

Thaddeus turned to Tom Durant. "We'll take it. But I expect from you a gentleman's wager. One hundred thousand dollars in cash payment, if we succeed."

It was Durant's turn to blanch. The Union Pacific vice-president seemed confused. His mouth worked, but no sound came out.

Now it was Brack who spoke.

"Done."

The meeting ended. Thaddeus led his companions Strobridge and Charlie Crocker to their waiting stagecoach. They climbed aboard and the driver lashed the horses into motion. "Yaaah!" The barren, dusty Utah landscape rolled past as they rocked westward.

"You've really put us on the line, Thaddeus," Charlie Crocker said. "I don't know what Stanford and the others are going to think about this." He mopped sweat from his face. "I just don't know what they're going to think." He hummed nervously, deep in his throat.

Three days later, at the railhead of the Central Pacific, Jim Strobridge glowered at Thaddeus's map and spat a stream of tobacco juice. "We might just beat the sons of bitches. What does Shingling say?"

Thaddeus smiled, despite his misgivings. Strobridge's fighting blood was up. When the field boss meant business, his face flushed and his bellow strengthened. Thaddeus folded the map and returned it to its leather case. The case was now worn and creased from more than six hundred and fifty miles of railroad building, from the Sierra crossing to the Great Salt Lake Desert, rugged badlands and endless plains. "Shingling says his men are ready. He says no problem."

"No problem, no problem. Did you ever hear that Chinaman say anything else?"

Thaddeus shook his head. "Come to think of it, I never did."

Charlie Crocker was still dubious. "It's going to take every bit of grit we've got. Jack Casement's boys damned near ate up the clock laying their eight miles of track last month. They started at three o'clock in the morning and kept going till midnight."

"Thaddeus has got a plan," Strobridge said.

"What kind of a plan? A miracle?"

"Organization, Charlie," Thaddeus replied softly. "Organization."

"Humph. We'll see."

They watched a grumbling Charlie Crocker ride away in the sunlight on a big dappled mare. "You've bit off a chaw this time, Thaddeus," Strobridge muttered.

He did not reply, but thought, Maybe you're right. Maybe I'm putting too much confidence in Shingling's gangs. But, my God, who would have expected those men to build so much track in less than a year?

And what a year they had just completed!

It was now the spring of 1869. In the spring of 1868 they had finally gotten across those damned mountains and Charlie Crocker had sent off his jubilant telegram from the raw plank town of Reno: "The track is connected." At the same time, Mark Hopkins and his accountants had announced that Central Pacific at last was turning a profit.

All this, plus the gentle terrain over which they worked after leaving the mountains, had spurred Shingling's tracklayers to spectacular feats. After crossing the biggest bend of the Truckee River, one hundred and eighty-nine miles from Sacramento, they had barreled toward the northeast across the Great Salt Lake Desert, one hundred and thirty miles of sand, sagebrush and alkaline deposits. Strobridge and Shingling drove the crews. Supply trains chuffed over open track around the clock carrying every scrap of material they required, from iron rails to great vats of drinking water and mountains of Chinese vegetables. To Thaddeus, the landscape had been haunting in its emptiness. To the south, a range of mountains made a blue haze on the horizon; to the north, ahead of this strange army of six thousand sweating men, lay a line of bleak hills. For a hundred miles there wasn't a drop of water to be had. "In this country," drawled Strobridge, "a jackrabbit's got to carry a canteen."

And yet, the rhythm of construction had quickened. The gangs moved with machine precision: five men to the five-hundred-pound rail, thirty spikes to the rail, three blows to the spike, two pairs of rails to the minute, four hundred rails to the mile. Their route was littered with the bones of animals left by the forty-niners. They'd worked through the terrible country west of where the Humboldt River, reduced to a trickle, simply vanished into the sand. From Wadsworth east for five hundred miles, there wasn't a tree. As summer waned into autumn, and cooler winds moaned across the wasteland, they had been pushing as much as six miles of track a day. By the end of December, the railhead spawned a new town of tents and board shacks.

"What's the name of this place, Mr. Stewart?"

"It's called Elko."

"Where the hell are we?"

"We're four hundred and seventy miles east of Sacramento and three-fourths of the way across Nevada."

"Well, I'll be damned."

And so winter had passed into spring. Five men to the five-hundred-pound rail, thirty spikes to the rail, three blows to the spike...

"Where do we link up with the Union Pacific?"

"It hasn't been decided."

"Somebody had better decide something. Our advance grading crews are looking down the Union Pacific's throat now. Crocker says there'll be trouble if they start grading side by side in opposite directions."

And there was trouble. Thaddeus galloped forward on horseback with picked men. Union Pacific grading gangs had set deliberate powder blasts near the Chinese crews. One Central Pacific workman was dead, several injured. Small groups of rival laborers had fought with fists and axe handles. Thaddeus met with the Union Pacific crew chief, a hostile Irishman named Crafton, and the two almost came to blows. He returned in an angry mood.

"What we do, Misser Stewart?"

"We'll light some black powder under their asses, too."

Shingling smiled broadly. "You bet!"

The Chinese had set multiple charges and timed the blasts for maximum fright, without injury. The sudden retaliation startled Union Pacific crews. Crafton and his men looked across in astonishment at a mass of Chinese workmen standing resolutely, armed with pick handles. The Union Pacific men had lost heart. The blastings stopped.

A telegraph message had arrived from Durant, inviting them to the meeting in his private car. Thus, the stage was set, and the confrontation between Thaddeus and Brack Stewart joined.

"Where is Promontory Point on the map, Strobridge?"

"Right here, at this spot."

"There's nothing there but rocks and sagebrush."

"There'll be one other thing, Thaddeus."

"What?"

"A railroad."

*   *   *

Brack Stewart's discovery was purely accidental, one of those fortuitous bursts of insight that open whole new paths of interest. He just happened to be passing through Pittsburgh, just happened to inquire about his mother's side of the family (Brack always drew this distinction with the Stewarts, that the Pittsburgh people were Maybelle's relatives and not really his own, because he recognized no formal kinships), and just happened to learn about a ne'er-do-well cousin, John Colby Stewart. The word came from the aunt of a business associate. She was one of those gossipy, disapproving old maids who lived alone in a great, musty house and tended to her store of malicious tidbits as lovingly as she did her African violets. "Scandalous! Positively scandalous, that child. Always in trouble with the law. Runs with the most unsavory people, cutthroats and thieves and the like. He deserted from the army. Oh, the constables know all about John Colby Stewart." She pursed her lips righteously. "They say he absolutely despises his cousin Thaddeus, would cut his heart out given half a chance." Other inquiries, of course, tended to substantiate her story. By the time Brack left Pittsburgh he had acquired a fascinating picture of this depraved, and murderous kinsman.

It was impossible to say precisely at what point the knowledge began to develop into a plan. Information was power, but worthless if not exercised. Brack had never been the type to do violence against another. It was one thing to best an opponent by business means—even chicanery—but quite another to plot his bodily harm. At first, the idea was simply too brazen to contemplate. Brack thrust it to the back of his mind. But as rivalry intensified between the Union Pacific and the Central Pacific, and Thaddeus emerged as his most troublesome nemesis, Brack pondered afresh the possibility of extreme measures. Naively, Thaddeus Stewart had not hesitated to help grease the palms of corrupt congressmen to win a more generous railroad act; but now, in the name of integrity he threatened Brack's enterprise, the Credit Mobilier. A stupid remark by Thaddeus in the wrong circles could blow the whole thing. As if this weren't nuisance enough, the man was spurring construction of the Central Pacific at a pace that would cost Brack and his associates a fortune, simply by snatching it from their hands.

Thus, by a series of rationalities, Brack Stewart was able to convince himself that the world would be better off without

Thaddeus. All he needed was the instrument of his rival's demise; and what better instrument could be desired than Thaddeus's own hate-filled cousin, John Colby Stewart? This point crystallized in Brack's mind after he received word that the renegade kinsman had turned up briefly in St. Joseph, Missouri, and was heading west. Brack alerted his network of information sources at helltowns and trading posts. A few weeks later, John Colby and several surviving companions arrived at General Heflin's headquarters to report an attack by the Cheyenne. Brack was able to make contact.

There came at last a blustery evening when a shadowy horseman arrived at Brack Stewart's private railroad car. The meeting was not notable for cordiality on either side. John Colby was a bloated, unkempt ruffian whose presence offended Brack's fastidious sensitivities. Brack thought, Lord, how did this family ever breed such a specimen? He managed to mask his dislike with a veneer of sociability while deftly sounding out, over whiskeys, the depths of John Colby's hatreds. The mention of Thaddeus's name brought a foxy glint to the bloodshot eyes. After two more whiskeys, Brack's visitor muttered darkly, "If I could get that bastard in range..." John Colby's right hand strayed to the butt of the pistol loosely holstered in a fold of grimy brown leather at his side.

"Perhaps if the two of you got together, you could work something out," Brack suggested evenly, "come to some mutual accord."

"Sure." John Colby drank again. His face was flushed, eyes reddened. He wore an expression of brute cunning. "But where am I supposed to find him?"

Brack leaned forward and filled the glass with another shot of hundred-proof whiskey. "I know exactly where he'll be one week from today..."

Fifteen minutes later, John Colby Stewart lurched into the night from the private car, cradling a half-empty bottle of whiskey and muttering to himself: "Kill the son of a bitch. Kill the son of a bitch."

He was quite drunk.

Central Pacific's big work engine *Jupiter* panted in predawn darkness. The railhead was poised just fourteen miles from Promontory Point. A group of Union Pacific officials, including Vice-President Durant and Chief Engineer Dodge, arrived by carriage and shared breakfast with Crocker, Thaddeus, Strobridge, and others. Durant, elegantly dressed and super-cilious of manner, trimmed a cigar and sipped scalding coffee. "Your Chinese will never pull it off, Stewart."

"We'll see."

"I'm sorry that you threw in your lot with this California crowd. We could have used your engineering talents. That would have harnessed Stewart family talents nicely, don't you think? Yours and Brack's..."

Thaddeus and Charlie Crocker exchanged glances. The portly contractor cleared his throat. "Sorry to intrude, Durant. But it's almost time."

Thaddeus left the table and hurried through the brightening morning to where Shingling had marshaled his workmen and was lecturing them in Chinese. Thaddeus quickly checked over equipment and rolling stock, glanced at his watch, eyed the eastern horizon and its spread of rosy light. Finally the gangs were mustered at the railhead, *Jupiter* blew its steady rhythm of steam, the spectators were arrayed in carriages alongside. Jim Strobridge stood in the cab of *Jupiter* with a hand on the whistle cord, eyeing his watch. At the click of seven, he yanked the cord and *Jupiter*'s steam whistle shrieked across the morning.

Shingling's work gangs sprang to action. Unloaders leaped onto waiting flatcars to hurl down iron rails, bundles of fishplates, keg loads of spikes and shackle bolts. Iron clanged. Already the right-of-way stretched ahead of them was strewn with ties, placed there by an advance party the previous day. Each flatcar bore sixteen rails and the supplies to lay them. Track gangs grabbed rails and rushed ahead at the trot. Behind them came spike-setters and sledgehammer wielders. Five men to the rail, thirty spikes to the rail, three blows to the spike... *Plang! Plang! Plang!* Sixteen flatcars waited, enough for two miles of track, and five loaded trains stood ready on the main line and sidings. A squadron of two-horse teams moved ahead, aligning ties. Sixteen flatcars were cleared in nine minutes; the train chuffed back to a siding and another came up. A portable track gauge set the rails at precisely four feet, eight and one-half inches apart. Each rail was down in thirty seconds. Spike men followed, eight to a rail, with a gang to set, a gang to finish spiking, a gang to tighten down bolts on the fishplates at rail joints. Behind them came the track levelers, hoisting up ties, shoveling dirt under the ties to bring them level. And at the end of the line, like a great human centipede on iron feet, came four hundred tampers, their tamping bars thumping down the earthen fill. The whole, from first tiesetter to last tamper, stretched two miles.

"My God, I've never seen such organization," said a cavalry officer. "It's an army, moving over the ground and leaving track."

Thaddeus hurried along the line, troubleshooting here, checking work there. The route now followed a gentle, curving rise which necessitated an extra process of rail-bending and slowed the work. Each rail now had to be placed in blocks and hammered to the curve.

He did not notice the arrival of the two men on horseback. They were trail-worn, their faces bearded and clothing dusty. A foremen came to him. "Thaddeus, there's a fellow here asking for you. I told him you were busy, but he says it's urgent. Says he's a relative of yours."

"A relative?" Thaddeus looked up from his chart, following the foreman's pointing finger. The men wore their hats low. His glance took in loose, black suits, high boots, holstered pistols slung low and tied at the thighs. Even from this distance there was an air of menace about them. His senses flashed a warning. The shorter of the men looked vaguely familiar, but the hard shadows of midday sunlight made recognition difficult. "I'll come," he said.

As he walked along the track, favoring his hip with the cane, the shorter of the men approached him a few paces and stopped planting his feet in an aggressive stance. The man's right hand hung loosely at the holster, as if ready to draw the pistol. Thaddeus recognized it as a heavy Colt model.

"Yes?" he called. Behind him, another train chugged forward and there were sounds of clanging iron, chattering workmen, tamping and spiking. "Are you looking for me?" He was five paces away when the man pushed his hat back and Thaddeus looked into the face of John Colby Stewart.

"Hello, cousin." The voice had a curious rasping sound and the mouth did not smile. "I see you're one of the big dogs around here."

"John Colby! My word, what are you doing here?" Confused, Thaddeus broke stride. John Colby Stewart? How many years had it been? He searched his mind for something to say. "Are you working on the railroad?" It was a stupid question. Of course John Colby wasn't working on the railroad. At least, not this railroad.

"Not exactly, Cousin Thaddeus." Deliberately, the right hand grasped the handle of the pistol and drew it free of the holster. The black metal gleamed dully in the sunlight. "I've come to kill you."

Thaddeus stopped walking, looking dumbly at the muzzle of the pistol. His mouth worked soundlessly. Then he heard himself saying, "But... but this is ridiculous. Why? This is a joke. Are you pulling one of your jokes, John Colby?"

They had drawn attention. Several men turned to watch, their faces blank with surprise. John Colby's companion seemed equally at a loss, struck by the audacity of the move. Thaddeus saw that the companion had stopped walking and was backing away toward a pair of saddle horses.

"The joke's on you, Thaddeus. That's what it all comes down to. The joke's on you."

The pistol rode the hand solidly. A thumb lifted, drew the hammer back. Thaddeus saw the chamber of the gun turning with the cocking hammer. His stomach tightened. His brain tumbled with thoughts, none of them making sense. Instinctively, he gauged the distance between them. He spoke rapidly, forcing himself to smile. "You always were a devil, John Colby..." He stepped closer.

"Get on your knees."

"...Always a card."

"I said, 'Get on your knees!'" The words spat out. The eyes were flat. "I want you to get on your knees and beg!"

Thaddeus moved forward another step, still talking, pretending not to hear. Madness blazed from the once handsome face, and there was no mistaking it. He had seen such a light in the eyes of Ruth, long ago. If he could just get within range.

The shot startled him. The hand had moved the pistol slightly, firing aslant and upward. Thaddeus felt the bullet nick his left ear and rip off his hat. He felt the trickle of warm blood. He smelled burnt gunpowder. He stopped walking and stared into John Colby's face. Suddenly, the confusion and nervousness had left him and he was calm. It was a calmness of certainty that the next shot would not stray.

"You go to hell, John Colby," he said.

The pistol lifted, aiming at a point between his eyes. The

hammer was pulled. He watched the finger tighten on the trigger...

A blow struck John Colby from the rear. It was a heavy, hollow sound. The pistol jerked and the shot caromed off the great boiler of the engine *Jupiter* behind Thaddeus. John Colby still stood, his bearded face frozen in surprise. And then he pitched forward onto the iron rail. A heavy pick was buried to the haft in his back.

Shingling had hurled it from ten feet away.

Men crowded in around Thaddeus, speaking in a babble. But even as the questions poured in upon him, the whistle-blast of *Jupiter* stilled the tumult. They looked up and saw Strobridge standing on top of the cab, glowering down, fists on hips. The field boss's voice came down with the power of a foghorn. "You men get back to work. We've got a race to win!"

The gangs moved back to their task. The rhythm resumed, in clangs and train noises and hammer beats. Thaddeus stood in the blazing sunshine looking down at the body of John Colby. His mind wondered. Why? A bulky figure came to his side, nudged the body with the toe of his boot and beckoned to several idle laborers. "Let's get this trash picked up," Charlie Crocker growled. "Haul it over there and bury it." He grasped Thaddeus by the arm. "Come on, Stewart. We've got a railroad to build."

The pace picked up. The morning gangs refused to be spelled, and so worked doggedly through the afternoon. *Clank! Bang! Pink! Bang! Pink!* Five men to the rail, thirty spikes to the rail, three blows to the spike...

At the click of seven, twelve hours after it had begun, *Jupiter's* whistle shrieked again. The work stopped. The gangs relaxed. The sweat was wiped. The sun settled. Big Jim Strobridge checked his charts, conferred with the gang foreman and Shingling, climbed back to the top of the locomotive cab. The crowd pressed around *Jupiter*, waiting for the word. Strobridge finished scribbling his notes, looked sternly down at them and announced: "The Central Pacific today laid ten miles and fifty-six feet of track in exactly twelve hours. And that's a record nobody can beat!"

Cheers rolled in volleys over the dry, harsh land.

*   *   *

May 10, 1869. At half past noon at Promontory Point, Utah, the golden spike was about to be driven linking the American continent by rail from coast to coast. A crowd gathered around two locomotives facing each other at the railhead. A nervous signal operator mopped sweat from his face and tapped out Morse Code to the nation's telegraphers: "To everybody. Keep quiet. When the last spike is driven we will say 'done.' Don't break the circuit, but watch for the signals of the blows of the hammer." (Silence.) "Almost ready. Hats off. Prayer is being offered." (Silence.) "We have got done praying. The spike is about to be presented." (Pause.) "All ready now." (Pause.) "Done!"

Across America, church bells rang. In New York, Philadelphia, Washington, Chicago, and San Francisco, roars of celebration erupted from waiting throngs. On New York's Hudson River, boats clanged their bells and loosed whistle blasts. Francesca Stewart stepped onto the verandah of her riverfront mansion, a newspaper in hand, and frowned. "The damned fools."

In Manhattan, Brack Stewart stood at the window of his corner office suite overlooking Fifth Avenue, smiled broadly and lit a cigar. Credit Mobilier had milked the Union Pacific of twenty-seven million dollars in clear profit on contracts to build eleven hundred miles of railroad from Omaha to Promontory Point. Brack had bought up vast land tracts along the route, creating his own thriving Amalgamated Land & Trust Company. His personal wealth now exceeded twelve million dollars. "Thank you, Cousin Thaddeus," he said softly.

In St. Joseph, Stephen Stewart put his arm around Catherine Bradley and Colette. The death of John Colby had come as a bitter blow, but the last of many involving this strange and wayward son. "I'm torn, Stephen," Catherine said, "between despair for him and joy for Thaddeus. But what's worst of all, I . . . I feel no grief."

At Promontory Point, Thaddeus stood with Jim Strobridge watching the celebration. He found no joy in it. John Colby's death had left him numbed. In emotional suspension, he had gone through the motions of the last tracklaying drive to Promontory Point, picking at the pieces of his memory. What had he done wrong? Could the tragedy have been averted? But he knew that nothing would have changed things. Shingling had saved his life. In recognition of this, Strobridge had recommended to the company that Shingling be made track maintenance foreman for the entire line. It was a timely event for the Chinaman, who was soon to marry his adoring Lotus. For Thaddeus, however, it all came pouring in on tides of remorse and guilt. He had telegraphed the news of John Colby's death to Stephen and Catherine, followed by two letters. But it seemed so perfunctory. Now that this golden spike was driven, he would go there, face them, try to explain how their eldest son had perished. In this dark mood, he pondered the twists his life had taken. He thought of Ruth, and the gulf of silence there. He thought of Marguerite, and the ache in his heart to see her again. He thought of Ted Judah, the dead engineer who should have been standing in his shoes today.

"This is history in the making, Stewart." Charlie Crocker clapped him on the shoulder. "It's a great day for America!"

Abruptly, Crocker's buoyance lifted him. It was true. This was a great day for America. A new era was opening, overwhelming everything else. By comparison, his petty broodings were nothing. Thaddeus turned to Strobridge and forced a smile. "It took my Aunt Maybelle six months to get to California by wagon train, with people dying along the way. The fastest clipper ship, my Cousin Drake's *Typhoon*, was three months sailing around the Horn. And now, New York to San Francisco in six days! Can you believe that, Strobridge?"

The big field boss nodded, eyeing him sharply.

"And it's merely the beginning, Stewart," he said. "This is merely the beginning."

XX

Congressman Pennington was ill at ease. Vanessa saw it in his eyes. Pale eyes they were, restless. The chairman of the House Subcommittee on Indian Affairs had not attained his position by strength of personality. The matter was too delicate in Congress for that. He attained it for being nonaggressive. Thus did Washington confer its small fiefdoms. By now, Vanessa was recognizing the pattern. There was no avenue in Congress for meaningful complaint about the ill-treatment of Indians. Nevertheless, for the tenth time in a week, she repeated her demand.

"I want a congressional investigation of the massacre at the Creek-of-Many-Branches. General Peter Heflin is a murderer and must be called to account for his slaughter of more than three hundred helpless men, women and children in that camp. The raid was unprovoked and uncalled for. I am willing to testify precisely to what went on there."

"Miss Stewart, please. You are asking the impossible. General Heflin is a highly respected soldier. He has served his country faithfully and well." The congressman was a slender, fussy man with pasty features and thinning hair. He suffered from an ulcer. His wife was unfaithful. He was deeply in debt. He did not intend to compound his troubles by taking on the cause of this young woman, however striking she may be. "The General has . . . has very important friends in Washington. No. It is out of the question."

"But I've told you what they did."

"Yes, I've already heard that."

"They attacked the camp without warning, crept up on it when everyone was asleep, and systematically murdered every man, woman and child."

"Except you and your son."

"We were spared because I'm white."

"Yes." He dragged out the word, giving it significance. "Yesss." His fingers fiddled with a paper on his desk. His eyes hooded slightly. "Miss Stewart, this Indian with whom you were living, he was not your husband?"

"No."

"He did not, er, force his intentions upon you?"—he licked his upper lip— "That is to say . . ."

"No, he did not, Congressman. I went to him of my own free will."

"I see." Pennington sighed. "And you had a child by this Indian, a son. And you lived with him openly without fear of censure. You would have had, I presume, other children by him?"

"I would have hoped to, yes."

The congressman settled back in his chair, waved a pale hand. "Well, there you have it, Miss, uh, Stewart."

"Have what, Congressman?"

"Any testimony you give would be regarded as totally without merit. Decent people—I mean to say, respectable people—would give your words no credence. Do you see what I mean? It would be a waste of your time, my time, the subcommittee's time." Seeing the anger kindling in her eyes, he drew out his pocket watch, snapped it open, stood up. "Now, if you don't mind . . ."

"Congressman Pennington . . ."

"Miss Stewart, I'm sorry. There is *nothing* I can do."

She walked out of his office into the marble corridor, where her mother waited with the child. Maybelle Stewart saw the expression on Vanessa's face and checked an impulse to embrace her. "Rejected again, eh?"

Vanessa compressed her lips and nodded. Her hair, beneath the black Parisian hat, had a golden tinge. Her eyes were an intense violet hue. Male passersby stared openly. Maybelle felt a surge of pride, thinking, Eat your hearts out, men. She fell into step, leading the child by the hand. He was a grave, dark boy with handsome features and strangely violet eyes. "Come, Van," she said.

They walked into the morning sunlight and descended the great steps of the Capitol. Before them, the green mall swept away toward the Washington Monument, flanked by flower beds. The summer sky was spotted with coasting clouds. "Washington is lovely when it's in a sunny mood," Maybelle said.

Vanessa was not listening. "I'm not going to be beaten, Mother," she said. "I'm not going to roll over like a dog and say, 'That's that. Sorry, Standing Bear. I tried.'"

"Of course not," Maybelle said.

"I've knocked on every door that I could find—bureaucrats, congressmen, your friends in the California delegation. Always it's the same thing. They're sorry. They would like to help. But General Heflin is a hero. General Heflin has important friends. Besides, we are at war with the Indians. The Sioux, Cheyenne, and Arapaho have committed too many crimes against white people to merit any sympathy in Washington . . ."

Maybelle listened in silence. It was better, she thought to

let Vanessa talk it out. Her own feelings were mixed. She could not have loved an Indian. It had appalled her, at first, to think that Vanessa's outrage and rebellion could go this far. But then, looking into her own past, Maybelle could see things more clearly. Vanessa was headstrong, vigorously independent. These were Stewart traits, which made them mixed blessings. She came from stubborn stock, this young woman whose beauty was such that it took people's breath away. She insisted, foremost, on being herself. And for what reason had Maybelle seen to her education and upbringing, if not to assert herself and her own values? The Indian Standing Bear had attracted Vanessa for reasons other than rebellion. Maybelle was now convinced of this. This dead Indian must have been a unique man indeed, to so captivate this daughter of the plainsman Van Harrison. Maybelle wished now, wished devoutly now, that she could have met the Indian, talked with him. She smiled ruefully. Hell, she would have brought him to the mansion on Nob Hill for a dinner party. And why not . . . ?

"Mother, why are you smiling?"

They were in a hansom cab now, riding along Pennsylvania Avenue. Everywhere, new government buildings—those massive bureaucratic mausoleums spawned in postwar prosperity—were under construction, raising dust and clatter. Maybelle fanned herself in irritation. Lord, would they never stop building this city? "I was just thinking," she said, "about little Van Harrison's education." She put her arm around the quiet boy. The name change had been her suggestion. They couldn't go on forever calling the child Spotted Deer. Van Harrison Stewart. Yes, that had a strong ring. "I think we should begin preparing him for Oxford, don't you? His great-uncle Nathan went there. And I'm sure he'll be the first Cheyenne Indian to graduate."

"Mother!" Vanessa spoke with mock vexation. For the first time that day, a smile softened her face. She looked at Maybelle and the boy, and the violet eyes were suddenly shining. "I think that would be a wonderful idea."

Later, as they arrived in the lobby of the Willard Hotel, Vanessa came to her ultimate decision. She stopped in her tracks and grasped Maybelle by the arm. "I'm going to see President Grant."

"President Grant! But Vanessa . . ."

"Yes. That's exactly what I'm going to do."

*   *   *

He was much shorter in stature than Vanessa had imagined
he would be. Ulysses S. Grant, commanding general of the
Union Army, conqueror of the Confederacy, now entering his
third year as the eighteenth President, was only an inch taller
than she herself. Moreover, he spoke softly and already was
being chastised by critics as a weak chief executive. But his
eyes seemed frank and sympathetic. As sunbeams stole through
banks of windows into his White House office, Grant listened
intently to what Vanessa had to say. When she had finished
speaking, he stroked his dark whiskers thoughtfully. "And this
is the boy?" he asked, looking kindly at Spotted Deer. "This is
your son?"

"Yes, Mr. President."

"A fine-looking lad. I know you're proud of him."

Vanessa searched the bearded face for a sign of double
meaning, saw none, smiled. "I am proud of him. He is
his father's child, and will grow to be his own man."

Grant looked at Vanessa, at Maybelle Stewart and nodded.
"Yes, I can see that." He rocked back in his chair and glanced
idly out the window as if to gather his thoughts. From this
angle, Vanessa was impressed by his youthful appearance as
well. And then she remembered that at the age of forty-six,
Ulysses S. Grant was the youngest man yet to be elected
President. But he was aging rapidly, she thought. They all
did.

"We're a growing, restless country, Miss Stewart," he
mused. "Out there, beyond those windows, America is forty
million people. We have just come through a dreadful ordeal
of war. And even as we try to heal the wounds there, and
redress the terrible lot of more than four million people who
until recently were held in slavery, we are pressured to come
to terms with multiple changes in other ways, too. Your
own sex is pushing for the vote, and leaders of women's
suffrage will not rest until they ahcieve it. American labor is
restless and organizing into unions; there are those who see
this as anticapital, anti-free enterprise, unpatriotic—indeed,
little short of anarchy. There is public scandal at large; greedy
men without principles feel they have license to plunder the
public treasury and private trust." His eye flicked to the two
women and the child. "And the Indian issue is terribly

complex, terribly difficult to resolve. These, too, are a people who have been plundered and whose status is unresolved. I don't know if we will ever resolve it, really; for where does fairness and probity lie, when a primitive people, as wild and free as the land upon which they roam and hunt, stand in the path of civilization? I honestly don't know. I know that we have attempted to arbitrate our differences with the tribes, but without success. And I know that few men in public life today will take up the cause of the Indian—an enormously unpopular stand anywhere in this country, especially west of the Mississippi—and see it through. To do so is to court political disaster."

Vanessa's heart sank. All this was nothing new. Others had said the same thing, in one way or another. But for some reason it had a ring of terrible finality when said by this man, who held the ultimate power to shape forces and events. What a fool she had been! How naive to think that even a President could wave his scepter and turn the tides of power. Power was too diffuse, too subtle and too complex a force for that.

"As for Peter Heflin, of course, I know the man well. He was one of my best cavalry generals during the war. In the field, he is an aggressive, committed soldier who does not hesitate to place himself in jeopardy at the head of his troops. I could, as Commander in Chief, simply strip him of command and order him home. Or I could kick him upstairs, give him another star and a desk job. But on what basis? The complaint of one white woman who bore a child by an Indiana chief whom Heflin killed?" Grant's eyes locked into her as he spoke, and something in the manner of the man made it clear that he spoke not in deference to Heflin but as a military and political realist. "My own adversaries, not to mention the press, would be screaming for my scalp."

He paused. The silence was intensified by the ticking of a heavy mantel clock. Vanessa whispered, "Yes, Mr. President."

Grant smiled. "On the other hand, Miss Stewart, public opinion can be a tremendous force in this republic. Public opinion sometimes can move mountains that no politician, not even a President, can budge." He reached for a pad and pencil and scribbled a note at his desk. "I don't want to leave you totally without recourse. There is a possibility, a slim possibility . . . Well, I'm going to pass this along to one of my aides with a suggestion that he follow up in an unofficial way

I don't know if it will work, or if you will care to follow
through. But someone will be calling on you at the Willard in
the next few days to discuss a possible alternative. Considering the delicacy of my, uh, position, I don't care to elaborate
further. And what you do about it is your own business.
Agreed?"

Vanessa nodded, heavy-hearted. "Agreed."

The President saw them to the door. He tousled the black
hair of the child Spotted Deer and looked thoughtfully into
the striking violet eyes. "I have a feeling, my young friend,"
he said softly, "that someday you will shake the world."

As they walked from the front portico of the White House
to the waiting carriage on Pennsylvania Avenue, Maybelle
asked, "What did he mean by that?"

Vanessa was preoccupied. "I haven't the slightest idea."

His name was Meriwether Crandon Putt. He was tall,
elegantly turned out in dark suit, soft hat, pearl gray vest,
trim mustache and silver-headed walking stick. He handed
his card to Maybelle. It identified him as a writer for Frank
Leslie's *Illustrated Weekly*. A short time later, over tea in the
sumptuous surroundings of the Willard suite, Vanessa was
dubious.

"Mr. Crandon, I really don't think..."

"Putt. Meriwether Crandon Putt. I see that you don't read
the *Illustrated Weekly*, Miss Stewart."

"Well, no. That is, I seldom read the journals."

"Quite understandable. Considering some of the writing
talent"—he sniffed delicately—"I can't say that I blame you."

"Yes. But I am curious to know how you found me, Mr.
Putt."

"Let us say that I have, er, certain contacts on the White
House staff. Very low-level, of course. Nonetheless, they do
provide me with some interesting leads from time to time."

"Oh?" Vanessa's eyes widened. "I see."

Putt was a skillful conversationalist and amiable personality. He spoke of the *Illustrated Weekly*, a journal with one of
the nation's largest circulations. He talked of his travels in the
West and articles about Indians. He had known, he said,
offhandedly, many of the Cheyenne. Vanessa's skepticism
began to fade. Gradually, almost imperceptibly, the conversation shifted to herself and her own experiences. She was not

conscious of what point Putt drew out his pencil and notebook. Suddenly it was there and he was scribbling as she
spoke; but quickly she adapted to this, too. And then,
without really knowing why, she was telling it—all of it—from
the decision to follow the cold trail of her dead father to her
arrival at the camp of the Shemkuk Cheyenne and her love
affair with Standing Bear. She spoke of his leadership, his
desire to be at peace with the white man, his battle to the
death with Black Feather. The pencil scribbled vigorously.
She described the birth of Spotted Deer, the attack on the
camp at Creek-of-Many-Branches, the massacre of the Shemkuk
tribe.

When she was done, a heavy quiet settled over them.
Merwether Crandon Putt picked up his cup of cold tea, his
hand trembling with suppressed excitement. "Sensational,"
he murmured, sipping distractedly. "Absolutely sensational."

The story of Sunset Woman fell like a bombshell upon the
nation's journal readers. Never had the *Illustrated Weekly*
enjoyed such a surge of single-copy sales. In New York,
Washington, Boston, Pittsburgh, Louisville, St. Louis, New
Orleans—wherever the magazine was sold—it was the stuff of
parlor debate and back-fence gossip. From the pulpit, ministers deplored the scarlet-haired woman who had lived in sin
with the heathen, bore his half-breed child out of wedlock
and then boasted about it. In New York, suffragettes paraded
in front of City Hall bearing placards demanding "Rights for
Vanessa," while feminist speakers urged the vote to give
women a voice in treatment of the Indians. Populists and
radicals called for a court-martial of Peter Heflin, while con-
servatives hailed him as "The Hero of the Indian Wars" and
demanded that Congress give him the Congressional Medal
of Honor. Accompanying the article was an artist's drawing in
the stunning likeness of Vanessa. So accurately was she
depicted that it became necessary for her to wear a veil in
public, to guard against recognition.

Official Washington welcomed the newest sensation as a
departure from a rising campaign in the public press against
corruption and thievery in public office. Newspaper accounts
of scandal ranged across such juicy targets as Boss Tweed,
whose Tammany empire was crumbling in New York City, to
new rumors of massive profiteering by the Credit Mobilier in
constructing the Union Pacific Railroad. The name of a
financial mystery man, Brack Stewart, kept popping up as the

diabolical manipulator of this monster, whose tentacles reached into the halls of Congress itself. No one made the connection between Vanessa Stewart and Brack, and even journalist Putt would have been aghast had he known they were brother and sister.

But if Vanessa had expected that her notoriety would awaken public conscience, her hopes were quickly dashed. In the wake of Putt's article and numerous adaptations by other newspapers, every government official she now attempted to see was unavailable, out of the city, busy in all-day hearings, not feeling well. The social circle of Washington, in which Vanessa and Maybelle had previously moved with the ease of wealth and powerful California connections, now seethed with gossip and ridicule. She began to feel the sting at parties from the dart of acid tongues: "My dear, what's it like wallowing on the ground like an animal?" and, "Is it true that Indians never bathe?" and, "When are you going to the reservation?" Very soon, invitations no longer came. And those women whom Vanessa naively had come to regard as friends avoided the taint of her company.

"We'll go back to San Francisco where we belong," Maybelle fumed. "There's no point in beating our heads against the wall here."

"I can't give up, Mother.. I'm going to keep on trying. Surely there's someone in this city, somewhere, who will see the evil that's been done and try to correct it."

Two days later, in the middle of the afternoon, there was a knock at the door of their suite. Vanessa answered it and found a well-dressed, roundfaced man of medium height and a manner of calm self-assurance.

He removed his hat. "Miss Vanessa Stewart?"

"Yes."

He smiled. "I'm Senator Poindexter Carp. May I come in?"

They came for him shortly after dawn, two United States marshals and a uniformed constable of the New York police. "Gentlemen, really," he began, "must we have all this display..?" But the cold eyes touched his heart and stilled the words. It would do no good complaining. Brack Stewart went to the hallway mirror, adjusted his cravat, put on his hat—a new silk topper, at the peak of style—and walked out into the gray morning flanked by his resolute escorts.

A mob packed the hearing room on the second floor of New York's old City Hall building. Eager journalists, black-garbed like birds of prey, crowded long tables set up along the barrier railing. As members of the congressional committee took their places and lawyers pawed through stacks of legal briefs, Brack sat in the witness chair thinking, My word, it's an inquisition.

The room was stuffy and he dabbed at his forehead with a handkerchief already soggy from use. In the audience he made out a few familiar faces of old financial associates, but they seemed to avoid his eyes. Indeed, the only friends he had in the entire world, it appeared, were the hired lawyers of Credit Mobilier.

One of the journalists unfolded a newspaper and the black headline splashed across his field of vision. "Credit Mobilier Mastermind on the Griddle."

A gavel sounded. A voice intoned, "These proceedings will come to order. Mr. Secretary, please call the roll of the committee." And it began.

Long afterward, Brack's memory would remain a clutter of disjointed impressions. They would come to haunt him in dreams: the accusative tones of committeemen, the guarded advice of lawyers at his ear, the never-ending questions, questions, questions...

"Mr. Stewart, what motivated you to incorporate the Credit Mobilier? Was it your intention to defraud the Union Pacific Railroad? How came it, Mr. Stewart, that there was no staff review of purchase orders and cost overruns? Are you telling this committee that the Union Pacific Railroad did not put out these supply contracts on competitive bidding?"

And when the questions were not being directed at him, they were addressed to others who took their turns in the witness chair. He listened incredulously to the questioning of railroad directors, executives and accountants; heard the implications of bribery of congressmen and other public officials, and felt with a sickening dread the relentless weaving of a set of circumstances designed to entrap and enmesh one man, and one alone: himself. Each fresh revelation of scandal sent journalists rushing from the hearing room to hand their notes to runners waiting outside, stirred the excited murmurs of audience response and brought the banging gavel and the chairman's hoarse command, "Order! Order, I say!"

Ultimately, the hearings ran their course, the public's lust for scandal was temporarily sated, the stories of Brack Stewart and his ring of thieves moved off the front pages. There were those, including congressmen who had profited by their own generous stock holdings in Credit Mobilier, who commiserated. "Frankly, old man, I think you're being thrown to the mob to appease them. There's so much in the public eye right now. The Navy Department is selling business to contractors, enriching Secretary Benson. Interior is conniving with land speculators. Swindle, in and out of government, is the order of the day. Too bad, but you happened to become a target—a scapegoat, if you will. Worse, your own cousin, Thaddeus, dropped the word into the right ears, fueling the whole thing. Mark my word, though, you won't stay in prison for long. And I suspect, when all this is done, that you will remain quite well-fixed. They can't take away your earnings, after all. What was the figure? Twelve million or so? Besides, old friends aren't likely to forget past favors you've done them. Especially if, uh, their remembrance will help to keep your lips sealed..."

Trial! Prison! The thought of it struck him cold. He drank far into the night, tried to find surcease in the arms of yet another young prostitute picked from the fleshpots of New York's waterfront, became haggard and drawn and terrified. He attempted to find Thaddeus—surely Thaddeus would let bygones be bygones; after all, they were blood kin—but was rebuffed. "He does not," came the reply, "care to see you, Mr. Stewart." The trial of Brack Stewart was a repeat of all the other miseries, only worse, infinitely worse. For now the accusations were clear and pointed, the evidence relentlessly mounting as fearful confederates rushed to turn evidence against him in order to protect themselves.

New York lay under a blanket of heat. Open windows and fluttering hand fans brought no relief to the packed, sweltering United States District Courtroom for the borough of Manhattan. A jury of twelve sweating men filed in after three days of deliberation to announce the verdict. And then Brack stood before the judge, a frowning, hawkfaced man with bulging eyes and the look of a dyspeptic. "You have been found guilty on all counts. Brack Stewart. Do you have anything to say to this court before I pronounce sentence?" Dumbly, he shook his head. The words came down like hammer blows and seemed to reverberate through his consciousness. "Twelve years... Twelve years... Twelve years..."

It broke in him, then, like the breaking of a dam. He heard himself shouting at the judge, felt himself turning to face the mob, felt their shocked recoil and glared into their staring eyes. "Bastards! Bastards! I'm not alone. Can't you see that? I'm not alone. You're all guilty, all of you. You're equally guilty, and more venal by your collective guilts than I shall ever be! Who are you to . . ."—he was only vaguely conscious of the strong hands grabbing at his arms, the force of the marshals bodily dragging him away, pinioning his hands behind his back, locking the shackles—"judge me? Who are you to judge meeeeeee!?"

Brack Stewart was taken immediately to the federal penitentiary. The next morning's newspapers led their front pages with the story of his twelve-year sentence and outburst in the courtroom. But even as the news was being hawked by paper boys on the street, certain powerful members of Congress were moving to reduce the actual jail term from twelve years to two.

"Tough break for old Brack," observed a Congressman from Ohio, himself the holder of a thousand shares of Credit Mobilier stock which had paid, at their peak, dividends of more than 300 per cent. "This is the least we can do for him."

As he spoke, a shattered Brack Stewart lay on the bunk in his cell, engulfed in the darkest night of his soul.

Carp. Poindexter Carp. The man was either a hopeless zealot or a fool, one could not be certain which. Brigadier General Peter Heflin brooded from the window of the Washington train, nursing his third glass of straight bourbon. He wore civilian clothing and had grown a mustache. His complexion was florid from perpetual drinking. Only the erect posture and hard, trim build gave evidence of his being a military man. Fellow passengers looked at him curiously, but from his unique appearance rather than recognition. For privacy, he had chosen to wear an expensive, well-tailored suit of lightweight wool. Summer heat sent sweat trickling down the back of his neck and sopped his armpits, but he kept his coat on. This was to conceal the heavy service revolver holstered there.

Later, they would ask why he had strapped on the gun to visit Washington on purely unofficial business. What was his intent? And he would say quite honestly that he did not know. It had been an automatic thing, especially since feelings against him were running so high among followers of that radical populist Carp. Carp had stirred them all up with his ridiculous speeches on the floor of the Senate demanding that General Peter Heflin be brought to Washington for a full-scale hearing on the massacre at Creek-of-Many-Branches. Heflin snorted at the thought, swigged from his glass, made a face. Liquid fire poured down his gullet. His face was pleasantly numbed. His temper was sour. He clenched and unclenched his big fists and studied the play of freckles on the backs of his hands. That bastard, Carp. And to think, they had once been brothers-in-law. No wonder Francesca had treated the man with such contempt.

Contempt. Contemptible. He ran it around the edges of his mind. Contemptible little piss-ass of a senator, making a name for himself at the expense of a general of the Army. Hell—he swigged again—he had seen more dead and dying and rotting bodies than piss-ass Carp even knew existed. He was a man of war and of battle, who stood for his country in its time of peril. And what did Carp do? Sit on his goddamned fat ass in the Senate, getting all his little goodies, making speeches, shuffling papers, playing the fool.

Well, this was too much. Too much. It was time for a showdown, time to shut that fat mouth once and for all. Caterwauling about the poor put-upon Indian, the poor innocent Cheyenne, murdered in their beds by this raving homicidal maniac Heflin.

What was it that that Confederate prisoner had said long ago? "Devil Heflin. May your soul rot in hell." Funny that he would remember that.

He was drunk. He looked around him at the other passengers in the coach. He had come here to sit because it was too goddamned lonely in his private stateroom. Peter Heflin was accustomed to people around him, Army officers, orderlies, troops. Oddly, the older he got the less he could stand being alone. He even hated to sleep alone, and more and more demanded the company of one of the female camp followers on the post. It was bad form for a general, but what the hell, a man had to have a bed partner, not to mention some ass.

Heflin's eye drifted to two women seated forward of him on the other side of the aisle. One of them, plump and blond, had given him the eye earlier. There was a pair of empty seats facing them, riding backward. He finished the glass of bourbon, eased the pint bottle into his inside coat pocket and lurched forward to join them. They looked up, startled, as he sat down heavily in the empty seats.

"Beg pardon, ladies. Mind if I join you?" He belched softly. "Sorry. The train. Somethin' I et." The blonde rolled her eyes at her companion and giggled. He straightened up, mustering his dignity. "I am . . . I am Brigadier General Peter Heflin, Unit . . . United States Cavalry. At yer service, misses." He affected a salute. "Where you pretty ladies going, might I ask?"

"We don't talk to strangers," the taller of the two replied. She was an angular young woman with the face of a hawk.

The blonde giggled. "Now, Priscilla, that ain't nice. This here gentleman just ast a question, that's all." The round face turned to him, simpering. Blue eyes batted their lashes. "We're goin' to Washington to see the sights. We're, uh, from Philadelphia. Proper ladies, you know." She wiggled in her seat. "We're goin' to the capital and do the social scene. Ain't that right, Priscilla?"

Hawkface did not reply. Heflin suppressed a snicker. God, what a homely one. He'd have to tell Colonel Sample when he got back to the post what a homely wench he'd met on the train. Man'd have to cover her head in a sack to get a piece.

"Charmed," he said.

"You're a Southerner, ain't you? I could tell by the accent. You from anywhere's around Baltimore? I got a friend in Baltimore. He sells things on the road, y'know. For a while he worked for Mr. Barnum's shows. Have you seen Mr. Barnum's shows? I used to get free tickets . . ."

It went on. Prattle. He disliked prattle. It bored him. The blonde had a lush little body, but Lord, what prattle. He belched again, drew out the pint from his pocket. "Snort?"

"No, thank you." Hawkface again, frowning. "I don't approve of spiritous liquors."

But Blondie giggled. "Well, maybe just a little." He handed her the bottle. She tipped it up, self-consciously. "Oh, ain't this awful? You'll think I'm perfectly awful, Mr. . . . . Mr. . . . ."

"General. General Peter Heflin. At yer service, Ma'am."

It was Hawkface who reacted. "Heflin!" Her eyes widened, as if in shock. "It's him. You're him! The general that killed all them Cheyenne at the creek of what's-its-name. I read it in the penny press. Mildred, it's him!"

"Who?"

"Heflin! You know, the one that senator's after, Senator Carp. He killed . . . he killed three hundred people with his cavalry, and—"

"Now hold on."

"Right in their beds they did it. The cavalry . . ."

Other passengers were looking. Heflin was conscious of the turning faces, the peering eyes. They peered and poked into his privacy, snooping with their dirty noses while this hawk-faced idiot woman gabbled at the top of her voice. Well, all right. "Shut your goddamned mouth for a minute, woman!" The mouth shut. The face appeared as if it had been slapped.

He let 'em have it then. Let all of 'em have it. By God, what'd they know about Indians? Scourge of the West, Indians. Scalpers of women and children in their beds. And Cheyenne, worst of the lot. Stinking Cheyenne smelling of bear grease and horse shit, thought nothing of plundering and raping and scalping. That's right, raping. "Take a respectable woman like you, Blondie, and strip you down and ram a red hot poker up your cunt. That's the Cheyenne, these helpless innocent people that Carp, little piss-ass senator, says I slaughtered. Well, I'll tell you what I'm going to do to Carp . . ."

They were ogling him now. All of 'em. Even Blondie had stopped wiggling her hot little ass and was ogling, eyes big as saucers.

Somebody came to his side, a presence in blue coat and brass buttons. A man was saying, "Sir? Sir, I must ask . . ." A hand came down firmly on his shoulder. Heflin looked up into the owlish face of a bespectacled conductor who said, "Sir, you are creating a disturbance. I must ask you to refrain."

Immediately, he was contrite. Immediately, he felt the eyes upon him. From some particle of conscious mind unnumbed by drink, he felt a flush of embarrassment. "Well, all right," he said. "I was just trying to . . ."

"Sir, please."

"All right. Sorry. Sorry." He came to his feet, towering over the conductor, swaying heavily. "Sorry." He lurched down the aisle, handhold-to-handhold, looking into the angry eyes and faces. "Sorry," he said. "Sorry." He left the coach and went to his private compartment. He sat down by the window and finished the pint bottle, muttering to himself.

The train pulled into the Washington station in the early afternoon. Peter Heflin ignored his baggage and caught a hansom cab to a saloon on Pennsylvania Avenue. There, witnesses would recall later, he drank for about an hour and talked loudly about what he intended to do to that son of a bitch, Carp, the piss-ass politician who wanted him hauled on the carpet. He talked about his wife in Washington, the socialite Marguerite Heflin, it was recalled. He mentioned the fact that Mrs. Heflin did not love him, had never loved him, but was in love with her first cousin. This was remembered distinctly, later, for the general said it several times. He also spoke of Vanessa Stewart, saying he should have killed the whore. He returned to the subject of Senator Carp and what he intended to do when he saw him. Several times during this rambling monologue, General Heflin displayed the holstered pistol inside his suit coat. He left the saloon at shortly before three o'clock, walking in the direction of the Capitol.

The whore. He should have killed the whore. He could have done it easily. Instead, he had saved her life, ordered her treated like any other released captive, saw that she was fed and clothed and taken to Fort Kearny. And this was the thanks he got. He walked along in the hot sunlight, conscious of the passing city. He bumped into a pedestrian, cursed, walked on. He lurched across Pennsylvania Avenue, swearing at the passing horse-drawn trolleys and carriage traffic. At last he arrived at the massive steps of the Capitol and climbed it, carefully taking each step at a time. He went into the Capitol, found a page in the corridor, asked about Senator Carp. The boy brought a Capitol usher, who looked at Heflin curiously. Heflin smiled, handed the usher a gold piece, asked his questions. The man shrugged. Yes, the senator usually left his office at about four o'clock. He came out this way to where his carriage usually waited. Yes, the senator had been in sessions today. Heflin thanked the usher, strolled back out onto the Capitol verandah and waited.

The time was twelve minutes after four when Senator Poindexter Carp emerged from the doors of the Capitol. He was accompanied by Senator Rufus Wilson of Missouri and Congressman Carson Minor of Illinois. Numerous other members of the Congress and their staffs also were leaving the building for the day.

Carp had begun to descend the steps when Heflin pushed away from the balustrade and lurched toward him. "Senator! Senator Carp, I want to see you!"

The senator stopped walking, turned. "Yes?" He did not recognize the man. "What is it, please?"

Heflin strode toward him. His step did not falter. The hated round face was half-smiling, eyebrows lifted. Carp was wearing glasses. Piss-ass, Heflin thought. At six feet away, he said, "You son of a bitch, I'm going to kill you!" And then the pistol was in his hand, blasting. He squeezed off six shots, very rapidly. Four of them made a neat pattern in the middle of Poindexter Carp's chest. The fifth struck the senator in the head as he was falling. The sixth went wild. "Kill you, son of a bitch! Kill you!"

Heflin was still squeezing the trigger on an empty chamber as the body of Poindexter Carp rolled down several steps, leaving a smear of blood.

A cold rain drizzled down over the city. It matched the mood of Marguerite Stewart Heflin as she rode with Thaddeus to the National Prison. He sat quietly, unobtrusively beside her. How natural it is that he should accompany me now, she thought. Even on such a day as this, on such a mission as this, Thaddeus was a stabilizing presence.

"He is not afraid," she said. "It is amazing. I would be terrified. I think anybody would. But Peter is . . . well, he is composed and accepting. What a cruel irony for this to happen."

Thaddeus did not reply. He took her hand and held it lightly. The closed carriage rocked along through the rain. She watched water streaking down the side windows, stared at the blurred outlines of the city flowing past, listened to the measured clip-clop of the trotters ahead. She thought of the bays, fine, strong horses, the pick of her stable.

It had been so difficult to make decisions. For days as this approached, she had been numb. Merely dressing was a chore, and today especially. She wore blue at Peter's request. ("For God's sake, Marguerite, don't wear black. It's so morbid.") She had put on the blue frock that he liked and a matching bonnet. But it had taken an infinity of time merely seeing to her hair and dressing properly. And now the time was slipping away, and suddenly it wasn't blue gowns or hairdos or bay horses that mattered; it was time that mattered. Time.

"He loved me, you know. He really did love me. Before the war, we lived in the house by the park, remember? Peter would putter about and cook, he enjoyed cooking. And the parties—you remember the parties, Thaddeus—they were divine." She dabbed at her eyes, Damn, she couldn't start weeping again. It wouldn't do to face him with red, swollen eyes. She sniffed and returned the hankie to her purse. "I don't think it was his fault, or mine either. It was circumstance, and the war." She turned to Thaddeus. "Do you understand?"

"I think I understand."

She patted his hand. "In the first place, his loyalties were so torn by the war. Torn between the Union and the South. Or maybe it was me and the South. He hated fighting against his own people. To do so, to see it through, he had to steel himself not to feel, not to regret, not to anguish. Peter did that, Thaddeus. He was a good officer. At the end, I think he became disoriented. I didn't understand it then. I thought he loved war and killing, loved playing general and leading cavalry charges. And in a way, he did; but it was a conditioned love, conditioned by the war. In going to war, you see, Peter cut himself off from the past and everything he'd held dear. He cut himself off from South Carolina and his friends and family, his boyhood, his heritage. Finally I was all that he had left, and then he cut himself off from me."

She looked at Thaddeus in the gray light. He was approaching forty handsomely. Maturity was in his hair and upon his face. It was a striking process. His suit was impeccably tailored, his body trim and fit. He was, of course, a millionaire now in his own right—the railroad had profited hugely and his share provided a fortune. Only in his eyes did the pain show. The gray eyes of Thaddeus Stewart mirrored all that had happened: Ruth's relentless decline and his decision to seek a divorce; the death of John Colby, for which he blamed himself; the Credit Mobilier scandal, which had enmeshed Brack Stewart and sent him to prison; the murder of Poindexter Carp, whom Thaddeus had admired; and now, the tragedy of Brigadier General Peter Heflin, the senator's killer and Marguerite's husband.

"I'm sorry, my dear," she said.

Thaddeus came out of his reverie. "I'm sorry for both of us," he said. "Do you remember when we first met and took that walk on the road in the moonlight? How naive we were.

We thought that the world was ours, that all we had to do was live and everything would turn out all right."

"Yes, I remember." Of course, she remembered. The memory had warmed her all these years, tucked away in a corner of her mind. Of course, she remembered. Her strange, emotional destiny had been forged that night. "Of course, I remember."

"What we did not consider is that life makes its own terms, and we're not necessarily the masters of our fate." Thaddeus peered grimly past her at the rain. "And yet we must come to an accommodation with it, find ways to live it. Do you know who I think of now, even more than I do of Ruth? I think of John Colby, and of how nothing went right for him. And I think of how I, a nephew of his parents, usurped his rightful place in the family so that he could never fully realize his potential. He was devastated in childhood. No wonder he hated me."

"It wasn't your fault, Thaddeus, any more than Peter's tragedy was mine. Our lives are directed by so many complex forces. Your parents were murdered, your grandfather took you in, your Uncle Stephen and Aunt Catherine adored you. It was . . . fate."

He sighed. "Yes, it was fate. But I can't stop thinking of John Colby's body lying on the railroad track, face down in the dirt. I'll carry that with me for the rest of my days."

The carriage driver turned into the rain-washed driveway of the prison. Marguerite showed her pass to the guard at the gate; he waved them on. The twin trotters stepped through the rain along a narrow roadway lined with elms, now leafless and gray. They stopped in front of the ugly brick building with its battlements and fortresslike stonework. Other carriages were arriving, most of them bearing members of the press, Army officers and official witnesses. They drew up in the rain and disgorged dark-clad men who hurried through the great double-doored entrance bearing shiny black umbrellas.

"Do you want me to go in with you?" he asked.

"No. This is something I must do alone."

He nodded. "I'll wait, then. I'll be here when it's over."

She stepped down from the carriage and walked through a portico, her footfalls echoing against wet walls. Rained drummed onto her umbrella. Uniformed guards and black-clad visitors stared at the stunning blond woman in the blue gown. Men whispered among themselves as she passed, and there were knowing nods. The set faces of guards came into her view, brass buttons gleaming, their hands respectfully saluting. Steel doors swung open. She was conscious of long, polished corridors, odors of sweat and wax, a constancy of reverberating voices and banging metal. A turn, and then the cold air came rushing with its smell of rain. She came into the main prison yard. A guard stopped her again, examined her pass. "Mrs. Heflin?" His eyes refused to meet hers. "That way, please." She felt his eyes following her as she walked away.

It was there, in the corner. One did not have to look. It was there. One felt it, a heavy, dark presence glistening in the rain, rising two stories above the main yard on raw, wet timbers bolted and nailed. She did not look immediately. She stopped walking and stood, letting her gaze drift upward along the brick facade of the prison, across the barred windows. Rain flecked her face and eyelashes, but she did not care. She thought, "How strange. What am I doing here? What is anybody doing here?"

Clackity-blamb!

The explosion of wood and metal struck her consciousness like a thunderbolt. Her head jerked to the left as she was looking at the gallows in the rain, glistening with angles and braces. A black-clad giant in a top hat stood on the platform looking down at her. Beneath him, suspended obscenely through the sprung trapdoor, a heavy sandbag swung gently from the rope. The eyes of the giant were dark orbs in a face the color of paste. The mouth twisted in a grimace.

She ducked her head and hurried across the yard.

The cell was on the ground floor just inside the first steel door. A cold dankness seeped into her bones. Two burly military guards in dress blue uniforms stood in the corridor watching her approach. From here she could see into the cell. He sat on a single cot with his hands clasped. Two men stood over him. One was the civilian lawyer Blackman, a robust figure with flushed features and a gold watch chain draped across his great, black-vested middle. The other was a tall, bony man with a gaunt, skull-like face. He wore a cleric's collar and carried a Bible. The faces turned as she was admitted by the guards.

"Gentlemen, my wife." Peter Heflin rose from the cot. He was thin and drawn in his prison clothes. The red hair was close-cropped now, the freckles pale upon his flesh. His lips were cold as they brushed her cheek. She could feel the bones in his hands. "Now, if you don't mind . . ."

They bowed and murmured, seeming confused. "We will keep on trying, General," the lawyer said. "The President . . ."

"Yes, Blackman. Do that."

And then they were gone. The cell door clanged shut. The backs of the guards turned to them, heavy and mobile beyond the bars. "The prison parson," he said, nodding after the cleric. "Wants to make sure my rotten soul is ready."

"Peter . . ."

"Forgive me." He sat down heavily, ran a hand through his hair, sighed. Outside, the trap door tripped again. The noise was unnaturally loud in the cell. "The hangman is a conscientious fellow."

"Is there a chance?"

He smiled wearily. "Frankly, no. All appeals have been exhausted. The President has not responded. The trial was fair, the testimony overwhelming. Even a general of the Army cannot murder a United States senator in cold blood on the Capitol steps and get away with it. There is . . . no choice."

She sat down beside him on the cot. It was a dreary cell with no furnishings except the cot, a chamber pot covered with a towel and a single window looking out upon the prison yard. Idly, she wondered how many men had waited here while the gallows was sprung repeatedly outside. One of them had scribbled something on the wall in pencil. "The Lord is my shepherd." The pathetic message lingered there, the last trace on earth of an anonymous soul.

"What will you do?" he was saying. "Will you remain here in Washington, after . . ."

"I don't know. I have not made up my mind. But I . . . I will remember how it was before all this."

"Yes." He smiled. The weight loss had ravaged his face and given it a fragile, ethereal quality. His skin seemed translucent. "Yes, before all this."

"And the war. Before the war."

"Yes. Before the war."

They were talking like strangers. The barrier lay between them, an invisible wall of silences. Tension throbbed at her temples. There must be something more, something more than this!

"Oh, Peter,"—she took his hands and held them—"I'm sorry. I'm so sorry."

He bit at his lower lip. "There is something I want to say."

"Certainly, darling. Anything. Say anything."

"It's about you and me, and... Thaddeus."

"Thaddeus?"

"Where is he now?"

"He's outside in the carriage. He did not come in. I wanted to be with you, alone."

"I've wanted to speak with you about Thaddeus for a long time. Years, actually. But I never seemed quite able to do it."

"What do you mean?"

"I've had time to think in these past months. I've thought about myself and about life. I've thought about you and Thaddeus. I've known from the beginning, you see, that you loved each other. It was not something threatening to me, honestly. From our first meeting at Marvella's house, I knew how things were. You were first cousins, you had a powerful attraction for each other going back a number of years."

"Peter..."

"No, please let me speak. I've done some terrible things in the past few years. I became a person warped, consumed by lust for war. But that was my own doing. I am responsible, and I intend now to bear that responsibility. At the same time, I've been thinking that maybe—just maybe—I can still do something for someone else. I can help you come to terms with the conflict that has lived within you all these years, the conflict over Thaddeus."

An outer door opened somewhere. There were footfalls in the corridor, a murmur of voices. His eyes seemed to flutter in their sockets. His words hurried on.

"You belong together, you and Thaddeus. This is the simple, basic truth of it. By a twist of fate you were born first cousins. Well, so be it. And so what? First cousins have loved before. They have married and borne children before. Why should you be afraid? Because of your family's disapproval? Because of Francesca's disapproval? Francesca disapproves of everything you've ever done, Marguerite, because of her insane jealousy. If you're bothered by what people think, then you and Thaddeus can simply go elsewhere. This is an enormous country, and there's plenty of room in it for privacy."

Keys jangled in the cell door. The door swung open.

"Peter..."

"I want you to be happy, Marguerite. I want you to be happy for my sake and have fine, strong sons, and name one

of them for me. There's nothing else that I can leave for
anybody. And if I can't leave anything behind, then my life
has been meaningless. If, because of me, you and Thaddeus
can find happiness, then I've achieved something besides
killing people. And suddenly—"

"General Heflin," a voice said. "It is time."

"—suddenly to create something living, something worthwhile, is terribly important to me."

She flung her arms about him and held him close. The
tears poured now, and she let them. She kissed him, fully,
and whispered, "You will always live in my heart."

They took him then. They took him by the arms and
moved slowly from the cell into the corridor while the voice
of the chaplain droned. A military guard came to her and
said, "Mrs. Heflin, if you'll come with me, please." He led
her in the other direction, through a maze of hallways and
finally through an exit onto the back side of the prison yard.
A crowd of military officers had gathered in the rain. They
made a path for her as the guard led the way to a place where
witnesses sat on a row of hard chairs. She took the last empty
chair among the civilians and military men. Several journalists glanced at her without speaking. Pencils scribbled on
notepads.

He was so thin and frail, walking with the escort. A
drumbeat sounded in slow, muffled rhythm. The rain intensified, beating down upon the umbrellas. He was hatless, red
hair plastered down. The cleric and the military guard accompanied him up the steep wooden steps. At last he stood
in the gray light looking down at her while they shackled his
hands behind his back and the giant in the top hat prepared a
black hood. The drum throbbed softly. The stark walls of the
prison soared behind the scaffold, its bricks the color of dried
blood. The provost marshal of the Washington military district, a colonel, mounted the platform and read from a
document, his voice filtering out in fragments.

"... tried by court martial and found guilty of... crime of
first degree murder... sentence of this court that defendant,
Peter James Heflin... hang by the neck until dead... have
mercy on your soul..."

The provost marshal handed the document to the black-
clad giant. The giant read, initialed, nodded and handed it
back. The provost marshal descended the wooden steps. The
hood dropped over the head of Peter Heflin and the rope loop

was arranged, its great knot jutting from behind the left ear, and jerked tight. The muffled drumbeat stopped. The cleric prayed. The drums took a new cadence, rolling, rolling, rolling. Tensions coursed across the prison yard. The condemned stiffened. The giant grasped a lever.

The rain beat down upon the umbrellas.

The lever tripped. The platform crashed open. The body plummeted down

Marguerite closed her eyes tightly and stifled a scream. When she opened them again, the hooded figure swung gently in the gray light.

They helped her to her feet. An officer offered to escort her away. She swayed, swallowed, and shook her head. Alone, she walked through the parting crowd and into the building, through the echoing corridor to the double doors, then along the portico and back out into the rain. The closed, black carriage waited in the driveway, the matched bays stamping restlessly. The driver snatched open the door and dropped the folding steps. She climbed into the carriage.

Thaddeus opened his arms.

"Hold me, darling," she whispered. "I'm cold. I'm so cold."

The driver snicked at the bays. The carriage jerked to life and moved smartly through the rain, back toward Washington.

ABOUT THE AUTHOR

CHARLES WHITED was born in West Virginia, attended the University of Virginia and was a paratrooper sergeant during the Korean War. He has been a journalist for twenty-five years and now writes a daily commentary column for the *Miami Herald*.

He ghostwrote Mrs. Elliott Roosevelt's autobiography *I Love a Roosevelt* for Doubleday. He later collaborated with treasure hunter Martin Meylach to write *Diving to a Flash of Gold*. His book about the true adventures of Dan Chiodo as a NYC decoy cop, *The Decoy Man*, was published in hard and soft cover by Playboy Press. He has published several paperback novels.

Charles Whited is now working on the third volume in the *Spirit of America* series.

THE SPIRIT OF AMERICA series
continues in spring 1983 with...

POWER
by Charles Whited

It is the turn of the 20th century and America is in the throes
of a turbulent new era—an era of expanding, inventing, brawling and building. Against this teeming backdrop, the Stewarts
of a new generation summon their fiery passions and ceaseless
ambition in a relentless struggle to forge a mighty empire.

Maurice—Handsome, resolute and determined to break free
of family tradition and an iron-willed father, he embarks
penniless and disinherited on his own. Amidst the fierce
challenges of ruthless competitors, confronted by women
who at once despise and adore him, he harnesses family
power in unprecedented ways.

Hope—Maurice's beautiful, restless and independent cousin,
she shocks New York society by marrying newspaper pub-
lisher Howard Langden, a man twenty-six years her senior.
Defying pressure to take a subservient place next to her
husband, she is a woman ahead of her times, carving a new
role for women all across America.

Isaiah—His creation of an internal combustion engine
launches the Stewarts to leadership in the burgeoning new
automobile industry. But triumph does not diminish his
loneliness as a man. When his adoration for a beautiful
courtesan leads him to the agony of betrayal, he seeks comfort from the woman he never thought he could love.

THE SPIRIT OF AMERICA
surges stronger than ever
in POWER—on sale in spring 1983

A stirring new novel by the World's
Bestselling Frontier Storyteller

THE CHEROKEE TRAIL
LOUIS L'AMOUR

Our foremost storyteller of the authentic West
with over 120 million copies of his books in
print around the world, Louis L'Amour has
thrilled a nation by bringing to vivid life
the bold men and women who settled the
American frontier. Now L'Amour introduces
us to Mary Breydon, a brave woman suddenly widowed and isolated with her young
daughter on the Colorado frontier. Though
everyone tells her that it is no work for a
woman, Mary takes a job managing a rundown stagecoach station on the Cherokee
Trail. With the support of a spirited Irish
woman, a fearless orphan boy and, most of
all, the mysterious gunman Temple Boone,
Mary finds the courage to face down the
constant danger of attacks by outlaws and
marauding Indians and shape Cherokee
Station into a vital stop on America's westward journey . . . Until the vicious murderer
whose bloody rampages stained her past
stalks Mary once again.

(#20846-2 • $2.95)